175
X

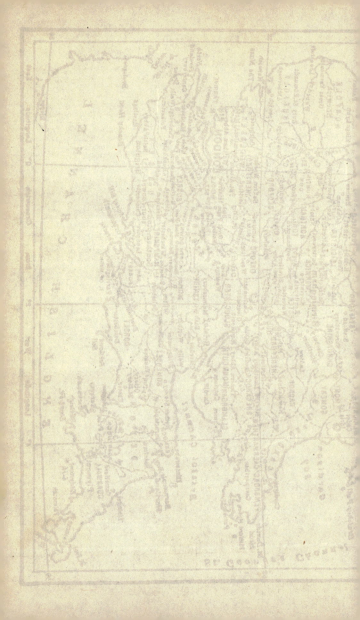

THE BEGINNINGS TO 1500

ENGLISH LITERATURE

THE BEGINNINGS TO 1500
JAMES DOW McCALLUM

THE RENAISSANCE
ROBERT WHITNEY BOLWELL

THE SEVENTEENTH CENTURY
EVERT MORDECAI CLARK

THE EIGHTEENTH CENTURY
JOSEPH P. BLICKENSDERFER

THE ROMANTIC PERIOD
ALBERT GRANBERRY REED

THE VICTORIAN PERIOD
GEORGE MOREY MILLER

This series of anthologies of English literature
is under the general editorship of
JAMES DOW McCALLUM

ENGLISH LITERATURE

THE
BEGINNINGS
TO 1500

EDITED BY

JAMES DOW MCCALLUM

CHARLES SCRIBNER'S SONS

NEW YORK

ACKNOWLEDGMENTS

The First Pennsylvania Company, Executors, Estate of S. Weir Mitchell, for "Pearl," translated by S. Weir Mitchell.

From the book *The Caedmon Poems*, edited by C. W. Kennedy. Published by E. P. Dutton & Co., Inc., and reprinted with their permission.

From the book *The Poems of Cynewulf*, edited by C. W. Kennedy. Published by E. P. Dutton & Co., Inc., and reprinted with their permission.

Holt, Rinehart and Winston, Inc., for "The Wanderer" and "The Sea-Farer" from *Early English Poems* selected and edited by Henry S. Pancoast and John Duncan Spaeth. All rights reserved.

The Princeton University Press and Professor Spaeth for "Beowulf."

CONTENTS

CONTENTS

Drama

INTRODUCTION

Old English Literature

ENGLISH literature has been running its course now for more than twelve centuries. An idea of that tremendous sweep of time may be gained by remembering that the history of our country from the American Revolution to the present year covers only one-eighth as much, and even if we reckon back to the death of Shakespeare in 1616 we are, in point of time, only one-quarter on our way!

Changes have taken place of course during those twelve centuries. To such an extent has our language changed that the earliest English writings cannot be understood today except by a student of Old English; new forms of literature have come in; and the subject matter of the present day shows surprising differences from that of the eighth century. To make clearer the course of English literature, then, it is customary to divide it into periods, the dates of which are rather arbitrary, by no means to be taken literally, and determined rather by the state of the language than by the content or form of the literature. The first division is the Old English period, often referred to as the Anglo-Saxon period, extending from some time in the seventh century to about 1100. This is followed by the Middle English period, which comes to a close about the year 1500; and from then on we are in the Modern English period.

To understand properly the beginnings of English

literature it is necessary to know something of the history of Britain in those early days. The reader will recall that in 55 B. C. Julius Caesar invaded Britain. It was not until a hundred years after Caesar's visit, however, that the Romans made a permanent settlement; in 42 A. D. the Emperor Claudius undertook the conquest of the island, and by the end of the century the Romans had conquered as far north as the Forth. Once established, the Romans set up a military government, made physical improvements such as new roads, protecting walls, baths, and villas, remains of which are still to be seen, and probably even left their imprint on the language in such words as street, Chester, port, wall, and wine. But while the Romans were conquering Britain they were having their own difficulties at home; internal dissensions and barbarian invasions caused the withdrawal of the legions from this far-away outpost, and by 410 A. D. the last legion had left the island. The Britons were thus left to govern themselves, and, a task more difficult, to protect themselves. From their inability to hold back the invaders arose, strange to say, our literature.

About the middle of the fifth century and after the withdrawal of the Romans, the Britons were once more invaded—this time by the Angles and Saxons from the northern part of Germany and by the Jutes from Denmark. Bede states that they came over at the invitation of Vortigern, King of Kent, to help against the Picts and the Scots. Whether that be so or not, come they did, and in such force that the country was soon in their hands. These are the peoples who begin English literature. One more element needs to be added: in 597 Augustine led missionaries from Rome to Britain and they began their conversions in Kent. Forty years later Aidan came from Iona into the northern part of England, and between the efforts of the missionaries in the north and those in the south, Britain was soon sufficiently converted to be called a Christian country.

Under Christianity letters flourished. From the northern centers of the new religion, especially from Whitby and Jarrow, came some of the outstanding literary figures of the period: Cædmon (end of the seventh century, at Whitby), Bede (673-735, at Jarrow), Alcuin (735-804, at York), and perhaps Cynewulf (late eighth century). The southern centers did not produce at this time any distinguished writers. These schools prospered in the north and south until the close of the eighth century, when the marauding Danes by repeated harryings reduced them to desolation. Alfred finally succeeded in arresting the invaders (in 878, at the battle of Edington), and learning was restored—this time in the south. We shall return to Alfred's program later.

Literature was well nourished in these early days, and although lacking many of the forms that were to develop in the succeeding centuries, includes a copious variety of types. In poetry we have the lyric, short descriptive poems, elegy, paraphrases of Biblical stories, charms, riddles, gnomic verses, battle poetry, and the long narrative poem *Beowulf;* and in prose, history, saints' legends, sermons, translations, and expositions of the rules of priestly conduct, to mention no more. Thus in spite of the primitive conditions of this early society, and in spite too of the many manuscripts that have been lost through vandalism and carelessness, enough material is available today to make the study of it not only profitable to the specialist but of interest to the general reader.

For the present let us disregard the distinctly Christian productions of this period and address ourselves to a study of the non-Christian poetry. The most significant poem is *Beowulf*, frequently described as the "first English epic." The description needs qualification. To begin with, it was not written in English but in Old English or Anglo-Saxon, which is as difficult for the uninitiated as German or Dutch. It was the language that had been brought by the Angles, Saxons, and Jutes, and having been slightly influenced by the language of the native Celts and to a slight degree also by Latin, developed into what we now know as Old English. The first three lines of *Beowulf* will serve as an example:

HWÆT, wē Gār-Dena in gēardagum
þēodcyninga þrym gefrūnon,
hū ðā æþelingas ellen fremedon.

(Hail! We have heard of the greatness in days past of the kings of the Spear-Danes, of how the nobles did mighty deeds!)

Furthermore, to continue the qualification, the material is not English: the scenes are laid in Denmark and Sweden; and the characters are not native to England, but are continental. In other words, the invaders brought with them the traditions which took shape in *Beowulf*. The poem was written probably in the first quarter of the eighth century, and the manuscript of it dates from the end of the tenth; the author is unknown. There is only a slight historical basis for the poem.

Beowulf is the fullest expression in verse of Old English values that has come down to us. As one might expect of such a society of roving, sea-faring, plundering warriors, physical prowess is one of the main virtues. Beowulf, the hero, has the strength of thirty men; he vanquishes the monster Grendel without weapons, pursues his dam to her lair and kills her, swims the ocean clad in his mail and beset by sea-monsters—and swims for five nights, too—and finally, after having ruled his people for fifty years, gives up his life for them in slaying another dragon. That keynote, struck so boldly in this early poem, sounds throughout Old English poetry. Years after the probable date of the composition of *Beowulf* we find in the *Battle of Brunanburh* (937) and in the *Battle of Maldon* (991) the same exaltation of the fighting man, the same willingness for personal encounter, the same zest for the clash of arms.

But a fighting man dealing blows right and left, careless of whom he struck, was by no means the ideal. The warrior must be true to his lord, to his kinsmen, to his word, and thus we find loyalty as a second prominent virtue. Beowulf fulfills the vow he had made with Breca to swim the ocean; he slays Grendel, as he had promised; and he bitingly silences Unferth by referring to his disloyalty to his kinsmen. In return for his faithfulness, the warrior expected of course to be rewarded. Mean was the earl who refused to expend rings and swords on his followers. The king, we are told in *Beowulf,* who generously rewards his men, binds faithful followers to himself for times of stress.

Even the casual reader of these pagan poems notices the strange injection of Christian material. In *Beowulf* we learn that Cain is the father of the ravaging monsters. God sends Beowulf as a help to the people. Beowulf, dying, gives thanks to the "God of Glory." These, and many other examples, are curious footprints of time dating clearly enough from the Christianizing of the country, and are the pious and not very happy additions of the monks. The pagan element is naturally very strong. Wyrd (Fate) rules all things. It often spares a "good man not yet doomed, if his strength avail;" but no man can withstand Wyrd when it comes for him. The mighty Wyrd, so the *Wanderer* runs, brings hardship on the earth; in the *Ruined City* Wyrd causes all glorious things to decay. And Beowulf, having thanked God for the dragon's treasure, laments that Wyrd has overwhelmed the line of the Wægmundings. Throughout this early poetry there is none of the introspection, the doubts, the qualms of the ethically undecided that we find in later poetry. The philosophy of life is clear. Strength counts, and loyalty counts, and generosity counts—but Wyrd rules all. And just as this pagan poetry as a whole lacks embellishments and is told simply and directly, so this philosophy is set forth without debate or qualifications. Yet there is a certain melancholy in many of these poems, the melancholy that Tennyson summed up in the tragic line: *Man comes and tills the field and lies beneath.*

Who wrote all these poems we do not know. Probably they are the songs, the recitations, of the scop, the singer-poet who occupied an honored place at the king's table. "There was heard the clear sound of the harp, the song of the gleeman" is the line in *Beowulf,* and the sequel informs us that the scop told of the forming of the earth. So likewise the scop would sing the deeds of his lord. *Widsith,* probably the oldest Old English poem, tells not very veraciously of the wide wanderings of such a poet, and *Deor's Lament* is the cry of the scop who has been cut off from the favors of his lord by one more skilful than he.

There is a certain directness, a literal stating of facts, a pruning of the expression that is quite refreshing in much of this early writing. In our later poetry we expect expansion and detail. Not so in these poems. Notice how swiftly Beowulf's men put off from shore, land, pass the sentinel, and enter Heorot, or how quickly the fight with Grendel is told. And still there is a certain redundancy, a repetitiousness that today we should say came from a lack of filing, and there is a wealth of vocabulary—observe the many synonyms for the sea—that is quite surprising.

The quality of these poems varies, of course. Many of the gnomic verses are merely trite statements of fact. The *Love-Letter* approaches daintiness; the *Banished Wife's Complaint* and *Deor's Lament* are plangent; the *Riddles*, some ninety-five in number, are interesting examples of the guess literature found all over the world; and the *Battle of Brunanburh* stirred Tennyson to translate it.

Old English poetry dispenses with rime, but has its own conventions, nevertheless. The unit is the line, which is broken into two parts by a cæsura (i.e., a pause). Each half line has two heavily stressed accents and a varying number of unaccented syllables, and the halves are joined by alliteration—that is, an important word in the first half of the line has the same initial letter as an important word in the second half. Thus:

Lixte se *l*eoma	*l*eoht inne stod.
*H*eard be *h*iltum	*H*igelaces þegn
*g*od and *g*eatolic	*g*iganta geweorc

The 3182 lines of *Beowulf*, as well as the rest of Old English poetry, preserve these conventions, and certain variations of them, with surprising care. Indeed, such is the attention given to style that the verse of this period, early as that verse is, shows decided evidence of decadence.

Christian poetry of this period is represented by two poets—Cædmon, from Whitby, in the seventh century, and Cynewulf, perhaps a Northumbrian also, in the eighth. All that we know of the life of the former has been told by Bede in his *Ecclesiastical History*. He tells how Cædmon, having slipped away from a feast, was visited by an angel and under his heavenly guidance composed his poems. Four poems have been ascribed to Cædmon and are now known as *Cædmon's Paraphrase;* present day scholarship does not assign them to him, however. In the longest of these poems, the *Genesis,* the poet sings of Creation, and at times with surprising power. His descriptions of the revolt of the angels, of the temptation scene, and of the flood are among his best; readers of Milton's *Paradise Lost* are struck by the similarity between the *Genesis* and the later epic. In these paraphrases Biblical material is expanded, embellished, and adapted to the times. His patriarch is really an Anglo-Saxon king, the leader of his men in battle, the dispenser of gifts. In the *Exodus* the wanderings of the Israelites form the subject; in *Daniel,* we have the struggles of the Jews with Nebuchadnezzar; and in *Christ and Satan,* the lament of the fallen angels, the harrowing of hell, and the temptation.

Of the two poets Cynewulf has always been the more favored, because we can see in his poetry the wistful singer that he was, and the lover of beauty. He is much the more personal poet of the two. Whether he was bishop or minstrel we do not know; he seems to have undergone a conversion and been convinced of the sinfulness of his youth; in his maturity he realized how fleeting the beauties of earth are, how imminent death is, and that God is merciful and just. The very mind of Cynewulf, not to take into account the advance of his style, is a product of a refined and cultured community.

Just what poems Cynewulf wrote is a matter of doubt. At one time most of the outstanding poems of the period were attributed to him, but at the present time only four poems are considered as his work, poems which he signed with a runic [1] signature: *Juliana,* describing the martyrdom of a fourth century saint; *Elene,* relating the journey of Saint Helena to Jerusalem and her finding of the Cross; *The Fates of the Apostles,* telling very briefly the lives of the apostles; and finally the *Christ* with its beautiful passages on the Advent and the Ascension, and the powerful account of Doomsday. Two other poems of the period, the *Phoenix* and the *Dream of the Rood,* used to be assigned to Cynewulf, but the authorship is doubtful. The latter is the more poetic of the two.

The name of Bede (673-735) has already been mentioned. The Venerable Bede, monk, scholar, historian, and teacher is a towering figure of this period. All of his work, except a translation of the Gospel of Saint John, was written in Latin. Of his many writings the most important are the *Ecclesiastical History of the English People;* the *De Natura Rerum,* a scientific treatise, long popular; and his *Lives of the Saints.* It was not so much any one work by Bede, however, but rather what we may call his whole scholarly personality that set him apart and made him a tremendous influence. Not only was he familiar with Greek and Latin and some Hebrew, but he had covered the scientific material of his day, and was well versed in Biblical lore. About him at Jarrow are said to have gathered some six hundred scholars. One of them, Egbert, founded the school at York, famous for its learned men; and one of Egbert's pupils, Alcuin, became Charlemagne's mainstay in his educational program. Bede's mind was of that capacious sort which we have come to associate with the scholars and artists of the Renaissance.

It was not from Bede but from Alfred (849-901) that Old English prose derived its greatest stimulus. After

[1] The letters of the ancient Teutonic alphabet are called *runes.*

his repulse of the Danes, Alfred was able to turn his energies not only to the physical improvement of the country but to literature, too, and thanks to him learning flourished once again as it had a century before. Times were sadly changed, though. Britain, instead of sending scholars abroad to educate her neighbors, was in dire need of men to lead the movement, and Alfred was forced to send to the continent for scholars. Under his direction translations were made: *The Pastoral Care* of Pope Gregory, a handbook for the clergy; Orosius's *History of the World;* and the *Consolation of Philosophy,* by a sixth century Roman senator, Boethius. We may credit Alfred also, in all probability, with changing the *Anglo-Saxon Chronicle* from a perfunctory and often fictitious account of English history to a literary monument, an actual history of his own times, and, as carried on by his successors, of the next two centuries and a half.

Important too in this later period is Ælfric (c. 955-1020?), the author of the *Homilies,* eighty-five in number, forceful, dignified examples of Old English prose at its best, and of the *Lives of the Saints.* His *Glossary and Colloquy* should be mentioned as a sample of the text-book of the day.

On the whole this later period is one of prose. The significant poetry of the Old English period had long before been produced in the north. Yet too much credit cannot be given to the southern centers of learning: they clearly preserved a love of letters during a most turbulent time.

MIDDLE ENGLISH LITERATURE

The literature of the Middle English period (1100-1500) is extensive and varied, and compared with that of the preceding period offers many new problems. In the first place, much more has come down to us from this second period than from the first. Then again, new subject matter has been introduced, and many new forms, such as the ballad, the play, and the romance have come in. To the Christian influence which was so important in Old English literature, and which continued in the following period unabated in force, is to be added a second and equally important influence, the French. In regard to extent of time the two periods are about equal, but the later is much more prolific. And finally, the conditions of the Middle English period are, as we should expect of a transitional era, much more complicated: the economic, political, and religious questions were by no means so clear-cut as they had been. All these elements then have contributed to make the study of Middle English literature by no means simple.

Story telling now came into its own, and, thanks to the French influence, underwent important modifications. This influence (subsequent, of course, to the Norman Conquest, 1066) softened the tone of English narrative, gave new material to work with, supplied a fresh technique, and on the whole added a more courtly, worldly-wise character to what are now called romances —long narratives in verse. No longer the brevity of *Beowulf* and, as we may say, the reckless waste of situation in that poem. Fullness of description was now required; we see the characters from many angles; the background is filled in with much detail, and the narrators often feel obliged to go back in history and sketch in all that books (and frequently imagination) supply.

In the Middle Ages there were various cycles of romances, of which the Arthurian is the most important. We shall accordingly confine our discussion to it.

First, the chronology of the writers on Arthurian material. About the middle of the twelfth century, Geoffrey of Monmouth, an archdeacon at Monmouth, and probably a Welshman, wrote his *History of the Kings of Britain*. We are not concerned with the authenticity of Geoffrey's work: whether he did or did not translate an ancient account written in Cymric, nor shall we complain with a writer at the end of the twelfth century that he has "made the little finger of his Arthur stouter than the back of Alexander." The significant point is that Geoffrey made of Arthur an important figure. This account was written in Latin; it was translated into Anglo-Norman verse by Geoffrey Gaimar, but his version was quickly superseded by Wace's French translation, completed in 1155 and called *Li Romans de Brut*. We come down now fifty years to Layamon, a priest in Worcestershire, who reworked Wace's translation, and, doubling it, produced his *Brut*. To him we owe a detailed description of the origin of the Round Table; in the *Brut* also Arthur stands forth more like an English than a French king; and in the account of the death of Arthur something of that mysticism has been introduced that we now associate with his passing.

The Arthurian cycle was very popular in the twelfth century and in the following. In France Chrétien de Troyes (middle of the twelfth century) is the outstanding poet; in England and France there were numerous *lais*, and romances both in verse and in prose. Of the metrical romances the best is *Sir Gawain and the Green Knight*, written shortly after the middle of the fourteenth century by an unknown author.

By the time that Sir Thomas Malory wrote his *Morte Darthur* (completed about 1470, published by Caxton in 1485), the material had been worked and re-worked. Added to early and quite simple accounts of Arthur, a British chieftain of the fifth century, were those other stories which today we find so significant: the Grail story, the love story of Tristram and Iseult, the story of Lancelot, the story of the magician Merlin. Other additions there are, but these are the most important. And so with much spade work done for him—and with so many blossoms to gather, too—Malory wrote his prose version. The wealth of material was of course embarrassing to Malory, and the reader of today is frequently conscious of the stringing out of episodes, the multiplying of effects without the expected emphasis, and above all the failure to make Arthur a dynamic, all-engrossing personality. But these defects a lover of Malory forgets and finds in the *Morte Darthur* the speed of narrative, the clear-cut delineation of Lancelot and Guinevere, the sweep of events, the quaintness of diction, and the personal, live touches that have made the work one of the living books of English literature.

To us today the Arthurian cycle is not merely a series of episodes: it is a group of symbols, a repository of the ideals of successive ages, an exposition in narrative of the mysticism and wonder which all of us at some time feel, and of those perennial human relationships which are the joy and tragedy of life.

Romances, as we have said, abounded in the Middle English period; they supplied the place of the novel of today. *King Horn* (antedating, probably, 1250, although the manuscript is about 1310) tells the story of the love of Horn for "King Aylmar's" daughter, Rimenhild, his banishment because of his love, his return and killing of a false friend, and his subsequent reunion with his lady. *Havelok the Dane* (composed before 1300) recounts in quaint and homely fashion the trials of Havelok and Goldeburgh, misused royal children, their marriage, and Havelok's revenge on his enemies. *The Squyr of*

Lowe Degre (c. 1450?) is the old story of the humble serving-man marrying the king's daughter. There is life in these stories and a pleasing zest.

But what of the church influence? Some there is of course, in these romances; God (not Wyrd by this time) rules, and it should be added, Cupid does too. But it is not in the romances that we find evidences of monkish handling: it is in the long and labored homilies and treatises of the period. The *Ormulum* (c. 1215) explains the portions of the Bible used in daily services; it is most complete, over ten thousand lines having come down to us, and is very dull. The *Ancren Riwle* (c. 1220) emphasises the love of Jesus and the joys to be found in religion. Robert Manning of Brunne wrote the *Handlyng Synne* (1303) explaining the commandments and illustrating with tales; in parts it is quite readable. The author of the *Cursor Mundi* (not known) tells us (c. 1300) that "All this world, ere this book ends, with Christ's help I shall run over"—to review for us the proper religious attitude and to retell stories from the Bible. Richard Rolle of Hampole's *Prick of Conscience,* important in its day as a religious influence, treats of the wickedness of man, the temptations of this world, and of judgment. In 1340 Dan Michel, in his *Ayenbite of Inwyt (Prick of Conscience)* describes the seven deadly sins as a tree, the twigs of which are the minor sins. It is tedious and wordy. And then, like a beautiful stream of light, the *Pearl* (c. 1370) gleams forth from the general dullness of these analyses, a charming expression of the love of a man for a lost child and for God. The depth of feeling in this poem is not surpassed by any writing of the period. Unfortunately, the author is unknown.

The influence of the church has been particularly noticeable also on the development of the drama; indeed, one wonders how the drama would have got its start without the church.

To find the origin of the English drama we must go even beyond the Norman Conquest. Imagine yourself attending an Easter Day mass at the end of the tenth century. A simple colloquy is introduced as part of the service: the three Marys are asked by the angels, "Whom seek you?" And they answer, "Jesus of Nazareth." In turn the angels reply, "He is not here, he is risen." That approximately is a specimen of our first drama! The text of this "play" is from a French manuscript, but of the sort that was in use in the early English church. From it, simple as it is, has developed the vast dramatic literature which is such an important part of English letters.

For the next three centuries (during the eleventh and twelfth centuries and the greater part of the thirteenth) the drama was almost entirely in the hands of the clergy. As the drama developed it became less sacred in character, and with the addition of secular elements—non-Biblical figures, clowns, native types—instead of being performed in the church proper was gradually removed to the churchyard, and from the churchyard to the town. Equipment became more elaborate. Carts drawn by horses were used for stages. Simple stage-settings such as the mouth of hell and a conventional representation of heaven were introduced. The guilds in the various towns were called on to present plays; thus, the water-leaders would present *Noah's Flood*, the cappers and linen drapers *Balaam and His Ass*. Originally called *Corpus Christi* plays or *Whitsun* plays, because performed on those church festivals, these plays are now known as *mystery* plays. The subject matter is Biblical: the sacrifice of Isaac, the Creation, the Slaughter of the Innocents, for example. Cycles of these plays were composed, the best known being the *York* (from a fifteenth century manuscript, including forty-nine plays), the *Wakefield* or *Townley* (from the second half of the fifteenth century, including thirty-two plays), the *Chester* (the oldest cycle, although the manuscript is late, some twenty-five plays), and the *Coventry* (the manuscript dating from 1468 and the cycle running to a little over forty plays).

Miracle plays dealing with the lives of the saints were popular also. The earliest is probably the play of *Saint Katharine,* at the beginning of the twelfth century. They were performed as late as the first quarter of the sixteenth century. After the mysteries and the miracle plays come the moralities: a dramatization of the conflict of good and evil for the possession of the soul of man. For the most part they are quite tiresome, although *Everyman* has now attained the rank of a classic. After the moralities comes another type, the interludes, generally brief and often farcical. By the time the drama had undergone these various changes it was ready for the skilled hands of the Elizabethan playwrights.

But the literature of the Middle English period has more than romance and drama to its credit. It has its grace notes, too. Some of our most delightful lyrics date from this period. Many of them are religious in character and have the Virgin Mary as the central theme. Others, and they are the lyrics that have survived by the appreciation of readers, show a fondness for nature and exhibit a pleasing vein of sentiment. Ballads, also, take their rise in this period. Of unknown authorship and of doubtful origin, they have continued for centuries to please by their freshness and quaintness.

All this earlier literature would seem to have been the preparation for the work of the great poet of the period, Geoffrey Chaucer. All that the monks had done to preserve and to encourage literature; the amalgamation of the French with the English; the interest in the romance; the development of the lyric; and the handling and refining of the language, all these elements contributed to the success of Chaucer (c. 1340-1400). Born in London—his father was a wine-merchant—he became a page in the household of the Duchess of Clarence in his seventeenth year. Two years were spent in France with the army of Edward III. Chaucer was made a prisoner, ransomed, and returned to England to spend the next ten years at the court of Edward III. It was but natural that he should have written first in the manner of the poets of the courts of love and that the courtly, French influence should have been the first important influence on him. The "ballades, roundels, and virelays," and his translation, probably not completed, of the *Romaunt of the Rose* show this influence; so too does the *Book of the Duchess* (1369), a typical French love-vision which in Chaucer's hands becomes a poignant elegy in which he laments the death of John of Gaunt's first wife. The second important influence was the Italian. In 1372 and again in 1375 Chaucer went on diplomatic missions to Italy, during the hey-day, that is, of the Italian Renaissance. To this time (1375-1385) belong the *House of Fame,* the *Parliament of Fowls, Troilus and Criseyde,* and the *Legend of Good Women.* But it is by the *Canterbury Tales* (begun about 1387) that Chaucer is best known today, and rightly so. Once more Chaucer appropriated a medieval convention—the gathering together of a number of men and women in order to have each one tell a tale. Chaucer was able, however, to eliminate much of the creaking machinery that is generally found in such collections of tales, or rather, the vividness of the writing makes us forget the machinery. In the *Prologue* the poet tells how he fell in with a group of pilgrims who were going to Canterbury, "Wel nyne and twenty in a companye." Then, having sketched inimitably the members of the group, he has the host, Harry Bailey, propose a supper, at the expense of the group, to the one who tells the best story. The host suggests that each one tell two stories on the way to Canterbury and two on the return: but Chaucer completed less than a fifth of the whole. The *Canterbury Tales* are truly remarkable: in them Chaucer's careful observation of medieval types, clerical and lay, his supreme gift as a story teller, his sensitiveness to shadings in character, his tenderness and at times his raciness, but above all his ability to present men and women who are actually alive and not mere puppets introduced to tell stories, place the *Canterbury Tales* in a rank that is not approached by any other collection of tales of the period.

Contemporary with Chaucer is John Gower (1325?-1408), not so versatile an artist, to be sure, and obviously trammeled by many of the medieval conventions of form and thought, but a figure of much interest. Gower wrote three works, each in a different language. The *Speculum Meditantis*, in French, sets forth in typical medieval fashion the seven deadly sins, and exhibits the existing corrupt conditions in London. The *Confessio Amantis*, in English, is a group of stories on the deadly sins. In the *Vox Clamantis*, written in Latin, Gower as an aristocrat arraigns the condition of the people and dwells at length on the evils of the time. Additional light is shed on the period by the *Vision of Piers the Plowman*, formerly attributed to William Langland, but now considered to be the work of various hands. Here we have a full and bitter criticism of the social structure of the fourteenth century. The wretched condition of the laboring man and the corruption of the courts and of the church are frankly assailed. The point of view is that of one of the masses, and sympathy is consequently directed to the people.

While the main emphasis in any account of the literature of Middle English must fall upon poetry, the prose of the time may not be neglected. We have said something already about the greatest prose work of the period—Malory's *Morte Darthur*. But the fourteenth century can show other great prose writers, particularly John Wycliff (1320?-1384), one of the most influential preachers that England has produced, a friend of the people, a castigator of the evil doers of his day, but above all the translator, with assistance, of the Bible. At the opposite pole from the writings of Wyclif is the *Voyage and Travel of Sir John Mandeville*, originally written in French, translated into English, and one of the most delightfully extravagant accounts that we have.

Suitably enough, the period closes with William Caxton, the first to introduce printing into England (1476). Through his labors much of the best literature of the century, and his own translations in addition, were made available to a wide range of readers. Caxton printed the *Canterbury Tales*, the works of Lydgate and of Gower, Malory's *Morte Darthur*, and numerous romances. His own translations into a lucid and vigorous English helped much to shape English prose.

JAMES DOW McCALLUM.

OLD ENGLISH

BEOWULF

The Myth of the Sheaf-Child

List to an old-time lay of the Spear-Danes,
Full of the prowess of famous kings,
Deeds of renown that were done by the heroes;
Scyld the Sheaf-Child from scourging foemen,
From raiders a-many their mead-halls wrested.
He lived to be feared, though first as a waif,
Puny and frail he was found on the shore.
He grew to be great, and was girt with power
Till the border-tribes all obeyed his rule,
And sea-folk hardy that sit by the whale-path   10
Gave him tribute, a good king was he.
Many years after, an heir was born to him,
A goodly youth, whom God had sent
To stay and support his people in need.
(Long time leaderless living in woe,
The sorrow they suffered He saw full well.)
The Lord of Glory did lend him honor,
Beowulf's fame afar was borne,
Son of old Scyld in the Scandian lands.
A youthful heir must be open-handed,   20
Furnish the friends of his father with plenty,
That thus in his age, in the hour of battle,
Willing comrades may crowd around him   (23)
Eager and true. In every tribe
Honorable deeds shall adorn an earl.

1

The aged Scyld, when his hour had come,
Famous and praised, departed to God.
His faithful comrades carried him down
To the brink of the sea, as himself had bidden,
The Scyldings' friend, before he fell silent,   30
Their lord beloved who long had ruled them.
Out in the bay a boat was waiting
Coated with ice, 'twas the king's own barge.
They lifted aboard their bracelet-bestower,
And down on the deck their dear lord laid,
Hard by the mast. Heaped-up treasure
Gathered from far they gave him along.
Never was ship more nobly laden
With wondrous weapons and warlike gear.
Swords and corslets covered his breast   40
Floating riches to ride afar with him
Out o'er the waves at the will of the sea.
No less they dowered their lord with treasure,
Things of price, than those who at first
Had launched him forth as a little child
Alone on the deep to drift o'er the billows.
They gave him to boot a gilded banner,
High o'er his head they hung it aloft.
Then set him adrift, let the surges bear him.
Sad were their hearts, their spirits mournful;   50
Man hath not heard, no mortal can say
Who found that barge's floating burden.

I

The Line of the Danish Kings and the Building of Heorot.

Now Beowulf was king in the burgs of the Scyldings
Famed among folk. (His father had left   (55)
The land of the living). From his loins was sprung

Healfdene the royal, who ruled to old age,
Gray and battlegrim, the bold-hearted Scyldings.
Children four to this chief of the people
Woke unto life, one after another;
Heorogar and Hrothgar, and Halga the brave, 60
And winsome Sigeneow, a Scylfing she wedded;
Saewela's queen they say she became.
To Hrothgar was given such glory in battle,
Such fame he won, that his faithful band
Of youthful warriors waxed amain.
So great had grown his guard of kinsmen,
That it came in his mind to call on his people
To build a mead-hall, mightier far
Than any e'er seen by the sons of men,
Wherein to bestow upon old and young, 70
Gifts and rewards, as God vouchsafed them,
Save folk-share lands and freemen's lives.
Far and wide the work was published;
Many a tribe, the mid-earth round,
Helped to fashion the folk-stead fair.
With speed they built it, and soon 'twas finished,
Greatest of halls. Heorot he named it,
Whose word was law o'er lands afar;
Nor failed in his promise, but freely dealt
Gifts at the feast. The fair hall towered 80
Wide-gabled and high, awaiting its doom, (82)
The sweep of fire; not far was the time
That ancient feuds should open afresh,
And sword-hate sunder sons from fathers.

In the darkness dwelt a demon-sprite,
Whose heart was filled with fury and hate
When he heard each night the noise of revel
Loud in the hall, laughter and song.
To the sound of the harp the singer chanted

Lays he had learned, of long ago; 90
How the Almighty had made the earth,
Wonder-bright lands, washed by the ocean;
How he set triumphant, sun and moon
To lighten all men that live on the earth.
He brightened the land with leaves and branches;
Life he created for every being,
Each in its kind, that moves upon earth.
So, happy in hall, the heroes lived,
Wanting naught, till one began
To work them woe, a wicked fiend. 100
The demon grim was Grendel called,
March-stalker huge, the moors he roamed.
The joyless creature had kept long time
The lonely fen, the lairs of monsters,
Cast out from men, an exile accurst.
The killing of Abel, on offspring of Cain
Was justly avenged by the Judge Eternal.
Naught gained by the feud the faithless murderer;
He was banished unblest from abode of men
And hence arose the host of miscreants, 110
Monsters and elves and eldritch sprites,
Warlocks and giants, that warred against God;
Jotuns and goblins; He gave them their due. (113)

II

The Ravaging of Heorot Hall by the Monster Grendel

When night had fallen, the fiend crept near
To the lofty hall, to learn how the Danes
In Heorot fared, when the feasting was done.
The aethelings all within he saw

Asleep after revel, not recking of danger,
And free from care. The fiend accurst,
Grim and greedy, his grip made ready; 120
Snatched in their sleep, with savage fury,
Thirty warriors; away he sprang
Proud of his prey, to repair to his home,
His blood-dripping booty to bring to his lair.
At early dawn, when day-break came,
The vengeance of Grendel was revealed to all;
Their wails after wassail were widely heard,
Their morning-woe. The mighty ruler,
The aetheling brave, sat bowed with grief.
The fate of his followers filled him with sorrow, 130
When they traced the tracks of the treacherous foe,
Fiend accurst. Too fierce was that onset,
Too loathsome and long, nor left them respite.
The very next night, anew he began
To maim and to murder, nor was minded to slacken
His fury of hate, too hardened in crime.
'Twas easy to find then earls who preferred
A room elsewhere, for rest at night, (139)
A bed in the bowers, when they brought this news
Of the hall-foe's hate; and henceforth all 140
Who escaped the demon, kept distance safe.

So Grendel wrongfully ruled the hall,
One against all till empty stood
That lordly mansion, and long remained so.
For the space of twelve winters the Scyldings' Friend
Bore in his breast the brunt of this sorrow,
Measureless woe. In mournful lays
The tale became known; 'twas told abroad
In gleemen's songs, how Grendel had warred
Long against Hrothgar, and wreaked his hate 150
With murderous fury through many a year,

Refusing to end the feud perpetual,
Or decently deal with the Danes in parley,
Take their tribute for treaty of peace;
Nor could their leaders look to receive
Pay from his hands for the harm that he wrought.
The fell destroyer kept feeding his rage
On young and old. So all night long
He prowled o'er the fen and surprised his victims,
Death-shadow dark. (The dusky realms   160
Where the hell-runes haunt are hidden from men.)
So the exiled roamer his raids continued;
Wrong upon wrong in his wrath he heaped.
In midnights dark he dwelt alone
'Mongst Heorot's trophies and treasures rich.
Great was the grief of the gold-friend of Scyldings,
Vexed was his mood that he might not visit
His goodly throne, his gift-seat proud,
Deprived of joy by the judgment of God.   (169)
Many the wise men that met to discover   170
Ways of escape from the scourge of affliction.
Often they came for counsel together;
Often at heathen altars they made
Sacrifice-offerings, beseeching their idols
To send them deliverance from assault of the foe.
Such was their practice, they prayed to the Devil;
The hope of the heathen on hell was fixed,
The mood of their mind. Their Maker they knew not,
The righteous Judge and Ruler on high.
The Wielder of Glory they worshipped not,   180
The Warden of Heaven. Woe be to him
Whose soul is doomed through spite and envy,
In utter despair and agony hopeless
Forever to burn. But blessed is he
Who, after this life, the Lord shall seek,
Eager for peace in the arms of the Father.

III

The Voyage of Beowulf to the Hall of Hrothgar

Thus boiled with care the breast of Hrothgar; *(189)*
Ceaselessly sorrowed the son of Healfdene,
None of his chieftains might change his lot.
Too fell was the foe that afflicted the people 190
With wrongs unnumbered, and nightly horrors.
Then heard in his home king Hygelac's thane,
The dauntless Jute, of the doings of Grendel.
In strength he outstripped the strongest of men
That dwell in the earth in the days of this life.
Gallant and bold, he gave command *(198)*
To get him a boat, a good wave-skimmer.
O'er the swan-road, he said, he would seek the king
Noble and famous, who needed men.
Though dear to his kin, they discouraged him not; 200
The prudent in counsel praised the adventure,
Whetted his valor, awaiting good omens.

So Beowulf chose from the band of the Jutes
Heroes brave, the best he could find;
He with fourteen followers hardy,
Went to embark; he was wise in seamanship,
Showed them the landmarks, leading the way.
Soon they descried their craft in the water,
At the foot of the cliff. Then climbed aboard
The chosen troop; the tide was churning 210
Sea against sand; they stowed away
In the hold of the ship their shining armor,
War-gear and weapons; the warriors launched
Their well-braced boat on her welcome voyage.

Swift o'er the waves with a wind that favored,
Foam on her breast, like a bird she flew.
A day and a night they drove to seaward,
Cut the waves with the curving prow,
Till the seamen that sailed her sighted the land,
Shining cliffs and coast-wise hills,   **220**
Headlands bold. The harbor opened,
Their cruise was ended. Then quickly the sailors,
The crew of Weder-folk clambered ashore,
Moored their craft with clank of chain-mail,   **(226)**
And goodly war-gear. God they thanked
That their way was smooth o'er the surging waves.

High on the shore, the Scylding coast-guard
Saw from the cliff where he kept his watch,
Glittering shields o'er the gunwale carried,
Polished weapons. It puzzled him sore,   **230**
He wondered in mind who the men might be.
Down to the strand on his steed came riding
Hrothgar's thane, with threatening arm
Shook his war-spear and shouted this challenge:
"Who are ye, men, all mailed and harnessed,
That brought yon ship o'er the broad sea-ways,
And hither have come across the water,
To land on our shores? Long have I stood
As coast-guard here, and kept my sea-watch,
Lest harrying foe with hostile fleet   **240**
Should dare to damage our Danish land.
Armed men never from overseas came
More openly hither. But how do ye know
That law of the land doth give ye leave
To come thus near? I never have seen
Statelier earl upon earth than him,—
Yon hero in harness. No house-carl he,
In lordly array, if looks speak true,

And noble bearing. But now I must learn
Your names and country, ere nearer ye come,   250
Underhand spies, for aught I know,
In Danish land. Now listen, ye strangers,
In from the sea, to my open challenge:
Heed ye my words and haste me to know
What your errand and whence ye have come."

IV

BEOWULF'S WORDS WITH THE COAST-GUARD

Him the hero hailed with an answer,   (258)
The war-troop's leader his word-hoard unlocked:
"In truth we belong to the tribe of the Jutes;
We are Hygelac's own hearth-companions.
Far among folk my father was known,   260
A noble chieftain; his name was Ecgtheow
Honored by all, he ended his days
Full of winters and famed in the land.
Wise men everywhere well remember him.
Hither we fare with friendly purpose
To seek thy lord, the son of Healfdene,
The land-protector. Instruct us kindly.
Bound on adventure we visit thy lord,
The prince of the Danes. Our purpose is open;
Naught keep we secret; thou surely wilt know   270
If the tale we were told is true or not:
That among the Scyldings a monster strange
A nameless demon, when nights are dark,
With cruel cunning, for cause unknown,
Works havoc and slaughter. I have in mind
A way to help your wise king Hrothgar,
Your ruler to rid of the ravening foe,
If ever his tide of troubles shall turn,

The billows of care that boil in his breast
Shall cool and subside, and his sorrow be cured;   280
Else, failing my purpose, forever hereafter
He shall suffer distress, while stands on its hill,
Mounting on high, his matchless hall."
Straight answered the coast-guard, astride his horse,
The warrior brave: "'Twixt words and deeds
A keen-witted thane, if he things aright,
Must well distinguish and weigh the difference.   (289)
Your words I believe, that you wish no evil
To the Scylding lord. I will let you bring
Your shields ashore and show you the way.   290
My comrades here shall keep the watch,
From meddling foe defend your craft,
Your fresh-tarred boat, fast by the beach,
And faithfully guard her till again she bear
With curving bow, o'er the bounding main,
Her master well-loved to the Wedermark.
Fortune oft favors the fighter who yields not;
Hero unflinching comes unhurt from the fray."
Landward they hastened, leaving behind them
Fast at her moorings the full-bosomed boat,   300
The ship at anchor. Shone the boar-heads
Gleaming with gold, o'er the guards of their helmets;
Bright and fire-forged the beast kept watch.
Forward they pressed, proud and adventurous,
Fit for the fight, till afar they descried
The high-peaked radiant roof of the hall.
Of houses far-praised 'neath heaven by the people
That inhabit the earth, this house was most famous,
The seat of king Hrothgar; its splendor gleamed bright
O'er many a land. Their leader well-armed,   310
Showed them the shining shield-burg of heroes,
And set them right on the road to their goal.
Then, wheeling his steed, he wished them farewell:

" 'Tis time that I leave you; the Lord of Heaven,
The Father Almighty in mercy keep you
Safe on your journey; seaward I turn,
Watch to keep and ward against foe."

V

BEOWULF'S ARRIVAL AT THE HALL AND THE MANNER OF HIS RECEPTION

The street was stone-paved; straight it led   *(320)*
To the goal of their journey. Glistened their byrnies
Stout and strong-linked; sang the rings   **320**
Of their iron mail as they marched along,
In armor and helmet right up to the hall.
Sea-voyage-sated, they set their shields,
Their linden-woods broad, along the wall.
As they bent to the bench, their byrnies clattered.
They stacked their spears that stood in a row,
Ashwood tipped with iron above;
Well-equipped was the warlike band.
A stately Dane the strangers addressed,
Asked who they were and whence they had come: **330**
"Whence do ye bear your burnished shields,
Your visored helmets and harness gray,
Your heap of spear-shafts? A servant of Hrothgar's
His herald, am I. Hardier strangers,
Nobler in mien, have I never seen.
'Tis clear you come to the court of Hrothgar,
Not outlaws and beggars, but bent on adventure."
To him gave answer the hero brave,
The lord of the Weders these words returned,
Bold 'neath his helmet: "We are Hygelac's men,   **340**
His board-companions. I am Beowulf called.
Ready am I the ruler to answer,

To say to thy lord, the son of Healfdene,   *(345)*
Why we have come his court to seek,
If he will graciously grant us a hearing."
Wulfgar replied (he was prince of the Wendles,
His noble renown was known to many,
His courage in war, and wisdom in counsel):
"I will carry thy quest to the king of the Danes,
And ask him whether he wishes to grant   350
The boon thou dost ask of the breaker-of-rings,
To speak to himself concerning thy journey;
And straight will I bring thee the answer he sends."
Swiftly he hied him where Hrothgar sat,
White-haired and old, his earls around him.
Stately he strode, till he stood in the presence
Of the king of the Danes,—in courtly ways
Was Wulfgar skilled; he spoke to his lord:
"Hither have fared from a far country,
A band of Jutes o'er the bounding sea.   360
Their leader and chief by his chosen comrades
Is Beowulf called; this boon they ask:
That they may find with thee, my lord,
Favor of speech; refuse them not,
But grant them, Hrothgar, gracious hearing.
In armor clad, they claim respect
Of choicest earls; but chiefly their lord
Who lately hither hath led his comrades."

VI

HROTHGAR'S WELCOME TO BEOWULF

Hrothgar spoke, the Scyldings' protector:
"Beowulf I knew in his boyhood days: 370
His aged father was Ecgtheow named.
To him, to take home, did Hrethel give   *(374)*

His only daughter. Their dauntless son
Now comes to my court in quest of a friend.
My sea-faring men whom I sent afar
To the land of the Jutes, with generous gifts,
In token of friendship, have told me this,
That the power of his grip was so great it equalled
The strength of thirty stout-armed thanes.
Him bold in battle, the blessed God   380
Hath sent in his mercy, to save our people
—So I hope in my heart—from the horror of Grendel.
I shall offer him gold for his gallant spirit.
Go now in haste, and greet the strangers;
Bid to the hall the whole of the company;
Welcome with words the warrior band,
To the home of the Danes." To the hall door went
Wulfgar the courtly, and called them in:
"My master commands me this message to give you,
The lord of the Danes your lineage knows;   390
Bids me to welcome you, brave-hearted warriors,
Bound on adventure o'er the billowy main.
Ye may rise now and enter, arrayed in your armor,
Covered with helmets, the king to greet.
But leave your shields, and your shafts of slaughter,
Here by the wall to await the issue."
Then rose the leader, around him his comrades,
Sturdy war-band; some waited without,
Bid by the bold one their battle-gear to guard.
Together they hastened where the herald led them,   400
Under Heorot's roof. The hero went first,
Strode under helmet, till he stood by the hearth. *(404)*
Beowulf spoke, his byrnie glistened,
His corslet chain-linked by cunning of smithcraft:
"Hail, King Hrothgar! Hygelac's thane
And kinsman am I. Known is the record
Of deeds of renown I have done in my youth.

Far in my home, I heard of this Grendel;
Sea-farers tell the tale of the hall:
How bare of warriors, this best of buildings   410
Deserted stands, when the sun goes down
And twilight deepens to dark in the sky.
By comrades encouraged, I come on this journey.
The best of them bade me, the bravest and wisest,
To go to thy succor, O good king Hrothgar;
For well they approved my prowess in battle,
They saw me themselves come safe from the conflict
When five of my foes I defeated and bound,
Beating in battle the brood of the monsters.
At night on the sea with nicors I wrestled,   420
Avenging the Weders, survived the sea-peril,
And crushed in my grip the grim sea-monsters
That harried my neighbors. Now I am come
To cope with Grendel in combat single,
And match my might against the monster, alone.
I pray thee therefore, prince of the Scyldings,
Not to refuse the favor I ask,
Having come so far, O friend of the Shield-Danes,
That I alone with my loyal comrades,
My hardy companions, may Heorot purge.   430
Moreover they say that the slaughterous fiend
In wanton mood all weapons despises.
Hence,—as I hope that Hygelac may,
My lord and king, be kind to me,—
Sword and buckler I scorn to bear,
Gold-adorned shield, as I go to the conflict.
With my grip will I grapple the gruesome fiend,
Foe against foe, to fight for our life.
And he that shall fall his faith must put
In the judgment of God. If Grendel wins   440
He is minded to make his meal in the hall
Untroubled by fear, on the folk of the Jutes,

As often before he fed on the Danes.
No need for thee then to think of my burial.
If I lose my life, the lonely prowler
My blood-stained body will bear to his den,
Swallow me greedily, and splash with my gore
His lair in the marsh; no longer wilt then
Have need to find me food and sustenance.
To Hygelac send, if I sink in the battle,   450
This best of corslets that covers my breast,
Heirloom of Hrethel, rarest of byrnies,
The work of Weland. So Wyrd will be done."

VII

THE FEASTING IN HEOROT AND THE CUSTOMS OF THE HALL

Hrothgar spoke, the Scyldings' defender:
"Thou hast come, dear Beowulf, to bring us help,
For the sake of friendship to fight our battles.   *(458)*
  (Hrothgar recounts the exploits of Beowulf's father.)
Sad is my spirit and sore it grieves me   *(473)*
To tell to any the trouble and shame
That Grendel hath brought me with bitter hate,
The havoc he wrought in my ranks in the hall.   460
My war-band dwindles, driven by Wyrd
Into Grendel's grasp; but God may easily
End this monster's mad career.
Full often they boasted, my beer-bold warriors,
Brave o'er their ale-cups, the best of my fighters,
They'd meet in the mead-hall the mighty Grendel,
End his orgies with edge of the sword.
But always the mead-hall, the morning after,
The splendid building, was blood-bespattered;
Daylight dawned on the drippings of swords,   470

Soiled with slaughter were sills and benches.
My liege-men perished, and left me poor.
Sit down to the board; unbend thy thoughts;
Speak to my men as thy mood shall prompt."
For the band of the Jutes a bench was cleared;
Room in the mead-hall was made for them all.
Then strode to their seats the strong-hearted heroes.
The warriors' wants a waiting-thane served;
Held in his hand the highly-wrought ale-cup,
Poured sparkling mead, while the minstrel sang   **480**
Gaily in Heorot. There was gladness of heroes,
A joyous company of Jutes and of Danes.

VIII

Unferth Taunts Beowulf

Then up spoke Unferth, Ecglaf's son,
Who sat at the feet of the Scylding ruler;
He vented his jealousy. The journey of Beowulf,
His sea-adventure, sorely displeased him.   *(502)*
It filled him with envy that any other
Should win among men more war-like glory,
More fame under heaven than he himself:
"Art thou the Beowulf that battled with Brecca,   **490**
Far out at sea, when ye swam together,
What time you two made trial of the billows,
Risking your lives in reckless folly,
On the open sea? None might dissuade you,
Friend nor foe, from the fool-hardy venture,
When straight from the shore you struck for the open,
Breasted the waves and beat with your arms
The mounting billows, measured the sea-paths
With lusty strokes. Stirred was the ocean
By wintry storms. Seven days and nights

Your sea-strife lasted; at length he beat you;
His strength was the better; at break of day
He made the beach where the Battle-Reamas
Dwell by the shore; and straightway returned
To his people beloved in the land of the Brondings,
Where liegemen and towns and treasure were his.
In sooth I say, the son of Beanstan
His boast against thee made good to the full.
But now I ween a worse fate awaits thee
Though thy mettle be proved in many a battle   510
And grim encounter, if the coming of Grendel
Thou darest abide, in the dead of the night."
Beowulf spoke, the son of Ecgtheow:
"What a deal of stuff thou hast talked about Brecca,
Garrulous with drink my good friend Unferth.
Thou hast lauded his deeds. Now listen to me!
More sea-strength had I, more ocean-endurance
Than any man else, the wide earth round.   *(534)*
 Tis true we planned in the pride of our youth
This ocean-adventure, and vowed we would risk   520
Our lives in the deep, each daring the other.
We were both of us boys, but our boast we fulfilled.
Our naked swords as we swam from the land,
We held in our grasp, to guard against whales.
Not a stroke could he gain on me, strive as he would,
Make swifter speed through the swelling waves,
Nor could I in swimming o'ercome him at sea.
Side by side in the surge we labored
Five nights long. At last we were parted
By furious seas and a freezing gale.   530
Night fell black; the norther wild
Rushed on us ruthless and roughened the sea.
Now was aroused the wrath of the monsters,
But my war-proof ring-mail, woven and hand-locked,
Served me well 'gainst the sea-beasts' fury;

The close-linked battle-net covered my breast.
I was dragged to the bottom by a blood-thirsty monster,
Firm in his clutch the furious sea-beast
Helpless held me. But my hand came free,
And my foe I pierced with point of my sword.   540
With my battle-blade good 'twas given me to kill
The dragon of the deep, by dint of my blow."

IX

BEOWULF COMPLETES THE STORY OF HIS SWIMMING ADVENTURE WITH BRECCA. HROTHGAR'S DEPARTURE FROM THE HALL.

"Thus sore beset me sea-beasts thronging,   *(559)*
Murderous man-eaters. I met their charges,
Gave them their due with my goodly blade.
They failed of their fill, the feast they expected
In circle sitting on the sea-floor together
With me for their meal. I marred their pleasure.
When morning came, they were cast ashore
By the wash of the waves; their wounds
          proved fatal;   550
Bloated and dead on the beach they lay.
No more would they cross the course of the ships,
In the chop of the channel charge the sailors.
Day broke in the east, bright beacon of God;
The sea fell smooth. I saw bold headlands,
Windy walls; for Wyrd oft saveth
A man not doomed, if he dauntless prove.
My luck did not fail me, my long sword finished
Nine of the nicors. Ne'er have I heard
Of fiercer battle fought in the night,   560
Of hero more harried by horrors at sea.
Yet I saved my life from the sea-beasts' clutch.

Worn with the struggle, I was washed ashore
In the realm of the Finns by the run of the tide,
The heave of the flood. I have failed to hear
Of like adventure laid to thee,
Battle so bitter. Brecca did never,—
Neither of you was known to achieve
Deed so valiant, adventure so daring,
Sword-play so nimble; not that I boast of it, *(586)* 570
But mark me, Unferth, you murdered your brothers,
Your closest of kin. The curse of hell
For this you will suffer, though sharp be your wit.
In sooth I say to you, son of Ecglaf,
Never had Grendel such grim deeds wrought,
Such havoc in Heorot, so harried your king
With bestial fury, if your boasted courage
In deeds as well as in words you had proved.
But now he has found he need not fear
Vengeance fierce from the Victory-Scyldings, 580
Ruthless attack in return for his raids.
He takes his toll of your tribe as he pleases,
Sparing none of your spearmen proud.
He ravens and rages and recks not the Dane folk,
Safe from their sword-play. But soon I will teach him
How the Jute-folk fight. Then freely may go
To the mead-hall who likes, when the light of the morning,
The next day's dawn, the dark shall dispel,
And the heaven-bright sun from the south shall shine."

Glad in his heart was the giver of rings, 590
Hoped to have help, the hoar-headed king;
The Shield-Danes' shepherd was sure of relief,
When he found in Beowulf so firm a resolve.
There was laughter of heroes. Loud was their revelry,
Words were winsome as Wealhtheow rose,

Queen of Hrothgar, heedful of courtesy,
Gold-adorned greeted the guests in the hall.
First to her lord, the land defender,   *(615)*
The high-born lady handed the cup;
Bade him be gleeful and gay at the board,   **600**
And good to his people. Gladly he took it,
Quaffed from the beaker, the battle-famed king.
Then leaving her lord, the lady of the Helmings
Passed among her people in each part of the hall,
Offered the ale-cup to old and young,
Till she came to the bench where Beowulf sat.
The jewel-laden queen in courteous manner
Beowulf greeted; to God gave thanks,
Wise in her words, that her wish was granted,
That at last in her trouble a trusted hero   **610**
Had come for comfort. The cup received
From Wealhtheow's hand the hardy warrior,
And made this reply, his mind on the battle;
Beowulf spoke, the son of Ecgtheow:
"I made up my mind when my mates and I
Embarked in our boat, outbound on the sea,
That fully I'd work the will of thy people,
Or fall in the fight, in the clutch of the fiend.
I surely shall do a deed of glory,
Worthy an earl, or end my days,   **620**
My morning of life, in the mead-hall here."
His words pleased well the wife of Hrothgar,
The Jutish lord's boast. The jewelled queen
Went to sit by the side of her lord.

Renewed was the sound of noisy revel,
Wassail of warriors. Brave words were spoken.
Mirth in the mead-hall mounted high,
Till Healfdene's son the sign did give
That he wished to retire. Full well he knew   *(646)*

The fiend would find a fight awaiting him,   630
When the light of the sun had left the hall,
And creeping night should close upon them,
And shadowy shapes come striding on
Dim through the dark. The Danes arose.
Hrothgar again gave greeting to Beowulf,
Wished him farewell; the wine-hall lofty
He left in his charge. These last words spoke he:
"Never before have I fully entrusted
To mortal man this mighty hall,
Since arm and shield I was able to lift.   640
To thee alone I leave it now,
To have and to hold it. Thy hardihood prove!
Be mindful of glory; keep watch for the foe!
No reward shalt thou lack if thou live through this fight."

X

BEOWULF'S WATCH IN HEOROT

Then Hrothgar went with his warrior-band,
The Arm-of-the-Scyldings, out of the hall.
Would the war-lord Wealhtheow seek,
The queen for his bed-mate. The best of kings
Had placed in the hall, so heroes report,
A watch against Grendel, to guard his house,   650
Deliverance bring to the land of the Danes.
But the lord of the Jutes joyfully trusted
In the might of his arm and the mercy of God.
Off he stripped his iron byrnie,
Helmet from head, and handed his sword,   (672)
Choicest of blades, to his body-thane,
And bade him keep the battle armor.
Then made his boast once more the warrior,
Beowulf the bold, ere his bed he sought,

Summoned his spirit: "Not second to Grendel   660
In combat I count me and courage of war.
But not with the sword will I slay this foeman,
Though light were the task to take his life.
Nothing at all does he know of such fighting,
Of hewing of shields, though shrewd be his malice
Ill deeds to contrive. We two in the night
Shall do without swords, if he dare to meet me
In hand to hand battle. May the holy Lord
To one or the other award the victory,
As it seems to Him right, Ruler all-wise."   670
Then he sought his bed. The bolster received
The head of the hero. In the hall about him,
Stretched in sleep, his sailormen lay.
Not one of them thought he would ever return
Home to his country, nor hoped to see
His people again, and the place of his birth.
They had heard of too many men of the Danes
O'ertaken suddenly, slain without warning,
In the royal hall. But the Ruler on High
Through the woof of fate to the Wederfolk gave   680
Friendship and help, their foes to o'ercome,
By a single man's strength to slay the destroyer.
Thus all may learn that the Lord Almighty
Wields for aye the Wyrds of men.   *(702)*

* * * * *

XI

Beowulf's Fight With Grendel

Now Grendel came, from his crags of mist   *(710)*
Across the moor; he was curst of God.
The murderous prowler meant to surprise
In the high-built hall his human prey.

He stalked 'neath the clouds, till steep before him
The house of revelry rose in his path,   690
The gold-hall of heroes, the gaily adorned.
Hrothgar's home he had hunted full often,
But never before had he found to receive him
So hardy a hero, such hall-guards there.
Close to the building crept the slayer,
Doomed to misery. The door gave way,
Though fastened with bolts, when his fist fell on it.
Maddened he broke through the breach he had made;
Swoln with anger and eager to slay,
The ravening fiend o'er the bright-paved floor   700
Furious ran, while flashed from his eyes
An ugly glare like embers aglow.
He saw in the hall, all huddled together,
The heroes asleep. Then laughed in his heart
The hideous fiend; he hoped ere dawn
To sunder body from soul of each;
He looked to appease his lust of blood,
Glut his maw with the men he would slay.
But Wyrd had otherwise willed his doom;
Never again should he get a victim   710
After that night. Narrowly watched
Hygelac's thane how the horrible slayer
Forward should charge in fierce attack.
Nor was the monster minded to wait: (739)
Sudden he sprang on a sleeping thane,
Ere he could stir, he slit him open;
Bit through the bone-joints, gulped the blood,
Greedily bolted the body piecemeal.
Soon he had swallowed the slain man wholly,
Hands and feet. Then forward he hastened,   720
Sprang at the hero, and seized him at rest;
Fiercely clutched him with fiendish claw.
But quickly Beowulf caught his forearm,

And threw himself on it with all his weight.
Straight discovered that crafty plotter,
That never in all mid-earth had he met
In any man a mightier grip.
Gone was his courage, and craven fear
Sat in his heart, yet helped him no sooner.
Fain would he hide in his hole in the fenland,   **730**
His devil's den. A different welcome
From former days he found that night!
Now Hygelac's thane, the hardy, remembered
His evening's boast, and bounding up,
Grendel he clenched, and cracked his fingers;
The monster tried flight, but the man pursued;
The ravager hoped to wrench himself free,
And gain the fen, for he felt his fingers
Helpless and limp in the hold of his foe.
'Twas a sorry visit the man-devourer   **740**
Made to the Hall of the Hart that night.
Dread was the din, the Danes were frighted
By the uproar wild of the ale-spilling fray.
The hardiest blenched as the hall-foes wrestled
In terrible rage. The rafters groaned;
'Twas wonder great that the wine-hall stood,   **(771)**
Firm 'gainst the fighters' furious onslaught,
Nor fell to the ground, that glorious building.
With bands of iron 'twas braced and stiffened
Within and without. But off from the sill   **750**
Many a mead-bench mounted with gold
Was wrung where they wrestled in wrath together.
The Scylding nobles never imagined
That open attack, or treacherous cunning,
Could wreck or ruin their royal hall,
The lofty and antlered, unless the flames
Should some day swallow it up in smoke.
The din was renewed, the noise redoubled;

Each man of the Danes was mute with dread,
That heard from the wall the horrible wail, 760
The gruesome song of the godless foe,
His howl of defeat, as the fiend of hell
Bemoaned his hurt. The man held fast;
Greatest he was in grip of strength,
Of all that dwelt upon earth that day.

XII

THE DEFEAT OF GRENDEL

Loath in his heart was the hero-deliverer
To let escape his slaughterous guest.
Of little use that life he deemed
To human kind. The comrades of Beowulf
Unsheathed their weapons to ward their leader, 770
Eagerly brandished their ancient blades,
The life of their peerless lord to defend.
Little they deemed, those dauntless warriors, *(798)*
As they leaped to the fray, those lusty fighters,
Laying on boldly to left and to right,
Eager to slay, that no sword upon earth
No keenest weapon could wound that monster:
Point would not pierce, he was proof against iron;
'Gainst victory-blades the devourer was charmed.
But a woeful end awaited the wretch, 780
That very day he was doomed to depart,
And fare afar to the fiends' domain.

Now Grendel found, who in former days
So many a warrior had wantonly slain,
In brutish lust, abandoned of God,
That the frame of his body was breaking at last.
Keen of courage, the kinsman of Hygelac
Held him grimly gripped in his hands.

Loath was each to the other alive.
The grisly monster got his death-wound: 790
A huge split opened under his shoulder;
Crunched the socket, cracked the sinews.
Glory great was given to Beowulf.
But Grendel escaped with his gaping wound,
O'er the dreary moor his dark den sought,
Crawled to his lair. 'Twas clear to him then,
The count of his hours to end had come,
Done were his days. The Danes were glad,
The hard fight was over, they had their desire.
Cleared was the hall, 'twas cleansed by the hero   800
With keen heart and courage, who came from afar.
The lord of the Jutes rejoiced in his work,
The deed of renown he had done that night.
His boast to the Danes he bravely fulfilled;   (829)
From lingering woe delivered them all;
From heavy sorrow they suffered in heart;
From dire distress they endured so long;
From toil and from trouble. This token they saw:
The hero had laid the hand of Grendel
Both arm and claws, the whole forequarter   810
With clutches huge, 'neath the high-peaked roof.

XIII

The Celebration of the Victory and the Song
of the Gleeman

When morning arrived, so runs the report,
Around the gift-hall gathered the warriors;
The folk-leaders fared from far and near,
The wide ways o'er, the wonder to view,
The wild beast's foot-prints. Not one of them felt
Regret that the creature had come to grief,

When they traced his retreat by the tracks on the moor;
Marked where he wearily made his way,
Harried and beaten, to the haunt of the nicors, 820
Slunk to the water, to save his life.
There they beheld the heaving surges,
Billows abrim with bloody froth,
Dyed with gore, where the gruesome fiend,
Stricken and doomed, in the struggle of death
Gave up his ghost in the gloom of the mere,
His heathen soul for hell to receive it.
Then from the mere the thanes turned back,
Men and youths from the merry hunt, (854)
Home they rode on their horses gray, 830
Proudly sitting their prancing steeds.
Beowulf's prowess was praised by all.
They all agreed that go where you will,
'Twixt sea and sea, at the south or the north,
None better than he, no braver hero,
None worthier honor could ever be found.
(They meant no slight to their master and lord
The good king Hrothgar, their ruler kind.)

Now and again the noble chiefs
Gave rein to their steeds, and spurred them to race, 840
Galloped their grays where the ground was smooth.
Now and again a gallant thane,
Whose mind was stored with many a lay,
With songs of battle and sagas old,
Bound new words in well-knit bars,
Told in verse the valor of Beowulf,
Matched his lines and moulded his lay. (872)

Here is introduced an episode of the Nibelungen Legend.
The gleeman tells how Sigmund the Volsung with his son and
nephew Fitela ranged the forests and slew wild beasts. Later
when Fitela was no longer with him, Sigmund killed a dragon
and won a great treasure.

When the lay was ended they urged once more
Their racers fleet to fly o'er the plain.   (916)
As the morning sped, and the sun climbed higher,   850
Many went in, the marvellous sight
More closely to scan. The king himself
With a troop of trusty retainers about him
Strode from his bower; the bestower-of-rings
Came, and with him the queen, in state,
The meadow-path trod, by her maidens attended.

XIV

HROTHGAR'S PRAISE OF BEOWULF, AND BEOWULF'S REPLY

Hrothgar spoke when he reached the hall,
Stood on the step, and stared at the roof
Adorned with gold, and Grendel's hand:
"Prompt be my heart to praise the Almighty   860
For the sight I behold. Much harm have I suffered,
And grief from Grendel, but God still works
Wonder on wonder, the Warden of Glory.
But a little while since, I scarcely dared,
As long as I lived, to look for escape
From my burden of sorrow, when blood-stained stood
And dripping with slaughter, this stately hall.
Wide-spread woe my warriors scattered;
They never hoped this house to rid,
While life should last, this land-mark of people,   870
Of demons and devils. 'Tis done by the hero.
By the might of the Lord this man has finished
The feat that all of us failed to achieve
By wit or by war. And well may she say,
—Whoever she be.—that bore this son,

That the Ancient of Days dealt with her graciously,
And blest her in child-birth. Now Beowulf, hear!
I shall henceforth hold thee, hero beloved,
As child of my own, and cherish thee fondly   (948)
In kinship new. Thou shalt never lack   880
Meed of reward that is mine to give.
For deeds less mighty have I many times granted
Fullest reward to warriors feebler,
In battle less brave. Thy boldness and valor
Afar shall be known; thy fame shall live
To be great among men. Now God the Almighty
With honor reward thee, as ever he doth."

Beowulf spoke, the son of Ecgtheow:
"Gladly we fought this good fight through,
Fearlessly faced the foe inhuman,   890
Grappled him gruesome; it grieves me sore
That the man-beast himself you may not see,
Dead in the hall, fordone in the fray.
I meant to master the monster quickly,
To his death-bed pin him by power of my grip,
Hold him hard till my hand could strangle him,
Bringing him low, but he broke away.
In vain I tried to prevent his escape.
The Lord was unwilling; I lost my hold
On the man-destroyer; too strong was the monster, 900
Too swift on his feet. But to save his life
He left behind him the whole of his fore-paw,
Arm and shoulder. 'Twas a useless shift,
Profiting nothing. He ne'er will prolong
His life by the loss, the loathly slayer,
Sunk in sin; but sorrow holds him,
Caught in the grasp of its grip relentless,
In woful bonds to await in anguish,

Guilty wretch, the rest of his doom,
As the Lord Almighty shall mete it to him." *(979)* 910
More silent seemed the son of Ecglaf
Less boastful in bragging of brave deeds done
When all of them, looking aloft, beheld
The hand on high, where it hung 'neath the roof,
The claw of the fiend; each finger was armed
With a steel-like spur instead of a nail,
The heathen's handspikes, the horrible paw
Of the evil fiend. They all declared
No iron blade could e'er have bit
On the monstrous bulk of the man-beast's hide,   920
Or hewn away that woful talon.

XV

THE FEASTING AND GIVING OF TREASURE IN THE HALL

Now orders were given the guest-hall to cleanse,
And furnish it fresh. Forth went hurrying
Men and maids. To the mead-hall they went
And busily worked. Woven tapestries,
Glinting with gold, hung gay on the walls,
Marvellous wonders for men to look upon.
Ruin and wreck had been wrought in the building,
Though braced within by iron bands.
The hinges were wrenched, the roof alone stood   930
Undamaged and sound, when the sin-spotted wretch
The demon destroyer, in despair of his life,
Turned and made off,—not easy it is
To escape from death, essay it who will.
(So each of us all to his end must come   *(1004)*
Forced by fate to his final abode
Where his body, stretched on the bier of death,
Shall rest after revel.) Now right was the hour
For Healfdene's heir to enter the hall,

The king himself would come to the feast.   **940**
I never have heard of nobler bearing
Mongst ranks of liegemen surrounding their lord
As they took their seats, the trusty comrades,
And fell to feasting. Freely quaffed
Many a mead-cup the mighty kinsmen
Hrothgar and Hrothulf, the high hall within.
Heorot was filled with a friendly host.
(Far was the day when the Scylding host
Should treachery plot, betraying each other.)
Then Healfdene's son bestowed on Beowulf   **950**
A gold-adorned banner for battle-reward,
A rich-broidered standard, breast-plate and helmet.
The swordmen assembled saw the treasures
Borne before the hero. Beowulf drank
The health of Hrothgar, nor had reason to feel
Ashamed before shieldmen to show his reward.
Never were offered by earls that I heard of,
In token of friendship four such treasures,
Never was equalled such ale-bench bounty.
Round the ridge of the helmet a rim of iron   **960**
Wound with wire, warded the head,
That the offspring of files, with fearful stroke,
The hard-tempered sword-blade, might harm it not,
When fierce in the battle the foemen should join.
At a sign from the king, eight stallions proud
Bitted and bridled were brought into hall.
On the back of one was a wondrous saddle,   *(1037)*
Bravely wrought and bordered with jewels,
The battle-seat bold of the best of kings
When Hrothgar himself would ride to the sword-   **970**
    play.
(Nor flinched from the foe the famous warrior
In the front of the fight where fell the slain.)
To the hero delivered the lord of the Scyldings
The heir of Ing, both armor and horses,

Gave them to Beowulf, and bade him enjoy them.
Thus royally, the ruler famous,
The heroes' hoard-guard, heaped his bounty;
Repaid the struggle with steeds and trophies,
Praised by all singers who speak the truth.

XVI

The King's Gifts To Beowulf's Men, and the Gleeman's Lay of Finn

The Lord of the earls then added gifts,   980
At the mead-bench remembered the men, each one,
That Beowulf brought o'er the briny deep,
With ancient heirlooms and offered to pay
In gold for the man that Grendel had slain,
As more of them surely the monster had killed
Had not holy God and the hero's courage
Averted their doom. (So daily o'errules
The Father Almighty the fortunes of men.
Therefore is insight ever the best,
And prudence of mind; for much shall suffer   990
Of lief and of loath who long endures
The days of his life in labor and toil.)
Now music and song were mingled together,   (1063)
In the presence of Hrothgar, ruler in war.
Harp was struck and hero-lays told.
Along the mead-bench the minstrel spread
Cheer in hall when he chanted the lay
Of the sudden assault on the sons of Finn.   (1068)

The episode which follows alludes obscurely to details of a
feud between Frisians and Danes. The Finnsburg fragment
contains a portion of the same story and one of the heroes,
Hnaef, is also mentioned in Widsith.

XVII

THE LAY OF FINN ENDED. THE SPEECH OF THE QUEEN

The lay was ended, (1159)

The gleeman's song. Sound of revelry   1000
Rose again. Gladness spread
Along bench and board. Beer-thanes poured
From flagons old the flowing wine.
Wealhtheow the queen walked in state,
Under her crown, where uncle and nephew
Together sat,—they still were friends.
There too sat Unferth, trusted counsellor,
At Hrothgar's feet; though faith he had broken
With his kinsmen in battle, his courage was proved.
Then the queen of the Scyldings spoke these words: 1010
"Quaff of this cup my king and my lord,
Gold-friend of men. To thy guests be kind,
To the men of the Jutes be generous with gifts.
Far and near thou now hast peace.
I have heard thou dost wish the hero for son
To hold as thy own, now Heorot is cleansed,   <i>(1176)</i>
The jewel-bright hall. Enjoy while thou mayest,
Allotment of wealth, and leave to thy heirs
Kingdom and rule when arrives the hour
That hence thou shalt pass to thy place appointed. 1020
Well I know that my nephew Hrothulf
Will cherish in honor our children dear
If thou leavest before him this life upon earth;
He will surely requite the kindness we showed him,
Faithfully tend our two young sons,
When to mind he recalls our care and affection
How we helped him and housed him when <i>he</i> was a
    child."
She turned to the bench where her two boys sat,

Hrethric and Hrothmund, and the rest of the youth,
A riotous band, and right in their midst,   1030
Between the two brothers, Beowulf sat.

XVIII

The Queen's Gifts to Beowulf

With courteous bow the cup she offered,
Greeted him graciously and gave him to boot
Two armlets rare of twisted gold,
A robe and rings, and the rarest collar;
A better was never known among men,
Since Hama brought to his bright-built hall
The jewelled necklace, the gem of the Brisings. *(1199)*

Lines 1200-1214 interrupt the narrative to tell of the subsequent history of Wealhtheow's gift; how Beowulf gave it
to Hygelac, who wore it on his famous raid against the Frisians, in which he was slain by the Franks.

Before the warriors Wealhtheow spoke: *(1215)*
"Accept, dear Beowulf, this bright-gemmed collar; 1040
Make happy use of this heirloom jewelled,
This ring and robe and royal treasure;
Be brave and bold. My boys instruct
In gentle manners; mine be the praise.
Thou hast done such a deed that in days to come
Men will proclaim thy might and valor
To the ends of the earth where the ocean-wave
Washes the windy walls of the land.
I wish thee joy of thy jewelled treasure,
Long be thy life; enlarge thy prosperity,   1050
Show thee a friend to my sons in deed.
Here each earl to the other is faithful,
True to his liege-lord, loyal and kind.
My warriors obey me, willing and prompt.

The Danes carousing, do as I bid."
She went to her seat, the wine flowed free;
'Twas a glorious feast. The fate that impended,
None of them knew, though near to them all.

When darkness came, the king of the Danes
Went to his rest in the royal bower;   1060
But a throng of his kinsmen kept the hall
As they used to do in the days of old.
They cleared the boards and covered the floor
With beds and bolsters. One beer-thane there
Lay down to sleep with his doom upon him.
They placed by their heads their polished shields,
Their battle-boards bright, on the bench nearby.
Above each earl, within easy reach,   *(1244)*
Was his helmet high and his harness of mail
And the spear-shaft keen. 'Twas their custom so,   1070
That always at rest they were ready for war
At home or abroad, where'er they might be,
At what hour soever for aid might call
Their lord and king; they were comrades true.

END OF THE FIRST ADVENTURE

XIX

The Coming of Grendel's Dam to Avenge Her Son

Then sank they to sleep, but sorely paid
One poor wretch for his rest that night.
The same fell, as in former days
When Grendel his raids on the gold-hall made,
Before the fiend had found his match,
Caught in his sins. 'Twas seen that night   1080
An avenger survived the villainous fiend,
Although they had ceased from their sorrow and care.

'Twas Grendel's mother, a monstrous hag.
She remembered her loss. She had lived in the deep,
In a water-hell cold since Cain had become
The evil slayer of his only brother,
His kin by blood; accursed he fled
Marked by murder from men's delights,
Haunted the wilds; from him there sprung
Ghastly demon-shapes, Grendel was one. *(1266)* 1090

The omitted lines break the narrative to turn back to the Grendel fight.

     Now grim and vengeful *(1276)*
His mother set out on her errand of woe,
Damage to wreak for the death of her son.
Arrived at Heorot, the Ring-Danes she found
Asleep in the hall. Soon was to come
Surprise to the earls when into the hall
Burst Grendel's dam. (Less grim was the terror
As terror of woman in war is less,
—The fury of maidens, than full-armed men's,
When the blood-stained war-blade with
  wire-bound hilt,   1100
Hard and hammer-forged, hurtling through air,
Hews the boar from the helmet's crest.)
Many the swords that were suddenly drawn,
Blades from the benches; buckler and shield
Were tightly grasped; no time for the helmet,
For harness of mail, when the horror was on them.
The monster was minded to make for the open;
Soon as discovered, she sought to escape.
Quickly she seized a sleeping warrior,
Fast in her clutch to the fens she dragged him. 1110
He was to Hrothgar of heroes the dearest,
Most trusted of liegemen between the two seas,
Comrade the nearest, killed in his sleep,
The bravest in battle. Nor was Beowulf there;

They had elsewhere quartered the earl that night,
After the giving of gifts in the hall.
There was shouting in Heorot; the hand she seized,
The bloody talon, she took away.
Sorrow was renewed in the nearby dwellings, *(1304)*
Bad was the bargain that both had made 1120
To pay for their friends with further lives lost.
With grief overcome was the gray-haired king
When he learned that his thane was alive no more,
His dearest comrade by death o'ertaken,
Quick from his bower was Beowulf fetched,
The hero brave. At break of dawn
He with his comrades came to the place
Where the king in sorrow was waiting to see
Whether God the Wielder of All would grant him
A turn in his tide of trouble and woe. 1130
Then entered the room the ready hero;
With his band of brave men the boards resounded.
He eagerly greeted the aged ruler,
Delayed not to ask the Lord of the Ingwines
If his night had passed in peace and quiet.

XX

HROTHGAR DESCRIBES THE HAUNT OF THE MONSTER AND ASKS BEOWULF TO UNDERTAKE A SECOND ADVENTURE

Hrothgar spoke, the Scylding defender:
"Speak not of peace, for pain is renewed
'Mongst all the Danes. Dead is Æschere,
Elder brother of Irmenlaf,
My comrade true and counsellor trusted, 1140
My right-hand friend when in front of the combat
We stood shoulder to shoulder, when shield-burg broke,

And boar-crests crashed in battle together.   (1328)
Earls should ever like Æschere be.
On Heorot's floor he was foully slain
By warlock wild. I wot not whither
The prey-proud fury hath fled to cover,
Glutted and gorged. With gruesome claws
And violence fierce she avenged thy deed,
The slaying of Grendel her son last night,   1150
Because too long my loyal thanes
He had hunted and hurt. In the hall he fell;
His life was forfeit. To the fray returned
Another as cruel, her kin to avenge;
Faring from far, the feud re-opened.
Hence many a thane shall mourn and think
Of the giver of gifts with grief renewed
And heart-woe heavy. The hand lies low
That fain would have helped and defended you all.
I have heard my people, the peasant folk   1160
Who house by the border and hold the fens,
Say they have seen two creatures strange,
Huge march-stalkers, haunting the moorland,
Wanderers outcast. One of the two
Seemed to their sight to resemble a woman;
The other manlike, a monster misshapen,
But huger in bulk than human kind,
Trod an exile's track of woe.
The folk of the fen in former days
Named him Grendel. Unknown his father,   1170
Or what his descent from demons obscure.
Lonely and waste is the land they inhabit,
Wolf-cliffs wild and windy headlands,
Ledges of mist, where mountain torrents
Downward plunge to dark abysses,   (1360)
And flow unseen. Not far from here
O'er the moorland in miles, a mere expands:

Spray-frosted trees o'erspread it, and hang
O'er the water with roots fast wedged in the rocks.
There nightly is seen, beneath the flood,   1180
A marvellous light. There lives not the man
Has fathomed the depth of the dismal mere.
Though the heather-stepper, the strong-horned stag,
Seek this cover, forspent with the chase,
Tracked by the hounds, he will turn at bay,
To die on the brink ere he brave the plunge,
Hide his head in the haunted pool.
Wan from its depths the waves are dashed,
When wicked storms are stirred by the wind,
And from sullen skies descends the rain.   1190
In thee is our hope of help once more.
Not yet thou hast learned where leads the way
To the lurking-hole of this hatcher of outrage.
Seek, if thou dare, the dreaded spot!
Richly I pay thee for risking this fight,
With heirlooms golden and ancient rings,
As I paid thee before, if thou come back alive."

XXI

The Arrival of Hrothgar and Beowulf at Grendel's Mere

Beowulf spoke, the son of Ecgtheow:
"Sorrow not, gray-beard, nor grieve o'er thy friend!
Vengeance is better than bootless mourning.   1200
To each of us here the end must come   *(1368)*
Of life upon earth: let him who may
Win glory ere death. I deem that best,
The lot of the brave, when life is over.
Rise, O realm-ward, ride we in haste,
To track the hag that whelped this Grendel.

I tell thee in truth, she may turn where she will,
No cave of ocean nor cover of wood,
No hole in the ground shall hide her from me.
But one day more thy woe endure,   121C
And nurse thy hope as I know thou wilt."
Sprang to his feet the sage old king,
Gave praise to God for the promise spoken.
And now for Hrothgar a horse was bridled,
A curly-maned steed. The king rode on,
Bold on his charger. A band of shield-men
Followed on foot. Afar they saw
Footprints leading along the forest.
They followed the tracks, and found she had crossed
Over the dark moor, dragging the body   1220
Of the goodliest thane that guarded with Hrothgar
Heorot Hall, and the home of the king.
The well-born hero held the trail;
Up rugged paths, o'er perilous ridges,
Through passes narrow, an unknown way,
By beetling crags, and caves of the nicors.
With a chosen few he forged ahead,
Warriors skilled, to scan the way.
Sudden they came on a cluster of trees
Overhanging a hoary rock,   1230
A gloomy grove; and gurgling below,
A stir of waters all stained with blood.
Sick at heart were the Scylding chiefs,   *(1418)*
Many a thane was thrilled with woe,
For there they beheld the head of Æschere
Far beneath at the foot of the cliff.
They leaned and watched the waters boil
With bloody froth. The band sat down,
While the war-horn sang its summons to battle.
They saw in the water sea-snakes a many,   1240
Wave-monsters weird, that wallowed about.

At the base of the cliff lay basking the nicors,
Who oft at sunrise ply seaward their journey,
To hunt on the ship-trails and scour the main,
Sea-beasts and serpents. Sudden they fled,
Wrathful and grim, aroused by the hail
Of the battle-horn shrill. The chief of the Jutes,
With a bolt from his bow a beast did sunder
From life and sea-frolic; sent the keen shaft
Straight to his vitals. Slow he floated,   **1250**
Upturned and dead at the top of the waves.
Eager they boarded their ocean-quarry;
With barb-hooked boar-spears the beast they gaffed,
Savagely broached him and brought him to shore,
Wave-plunger weird. The warriors viewed
The grisly stranger. But straightway Beowulf
Donned his corslet nor cared for his life. . . . *(1442)*

Lines 1443-1472 break the narrative with a description of
Beowulf's armor and the sword Hrunting, lent him by Unferth.

XXII

BEOWULF'S FIGHT WITH GRENDEL'S DAM

To Hrothgar spoke the son of Ecgtheow: *(1473)*
"Remember, O honored heir of Healfdene,
Now that I go, thou noble king,   **1260**
Warriors' gold-friend, what we agreed on,
If I my life should lose in thy cause,
That thou wouldst stand in stead of my father,
Fulfil his office when I was gone.
Be guardian thou, to my thanes and kinsmen,
My faithful friends, if I fail to return.
To Hygelac send, Hrothgar beloved,
The goodly gifts thou gavest to me.
May the lord of the Jutes, when he looks on this
    treasure,

May Hrethel's son, when he sees these gifts,   1270
Know that I found a noble giver,
And joyed while I lived, in a generous lord.
This ancient heirloom to Unferth give,
To the far-famed warrior, my wondrous sword
Of matchless metal. I must with Hrunting
Glory gain, or go to my death."

After these words the Weder-Jute lord
Sprang to his task, nor staid for an answer.
Swiftly he sank 'neath the swirling flood;
'Twas an hour's time ere he touched the bottom.   1280
Soon the sea-hag, savage and wild,
Who had roamed through her watery realms at will,
For winters a hundred, was 'ware from below,
An earthling had entered her ocean domain.
Quickly she reached and caught the hero;   (1501)
Grappled him grimly with gruesome claws.
Yet he got no scratch, his skin was whole;
His battle-sark shielded his body from harm.
In vain she tried, with her crooked fingers,
To tear the links of his close-locked mail.   1290
Away to her den the wolf-slut dragged
Beowulf the bold, o'er the bottom ooze.
Though eager to smite her, his arm was helpless.
Swimming monsters swarmed about him,
Dented his mail with dreadful tusks.
Sudden the warrior was 'ware they had come
To a sea-hall strange and seeming hostile,
Where water was not nor waves oppressed,
For the caverned rock all round kept back
The swallowing sea. He saw a light,   1300
A flicker of flame that flashed and shone.
Now first he discerned the sea-hag monstrous,
The water-wife wolfish. His weapon he raised,
And struck with his sword a swinging blow.

Sang on her head the hard-forged blade
Its war-song wild. But the warrior found
That his battle-flasher refused to bite,
Or maim the foe. It failed its master
In the hour of need, though oft it had cloven
Helmets, and carved the casques of the doomed   1310
In combats fierce. For the first time now
That treasure failed him, fallen from honor.
But Hygelac's earl took heart of courage;
In mood defiant he fronted his foe.
The angry hero hurled to the ground,
In high disdain, the hilt of the sword,
The gaudy and jewelled; rejoiced in the strength
Of his arm unaided. So all should do   *(1534)*
Who glory would find and fame abiding,
In the crash of conflict, nor care for their lives.   1320
The Lord of the Battle-Jutes braved the encounter;
The murderous hag by the hair he caught;
Down he dragged the dam of Grendel
In his swelling rage, till she sprawled on the floor.
Quick to repay in kind what she got,
On her foe she fastened her fearful clutches;
Enfolded the warrior weary with fighting;
The sure-footed hero stumbled and fell.
As helpless he lay, she leapt on him fiercely;
Unsheathed her hip-knife, shining and broad,   1330
Her son to avenge, her offspring sole.
But the close-linked corslet covered his breast,
Foiled the stroke and saved his life.
All had been over with Ecgtheow's son,
Under the depths of the ocean vast,
Had not his harness availed to help him,
His battle-net stiff, and the strength of God.
The Ruler of battles aright decided it;
The Wielder all-wise awarded the victory:
Lightly the hero leaped to his feet.   1340

XXIII

Beowulf's Victory and Return to Heorot

He spied 'mongst the arms a sword surpassing,
Huge and ancient, a hard-forged slayer,
Weapon matchless and warrior's delight,
Save that its weight was more than another   *(1560)*
Might bear into battle or brandish in war;
Giants had forged that finest of blades.
Then seized its chain-hilt the chief of the Scyldings;
His wrath was aroused, reckless his mood,
As he brandished the sword for a savage blow.
Bit the blade in the back of her neck,   1350
Cut the neck-bone, and cleft its way
Clean through her flesh; to the floor she sank;
The sword was gory; glad was the hero.
A light flashed out from the inmost den,
Like heaven's candle, when clear it shines
From cloudless skies. He scanned the cave,
Walked by the wall, his weapon upraised;
Grim in his hand the hilt he gripped.
Well that sword had served him in battle.
Steadily onward he strode through the cave,   1360
Ready to wreak the wrongs untold,
That the man-beast had wrought in the realm of
        Danes. . . .   *(1578)*
He gave him his due when Grendel he found *(1584)*
Stretched as in sleep, and spent with the battle.
But dead was the fiend, the fight at Heorot
Had laid him low. The lifeless body
Sprang from the blows of Beowulf's sword,
As fiercely he hacked the head from the carcass.
But the men who were watching the water with
        Hrothgar
Suddenly saw a stir in the waves,   1370

The chop of the sea all churned up with blood
And bubbling gore. The gray-haired chiefs
For Beowulf grieved, agreeing together   (1595)
That hope there was none of his home-returning,
With victory crowned, to revisit his lord.
Most of them feared he had fallen prey
To the mere-wolf dread in the depths of the sea.
When evening came, the Scyldings all
Forsook the headland, and Hrothgar himself
Turned homeward his steps. But sick at heart   1380
The strangers sat and stared at the sea,
Hoped against hope to behold their comrade
And leader again.

           Now that goodly sword
Began to melt with the gore of the monster;
In bloody drippings it dwindled away.
'Twas a marvellous sight: it melted like ice,
When fetters of frost the Father unlocks,
Unravels the ropes of the wrinkled ice,
Lord and Master of months and seasons.   1390
Beheld in the hall the hero from Juteland
Treasures unnumbered, but naught he took,
Save Grendel's head, and the hilt of the sword,
Bright and jewelled,—the blade had melted,
Its metal had vanished, so venomous hot
Was the blood of the demon-brute dead in the cave.

Soon was in the sea the slayer of monsters;
Upward he shot through the shimmer of waves;
Cleared was the ocean, cleansed were its waters,
The wolfish water-hag wallowed no more;   1400
The mere-wife had yielded her miserable life.
Swift to the shore the sailors' deliverer
Came lustily swimming, with sea-spoil laden;
Rejoiced in the burden he bore to the land.   (1625)

Ran to meet him his mailèd comrades,
With thanks to God who gave them their leader
Safe again back and sound from the deep.
Quickly their hero's helmet they loosened,
Unbuckled his breastplate. The blood-stained waves
Fell to a calm 'neath the quiet sky.   1410
Back they returned o'er the tracks with the footprints,
Merrily measured the miles o'er the fen,
Way they knew well, those warriors brave;
Brought from the holm-cliff the head of the monster;
'Twas toil and labor to lift the burden,
Four of their stoutest scarce could carry it
Swung from a spear-pole, a staggering load. . . . (1638)
Thus the fourteen of them, thanes adventurous,
Marched o'er the moor to the mead-hall of Hrothgar.
Tall in the midst of them towered the hero;   1420
Strode among his comrades, till they came to the hall.
In went Beowulf, the brave and victorious,
Battle-beast hardy, Hrothgar to greet.
Lifting by the hair the head of Grendel,
They laid it in the hall, where the heroes were carous-
    ing,
Right before the king, and right before the queen;
Gruesome was the sight that greeted the Danes.

XXIV XXV

BEOWULF'S STORY OF HIS FIGHT, AND HROTHGAR'S COUNSEL

Beowulf spoke, the son of Ecgtheow: (1651)
"Gladly we offer this ocean-booty,
That here thou lookest on, lord of the Scyldings,   1430
For sign of victory, son of Healfdene.
Hard was the fight I fought under water;
That combat nearly cost me my life.

Soon had been ended the ocean-encounter,
Had God in his mercy not given me aid.
No help I got from the good blade Hrunting,
The well-tried weapon worthless proved.
By the grace of God, who guided me friendless,
A splendid old sword I spied on the wall,
Hanging there, huge; by the hilt I grasped it,   1440
And seeing my chance, I struck amain
At the sea-cave's wardens, when sudden the blade
Melted and burned, as the blood gushed out,
The battle-gore hot. The hilt I saved
From the villainous fiends, and avenged their crimes,
The murder of the Danes, as was meet and due.
I promise thee now, in peace thou shalt sleep
In Heorot hall, with the whole of thy band.
Thou and thy thanes may throng within
As ye used of yore, both young and old.   1450
Thou need'st not fear renewal of strife,
Harm to thy folk at the hands of the fiends."
The golden hilt was given to the king;
The jewelled work of the giants of old
Came into hand of the hoary warrior.
On the death of the demons, the Danish lord kept it,
Wondersmiths' work. When the world was rid
Of the evil fiend, the enemy of God,   (1682)
Guilty of murder, and his mother too,
The trophy passed to the peerless lord,   1460
The goodliest king, that gave out treasure
Between the two seas on Scandia's isle.
Hrothgar gazed on the golden hilt,
Relic of old, where was writ the tale
Of a far-off fight, when the flood o'erwhelmed,
The raging sea, the race of the giants.
(They wantonly dared to war against God;
Then rose in his wrath the Ruler Eternal,

'Neath the heaving billows buried them all.)
On the polished gold of the guard of the hilt,　　1470
Runes were writ that rightly told,
To him that read them, for whom that weapon,
Finest of sword-blades, first was made,
The splendid hilt with serpents entwined.
All were silent, when the son of Healfdene,
The wise king spoke: "Well may he say,
The aged ruler, who aye upholds
Truth and right, 'mid the ranks of his people,
Whose mind runs back to by-gone days,
This guest is born of a goodly breed.　　1480
Thy fame shall fly afar among men,
Beowulf my friend, firmly thou holdest
Both wisdom and might. My word will I keep,
The love that I proffered. Thou shalt prove a deliverer
To thy folk and followers in far-off years,
A help to the heroes. Not Heremod thus
Ecgwela's heir, did offer at need　　(1710)
His strength to the Scyldings; instead, he brought
Slaughter and death on the sons of the Danes.
Swoln with wrath he slew his comrades,　　1490
His friends at the board and fled alone,
Ill-famed earl, an outcast from men.
Though God endowed him with gifts of strength,
With boldness and might above all men,
And prospered him greatly, yet he grew to be
Blood-thirsty and cruel. No bracelets he gave
To the Danes as was due, but dwelt in gloom,
Reaped the reward of the woful strife,
And wearisome feud. Take warning from him　　(1722)

•　　•　　•　　•　　•　　•

Hrothgar now delivers a long sermon to Beowulf on the
dangers of pride, the fickleness of fortune, and the brevity
of life, and ends by asking him to sit down to the feast, promising more gifts on the morrow.

Beowulf hastened, happy in mood,   *(1785)*   1500
To seek his bench as bid by the king.
Once more, as of old, for the earls in hall,
The famous in battle, the board was set
For feasting anew. When night with its shadows
O'erwhelmed the world, the heroes arose.
The gray-haired ruler his rest would seek,
The Scylding his bed; and Beowulf too,
The lusty warrior, longed for his sleep.
Soon an attendant showed the way
To the stranger from far, spent with his faring.   1510
With courtly custom, he cared for his needs.
All that to warriors, overseas wandering,
Was due in those days, he did for the guest.
High-gabled and gold-decked, the gift-hall towered;
The stout-hearted hero slept soundly within,   *(1800)*
Till the raven black, with blithe heart hailed
The bliss of heaven, and bright the sun
Came gliding o'er earth. Then, eager to start,
The warriors wakened; they wished to set out
On their homeward journey. The hero brave   1520
Would board his ship, and back again sail.
The hardy one bade that Hrunting be brought
To the son of Ecglaf: the sword he offered him;
Thanked him for lending the lovely weapon;
Called it a war-friend, keen in the battle;
Not a word in blame of the blade he uttered,
Great-hearted hero. Now hastened the guests,
Eager to part, and armed for their voyage.
Their dauntless leader, beloved of the Danes,
Came to the high-seat, and to Hrothgar the king   1530
The bold-in-battle now bade farewell.   *(1816)*

XXVI

Beowulf's Leave-Taking of Hrothgar

Beowulf spoke, the son of Ecgtheow:
"Now we sea-farers would make known our desire;
Far-travelled wanderers, we wish to return
To Hygelac now. A hearty welcome
We here have found, thou hast harbored us well.
If ever on earth I may anywise win,
Master of men, more of thy love
Than now I have won, for another adventure
Of arms and war I am eager and willing.   1540
If ever I hear, o'er the ocean-ways   *(1826)*
That neighbor-tribes threaten annoyance or war,
As feud-seeking foemen aforetime assailed thee,
A thousand thanes to thee will I bring,
Heroes to help thee. For Hygelac, I know,
Though young in years will yield me aid;
The people's Shepherd will surely help me
By word and deed to do thee service,
And bring thee spear-shafts to speed thee in battle,
Thy might to strengthen when men thou needest.   1550
If ever Hrethric, heir of thy line,
Should come to sojourn at the court of the Jutes,
A host of friends he will find awaiting him.
Who boasts himself brave, abroad should travel."
The aged Hrothgar answering spoke:
"To utter these words, the All-wise Lord
Hath prompted thy heart; more prudent counsel
From one in years so young as thou,
I never have heard. Thou art hardy in strength,
And sage in spirit, and speakest well.   1560
If ever it happen that Hrethel's heir
Be stricken by spear and slain in battle,
If sickness or sword assail thy lord,

And thou survive him, I think it likely
The Sea-Jutes in vain will seek for a better
As choice for their king, their chief to become
And rule o'er the thanes, if thou be willing
The lordship to hold. The longer I know thee
The better I like thee, Beowulf my friend.
Thou hast brought it about that both our peoples   1570
Jutes and the Spear-Danes shall be joined in peace.
They shall cease from war, the strife shall be ended,
The feuds of aforetime, so fiercely waged.   *(1858)*
While I rule this realm, our riches we share;
Many shall travel with treasure laden,
Each other to greet, o'er the gannet's bath;
O'er the rolling waves the ringèd prow
Tokens of friendship shall freely bring
And bind our people in peace together,
Toward friend and foe, in faith as of old."   1580

Still other treasures, twelve in all,
Healfdene's heir in the hall bestowed
On Beowulf brave, and bade him take them
And seek his people, and soon return.
Then kissed the king, of kin renowned,
The thane beloved. The lord of the Scyldings
Fell on his neck. Fast flowed the tears
Of the warrior gray; he weighed both chances,
But held to the hope, though hoary with years,
That each should see the other again,   1590
And meet in the mead-hall. The man was so dear
That he could not restrain the storm in his breast.
Locked in his heart, a hidden longing
For the man he loved so, left him no peace,
And burnt in his blood. But Beowulf went;
The gold-decked hero the grass-way trod
Proud of his booty. The boat awaited
Its owner and master, where at anchor it rode.

As they went on their way, the warriors praised
The bounty of Hrothgar, the blameless king.   1600
None was his equal till age snatched away
The joy of his manhood,—no mortal it spares.

XXVII

Beowulf's Return Voyage to Hygelac

Then came to the coast the comrades brave   (1888)
The lusty warriors, wearing their ring-nets,
Their chain-linked corslets. The coast-guard saw them,
The same that at first had spied them coming;
This time he chose not to challenge them harshly,
But gave them his greeting, galloping toward them.
Said the Weder-folk would welcome the sight of them
Boarding their ship in shining armor.   1610
Then by the sands, the seaworthy craft,
The iron-ringed keel, with arms was laden,
With horses and treasure. On high the mast
Towered above the treasures of Hrothgar.
To the man who had waited as watchman aboard,
Beowulf gave a gold-bound sword.
(Oft on the mead-bench that heirloom precious
Its owner would honor.) When all had embarked,
They drove for the deep, from Daneland's shore.
Then soon did the mast its sea-suit wear,   1620
A sail was unfurled, made fast with ropes,
The sea-wood sang as she sped o'er the ocean,
No baffling head-wind hindered her course;
The foamy-necked floater flew o'er the billows,
The sea-craft staunch o'er the salt-sea waves,
Till they came in sight of the cliffs of Jutland,
The well known capes, and the wind-driven keel
Grating the sand, stood still on the shore.

Soon was at hand the harbor-watch eager.
Long had he looked for his loved companions   1630
Scanning the sea for their safe return.   *(1916)*
The broad-bosomed boat to the beach he moored
With anchor-ropes fast, lest the force of the waves
That comely craft should cast adrift.
Then Beowulf bade them bring ashore
His treasure-cargo of costly gold
And weapons fine; not far was the way
To Hygelac's hall, where at home he dwelt
The king and his comrades, close by the sea.

END OF THE SECOND ADVENTURE

After the death of Hygelac and his son, Beowulf became king of the Jutes, and ruled over them fifty years. In his old age his people were harried by a fire-dragon whom the hero went out to fight. It seems that an outlaw, banished and flying for shelter, had come upon a treasure hid in a deep cave or barrow, guarded by a dragon. Long years before, an earl, the last of his race, had buried the treasure. After his death the dragon, sniffing about the stones, had found it and guarded it three hundred years, until the banished man discovered the place, and carried off one of the golden goblets. In revenge the dragon made nightly raids on Beowulf's realm, flying through the air, spitting fire, burning houses and villages, even Beowulf's hall, the "gift-stool" of the Jutes. Beowulf had an iron shield made against the dragon's fiery breath, and with eleven companions, sought out the hill-vault near the sea. These events are related in Sections XXVIII-XXXV of the Beowulf MS.

XXXV

BEOWULF'S FIGHT WITH THE FIRE DRAGON

Before attacking the fire-dragon Beowulf once more and for the last time makes his "battle-boast" in the presence of his followers.

Beowulf said to them, brave words spoke he: *(2510)*
                                                      1640

"Brunt of battles I bore in my youth:

One fight more I make this day.
I mean to win fame defending my people,
If the grim destroyer will seek me out,
Come at my call from his cavern dark."
Then he greeted his thanes each one,
For the last time hailed his helmeted warriors,
His comrades dear. "I should carry no sword,
No weapon of war 'gainst the worm should bear,
If the foe I might slay by strength of my arm,   1650
As Grendel I slew long since by my hand.
But I look to fight a fiery battle,
With scorching puffs of poisonous breath.
For this I bear both breastplate and shield;
No foot will I flinch from the foe of the barrow.
Wyrd is over us, each shall meet
His doom ordained at the dragon-cliff!
Bold is my mood, but my boast I omit
'Gainst the battle-flier. Abide ye here,
Heroes in harness, hard by the barrow,   1660
Cased in your armor the issue await:
Which of us two his wounds shall survive.
Not yours the attempt, the task is mine.
'Tis meant for no man but me alone
To measure his might 'gainst the monster fierce.
I get you the gold in glorious fight,
Or battle-death bitter shall bear off your lord."

  Uprose with his shield the shining hero,
Bold 'neath his helmet. He bore his harness
In under the cliff; alone he went,   1670
Himself he trusted; no task for faint-heart.
Then saw by the wall the warrior brave,
Hero of many a hard-fought battle,   (2543)
Arches of stone that opened a way;
From the rocky gate there gushed a stream,

Bubbling and boiling with battle-fire.
So great the heat no hope was there
To come at the hoard in the cavern's depth,
Unscathed by the blast of the scorching dragon.
He let from his breast his battle-cry leap;　　1680
Swoln with rage was the royal Jute,
Stormed the stout-heart; strong and clear
Through the gloom of the cave his cry went ringing.
Hate was aroused, the hoard-ward knew
The leader's hail. Too late 'twas now
To parley for peace. The poisonous breath
Of the monster shot from the mouth of the cave,
Reeking hot. The hollow earth rumbled.
The man by the rock upraised his shield,
The lord of the Jutes, 'gainst the loathly dragon.　1690
Now kindled for battle the curled-up beast;
The king undaunted with drawn sword stood,
'Twas an heirloom olden with edge of lightning.
Each was so fierce he affrighted the other.
Towering tall 'neath tilted shield,
Waited the king as the worm coiled back,
Sudden to spring: so stood he and waited.
Blazing he came in coils of fire
Swift to his doom. The shield of iron
Sheltered the hero too short a while,—　　1700
Life and limb it less protected
Than he hoped it would, for the weapon he held
First time that day he tried in battle;
Wyrd had not willed he should win the fight.　(2575)
But the lord of the Jutes uplifted his arm,
Smote the scaly worm, struck him so fierce
That his ancient bright-edged blade gave way,
Bent on the bone, and bit less sure
Than its owner had need in his hour of peril.

That sword-stroke roused the wrath of the
    cave-guard; 1710
Fire and flame afar he spirted,
Blaze of battle; but Beowulf there
No victory boasted: his blade had failed him,
Naked in battle, as never it should have,
Well-tempered iron. Nor easy it was
For Ecgtheow's heir, honored and famous,
This earth to forsake, forever to leave it;
Yet he must go, against his will
Elsewhere to dwell. So we all must leave
This fleeting life.—Erelong the foes 1720
Bursting with wrath the battle renewed.
The hoard-ward took heart, and with heaving breast
Came charging amain. The champion brave,
Strength of his people, was sore oppressed,
Enfolded by flame. No faithful comrades
Crowded about him, his chosen band,
All æthelings' sons, to save their lives,
Fled to the wood. One of them only
Felt surging sorrow; for naught can stifle
Call of kin in a comrade true. 1730

XXXVI

WIGLAF'S REPROACH TO HIS COMRADES. BEOWULF MORTALLY WOUNDED.

The shield-thane beloved, lord of the Scylfings,
Wiglaf was called; 'twas Weohstan's son (2603)
Ælfhere's kinsman. When his king he saw
Hard by the heat under helmet oppressed,
He remembered the gifts he had got of old,
Lands and wealth of the Wægmunding line,

The folk-rights all that his father's had been;
He could hold no longer, but hard he gripped
Linden shield yellow and ancient sword. . . . *(2610)*

The intervening lines tell the history of the sword and the
feuds in which it has participated.

For the first time there the faithful thane, *(2625)* 1740
Youthful and stalwart, stood with his leader,
Shoulder to shoulder in shock of battle.
Nor melted his courage, nor cracked his blade,
His war-sword true, as the worm found out
When together they got in grim encounter.

   Wiglaf in wrath upbraided his comrades,
Sore was his heart as he spake these words:
"Well I mind when our mead we drank
In the princely hall, how we promised our lord
Who gave us these rings and golden armlets,   1750
That we would repay his war-gifts rich,
Helmets and armor, if haply should come
His hour of peril; us hath he made
Thanes of his choice for this adventure;
Spurred us to glory, and gave us these treasures
Because he deemed us doughty spearmen,   *(2641)*
Helmeted warriors, hardy and brave.
Yet all the while, unhelped and alone,
He meant to finish this feat of strength,
Shepherd of men and mightiest lord   1760
Of daring deeds. The day is come,—
Now is the hour he needs the aid
Of spearmen good. Let us go to him now,
Help our hero while hard bestead
By the nimble flames. God knows that I
Had rather the fire should ruthlessly fold

My body with his, than harbor me safe.
Shame it were surely our shields to carry
Home to our lands, unless we first
Slay this foe and save the life   1770
Of the Weder-king. Full well I know
To leave him thus, alone to endure,
Bereft of aid, breaks ancient right.
My helmet and sword shall serve for us both;
Shield and armor we share to-day."

Waded the warrior through welter and reek;
Buckler and helmet he bore to his leader;
Heartened the hero with words of hope:
"Do thy best now, dearest Beowulf.
Years ago, in youth, thou vowedst   1780
Living, ne'er to lose thine honor,
Shield thy life and show thy valor.
I stand by thee to the end!"
After these words the worm came on,
Snorting with rage, for a second charge;
All mottled with fire his foes he sought,
The warriors hated. But Wiglaf's shield   (2672)
Was burnt to the boss by the billows of fire;
His harness helped not the hero young.
Shelter he found 'neath the shield of his kinsman, 1790
When the crackling blaze had crumbled his own.
But mindful of glory, the mighty hero
Smote amain with his matchless sword.
Down it hurtled, driven by anger,
Till it stuck in the skull, then snapped the blade,
Broken was Nægling, Beowulf's sword,
Ancient and gray. 'Twas granted him never
To count on edge of iron in battle;
His hand was too heavy, too hard his stroke,

As I have heard tell, for every blade   1800
He brandished in battle: the best gave way,
And let him helpless and hard bestead.
Now for a third time neared the destroyer;
The fire-drake fierce, old feuds remembering,
Charged the warrior who wavered an instant;
Blazing he came and closed his fangs
On Beowulf's throat; and throbbing spirts
Of life-blood dark o'erdrenched the hero.

XXXVII

The Slaying of the Dragon

Then in the hour of utmost peril,
The stripling proved what stock he came of;   1810
Showed his endurance and dauntless courage.
Though burnt was his hand when he backed his
        kinsman,
With head unguarded the good thane charged,
Thrust from below at the loathly dragon,   (2699)
Pierced with the point and plunged the blade in,
The gleaming-bright, till the glow abated
Waning low. Ere long the king
Came to himself, and swiftly drew
The war-knife that hung at his harness' side,
And cut in two the coilèd monster.   1820
So felled they the foe and finished him bravely,
Together they killed him, the kinsmen two,
A noble pair. So needs must do
Comrades in peril. For the king it proved
His uttermost triumph, the end of his deeds
And work in the world. The wound began,
Where the cave-dragon savage had sunk his teeth,

To swell and fever, and soon he felt
The baleful poison pulse through his blood,
And burn in his breast. The brave old warrior   1830
Sat by the wall and summoned his thoughts,
Gazed on the wondrous work of the giants:
Arches of stone, firm-set on their pillars,
Upheld that hill-vault hoar and ancient.

Now Beowulf's thane, the brave and faithful,
Dashed with water his darling lord,
His comrade and king all covered with blood
And faint with the fight; unfastened his helmet.
Beowulf spoke despite his hurt,
His piteous wound; full well he knew   1840
His years on earth were ended now,
His hours of glad life gone for aye
His days allotted, and death was near:
"Now would I gladly give to a son   *(2729)*
These weapons of war, had Wyrd but granted
That heir of my own should after me come,
Sprung from my loins. This land have I ruled
Fifty winters. No folk-king dared,
None of the chiefs of the neighboring tribes,
To touch me with sword or assail me with terror   1850
Of battle-threats. I bided at home,
Held my peace and my heritage kept,
Seeking no feuds nor swearing false oaths.
This gives me comfort, and gladdens me now,
Though wounded sore and sick unto death.
As I leave my life, the Lord may not charge me
With killing of kinsmen. Now quickly go,
Wiglaf beloved, to look at the hoard,
Where hidden it rests 'neath the hoary rock.
For the worm lies still, put asleep by his wound,   1860
Robbed of his riches. Then rise and haste!

Give me to see that golden hoard,
To gaze on the store of glorious gems,
The easier then I may end my life,
Leave my lordship that long I held."

XXXVIII

THE RESCUE OF THE HOARD AND THE DEATH OF BEOWULF

Swiftly, 'tis said, the son of Weohstan
Obeyed the words of his bleeding lord,
Maimed in the battle. Through the mouth of the
    cave
Boldly he bore his battle-net in.
Glad of the victory, he gazed about him   *(2756)* **1870**
Many a sun-bright jewel he saw,
Glittering gold, strewn on the ground,
Heaped in the den of the dragon hoary,
Old twilight-flier,—flagons once bright,
Wassail cups wondrous of warriors departed
Stript of their mountings, many a helmet
Ancient and rusted, armlets a many,
Curiously woven. (Wealth so hoarded,
Buried treasure, will taint with pride
Him that hides it, whoever it be.)   **1880**
Towering high o'er the hoard he saw
A gleaming banner with gold inwoven,
Of broidure rare; its radiance streamed
So bright, he could peer to the bounds of the cave,
Survey its wonders; no worm was seen.
Edge of the sword had ended his life.
Then, as they say, that single adventurer
Plundered the hoard that was piled by the giants;
Gathered together old goblets and platters,

Took what he liked; the towering banner 1890
Brightest of beacons he brought likewise.
The blade of Beowulf, his brave old chief,
With edge of iron had ended the life
Of him that had guarded the golden hoard
For many a year, and at midnight hour
Had spread the terror of surging flames
In front of the den, till death o'ertook him.
So Wiglaf returned with treasure laden.
The high-souled hero hastened his steps,
Anxiously wondered if he should find 1900
The lord of the Weders alive where he left him
Sapped of his strength and stretched on the ground.
As he came from the hill he beheld his comrade,
His lord of bounty, bleeding and faint, *(2789)*
Near unto death. He dashed him once more
Bravely with water, till burden of speech
Broke from his breast, and Beowulf spoke,
Gazing sad at the gold before him:
"For the harvest of gold that here I look on,
To the God of Glory I give my thanks. 1910
To the Ruler Eternal I render praise
That ere I must go, he granted me this,
To leave to my people this priceless hoard.
'Twas bought with my life; now look ye well
To my people's need when I have departed.
No more I may bide among ye here.
Bid the battle-famed build on the foreland
A far-seen barrow when flames have burnt me.
High o'er the headland of whales it shall tower,
A beacon and mark to remind my people. 1920
And sailors shall call it in years to come
Beowulf's Barrow, as bound from afar
Their tall ships stem the storm-dark seas.

The great-hearted king unclasped from his neck
A collar of gold and gave to his thane,
The brave young warrior, his bright-gilt helmet,
Breastplate and ring. So bade him farewell:
"Thou art the last to be left of our house.
Wyrd hath o'erwhelmed our Wægmunding line,
Swept my kinsmen swift to their doom,   1930
Earls in their prime. I must follow them."
These words were the last that the warrior gray
Found, ere the funeral-flames he chose.
Swift from his bosom his soul departed
To find the reward of the faithful and true.   *(2820)*

In lines 2821-2891, Section XXXIX of the MS., the narrative doubles back upon itself to repeat the description of
Beowulf and the dragon lying dead before the cave, and to
report Wiglaf's reproach to the returning deserters.

XL

Beowulf's Death Announced to the People. The Speech of the Herald.

Then Wiglaf bade the battle-work tell   *(2892)*
To the sorrowful troop that had sat all day
At the sea-cliff's edge, their shields in hand,
In dread and in hope, yet doubtful of either:
Their dear lord's return, or his death in the fight. 1940
The herald that came to the headland riding,
Naught kept back of the news that befell,
But truthfully told them the tidings all:
"Now lies low the lord of the Weders;
The generous giver of gifts to the Jutes,
Sleeps his battle-sleep, slain by the worm.
At his side lies stretched his slaughterous foe,
Fordone by the dagger. The dragon fierce

Would take no wound from touch of sword;
Its blade would not bite. At Beowulf's side   1950
Wiglaf sits, the son of Weohstan;
By the hero dead, the hero living
At his head keeps watch with woful heart
O'er friend and foe.   *(2910)*

.   .   .   .   .   .

The herald now warns of renewed attacks on the Jutes by
Franks and Frisians, and alludes to the origin of the feud in
the famous raid in which Hygelac was slain. He further
warns of renewed attacks by the Swedes, now that Beowulf
is dead, and refers to the origin of the wars between Swedes
and Jutes and to a famous battle at "Ravenswood." The
episodic digression over, the herald returns to present events.

XLI

The Herald's Speech Concluded

'Tis time we hasten   *(3007)*
To see where lies our lord and king,
Our giver of bounty, and bear him away
To the funeral pyre; of precious gems
Not a few shall melt in the fire with him.
The hoard he won, the wealth untold,   1960
The priceless treasure he purchased so dear,
And bought with his life at the bitter end,
The flame shall enfold it, the fire consume.
No warrior one keepsake shall carry away,
No necklace be worn by winsome maid.
In sorrow rather, and reft of her gold,
Alone she shall tread the track of an exile,
Now our lord lies low, his laughter stilled,
His mirth and revel. Now many a spear

Shall morning-cold be clasped in the hand   1970
And held on high. No harp shall sound
The warriors to wake, but the wan-hued raven
Shall croak o'er the carcass and call to the eagle,
To tell how he fared at the feast after battle
When he and the gray wolf gorged on the slain."
Thus ended his tale, his tidings of woe,   (3028)
The faithful thane, nor falsely reported
Wyrd or word. The warriors rose;
To the Eagles' Cliff they came in sadness,
With welling tears, the wonder to see.   1980
Lying helpless, their lord they found
Stretched on the ground, the giver of rings.
The end had come to him, open-handed
King of the Weders, warrior brave.
That day a fearful death he had found.
A stranger thing they saw near by:
The loathsome monster lying dead
On the field where they fought, the fiery dragon,
The gruesome beast was burnt and charred.
Fifty feet in full he measured   1990
In length, as he lay, along the ground.
'Twas his wont at night to wing aloft
And dip to earth as his den he sought;
Now he lay dead, his night-revels over.
Scattered about were bowls and flagons,
Golden platters, and priceless swords,
With rust eaten through, as though they had lain
Winters a thousand in the womb of the earth.
O'er that heritage huge, the hoard of afore-time,
A spell had been woven to ward off despoilers,   2000
And none might touch the treasure-vault hidden;
Save that God alone, the Lord of victory,
The Guardian of men, might grant the power

To unlock the hoard, and lift the treasure,
To such a hero as to Him seemed meet.   *(3057)*

. . . . . .

XLII

BEOWULF'S BODY CARRIED TO THE FUNERAL PYRE AND THE DRAGON CAST INTO THE SEA.

Wiglaf spoke, the son of Weohstan: *(3076)*
"Let us go once more to gaze at the marvels   *(3101)*
Still left 'neath the rock; I will lead you in
Where your hands may touch great heaps of gold,
Bracelets and rings. Let the bier be ready   2010
When out of the cave we come again,
To bear away the warrior brave,
Our lord beloved, where long he shall bide,
Kept in the sheltering care of God."
The son of Weohstan, warrior brave,
Called on the folk-men, far and wide,
From house and home to hasten and bring
Wood for the pyre of the peerless man,
His funeral pile. "Now fire shall consume,
The wan flame wax o'er the warrior strong,   2020
Who oft stood firm in the iron shower
When the storm of arrows, sent from the bow-string,
Flew o'er the shield-wall, and the fleet-winged shaft,
Feather behind, pushed home the barb."
Now the wise young warrior, Weohstan's son,
Seven men called, of the king's own thanes,
The best of the band; the bravest he gathered;
Himself the eighth, they sought the den
Of the hateful beast; one bore in his hand
A lighted torch and led the way.   2030
No lots were drawn for the dragon's hoard

When they saw it lying, loose in the cave,
Uncared for, unguarded, unclaimed by a soul;
There was none to hinder as they hurried away,
Laden with spoils and splendid heirlooms.   *(3130)*
O'er the edge of the cliff they cast the dragon,
Into the sea, the scaly worm;
Let the waves engulf the gold-hoard's keeper.
On a wagon they loaded the wondrous treasure,
Gold past counting. The gray-haired king   2040
They bore to the pyre, on the Point of Whales.

XLIII

The Burning of Beowulf's Body

Then built for Beowulf the band of the Jutes
A funeral pyre; 'twas firmly based.
They hung it with helmets as he had bidden,
With shining byrnies and battle-shields.
In the midst they laid, with loud lament,
Their lord beloved, their leader brave.
On the brow of the cliff they kindled the blaze,
Black o'er the flames the smoke shot up;
Cries of woe, in the windless air,   2050
Rose and blent with the roar of the blast,
Till the frame of the body burst with the heat
Of the seething heart. In sorrowing mood
They mourned aloud their leader dead.
Joined in the wail a woman old,
With hair upbound for Beowulf grieved,
Chanted a dreary dirge of woe,
Dark forebodings of days to come,
Thick with slaughter and throes of battle,
Bondage and shame. The black smoke rose.   2060
High on the headland they heaped a barrow,   *(3156)*

Lofty and broad 'twas built by the Weders,
Far to be seen by sea-faring men.
Ten days long they toiled to raise it,
The battle-king's beacon. They built a wall
To fence the brands of the funeral burning,
The choicest and best their chiefs could devise.
In the barrow they buried the bracelets and rings,
All those pieces of precious treasure
That bold-hearted men had brought from the cave, 2070
Returned to earth the heirloom of heroes,
The gold to the ground, again to become
As useless to men as of yore it had been.

Around the barrow the battle-brave rode,
Twelve in the troop, all true-born æthelings,
To make their lament and mourn for the king;
To chant a lay their lord to honor.
They praised his daring; his deeds of prowess
They mentioned in song. For meet it is
That men should publish their master's praise, 2080
Honor their chieftain, and cherish him dearly
When he leaves this life, released from the body.

Thus joined the men of the Jutes in mourning
Their hero's end. His hearth-companions
Called him the best among kings of the earth,
Mildest of men, and most beloved,
Kindest to kinsmen, and keenest for fame. 2087

DEOR'S LAMENT

WELAND well knew the power of sorrow,
The stout-hearted earl endured distress,
Sadness and longing he had for his comrades,
Woe cold as winter; woe oft-times he suffered,
When Nithhad laid misfortune upon him,
Made the strong man weak with laming wounds.

Yet that he overcame; so this may I.

Not for her brothers' death was Beadohild
So sore at heart as for her own distress,
When she at last had fully understood   10
She was with child; never might she
Without shame think how this should come to be.
Yet that she overcame; so this may I.

We have heard much about Mæthilde;
The desires of the Geat so boundless were
That pain took all his sleep from him.
Yet that he overcame; so this may I.

What way Theodoric ruled the Mærings' burg
For thirty winters long, is widely known.
Yet that he overcame; so this may I.   20

We have heard of Eormanric,
Wolf-hearted king; a wide folk he ruled,
The country of the Goths; that was a grim king.
Sat many a man in sorrow bound,
Woeful of mind, and wishing desperately
That kingdom were o'erthrown.
Yet that they overcame; so this may I.

Seated, weary with care, deprived of joy,
His heart is dark with sorrow; and he thinks
His share of misery will never end.   30
But let him rather think, that in this world
The mighty Lord draws near,
To many a man shows mercy,
A certain joy, to some a deal of woe.

Of my own story this I tell,
I once was minstrel to the Heodenings,
Dear to my lord; and Deor was my name.
For many winters long I knew a pleasant place,
A noble lord, 'til Heorrenda now,
Song-crafty man, has taken all the land   40
That once the earl my patron gave to me.
Yet that he overcame; so this may I.

THE WANDERER

MANY a lonely man at last comes to honor,
Merits God's mercy, though much he endured
On wintry seas, with woe in his heart,
Dragging his oar through drenching-cold brine,
Homeless and houseless and hunted by Wyrd.

These are the words of a way-faring wanderer,
This is his song of the sorrow of life,
Slaughter of foemen, felling of kinsmen:

Often alone in the dark before dawning,
All to myself my sorrow I tell.   10
Friend have I none to whom I may open
My heart's deep secret, my hidden spring of woe.
Well do I know 'tis the way of the high-born,
Fast in his heart to fetter his feelings,
Lock his unhappiness in the hold of his mind.
Spirit that sorrows withstandeth not destiny,
Heart that complaineth plucketh no help.
A haughty hero will hide his suffering,
Manfully master misery's pang.
Thus stricken with sorrow, stript of my heritage,   20
Far from kinsmen and country and friends,
Grimly I grappled my grief to my bosom,
Since long time ago, my giver of bounty
Was laid in the earth, and left me to roam
Watery wastes, with winter in my heart.
Forsaken I sought a shielder and protector;
Far and near I found none to greet the wanderer,
No master to make him welcome in his wine-hall;
None to cheer the cheerless, or the friendless to be-
        friend.

He who hath lost all his loved companions   30
Knoweth how bitter a bedfellow is sorrow.
Loneliness his lot, not lordly gold,

Heart-chilling frost, not harvest of plenty.
Oft he remembers the mirth of the mead-hall,
Yearns for the days of his youth, when his dear lord
Filled him with abundance. Faded are those joys!
He shall know them no more; no more shall he listen
To the voice of his lord, his leader and counsellor.
Sometimes sleep and sorrow together
Gently enfold the joyless wanderer: 40
Bright are his dreams, he embraces his lord again,
Kisses his liege, and lays on his knee
Head and hands as in happy days,
When he thanked for a boon his bountiful giver.

Wakes with a start the homeless wanderer;
Nought he beholds but the heaving surges,
Seagulls dipping and spreading their wings,
Scurries of snow and the scudding hail.
Then his heart is all the heavier,
Sore after sweet dreams sorrow reviveth.   50
Fain would he hold the forms of his kinsmen,
Longingly leans to them, lovingly greets them;
Slowly their faces swim into distance;
No familiar greeting comes from the fleeting
Companies of kinsmen. Care ever shadows
The way of the traveller, whose track is on the waters,
Whose path is on the billows of the boundless deep.

Surely I see not how I should keep
My heart from sinking, heavy with sorrow,
When all life's destiny deeply I ponder,—   60
Men that are suddenly snatched in their prime,
High-souled heroes; so the whole of this earth
Day by day droopeth and sinketh to decay . . .
How dread is the doom of the last desolation,
When all the wealth of the world shall be waste,
He that is wise may learn, if he looks

Abroad o'er this land, when lonely and ruinous,
Wind-swept walls, waste are standing;
Tottering towers, crusted with frost,
Crumbling wine-halls, bare to the sky.   70
Dead is their revelry, dust are the revellers!
Some they have fallen on far fields of battle,
Some have gone down in ships on the sea;
Some were the prey of the prowling gray wolf,
Some by their loved ones were laid in the earth.
The Lord of the living hath levelled their mansions,
Silenced the sound of the singing and laughter.
Empty and bare are all their habitations,
Wondrous works of the giants of old.

He that considers this scene of desolation,   80
And this dark life deeply doth ponder,—
Battle and blood-shed, burning and slaughter,
It bringeth to mind, and mournfully he asks:
Where is the warrior, where is the war-horse?
Where is the giver of bounty, where are the boon-
      companions,
The "dream and the gleam" that gladdened the hall?
Alas the bright ale-cup, alas the brave warrior!
Alas the pride of princes! Their prime is no more;
Sunk under night's shadow, as though it had never
      been!
Where lusty warriors thronged, this lone wall towers, 90
Weird with dragon-shapes, wondrously carven;
Storm of ash-spears hath stricken the heroes,
Blood-thirsty weapons, Wyrd the supreme.
Wintry blasts now buffet these battlements;
Dreary snow-storms drift up the earth,
The terror of winter when wild and wan
Down from the north with the darkness drives
The ruinous scourge of the ruthless hail.

All this life is labor and sorrow,
Doom of destiny darkens o'er earth.   100
Wealth is fleeting, friends are fleeting,
Man is fleeting, maid is fleeting,
All this earth's foundations utterly shall pass.

THE SEA-FARER

The Old Sailor:

TRUE is the tale that I tell of my travels,
Sing of my sea-faring sorrows and woes;
Hunger and hardship's heaviest burdens,
Tempest and terrible toil of the deep,
Daily I've borne on the deck of my boat.
Fearful the welter of waves that encompassed me,
Watching at night on the narrow bow,
As she drove by the rocks, and drenched me with
　　　spray.
Fast to the deck my feet were frozen,
Gripped by the cold, while care's hot surges   10
My heart o'erwhelmed, and hunger's pangs
Sapped the strength of my sea-weary spirit.

Little he knows whose lot is happy,
Who lives at ease in the lap of the earth,
How, sick at heart, o'er icy seas,
Wretched I ranged the winter through,
Bare of joys, and banished from friends,
Hung with icicles, stung by hail-stones.
Nought I heard but the hollow boom
Of wintry waves, or the wild swan's whoop.   20
For singing I had the solan's scream;
For peals of laughter, the yelp of the seal;
The sea-mew's cry, for the mirth of the mead-hall.
Shrill through the roar of the shrieking gale
Lashing along the sea-cliff's edge,

Pierces the ice-plumed petrel's defiance,
And the wet-winged eagle's answering scream.

Little he dreams that drinks life's pleasure,
By danger untouched in the shelter of towns
Insolent and wine-proud, how utterly weary   30
Oft I wintered on open seas.
Night fell black, from the north it snowed
Harvest of hail.

The Youth:
           Oh wildly my heart
Beats in my bosom and bids me to try
The tumble and surge of seas tumultuous,
Breeze and brine and the breakers' roar.
Daily hourly drives me my spirit
Outward to sail, far countries to see.
Liveth no man so large in his soul,   40
So gracious in giving, so gay in his youth,
In deeds so daring, so dear to his lord,
But frets his soul for his sea-adventure,
Fain to try what fortune shall send.
Harping he heeds not, nor hoarding of treasure;
Nor woman can win him, nor joys of the world.
Nothing doth please but the plunging billows;
Ever he longs, who is lured by the sea.
Woods are abloom, the wide world awakens,
Gay are the mansions, the meadows most fair;   50
These are but warnings, that haste on his journey
Him whose heart is hungry to taste
The perils and pleasures of the pathless deep.

The Old Sailor:
Hearest the cuckoo mournfully calling?
The summer's watchman sorrow forebodes.

What does the landsman that wantons in luxury,
What does he reck of the rough sea's woe,
The cares of the exile, whose keel has explored
The uttermost parts of the Ocean-ways!

The Youth:

Sudden my soul starts from her prison-house,   60
Soareth afar o'er the sounding main;
Hovers on high, o'er the home of the whale;
Back to me darts the bird-sprite and beckons,
Winging her way o'er woodland and plain,
Hungry to roam, and bring me where glisten
Glorious tracts of glimmering foam.
This life on land is lingering death to me,
Give me the gladness of God's great sea.

SWALLOWS

THE breeze bears a small folk
Over the mountain-side. Very dark they are,
Swart and black-coated. They fly in a flock
Singing strongly; loudly they call.
They live in wild places, but sometimes they come
To the houses in town, to the dwellings of men.
What is their name?

BOOK-MOTH

A MOTH ate a word; that I thought
A curious thing, when I heard that marvel,
That a worm should devour the word of a man,
A thief in the dark eat a mighty saying,
In its strong abode. Yet the thieving sprite
Was no whit the wiser for the words he ate.

SWAN

My GARMENT is silent when I move on the earth,
Whether I dwell in a village or swim in the sea.
Sometimes my wings and the high air
Lift me over the dwellings of men,
And the strength of the clouds
Carries me wide over the folk. My fretted wings
Loudly resound and make a song;
Clearly they sing when I am far above
Fold and flood, a flying spirit.

CÆDMON'S HYMN

PRAISE we the Lord
Of the heavenly kingdom,
God's power and wisdom,
The works of His hand;
As the Father of glory,
Eternal Lord,
Wrought the beginnings
Of all His wonders!
Holy Creator!
Warden of men!   10
First, for a roof,
O'er the children of earth,
He stablished the heavens,
And founded the world,
And spread the dry land
For the living to dwell in.
Lord Everlasting!
Almighty God!

CÆDMON (LATE SEVENTH CENTURY)

(Beginning of *Genesis B*)

"EAT freely of the fruit of every other tree. From that one tree refrain. Beware of its fruit. And ye shall know no dearth of pleasant things."

Eagerly they bowed them down before the King of heaven, and gave Him thanks for all, for His teachings and counsels. And He gave them that land to dwell in. Then the Holy Lord, the Steadfast King, departed into heaven. And the creatures of His hand abode together on the earth. They had no whit of care to grieve them, but only to do the will of God for ever. Dear were they unto God as long as they would keep His holy word.

The Holy Lord, All-wielding God, with mighty hand wrought ten angel-orders in whom He trusted well, that they would do Him service, and work His will. Therefore God gave them reason, with His own hands shaped them, and stablished them in bliss. But one He made so great and strong of heart, He let him wield such power in heaven next unto God, so radiant-hued He wrought him, so fair his form in heaven which God had given, that he was like unto the shining stars. He should have sung his Maker's praise, and prized his bliss in heaven. He should have thanked his Lord for the great boon He showered on him in the heavenly light, and let him long enjoy. But he turned him to a worse thing, and strove to stir up strife against the Highest Lord of heaven, who sitteth on the throne of glory.

Dear was he to our Lord. Nor could it long be hid from God that pride was growing in His angel's heart. He set himself against his Leader, scoffed at God with boasting, and would not serve Him. He said his form was beautiful and bright, gleaming and fair of hue. Nor could he find it in his heart to serve the Lord God, or be subject to Him. It seemed to him that he had greater strength and larger following than Holy God might have. Many words the angel spake in his presumption. By his own power alone he thought to build a stronger throne and mightier in heaven. He said his heart was urging him to toil, to build a stately palace in the north and west. He said he doubted in his heart if he would still be subject unto God:

"Why should I slave?" quoth he. "I need not serve a master. My hands are strong to work full many a wonder. Power enough have I to rear a goodlier throne, a higher in the heavens. Why should I fawn for His favour, or yield Him such submission? I may be God as well as He! Brave comrades stand about me; stout-hearted heroes who will not fail me in the fray. These valiant souls have chosen me their lord. With such peers one may ponder counsel, and gain a following. Devoted are these friends and faithful-hearted; and I may be their lord and rule this realm. It seemeth no wise right to me that I should cringe a whit to God for any good. I will not serve Him longer."

Now when God had heard all this, how His angel was beginning to make presumptuous head against his Leader, speaking rash words of insolence against his Lord, needs must he make atonement for that deed, endure the woe of strife, and bear his punishment, most grievous of all deaths. And so doth every man who wickedly thinketh to strive with God, the Lord of might.

Then Almighty God, High Lord of heaven, was filled

with wrath, and hurled him from his lofty throne. He had gained his Master's hate, and lost His favour. God's heart was hardened against him. Wherefore he needs must sink into the pit of torment because he strove against the Lord of heaven. He banished him from grace and cast him into hell, into the deep abyss where he became a devil. The Fiend and all his followers fell from heaven; three nights and days the angels fell from heaven into hell. God changed them all to devils. Because they heeded not His deed and word, therefore Almighty God hurled them into darkness, deep under earth, crushed them and set them in the murk of hell. There through the never-ending watches of the night the fiends endure an unremitting fire. Then at the dawn cometh an east wind, and bitter frost, ever a blast of fire or storm of frost. And each must have his share of suffering wrought for his punishment. Their world was changed when God filled full the pit of hell with His foes!

But the angels who kept their faith with God dwelt in the heights of heaven. The other fiends who waged so fierce a war with God lay wrapped in flames. They suffer torment, hot and surging flame in the midst of hell, broad-stretching blaze of the fire and bitter smoke, darkness and gloom, because they broke allegiance unto God. Their folly and the angel's pride deceived them. They would not heed the word of God. Great was their punishment! They fell, through folly and through pride, to fiery depths of flame in hell. They sought another home devoid of light and filled with fire—a mighty flaming death. The fiends perceived that through the might of God, because of their presumptuous hearts and boundless insolence they had won a measureless woe.

Then spake their haughty king, who formerly was

fairest of the angels, most radiant in heaven, beloved of his Leader and dear unto his Lord, until they turned to folly, and Almighty God was moved to anger at their wantonness, and hurled him down to depths of torment on that bed of death. He named him with a name, and said their leader should be called from thenceforth Satan. He bade him rule the black abyss of hell in place of striving against God. Satan spake— who now must needs have charge of hell and dwell in the abyss—in bitterness he spake who once had been God's angel, radiant-hued in heaven, until his pride and boundless arrogance betrayed him, so that he would not do the bidding of the Lord of hosts. Bitterness was welling in his heart; and round him blazed his cruel torment. These words he spake:

"This narrow place is little like those other realms we know on high in heaven, allotted by my Lord, though the Almighty hath not granted us to hold our state, or rule our kingdom. He hath done us wrong to hurl us to the fiery depths of hell, and strip us of our heavenly realm. He hath ordained that human kind shall settle there. That is my greatest grief, that Adam—wrought of earth—should hold my firm-set throne and live in joy, while we endure this bitter woe in hell.

"Alas! Could I but use my hands and have my freedom for an hour, one winter hour, then with this host I would—But bands of iron crush me down, the bondage of my chains is heavy. I am stripped of my dominion. Firmly are hell's fetters forged upon me. Above me and below a blaze of fire! Never have I seen a realm more fatal—flame unassuaged that surges over hell. Ensnaring links and heavy shackles hold me. My ways are trammelled up; my feet are bound; my hands are fastened. Closed are the doors of hell, the way cut off. I may not escape out of my bonds, but mighty gyves of tempered iron, hammered hot, press hard upon me. God hath set His foot upon my neck. So I know the Lord of hosts hath read the purpose of my heart, and knew full well that strife would grow between our host and Adam over the heavenly realm, had I the freedom of my hands.

"But now we suffer throes of hell, fire and darkness, bottomless and grim. God hath thrust us out into the black mists. He cannot charge upon us any sin or evil wrought against Him in His realm! Yet hath He robbed us of the light and cast us into utter woe. Nor may we take revenge, nor do Him any evil because He stripped us of the light. He hath marked out the borders of the world, and there created man in His own image, with whom He hopes again to people heaven, with pure souls. We needs must ponder earnestly to wreak this grudge on Adam, if we may, and on his children, and thwart His will if so we may devise.

"No longer have I any hope of light wherein He thinketh long to joy, in bliss among His angel hosts; nor may we ever bring this thing to pass, that we should change the purpose of Almighty God. Let us therefore turn the heavenly kingdom from the sons of men, since we may not possess it, cause them to lose His favour and turn aside from the command He laid upon them. Then shall His wrath be kindled, and He shall cast them out from grace. They shall seek out hell and its grim gulf, and in this heavy bondage we may have the sons of men to serve us.

"Begin now and plan this enterprise. If ever in older days, when happily we dwelt in that good kingdom, and held possession of our thrones, I dealt out princely treasure to any thane, he could not make requital for my gifts at any better time than now, if some one of my thanes would be my helper, escaping outward through these bolted gates, with strength to wing his way on high where, new-created, Adam and Eve, surrounded with abundance, dwell on earth—and we are cast out hither in this deep abyss. They are now much dearer unto God, and own the high estate and rightful realm which we should have in heaven! Good fortune is allotted to mankind.

"My soul is sorrowful within me, my heart is sore, that they should hold the heavenly realm for ever. But if in any wise some one of you could bring them to forsake God's word and teaching, soon would they be less pleasing unto Him! If they break His commandment, then will His wrath be kindled. Their high estate shall vanish; their sin shall have requital, and some grim penalty. Take thought now how ye may ensnare them. I shall rest softly in these chains if they lose heaven. Whoso shall bring this thing to pass shall have reward for ever, of all that we may win to our advantage, amid these flames. I will let him sit next me, whoever shall return to hell proclaiming that they have set at naught, by word and deed, the counsels of the King of heaven and been displeasing to the Lord."

Then God's enemy began to make him ready, equipped in war-gear, with a wily heart. He set his helm of darkness on his head, bound it full hard, and fastened it with clasps. Many a crafty speech he knew, many a crooked word. Upward he beat his way and darted through the doors of hell. He had a ruthless heart. Evil of purpose he circled in the air, cleaving the flame with fiendish craft. He would fain ensnare God's servants unto sin, seduce them and deceive them that they might be displeasing to the Lord. With fiendish craft he took his way until he came on Adam upon earth, the finished handiwork of God, full wisely wrought, and his wife beside him, loveliest of women, performing many a goodly service since the Lord of men appointed them His ministers.

And by them stood two trees laden with fruit and clothed with increase. Almighty God, High King of heaven, had set them there that the mortal sons of men might choose of good and evil, weal and woe. Unlike was their fruit! Of the one tree the fruit was pleasant, fair and winsome, excellent and sweet. That was the tree of life. He might live for ever in the world who ate of that fruit, so that old age pressed not heavily upon him, nor grievous sickness, but he might live his life in happiness for ever, and have the favour of the King of heaven here on earth. And glory was ordained for him in heaven, when he went hence.

The other tree was dark, sunless, and full of shadows: that was the tree of death. Bitter the fruit it bore! And every man must know both good and evil; in this world abased he needs must suffer, in sweat and sorrow, who tasted of the fruit that grew upon that tree. Old age would rob him of his strength and joy and honour, and death take hold upon him. A little time might he enjoy this life, and seek out the murky realm of flame, and be subject unto fiends. There of all perils are the worst for men for ever. And that the evil one knew well, the wily herald of the fiend who fought with God. He took the form of a serpent, coiled round the tree of death by devil's craft, and plucked the fruit, and turned aside again where he beheld the handiwork of the King of heaven. And the evil one in lying words began to question him:

"Hast thou any longing, Adam, unto God? His service brings me hither from afar. Not long since I was sitting at His side. He sent me forth upon this journey to bid thee eat this fruit. He said thy strength and power would increase, thy mind be mightier, more beautiful thy body, and thy form more fair. He said thou wouldest lack no good thing on the earth when thou hast won the favour of the King of heaven, served thy Lord with gladness, and deserved His love.

"In the heavenly light I heard Him speaking of thy life, praising thy words and works. Needs must thou do His bidding which His messengers proclaim on earth. Broad-stretching are the green plains of the world, and from the highest realms of heaven God ruleth all things here below. The Lord of men will not Himself endure the hardship to go upon this journey, but sendeth His ministers to speak with thee. He sendeth tidings unto thee to teach thee wisdom. Do His will with gladness! Take this fruit in thy hand; taste and eat. Thy heart shall grow more roomy and thy form more fair. Almighty God, thy Lord, sendeth this help from heaven."

And Adam, first of men, answered where he stood on earth: "When I heard the Lord, my God, speaking with a mighty voice, He bade me dwell here keeping His commandments, gave me this woman, this lovely maid, bade me take heed and be not tempted to the tree of death and utterly beguiled, and said that he who taketh to his heart one whit of evil shall dwell in blackest hell. Though thou art come with lies and secret wiles, I know not that thou art an angel of the Lord from heaven. Lo! I cannot understand thy precepts, thy words or ways, thy errand or thy sayings. I know what things our Lord commanded when I beheld Him nigh at hand. He bade me heed His word, observe it well, and keep His precepts. Thou art not like to any of His angels that ever I have seen, nor hast thou showed me any token that my Lord hath sent of grace and favour. Therefore I cannot hearken to thy teachings.

Get thee hence! I have my faith set firm upon Almighty
God, who with His own hands wrought me. From His
high throne He giveth all good things, and needeth not
to send His ministers."

Then turned the fiend with wrathful heart to where
he saw Eve standing on the plains of earth, a winsome
maid. And unto her he said, the greatest of all ills
thereafter would fall on their descendants in the world:

"I know God's anger will be roused against you,
when from this journey through far-stretching space I
come again to Him, and bring this message, that ye
refuse to do His bidding, as He hath sent commandment
hither from the East. He needs must come to speak
with you, forsooth, nor may His minister proclaim His
mission! Truly I know His wrath will be kindled against
you in His heart!

"But if thou, woman, wilt hearken to my words, thou
mayest devise good counsel. Bethink thee in thy heart
to turn away His vengeance from you both, as I shall
show thee. Eat of this fruit! Then shall thine eyes
grow keen, and thou shalt see afar through all the world,
yea! unto the throne of God, thy Lord, and have His
favour. Thou mayest rule the heart of Adam, if thou
incline to do it and he doth trust thy words, if thou
wilt tell him truly what law thou hast in mind, to keep
God's precepts and commandments. His heart will
cease from bitter strife and evil answers, as we two
tell him for his good. Urge him earnestly to do thy
bidding, lest ye be displeasing to the Lord your God.
If thou fulfill this undertaking, thou best of women,
I will not tell our Lord what evil Adam spake against
me, his wicked words accusing me of falsehood, saying
that I am eager in transgression, a servant of the Fiend
and not God's angel. But I know well the angel race,
and the high courts of heaven. Long ages have I

served the Lord my God with loyal heart. I am not
like a devil."

So he urged with lies and luring wiles, tempting
the woman unto sin, until the serpent's counsel worked
within her—for God had wrought her soul the weaker—
and her heart inclined according to his teaching. Trans-
gressing God's commandment, from the fiend she took
the fatal fruit of the tree of death. Never was worse
deed wrought for men! Great is the wonder that Eternal God, the Lord, would let so many of His thanes be
tricked with lies by one who brought such counsel.
She ate the fruit and set at naught the will and word
of God.

Then could she see afar by gift of the fiend, whose
lies deceived and artfully ensnared her, so that it came
to pass the heavens appeared to her more radiant, and
the earth and all the world more fair, the great and
mighty handiwork of God, though she beheld it not by
human wisdom; but eagerly the fiend deceived her soul
and gave her vision, that she might see afar across the
heavenly kingdom. Then spake the fiend with hostile
purpose—and naught of profit did he counsel:

"Now mayest thou behold, most worthy Eve, nor
need I tell thee, how fair thy beauty and thy form
how changed, since thou didst trust my words and do
my bidding. A radiance·shineth round about thee,
gleaming splendour, which I brought forth from God
on high. Thou mayest touch it! Tell Adam what vision
thou hast and power by my coming. And even yet,
if he will do my bidding with humble heart, I will give
him of this light abundantly, as I have given thee, and
will not punish his reviling words, though he deserves
no mercy for the grievous ill he spake against me. So
shall his children live hereafter! When they do evil,

they must win God's love, avert His doom, and gain the favour of their Lord for ever!"

Then the lovely maid, fairest of women that ever came into this world, went unto Adam. She was the handiwork of the King of heaven, though tricked with lies and utterly undone, so that through fiendish craft and devil's fraud she needs must be displeasing to the Lord, forfeit God's favour, and lose her glory and her heavenly home. So often evil dwelleth with that man who doth not shun it when he hath the power.

Of the fatal apples some she carried in her hands and some lay on her breast, the fruit of the tree of death whereof the Lord of lords, the Prince of glory, had forbidden her to eat, saying His servants need not suffer death. The Holy Lord bestowed a heavenly heritage and ample bliss on every race, if they would but forgo that fruit alone, that bitter fruit, which the mortal tree brought forth upon its boughs. That was the tree of death which the Lord forbade them!

But the fiend, who hated God, and loathed the King of heaven, deceived with lies Eve's heart and erring wisdom, and she believed his words and did his bidding, and came at last to think his counsels were indeed from God, as he so cunningly had said. He showed to her a token, and gave her promise of good faith and friendly purpose. Then to her lord she said:

"Adam, my lord! This fruit is sweet and pleasing to the heart; this radiant messenger is God's good angel! I know by his attire he is a herald of our Lord, the King of heaven. Better to win his favour than his wrath! If thou to-day hast spoken aught of evil, yet will he still forgive thee, if we will do his will. Of what avail this bitter strife against the herald of thy Lord? We need his favour. For he may plead our cause before Almighty God, the King of heaven.

"I can behold where in the south and east He who shaped the world sits veiled in splendour. I see the angels circling round His throne, in winged flight, unnumbered myriads, clothed in beauty. Who could give me such discernment, except it be sent straight from God, the Lord of heaven? Widely may I hear and widely see through all the world across the broad creation. I hear the hymns of rapture from on high. Radiance blazes on my soul without and within since first I tasted of the fruit. Lo! my good lord! I bring thee in my hand this fruit, and give thee freely of it. I do believe that it is come from God, and brought by His command, as this messenger declared in words of truth. It is not like aught else on earth except, as this herald saith, it cometh straight from God."

Long she pled, and urged him all the day to that dark deed, to disobey their Lord's command. Close stood the evil fiend, inflaming with desire, luring with wiles, and boldly tempting him. The fiend stood near at hand who on that fatal mission had come a long, long way. He planned to hurl men down to utter death, mislead them and deceive them, that they might lose the gift of God, His favour and their heavenly realm. Lo! well the hell-fiend knew they must endure God's anger and the pains of hell, suffer grim misery and woe, since they had broken God's commandment, when with his lying words he tricked the beauteous maid, fairest of women, unto that deed of folly, so that she spake according to his will; and aided her in tempting unto evil the handiwork of God.

Over and over the fairest of women pled with Adam, until she began to incline his heart so that he trusted the command the woman laid upon him. All this she did with good intent, and knew not that so many evils, such grim afflictions, would come upon mankind, when

she was moved to hearken to the counsels of the evil
herald; but she hoped to win God's favour by her
words, showing such token and such pledge of truth
unto the man that the mind of Adam was changed
within his breast, and his heart began to bend according
to her will.

From the woman he took both death and hell, although it did not bear these names, but bore the name
of fruit. The sleep of death and fiends' seduction;
death and hell and exile and damnation—these were the
fatal fruit whereon they feasted. And when the apple
worked within him and touched his heart, then laughed
aloud the evil-hearted fiend, capered about, and gave
thanks to his lord for both:

"Now have I won thy promised favour, and wrought
thy will! For many a day to come is man undone,
Adam and Eve! God's wrath shall be heavy upon them,
for they have scorned His precepts and commandments.
Wherefore they may no longer hold their heavenly
kingdom, but they must travel the dark road to hell.
Thou needest not feel sorrow in thy heart, as thou liest
in thy bonds, nor mourn in spirit that men should dwell
in heaven above, while we now suffer misery and pain
in realms of darkness, and through thy pride have lost
our high estate in heaven and goodly dwellings. God's
anger was kindled against us because in heaven we
would not bow our heads in service before the Holy
Lord. It pleased us not to serve Him. Then was
God moved to wrath and hard of heart, and drove us
into hell; cast a great host into hell-fire, and with His
hands prepared again in heaven celestial thrones, and
gave that kingdom to mankind.

"Blithe be thy heart within thy breast! For here
to-day are two things come to pass: the sons of men
shall lose their heavenly kingdom, and journey unto

thee to burn in flame; also heart-sorrow and affliction are visited on God. Whatever death we suffer here is now repaid on Adam in the wrath of God and man's damnation and the pangs of death. Therefore my heart is healed, my soul untrammelled in my breast. All our injuries are now avenged, and all the evil that we long have suffered. Now will I plunge again into the flame, and seek out Satan, where he lieth in hell's shadows, bound with chains."

Then the foul fiend sank downward to the wide-flung flames and gates of hell wherein his lord lay bound. But Adam and Eve were wretched in their hearts; sad were the words that passed between them. They feared the anger of the Lord their God; they dreaded the wrath of the King of heaven. They knew that His command was broken.

The woman mourned and wept in sorrow (she had forfeited God's grace and broken His commandment) when she beheld the radiance disappear which he who brought this evil on them had showed her by a faithless token, that they might suffer pangs of hell and untold woe. Wherefore heartsorrow burned within their breasts. Husband and wife they bowed them down in prayer, beseeching God and calling on the Lord of heaven, and prayed that they might expiate their sin, since they had broken God's commandment. They saw that their bodies were naked. In that land they had as yet no settled home, nor knew they aught of pain or sorrow; but they might have prospered in the land if they had done God's will. Many a rueful word they uttered, husband and wife together. And Adam spake unto Eve and said:

"O Eve! a bitter portion hast thou won us! Dost thou behold the yawning gulf of hell, sunless, insatiate? Thou mayest hear the groans that rise therefrom! The heavenly realm is little like that blaze of fire! Lo! fairest of all lands is this, which we, by God's grace, might have held hadst thou not hearkened unto him who urged this evil, so that we set at naught the word of God, the King of heaven. Now in brief we mourn that evil mission! For God Himself bade us beware of sin and dire disaster. Now thirst and hunger press upon my heart whereof we formerly were ever free. How shall we live or dwell now in this land if the wind blow from the west or east, south or north, if mist arise and showers of hail beat on us from the heavens, and frost cometh, wondrous cold, upon the earth, or, hot in heaven, shineth the burning sun, and we two stand here naked and unclothed? We have no shelter from the weather, nor any store of food. And the Mighty Lord, our God, is angry with us. What shall become of us? Now I repent me that I prayed the God of heaven, the Gracious Lord, and of my limbs He wrought thee for my helpmeet, since thou hast led me unto evil and the anger of my Lord. Well may I repent to all eternity that ever I beheld thee with mine eyes!"

Then spake Eve, the lovely maid, fairest of women. (She was the work of God, though led astray by power of the fiend):

"Well mayest thou upbraid me, my dear Adam! But thou canst not repent one whit more bitterly in thy heart than my heart repenteth."

And Adam answered her: "If I but knew the will of God, the penalty I needs must pay, thou couldest not find one more swift to do it, though the Lord of heaven bade me go forth and walk upon the sea. The ocean-stream could never be so wondrous deep or wide that ever my heart would doubt, but I would go even unto the bottom of the sea, if I might work the will of God.

I have no wish for years of manhood in the world now
that I have forfeited the favour of my Lord, and lost
His grace. But we may not be thus together, naked.
Let us go into this grove, and under the shelter of this
wood."

And they turned and went weeping into the green
wood, and sat them down apart from one another to wait
the fate the Lord of heaven should assign them, since
they had lost their former state and portion which Almighty God had given them. And they covered their
bodies with leaves, and clothed them with the foliage of
the wood, for they had no garments. And both together
bowed in prayer; and every morning they besought
Almighty God, the Gracious Lord, that He would not
forget them, but would teach them how to live thence-
forward in the light.

BEDE (673-735)

From *The Ecclesiastical History of the English People, Book I, chap.* 1. Of the Situation of Britain
and Ireland, and of their ancient inhabitants.

BRITAIN, an island in the ocean, formerly called
ALBION, is situated between the north and west, facing,
though at a considerable distance, the coasts of Germany, France, and Spain, which form the greatest part
of Europe. It extends 800 miles in length towards
the north, and is 200 miles in breadth, by which its
compass is made to be 3675 miles. To the south, as
you pass along the nearest shore of the Belgic Gaul,
the first place in Britain which opens to the eye is
the city of Rutubi Portus, by the English corrupted into
Reptacestir. The distance from hence across the sea
to Gessoriacum, the nearest shore of the Morini, is fifty

miles, or as some writers say, 450 furlongs. On the back of the island, where it opens upon the boundless ocean, it has the islands called Orcades. Britain excels for grain and trees, and is well adapted for feeding cattle and beasts of burden. It also produces vines in some places, and has plenty of land and water-fowls of several sorts; it is remarkable also for rivers abounding in fish, and plentiful springs. It has the greatest plenty of salmon and eels; seals are also frequently taken, and dolphins, as also whales; besides many sorts of shell-fish, such as mussels, in which are often found excellent pearls of all colors, red, purple, violet, and green, but mostly white. There is also a great abundance of cockles, of which the scarlet dye is made; a most beautiful color, which never fades with the heat of the sun or the washing of the rain; but the older it is, the more beautiful it becomes. It has both salt and hot springs, and from them flow rivers which furnish hot baths, proper for all ages and sexes, and arranged according. For water, as St. Basil says, receives the heating quality when it runs along certain metals, and becomes not only hot but scalding. Britain has also many veins of metals, as copper, iron, lead and silver; it has much and excellent jet, which is black and sparkling, glittering at the fire, and when heated, drives away serpents; being warmed with rubbing, it holds fast whatever is applied to it, like amber. The island was formerly embellished with twenty-eight noble cities, besides innumerable castles, which were all strongly secured with walls, towers, gates, and locks. And, from its lying almost under the North Pole, the nights are light in summer, so that at midnight the beholders are often in doubt whether the evening twilight still continues, or that of the morning is coming on; for the sun, in the night, returns under the earth, through the northern regions at no great distance from them. For this reason the days are of a great length in summer, as, on the contrary, the nights are in winter, for the sun then withdraws into the southern parts, so that the nights are eighteen hours long. Thus the nights are extraordinarily short in summer, and the days in winter, that is, of only six equinoctial hours. Whereas, in Armenia, Macedonia, Italy, and other countries of the same latitude, the longest day or night extends but to fifteen hours, and the shortest to nine.

This island at present, following the number of the books in which the Divine law was written, contains five nations, the English, Britons, Scots, Picts, and Latins, each in its own peculiar dialect cultivating the sublime study of Divine truth. The Latin tongue is, by the study of the Scriptures, become common to all the rest. At the first this island had no other inhabitants but the Britons, from whom it derived its name, and who, coming over into Britain, as is reported, from Armorica, possessed themselves of the southern parts thereof. When they, beginning at the south, had made themselves masters of the greatest part of the island, it happened that the nation of the Picts, from Scythia, as is reported, putting to sea in a few long ships, were driven by the winds beyond the shores of Britain, and arrived on the northern coasts of Ireland, where, finding the nation of the Scots, they begged to be allowed to settle among them, but could not succeed in obtaining their request. Ireland is the greatest island next to Britain, and lies to the west of it; but as it is shorter than Britain to the north, so, on the other hand, it runs out far beyond it to the south, opposite to the northern parts of Spain, though a spacious sea lies between them. The Picts, as has been said, arriving in this island by sea, desired to have a place granted them, in which they might settle. The Scots answered that the island could not contain them both; but "We can give you good advice," said they, "what to do; we know there is another island, not far from ours, to the eastward, which we often see at a distance, when the days are clear. If you will go thither, you shall have our assistance." The Picts, accordingly, sailing over into Britain, began to inhabit the northern parts thereof, for the Britons were possessed of the southern. Now the Picts had no wives, and asked them of the Scots; who would not consent to grant them upon any other terms, than that when any difficulty should arise, they should choose a king from the female royal race than from the male; which custom, as is well known, has been observed among the Picts to this day. In process of time, Britain, besides the Britons and the Picts, received a third nation, the Scots, who, migrating from Ireland under their leader, Reuda, either by fair means, or by force of arms, secured to themselves those settlements among the Picts which they still possess. From the name of their commander, they are to this day called Dalreudins; for, in their language, Dal signifies a part.

Ireland, in breadth, and for wholesomeness and serenity of climate, far surpasses Britain; for the snow scarcely ever lies there above three days: no man makes hay in the summer for winter's provision, or builds stables for his beasts of burden. No reptiles are found there, and no snake can live there; for, though often carried thither out of Britain, as soon as the ship comes near the shore, and the scent of the air reaches them, they die. On the contrary, almost all things in the island are good against poison. In short, we have known that when some persons have been bitten by serpents, the scrapings of leaves of books that were brought out of Ireland, being put into water, and given them to drink, have immediately expelled the spreading poison, and assuaged the swelling. The island abounds in milk and honey, nor is there any want of vines, fish, or fowl; and it is remarkable for deer and goats. It is properly the country of the Scots, who, migrating from thence, as has been said, added a third nation in Britain to the Britons and the Picts. There is a very large gulf of the sea, which formerly divided the nation of the Picts from the Britons; which gulf runs from the west very far into the land, where, to this day, stands the strong city of the Britons, called Alcluith. The Scots, arriving on the north side of this bay, settled themselves there.

Book I, chap. 12

THE ROMANS AID THE BRITONS

From that time, the south part of Britain, destitute of armed soldiers, of martial stores, and of all its active youth, which had been led away by the rashness of the tyrants, never to return, was wholly exposed to rapine, as being totally ignorant of the use of weapons. Whereupon they suffered many years under two very savage foreign nations, the Scots from the west, and the Picts from the north. We call these foreign nations, not on account of their being seated out of Britain, but because they were remote from that part of it which was possessed by the Britons; two inlets of the sea lying between them, one of which runs in far and broad into the land of Britain, from the Eastern Ocean, and the other from the Western, though they do not reach so as to touch one another. The eastern has in the midst of it the city Giudi. The western has on it, that is, on the right hand thereof, the city Alcluith, which in their language signifies the Rock Cluith, for it is close by the river of that name.

On account of the irruption of these nations, the Britons sent messengers to Rome with letters in mournful manner, praying for succors, and promising perpetual subjection, provided that the impending enemy should be driven away. An armed legion was immediately sent them, which, arriving in the island, and engaging the enemy, slew a great multitude of them, drove the rest out of the territories of their allies, and having delivered them from their cruel oppressors, advised them to build a wall between the two seas across the island, that it might secure them, and keep off the enemy; and thus they returned home with great triumph. The islanders raising the wall, as they had been directed, not of stone, as having no artist capable of such a work, but of sods, made it of no use. However, they drew it for many miles between the two bays or inlets of the seas, which we have spoken of; to the end that where the defense of the water was wanting, they might use the rampart to defend their borders from the irruptions of the enemies. Of which work there erected, that is, of a rampart of extraordinary breadth and height, there are evident remains to be seen at this day. It begins at about two miles' distance from the monastery of Abercurnig, on the west, at a place called in the Pictish language, Peanfahel, but in the English tongue, Penneltun, and running to the westward, ends near the city Alcluith.

But the former enemies, when they perceived that the Roman soldiers were gone, immediately coming by sea, broke into the borders, trampled and overran all places, and like men mowing ripe corn, bore down all before them. Hereupon messengers are again sent to Rome, imploring aid, lest their wretched country should be utterly extirpated, and the name of a Roman province, so long renowned among them, overthrown by the cruelties of barbarous foreigners, might become utterly contemptible. A legion is accordingly sent again, and, arriving unexpectedly in autumn, made great slaughter of the enemy, obliging all those that could escape, to flee beyond the sea; whereas before, they were wont yearly to carry off their booty without any opposition. Then the Romans declared to the Britons, that they could not for the future undertake such troublesome expeditions for their sake, advising them rather to handle their weapons like men, and undertake themselves the charge of engaging their enemies, who would not prove too powerful for them, unless they were deterred by cowardice; and, thinking that it might be some help to the allies, whom they were forced to abandon, they built a strong stone wall from sea to sea, in a straight line between the towns that had been there built for fear of the enemy, and not far from the trench of Severus. This famous wall, which is still to be seen, was built at the public and private expense, the Britons also lending their assistance. It is eight feet in breadth, and twelve in height, in a straight line from east to west, as is still visible to beholders. This being finished, they gave that dispirited people good advice, with patterns to furnish them with arms. Besides, they built towers on the sea-coast to the southward, at proper distances, where their ships were, because there also the interruptions of barbarians were apprehended, and so took leave of their friends, never to return again.

After their departure, the Scots and Picts, understanding that they had declared they would come no more, speedily returned, and growing more confident than they had been before, occupied all the northern and farthest part of the island, as far as the wall. Hereupon a timorous guard was placed upon the wall,

where they pined away day and night in the utmost fear.
On the other side, the enemy attacked them with
hooked weapons, by which the cowardly defendants were
dragged from the wall, and dashed against the ground.
At last, the Britons, forsaking their cities and wall, took
to flight and were dispersed. The enemy pursued, and
the slaughter was greater than on any former occasion;
for the wretched natives were torn in pieces by their
enemies, as lambs are torn by wild beasts. Thus, being
expelled from their dwellings and possessions, they
saved themselves from starvation, by robbing and plundering one another, adding to the calamities occasioned
by foreigners, by their own domestic broils, till the
whole country was left destitute of food, except such
as could be procured in the chase.

Book I, chap. 15

THE ARRIVAL OF THE ANGLES

In the year of our Lord 449, Martian being made
emperor with Valentinian, and the forty-sixth from Augustus, ruled the empire seven years. Then the nation
of the Angles, or Saxons, being invited by the aforesaid king, arrived in Britain, with three long ships, and
had a place assigned them to reside in by the same king,
in the eastern part of the island, that they might thus
appear to be fighting for their country, whilst their
real intentions were to enslave it. Accordingly they
engaged with the enemy, who were come from the north
to give battle, and obtained the victory; which, being
known at home in their own country, as also the fertility
of the country, and the cowardice of the Britons, a
more considerable fleet was quickly sent over, bringing
a still greater number of men, which, being added to

the former, made up an invincible army. The new-comers received of the Britons a place to inhabit, upon condition that they should wage war against their enemies for the peace and security of the country, whilst the Britons agreed to furnish them with pay. Those who came over were of the three most powerful nations of Germany—Saxons, Angles, and Jutes. From the Jutes are descended the people of Kent, and of the Isle of Wight, and those also in the province of the West-Saxons who are to this day called Jutes, seated opposite to the Isle of Wight. From the Saxons, that is, the country which is now called Old Saxony, came the East-Saxons, the South-Saxons, and the West-Saxons. From the Angles, that is, the country which is called Anglia, and which is said, from that time, to remain desert to this day, between the provinces of the Jutes and the Saxons, are descended the East-Angles, the Midland-Angles, Mercians, all the race of the Northumbrians, that is, of those nations that dwell on the north side of the river Humber, and the other nations of the English. The two first commanders are said to have been Hengist and Horsa, of whom Horsa, being afterwards slain in battle by the Britons, was buried in the eastern parts of Kent, where a monument, bearing his name, is still in existence. They were the sons of Victgilsus, whose father was Vecta, son of Woden; from whose stock the royal race of many provinces deduce their original. In a short time, swarms of the aforesaid nations came over into the island, and they began to increase so much that they became terrible to the natives themselves who had invited them. Then, having on a sudden entered into league with the Picts, whom they had by this time repelled by the force of their arms, they began to turn their weapons against their confederates. At first they obliged them to furnish a greater quantity of provisions; and, seeking an occasion to quarrel, protested that unless more plentiful supplies were brought them, they would break the confederacy and ravage all the island; nor were they backward in putting their threats in execution. In short, the fires kindled by the hands of these pagans, proved God's just revenge for the crimes of the people; not unlike that which, being once lighted by the Chaldeans, consumed the walls and city of Jerusalem. For the barbarous conquerors acting here in the same manner, or rather the just Judge ordaining that they should so act, they plundered all the neighboring cities and country, spread the conflagration from the eastern to the western sea, without any opposition, and covered almost every part of the devoted island. Public as well as private structures were overturned; the priests were everywhere slain before the altars; the prelates and the people, without any respect of persons, were destroyed with fire and sword; nor was there any to bury those who had been thus cruelly slaughtered. Some of the miserable remainder, being taken in the mountains, were butchered in heaps. Others, spent with hunger, came forth and submitted themselves to the enemy for food, being destined to undergo perpetual servitude, if they were not killed even upon the spot. Some, with sorrowful hearts, fled beyond the seas. Others, continuing in their own country, led a miserable life among the woods, rocks, and mountains, with scarcely enough food to support life, and expecting every moment to be their last.

Book I, chap. 23

THE MISSION OF AUGUSTINE

In the year of our Lord 582, Maurice, the fifty-fourth from Augustus, ascended the throne, and reigned twenty-one years. In the tenth year of his reign, Gregory, a man renowned for learning and behavior, was promoted to the apostolical see of Rome, and presided over it thirteen years, six months and ten days. He, being moved by Divine inspiration, in the fourteenth year of the same emperor, and about the one hundred and fiftieth after the coming of the English into Britain, sent the servant of God, Augustine, and with him several other monks, who feared the Lord, to preach the word of God to the English nation. They having, in obedience to the pope's commands, undertaken that work, were, on their journey, seized with a sudden fear, and began to think of returning home, rather than proceed to a barbarous, fierce, and unbelieving nation, to whose very language they were strangers; and this they unanimously agreed was the safest course. In short, they sent back Augustine, who had been appointed to be consecrated bishop in case they were received by the English, that he might, by humble entreaty, obtain of the holy Gregory that they should not be compelled to undertake so dangerous, toilsome, and uncertain a journey. The pope, in reply, sent them a hortatory epistle, persuading them to proceed in the work of the Divine word, and rely on the assistance of the Almighty. The purport of which letter was as follows:—

"Gregory, the servant of the servants of God, to the servants of our Lord. Forasmuch as it had been better not to begin a good work, than to think of desisting from that which has been begun, it behooves you, my beloved sons, to fulfill the good work, which, by the help of our Lord, you have undertaken. Let not, therefore, the toil of the journey, nor the tongues of evil-speaking men, deter you; but with all possible earnestness and zeal perform that which, by God's direction, you have undertaken; being assured that much labor is followed by an eternal reward. When Augustine, your chief, returns, whom we also constitute your abbot, humbly obey him in all things; knowing that whatsoever you shall do by his direction, will in all respects be available to your souls. Almighty God protect you with his grace, and grant that I may, in the heavenly country, see the fruits of your labor. Inasmuch as, though I cannot labor with you, I shall partake in the joy of the reward, because I am willing to labor. God keep you in safety, my most beloved sons. Dated the 23rd of July, in the fourteenth year of the reign of our pious and most august lord, Mauritius Tiberius, the thirteenth year after the consulship of our said lord. The fourteenth indiction."

Book I, chap. 25

THE ENDEAVORS OF AUGUSTINE

Augustine, thus strengthened by the confirmation of the blessed Father Gregory, returned to the work of the word of God, with the servants of Christ, and arrived in Britain. The powerful Ethelbert was at that time king of Kent; he had extended his dominions as far as the great river Humber, by which the Southern Saxons are divided from the Northern. On the east of Kent is the large Isle of Thanet containing according to the English way of reckoning, 600 families, divided from the other land by the river Wantsum, which is about three furlongs over, and fordable only in two places, for both ends of it run into the sea. In this island landed the servant of our Lord, Augustine, and his companions, being, as is reported, nearly forty men. They had, by order of the blessed Pope Gregory, taken interpreters of the nation of the Franks, and sending to Ethelbert, signified that they were come from Rome, and brought a joyful message, which most undoubtedly assured to all that took advantage of it everlasting joys in heaven, and a kingdom that would never end, with the living and true God. The king having heard this, ordered them to stay in that island where they had landed, and that they should be furnished with all necessaries, till he should consider what to do with them. For he had before neard of the Christian religion, having a Christian wife of the royal family of the Franks, called Bertha; whom he had received from her parents, upon condition that she should be permitted to practise her religion with the Bishop Luidhard, who was sent with her to preserve her faith. Some days after, the king came into the island, and sitting in the open air, ordered Augustine and his companions to be brought into his presence. For he had taken precaution that they should not come to him in any house, lest, according to an ancient superstition, if they practised any magical arts, they might impose upon him, and so get the better of him. But they came furnished with Divine, not with magic virtue, bearing a silver cross for their banner, and the image of our Lord and Savior painted on a board; and singing the litany, they offered up their prayers to the Lord for the eternal salvation both of themselves and of those to whom they were come. When he had sat down, pursuant to the king's commands, and preached to him and his attendants there present, the word of life, the king answered thus: "Your words and promises are very fair, but as they are new to us, and of uncertain import, I cannot approve of them so far as to forsake that which I have so long followed with the whole English nation. But because you are come from far into my kingdom, and, as I conceive, are desirous to impart to us those things which you believe to be true, and most beneficial, we will not molest you, but give you favorable entertainment, and take care to supply you with your necessary sustenance; nor do we forbid you to preach and gain as many as you can to your religion. Accordingly he permitted them to reside in the city of Canterbury, which was the metropolis of all his dominions, and, pursuant to his promise, besides allowing them sustenance, did not refuse them liberty to preach. It is reported that, as they drew near to the city, after their manner, with the holy cross, and the image of our sovereign Lord and King, Jesus Christ, they, in concert, sung this litany: "We beseech thee, O Lord, in all thy mercy, that thy anger and wrath be turned away from this city, and from thy holy house, because we have sinned. Hallelujah."

Book I, chap. 26

As soon as they entered the dwelling-place assigned them, they began to imitate the course of life practised in the primitive church; applying themselves to frequent prayer, watching and fasting; preaching the word of life to as many as they could; despising all worldly things, as not belonging to them; receiving only their necessary food from those they taught; living themselves in all respects conformably to what they prescribed to others, and being always disposed to suffer any adversity, and even to die for that truth which they preached. In short, several believed and were baptized, admiring the simplicity of their innocent life, and the sweetness of their heavenly doctrine. There was on the east side of the city, a church dedicated to the honor of St. Martin, built whilst the Romans were still in the island, wherein the queen, who, as has been said before, was a Christian,

used to pray. In this they first began to meet, to sing,
to pray, to say mass, to preach, and to baptize, till the
king, being converted to the faith, allowed them to
preach openly, and build or repair churches in all
places.

When he, among the rest, induced by the unspotted
life of these holy men, and their delightful promises,
which, by many miracles, they proved to be most certain, believed and was baptized, greater numbers began
daily to flock together to hear the word, and, forsaking
their heathen rites, to associate themselves, by believing,
to the unity of the church of Christ. Their conversion
the king so far encouraged as that he compelled none
to embrace Christianity but only showed more affection
to the believers, as to his fellow citizens in the heavenly
kingdom. For he had learned from his instructors and
leaders to salvation that the service of Christ ought to
be voluntary, not by compulsion. Nor was it long before
he gave his teachers a settled residence in his metropolis
of Canterbury, with such possessions of different kinds
as were necessary for their subsistence.

Book IV, chap. 24

CÆDMON

There was in this abbess's monastery a certain brother,
particularly remarkable for the grace of God, who was
wont to make pious and religious verses, so that whatever was interpreted to him out of Scripture, he soon
after put the same into poetical expressions of much
sweetness and humility, in English, which was his native
language. By his verses the minds of many were often
excited to despise the world, and to aspire to heaven.
Others after him attempted, in the English nation, to

compose religious poems, but none could ever compare
with him, for he did not learn the art of poetry from
men, but from God; for which reason he never could
compose any trivial or vain poem, but only those which
relate to religion suited his religious tongue; for having
lived in a secular habit till he was well advanced in
years, he had never learned any thing of versifying; for
which reason being sometimes at entertainments, when
it was agreed for the sake of mirth that all present
should sing in their turns, when he saw the instrument
come towards him, he rose up from table and returned
home.

Having done so at a certain time, and gone out of
the house where the entertainment was, to the stable,
where he had to take care of the horses that night, he
there composed himself to rest at the proper time; a
person appeared to him in his sleep, and saluting him by
his name, said, "Cædmon, sing some song to me." He
answered, "I cannot sing; for that was the reason why
I left the entertainment, and retired to this place, because I could not sing." The other who talked to him,
replied, "However, you shall sing."—"What shall I
sing?" rejoined he. "Sing the beginning of created
beings," said the other. Hereupon he presently began
to sing verses to the praise of God, which he had never
heard, the purport whereof was thus:—We are now
to praise the Maker of the heavenly kingdom, the power
of the Creator and his counsel, the deeds of the Father
of glory. How he, being the eternal God, became the
author of all miracles, who first, as almighty preserver
of the human race, created heaven for the sons of men
as the roof of the house, and next the earth. This is
the sense, but not the words in order as he sang them
in his sleep; for verses, though never so well composed,
cannot be literally translated out of one language into

another, without losing much of their beauty and lofti-
ness. Awakening from his sleep, he remembered all
that he had sung in his dream, and soon added much
more to the same effect in verse worthy of the Deity.

In the morning he came to the steward, his superior,
and having acquainted him with the gift he had received, was conducted to the abbess, by whom he was
ordered, in the presence of many learned men, to tell
his dream, and repeat the verses, that they might all give
their judgment what it was, and whence his verse pro-
ceeded. They all concluded that heavenly grace had
been conferred on him by our Lord. They expounded
to him a passage in Holy Writ, either historical, or doc-
trinal, ordering him, if he could, to put the same into
verse. Having undertaken it, he went away, and returning the next morning, gave it to them composed in
most excellent verse; whereupon the abbess, embracing
the grace of God in the man, instructed him to quit the
secular habit, and take upon him the monastic life;
which being accordingly done, she associated him to the
rest of the brethren in her monastery, and ordered that
he should be taught the whole series of sacred history.
Thus Cædmon, keeping in mind all he heard, and as
it were chewing the cud, converted the same into most
harmonious verse; and sweetly repeating the same
made his masters in their turn his hearers. He sang
the creation of the world, the origin of man, and all
the history of Genesis: and made many verses on the
departure of the children of Israel out of Egypt, and
their entering into the land of promise, with many other
histories from Holy Writ; the incarnation, passion,
resurrection of our Lord, and his ascension into heaven;
the coming of the Holy Ghost, and the preaching of
the apostles; also the terror of future judgment, the
horror of the pains of hell, and the delights of heaven;

besides many more about the Divine benefits and judgments, by which he endeavored to turn away all men from the love of vice, and to excite in them the love of, and application to, good actions; for he was a very religious man humbly submissive to regular discipline, but full of zeal against those who behaved themselves otherwise; for which reason he ended his life happily.

For when the time of his departure drew near, he labored for the space of fourteen days under a bodily infirmity which seemed to prepare the way, yet so moderate that he could talk and walk the whole time. In his neighborhood was the house to which those that were sick, and like shortly to die, were carried. He desired the person that attended him, in the evening, as the night came on in which he was to depart this life, to make ready a place there for him to take his rest. This person, wondering why he should desire it, because there was as yet no sign of his dying soon, did what he had ordered. He accordingly went there, and conversing pleasantly in a joyful manner with the rest that were in the house before, when it was past midnight, he asked them whether they had the Eucharist there. They answered, "What need of the Eucharist? for you are not likely to die, since you talk so merrily with us, as if you were in perfect health."—"However," said he, "bring me the Eucharist." Having received the same into his hand, he asked whether they were all in charity with him, and without any enmity or rancor? They answered, that they were all in perfect charity, and free from anger; and in their turn asked him, whether he was in the same mind towards them? He answered, "I am in charity, my children, with all the servants of God." Then strengthening himself with the heavenly viaticum, he prepared for the entrance into another life, and asked how near the time was when the brothers were to be awakened to sing the nocturnal praises of our Lord? They answered, "It is not far off." Then he said, "Well, let us wait that hour"; and signing himself with the sign of the cross, he laid his head on the pillow, and falling into a slumber, ended his life so in silence.

Thus it came to pass, that as he had served God with a simple and pure mind, and undisturbed devotion, so he now departed to His presence, leaving the world by a quiet death; and that tongue, which had composed so many holy words in praise of the Creator, uttered its last words whilst he was in the act of signing himself with the cross, and recommending himself into His hands, and by what has been here said, he seems to have had foreknowledge of his death.

CYNEWULF

(LATE EIGHTH CENTURY)

DOOMSDAY

(from *Christ*)

THEN in the midnight the great day of the Lord of might shall come with power unto mortal men, the radiant world, even as a crafty thief, a robber bold, who creepeth in the darkness, in the black night, and falleth suddenly on care-free men bound in slumber; evilly assaileth earls all unprepared.

So on Mount Sion shall gather a mighty host, faithful unto the Lord, bright and blithe; and unto them shall blessedness be given. Then from the four borders of the world, from the uttermost kingdom of earth, four radiant angels in accord shall blow upon the trumpet in one great blast. Then shall the earth tremble, the ground under the foot of man. They shall sound together, steadfast, glorious, unto the path of the stars; they shall peal and send their voice south and north, east and west over all creation. They shall wake from death, out of the ancient earth, in terror, the sons of warriors, the race of man, unto the judgment. They shall bid arise out of firm slumber suddenly.

Then shall be heard a wailing folk, sorrowful in soul, bitterly disquieted, lamenting in woe the deeds of their days of life, trembling in terror. That shall be the greatest of portents, of all such as early or late have ever been revealed to man. There shall meet together the secret hosts of angels and of devils, the radiant and the dark. And both shall come, the white and black, according as a home is wrought for them, in different wise for angels and for fiends.

Then suddenly from out the south and east cometh upon Mount Sion, from the Lord, the radiance of the sun, gleaming more brightly than men may imagine it in their hearts, shining in splendor, when the Son of God, through the arching heavens, appeareth hither. Then cometh the wondrous presence of Christ, the beauteous radiance of the noble King, eastward from the skies, pleasant in spirit unto His own people, bitter unto the sinful, varied in wondrous measure, unto the blessed and unto the wretched unlike.

Unto the good shall He be gracious, winsome and fair to see unto that holy host, beautiful in joy, a gentle friend. Pleasing and blissful shall it be to well-loved men to see that radiant splendor, mild in pleasure, the coming of their Lord, the King of might, unto such as pleased Him well of old in heart, in their words and works. But unto evil men He shall be fearsome, terrible to see, unto the sinful, unto such as thither come with transgressions all undone. That may be a warning of punishment to him that hath wise thought, so that he may be no whit afraid; for the terror of that presence he shall have no dread of heart when he beholdeth the Lord of all creation moving on with mighty wonders to judge the hosts. And round about him on either hand fly thronging angel-troops, a band of radiant beings, hosts of the holy, in ample train.

Then shall resound the vast creation, and before the Lord there shall go forth the mightiest of surging fires over the wide earth; the hot flame shall leap. Then shall the heavens crash, the steadfast stars and radiant shall fall. The sun shall be turned dark unto the hue of blood, which gleamed so brightly over the ancient world unto the sons of men. The very moon, that in the night of old shed her light on men, shall sink from her station; so also shall the stars fade from heaven, through the fierce air, smitten with storms.

And the Almighty with His angel-throng, the Lord of mighty kings, the glorious Prince will come unto the assemblage. There shall be an exultant throng of thanes. Holy souls shall fare forth with their Lord, what time the Warden of peoples, with menace of terror, shall Himself seek out the tribes of earth. Then loud shall be heard throughout the spacious earth the noise of the trumpets of heaven, and on the seven sides the winds shall roar, shall blow, howling in mightiest tumult. They shall wake and wither the earth with tempest, filling the world with their breath. Then shall be heard a heavy crash, loud and measureless, deafening, violent, mightiest of thunders, terrible to men.

The weary hosts of men in multitudes shall depart into the wide flame, where a destroying fire shall come upon them still alive, some up, some down, smitten of the flame. Sure is it that then, all fulfilled of care,

the race of Adam shall wail in sore affliction; nor for
little cause, these woeful tribes, but for the greatest of
heavy hardships, when in one embrace the wan surge
of fire, the dusky flame, far and wide shall seize on
all three together, the seas with their fish, the earth and
her hills, and the heaven above with all its stars. Fierce
and furious the consuming flame shall burn all three.
And all the world shall wail in woe in that dread hour.

So shall the greedy spirit run through earth, the
destroying flame through high-built halls. The wide-
known blast of fire, hot and devouring, shall fill the
plain of earth, the very world with the terror of its
flame. Broken city-walls shall fall together, mountains
shall melt and lofty cliffs, that shielded earth of old
against the sea, firm against the floods, secure and
steadfast, barriers against the waves, the rolling surge.
Then on every creature, on bird and beast, that fire
of death shall seize, and over earth shall fare the dusky
flame, a raging warrior. As of old waters flowed, the
driving seas, then in that bath of fire the sea fish shall
burn, sundered from the deep. All forspent each monster of the sea shall be consumed, water shall burn as
wax.

Then shall be more of marvels than any may imagine
in his heart, when the whirlwind and the storm and the
fierce air shall rend the broad creation. Men shall
mourn, sorrowing with tears and woeful voices, downcast and sad of soul, distressed with sorrow. The dusky
flame shall blaze on those undone by sin, and fire shall
devour golden jewels, the olden treasure of the kings
of the land. Then in the thunder of heaven there
shall be tumult and woe, strife of the living, lament,
loud wailing, the pitiful plaint of men. Then may not
any stained with sin win peace, or ever on earth escape
away from that burning. But the fire shall take all

things in the world, shall burrow grimly, eagerly search out all the folds of earth within and without, till that the heat of its flame hath burned away all the stain of the sin of the world in its billowing surge.

Then shall mighty God come unto that glorious mount with the greatest of angel-bands, the King of heaven's angels shining in holiness, resplendent above His train: the all-wielding God. And round about Him shall gleam in glory the best of noble hosts, holy armies, the blessed angel-throng. Troubled in their innermost thoughts they shall tremble in the fear of God, the Father. No marvel is it if the impure race of mortal men, sorrowing in care, have heavy dread when this holy order, white and heavenly bright, the Spirit-host, are smitten with terror before His presence, when these bright creatures await with trembling the judgment of the Lord. Direst of days shall that be in the world, when the King of Glory in majesty chasteneth every people; biddeth mortal men dowered with speech rise up from out the graves of earth; biddeth the nations come to judgment, all mankind.

Then straight shall all the race of Adam put on flesh; they shall be at an end of their tarrying, their rest in the earth. At the coming of Christ shall each one rise to life, put on limbs and body, grow young again. He shall have upon him all of good or evil that in days of yore upon earth he garnered into his soul as years passed by. He shall have both together, body and soul. And then shall come to light before the King of heaven the form of his works and the memory of his words, and the musing of his heart.

Mankind shall be enlarged and renewed by the Creator; a mighty host shall rise to judgment when the Lord of life looseth the bonds of death. Then shall the air be kindled, the heavenly stars shall fall; widely the greedy flame shall pillage. Spirits shall turn away unto their long home. For the deeds of men shall be known on earth, nor may they at all dissemble before their Lord the hoard of their hearts, their secret thoughts. No deeds are dark to Him, but God shall know on that great day how each one of men hath deserved eternal life, and all that early or late they wrought in the world shall come to light. Nor shall any of the musings of men be secret, but that great day will reveal the hoard of the casket of the soul, all the thoughts of the heart. Wherefore he should early be mindful of his spirit's need, whoso would bring a beauteous aspect unto God, when the hot, consuming fire testeth in the presence of the Victor-Judge how souls are held against the storms of sin.

Then the sound of the trump and the gleaming standard, the burning flame and the heavenly host, the angelband and the menace of terror, the day of wrath and the lofty cross, lifted on high for a sign of sway, shall muster before Him all the multitudes of men, every soul of those that early or late put on limbs in the flesh. Then this mighty host shall pass before the Lord, forever living and ever young, with desire and heavy need. Named by name they shall bear the hoard of their hearts, the treasure of their souls, before the Son of God. Then will the Father know how His children bring their souls unmarred from that land wherein they dwelt. They shall be of good courage who bring a radiant beauty unto God. Their might and joy shall be exceeding full to recompense their souls, reward their works. Well is it with them that in that awful hour find grace with God.

Then shall sin-stained men with woe of heart for their lot behold the greatest of sorrows. Nor shall it bring them grace that there, present before all peoples, standeth the cross of our Lord, brightest of beacons, with the blood of the King of heaven all bedewed, drenched with His pure blood. And it shineth resplendent over the wide creation. Shadows shall be dispelled where that radiant tree casteth its light on men. Yet shall it become an affliction, a woe unto the nations, unto all such as working iniquity knew no thanks to God, for that He was hung upon the holy tree for the sins of men. There for mankind with love He purchased life, He, the Prince, on that day with the ransom—His body, which had wrought no evil, no transgression nor sin—wherewith He set us free. Yet will He sternly take recompense again for all, when the red cross shineth over all the heavens in the place of the sun.

And the timid, undone in transgression, swart workers of sin, shall behold it in sorrow. They shall see it as a bale, which came best of all things unto them, had they but known it as good. Ruefully they shall see the former wounds upon their Lord, and the open gashes where plotters of hatred pierced with nails the white hands and the holy feet; yea! from His side let blood, and water and blood come forth together in the sight of all, ran out before the eyes of men, when He was on the cross. All this then may they see, open and clear, that for the love of sinful men He suffered many sorrows. Truly may the sons of men perceive how they denied Him in their lying hearts, flouted Him with words of insolence, spat their spittle in His face, deriding Him. With their hands hell-destined men struck that blessed face with outstretched palm and fist, and round about His head they bound a bitter crown of thorns, blind in heart, strayed and erring men.

They saw the dumb creation, the radiant-green earth and upper sky, with trembling feel its Savior's agonies; and though they lived not, woefully they wailed when

men of evil seized upon their Maker with sinful hands.
The sun was darkened, veiled in sorrow, and in Jerusalem men saw the best of goodly webs, whereon the
multitude had gazed of old, the glory of that holy
house, rent from above so that in two halves it lay upon
the earth. The temple-veil, wrought with wondrous
color to be the beauty of that house, was cleft in twain
even as though a keen sword-edge had pierced it through.
Many walls and rocks throughout the world were burst
asunder; also the earth, shaken with terror, trembled
in tumult. The broad sea made known the strength of its
might, and from its bonds in wrath broke forth unto
the lap of earth; and from their shining stations the
stars forsook their splendor sweet. In that same hour
heaven clearly knew who decked it brightly with its
starry gems; wherefore it sent its herald when first was
born the radiant King of all the world. Lo! sinful men
saw truly, on that very day whereon He suffered, a
mighty wonder, when earth gave up all those who lay
within. Quickened they rose to life whom she of old
had firm constrained, the dead and buried, who held
within their hearts the Lord's behests. And Hell perceived, she who avenges sin, that the Creator, the all-
wielding God, was come, when she gave that horde the
hosts from out her burning bosom.

Then was blessing come to many a heart, and from
their souls sorrow stole away. Yea! the sea made
known who stablished it upon the spacious earth, the
mighty King of glory. Wherefore it yielded Him a way
when God would walk upon the waves, nor dared the
ocean-stream to cover with its flood the feet of God.
And many a tree, no little number, revealed who shaped
them with their blossoms, when mighty God mounted
on one of them, whereon He knew affliction for the
need of human kind, a baleful death to succor men.

Then many a tree wept bloody tears under its bark, ruddy, abundant tears; the sap was turned to blood. Nor may the dwellers of the world unriddle that, by craft of wisdom, how many lifeless things, that might not feel, still knew the Passion of our Lord. They that are the noblest of the tribes of earth, and eke the heaven's high halls, for that alone grew sorrowful and smitten with fear. For though by nature they had no understanding hearts, yet wondrously they weened it when the Lord departed from the flesh.

But the tribes of men, blind of heart, harder than stones of flint, knew not to confess their God that the Prince, the Lord Almighty, delivered them from the torments of Hell, by His holy might, and that from the first beginnings of the world far-seeing men, prophets of the Lord, holy and sage of heart, with searching wisdom, full oft nor once alone spake to the sons of men anent that noble Son that, through the holy maid, the Precious Stone, the Lord of glory, Prince of bliss, would become a refuge and a comfort unto human kind.

What weeneth he who is not mindful in his heart of the gentle teachings of his Lord, and of all the sorrows that He suffered for the sons of men, since He was fain that we might have for ever a heavenly home. In the grim day of the great doom it shall go sadly with that man who, all defiled by deadly sin, gazeth on the gashes of the Lord, his wounds and woe. With weary hearts they shall behold that greatest of sorrows, how with His body, with pitying heart, the King himself redeemed them from their sin, that they might live set free from their transgressions and have the everlasting blessedness of glory. But for that gift they knew no thanks unto their Lord; wherefore in God shall they behold the token of their woeful lot, manifest, boding ill.

Then Christ shall sit upon His royal throne, on His high judgment-seat; the God of heaven's hosts, the Almighty Father, the Shining Lord, the Sovereign of the skies, shall adjudge unto every folk rightfully according to the things they have wrought. On the right hand shall be mustered the multitude of the pure, chosen unto Christ Himself for all that is choicest, for that they eagerly fulfilled His words in the days of their life. And the workers of sin shall be sundered unto a harder lot before their Lord. The true King of victory shall bid that sinful horde on the left hand depart. Then detected they shall wail and tremble in terror before God. As foul as goats, an unclean folk, they may not hope for mercy. Thus before God shall the soul's judgment be decreed unto the generations of men according to the things that formerly they wrought.

There among the blessed, easily to be discerned, shall be three tokens that they have heeded well their Master's will in their words and works. The first clear token is that they gleam with light before the peoples, with glory and splendor through the dwellings of the cities. And on them shine the works that formerly they wrought, on every one of them, more radiant than the sun.

And a second token shall be shown that they in glory know the grace of God, beholding with enraptured eyes that in the heavenly kingdom they may know bright joys in blessedness among the angels. And the third token shall be that the blessed hosts may see how those undone by sin suffer sorely in requital of their transgression—the raging flame and the sting of serpents with bitter jaws, a host of burning souls. And in their heart waxeth a winsome joy. When they see others suffer that evil which by God's mercy they escaped, then the more eagerly do they give thanks to God for blessedness and bliss—they who see that He redeemed them from that evil torment and granted them eternal joy. For them is Hell fast locked and the Kingdom of Heaven yielded up. So shall recompense be given them who heeded well in love their Maker's will.

But to those others shall unlike decree go forth. Full too many a woe must they behold upon themselves, abundant evil, suffering for transgressions done. Unto them sorrowing cleaveth sore distress, a grievous widespread evil on three sides. And of those many miseries whereon they gaze one shall be the dreadful fire of Hell before them, prepared in punishment, wherein forever they must strive and suffer curse and exile.

Likewise there shall be a second misery to the shame of guilty men that they, by sin defiled, must needs endure most deep disgrace. In them the Lord beholdeth no small toll of loathsome sins; likewise the radiant throng of heavenly angels and the sons of men, all they that dwell on earth and the grim fiend shall know their dark craft and every deed of evil. Through the flesh may they behold the stains of vice upon the soul. The sinful flesh shall be shot through with shame as a bright glass, that men most easily may gaze it through. And in their heavy need a third sorrow, a wailing woe, shall be that they behold how guiltless men in gladsomeness rejoice in their good deeds, which they, unhappy men, disdained to do while yet their days endured. And for their deeds shall come distress and weeping, that formerly so freely they accomplished sin.

They shall see better men shining in bliss, nor shall their misery only be a torment unto them, but the blessedness of those others shall be a sorrow, that they in former days passed by so fair and winsome joy through the deceitful pleasures of the body, the idle lust of sinful flesh. Then confounded, smit with shame, they shall stray dizzily, bearing their sinful burden, their deeds of guilt which all that folk doth see. Then were it better for them had they humbled them before one man aforetime for their works of sin, every iniquity and wrongful act, and to God's messenger confessed that to their shame they knew their deeds of evil. Neither may he that shriveth see through the flesh upon the soul whether one speaketh truth or lying words when he confesseth sin. Yet man may heal his every evil and unclean act if he but tell it to one single man. And none may hide on that grim day an evil unatoned; but then the host shall see it. Yea! with the body's eyes shall we behold upon our souls hateful transgressions, the wounds of sin, impure meditations, musings of ill. Nor may any man tell it to another with what eagerness each one of us by every act is fain in striving after life, anxiously endeavoring after days of living, to purge away the rust of sin to chasten self, to heal the scars of former wounds, what little time of life remaineth, that pure and undismayed before the eyes of them that dwell on earth he may enjoy his heritage with men so long as soul and body live together.

But with the heart's eyes should we eagerly and wisely gaze through the soul's casing to the sins within. For with those other eyes, the jewels of the head, in no wise may we penetrate the spirit of the secret thought, whether below it evil dwell or good, that it may be pleasing unto God in that dread hour.

Then in glory He shall shine above all hosts, in radiant flame from His high seat, where before angels and all the tribes of men He first shall speak to the most blessed, with loving kindness grant them grace in holy words. The High-King of heaven shall show them gentle comfort and bring them peace. He shall bid them, free of stain, and full of blessing, depart unto the land of the joy of angels, and ever gladsomely enjoy it.

"Now with friends receive ye the Kingdom of My Father, that was prepared for you in winsomeness before all worlds, blessedness with bliss, bright beauty of home, where ye with well-loved men may see true weal of life, sweet heavenly joy. This have ye merited since joyfully ye received with gracious heart wretched men, the needy of the world; when in My name they humbly craved your pity then did ye grant them help and shelter, unto the hungry bread, clothes to the naked, and those that lay diseased in pain, enthralled of sickness, their souls ye softly stayed with love of heart. All that ye did unto Me what time ye sought them out with kindly love, ever strengthening their souls with comfort. Wherefore in blessedness with My beloved long shall ye reap reward."

Then shall all-wielding God in the menace of terror begin to speak unto the evil, unto those on His left hand in unlike wise. They may not look for mercy from the Lord, nor life nor pity, but there a reward shall come unto all men, unto all with speech endowed, according to their acts of word and deed. They shall suffer a righteous doom full of terror. And on that day the great mercy of the Almighty Lord shall be cut off from all the tribes of men when wrathfully He imputeth to that folk perverse their sinful deeds; in words of anger biddeth them make accounting of their life which formerly He gave for blessedness unto so wicked men. Almighty God shall begin to speak as He were speaking to one only man, yet shall He mean all sinful folk.

"Lo! man! with my hand I wrought thee first, gave thee reason, shaped thy limbs of clay, yea! and breathed a living spirit in thee. Over all created things I honored thee. I gave thee form and aspect like to Me;

granted thee fulness of might, weal over all wide lands. No deal of woe thou knewest for thy portion, nor of the darkness thou must now endure. Yet knewest thou no thanks that I shaped thee in beauty, wrought thee winsome, granted thee wealth of riches that thou mightest wield it over the things of the world, where I set thee on the fair earth that thou mightest enjoy the bright profusion of Paradise, radiant of hue. Thou wouldest not keep the word of life, but broke My bidding at thy Bane's behest, hearkening rather unto scathing spoilers than to the Lord that made thee.

"Now I pass by that ancient tale how thou in the beginning wroughtest evil, squandering in deeds of sin that I gave thee as profit. That I gave to thee abundantly of good and in it all there seemed unto thy heart too little of felicity, if thou mightest not have fulness of might of like greatness with God's, therefore thou grewest estranged from that delight, cast out afar after the will of thy foes. The beauty of Paradise, the home of spirits, thou must needs forego, sorrowful in soul, wicked and wretched, shorn of all thy bounty and blessedness. Then wast thou driven out into the gloomy world to undergo heavy affliction all this weary while, pain and toilsome strife and darksome death, and on thy going hence must needs in Hell abjectly perish, bereft of helping hands. Then was I rueful that My handiwork should fare forth into fiends' dominion, that the sons of men should know destruction, make trial of a dwelling all unknown, and grievous fortune.

"Then I Myself descended as a son unto his mother; yet was her maidenhood inviolate of man. I only was born a comfort unto men; and with their hands men swathed Me, clad Me in weeds of the needy, and laid Me in darkness wrapped in swarthy raiment. Lo! that have I endured for the world. Little I seemed unto the children of men. I lay on the hard stone, an infant in a manger, that I might save thee from torment, and the burning bale of Hell. That misery I suffered that thou mightest shine holy and blessed in eternal life.

"No pride it was to Me; but I suffered in My youth misery and shameless pain of body that I might be like thee, and that thou, purged of sin, mightest grow like to My winsome beauty. And for My love of man My face and head have suffered, enduring grievous blows. Oft on My face I received the spittle of sinners, from the mouths of graceless men. Bitterly they blended unto Me an unsweet drink of vinegar and gall. There before that folk I suffered the hatred of hostile men; they afflicted Me with outrage, shrank not from enmity, with scourges scourged Me. That misery in meekness all for thee I suffered, insult and reviling word. About My head they wreathed a wounding crown, heavily pressed it home, all wrought of thorns. Then was I hung upon the lofty rood, fastened upon the cross. And straight with spear from out My side they let My blood flow forth, My gore into the ground, that thou thereby mightest be freed from the dominion of devils. So, unstained of sin, I suffered torment, evil affliction, till I sent forth alone from out its house of flesh My living spirit. Behold the deadly wounds they wrought of old upon My hands and feet, whereby made fast I hung in agony. Still mayest thou behold clearly in My side the bloody gash. How is the account unequal 'twixt us twain! I bore thy suffering that in blessedness thou mightest happily enjoy My native kingdom; for thee I purchased dearly by My death long life that thenceforth in the light, unstained of sin, thou mightest dwell in beauty. My body, which wrought no harm to any, lay enfolded in the earth, buried in the sepulchre

below, that thou mightest be on high brightly exalted
'mid the host of heaven. Why didst thou forsake that
shining life that with My body I kindly bought in love
for thee, a succor unto wretched men? Surely thou
wast void of understanding that thou knewest not thanks
to God for thy redemption. I ask nought for that
bitter death I suffered for thee. Yield Me thy life;
that life for which I gave Mine own in ransom, in
martyrdom, that life I now demand, which thou hast
slain with evil to thy shame. The holy temple which
I had hallowed in thee, a house of joy—why hast thou
fouled it of thine own self-will in lust of sin and filthy
deed?

"Yea! the very body that I redeemed from out the
clutch of fiends, forbade it sin, working thy wickedness,
thou hast stained with shames. Why didst thou hang
Me on a cross of thy hand's making in greater agony
than I hung of old? Lo! this to Me the harder seemeth.
Severer unto Me thy cross of sins whereon I am re-
luctant hung, than was that other cross whereon I
mounted up of Mine own will, when urgently thy woe
repented Me in heart, when forth from Hell I drew
thee, where thenceforth thou wast fain to dwell. In
the world was I poor that in heaven thou mightest have
wealth; wretched was I in thy kingdom that thou
mightest have bliss in Mine. Yet for all in thy heart
thou knewest no thanks unto thy Savior-God. Lo!
I gave you bidding to cherish well My brothers in the
world, with all the goods I gave you on the earth to
help the poor; ye have fulfilled it ill. Ye have denied
the needy to enter in under your roof, refused them
everything with stony heart, clothes unto the naked,
meat unto those anhungered, though in My name weary,
in sickness, they besought for water, bountiless, plagued
of thirst, distressed for drink. Roughly ye refused;

the sorrowful ye visited not, spake unto them no gentle word of comfort, that they might gain a better cheer. All this ye did to Me, unto the scorn of the King of heaven. Wherefore ye shall suffer grievous, endless torment, endure exile with fiends."

Then over all the Warden of victory shall issue an awful sentence, abounding in pain, over that fated folk. He shall say to that band of sinful souls:

"Fare ye now accursed, by your own wills bereft of angel's joy, unto eternal fire, hot and grim, that was prepared of old for Satan and his fellows, the Fiend and his dark host. Ye shall sink therein."

Shorn of counsel they may not scorn the sentence of the King of heaven, but swiftly they shall sink into the deep pit, into the dusky flame the host of the sinful, spirits doomed under the folds of earth, unto the dwelling of fiends the horde of the guilty, to destruction the cursed, unto the house of torment, death hall of the devil. Never again shall they seek remembrance of God, nor escape out of their sins, but stained of evil, bound in burning flame they shall suffer death. Ever vengeance for their sins shall be upon them, that is eternal torment. Nor may that flaming pit ever in the eternal night burn away sin from the sons of men, pollution from their souls forever. But ever the deep abyss feedeth those wretched souls; bottomless it holdeth spirits in the darkness, consumeth them with ancient flame and chilling terror, with serpents dire and many a torment, with bitter jaws it scatheth all that folk.

Of that may we have heed, declaring straightway, telling truly that the warden of the soul hath lost life's wisdom, he who regardeth not whether his soul know misery or bliss, where, after his going hence, he shall dwell forever. He feareth not to work his wickedness, rash-hearted man, nor any whit hath he of rue in heart,

that the Holy Ghost depart away from him by reason
of his sins in this fleeting life. Then the worker of
evil, trembling before God, shall stand black-hearted at
the judgment, stained with death, accursed with his sins.
The faithless shall be filled with fire, unworthy of life,
smitten of dread before the face of God. Dusky, devoid
of beauty, he shall have the hue of the damned, a sign
of the guilt of the soul. Then when there is no time
the sons of men shall weep their tears and wail for their
transgressions. Too late they shall do to the comfort
of their souls, when the Lord of hosts will not regard
how sinful men bewail in bitterness their olden treasure in that revealing hour. Nor shall any time of sorrow be vouchsafed to men, that he, who will not win
his soul's salvation, while still he dwelleth here on
earth, may then find healing. On no good man shall
woe be visited, nor weal on any evil, but every wight
shall bear his works alone.

Wherefore he who would fain win life at his Creator's
hand must haste while soul and body dwell together.
Let him cherish eagerly the beauty of his soul after the
will of God, be heedful of his words and deeds, his
bearing and his inward thoughts, so long as this world
gliding in the shadow may shine for him, that in this
fleeting hour he lose not the bounty of his joy, his toll
of days, and comely deeds, and his reward of glory that
the King of heaven in that holy hour justly granteth, as
guerdon of their triumph, unto all such as hearken unto
Him with eager hearts.

Then heaven and hell shall be filled with the children
of heroes, the souls of men. The gulf shall swallow
up God's enemies; the hurtling flame shall seize on
wicked men, mortal transgressors, neither allow them
thence to flee away with joy to any refuge. But fire
shall bind the fast imprisoned horde and scourge the

children of sin. Insolent to me it seemeth that men endowed with spirit will not heed in their hearts what the Ruler layeth on them in His vengeance, upon hostile men. Then life and death shall take their fill of souls; the house of torment shall be open and revealed to faithless men. Men swift to sin shall fill it with their blackened souls. Then to avenge their guilt the wicked horde shall be sundered, the cursed from the holy, unto destroying pain. There shall thieves and spoilers and liars and adulterers have no hope of life; and perjurers shall know the guerdon of sin, bitter and terrible. Then shall hell take in the host of the faithless and God shall give them over to destruction unto fiends. The damned shall suffer grievous mortal bale. Wretched shall be that man who willeth to work transgression so that in his sin he shall be sundered from the Lord at the day of doom to death below, among the race of hell, in that burning fire, under locks of flame. There shall they yield their limbs to be bound, to be burned, to be scourged in vengeance of sin.

Then at the word of the King, by the might of God, shall the Holy Spirit fasten the locks of hell, that greatest of torture-houses, filled with fire and the horde of fiends. Direst of deaths shall that be of devils and of men. That is a joyless house. Thence may not any ever flee away from out his icy bonds. They broke the King's behest, the bright commandments of the Books. Wherefore they must dwell in everlasting darkness, endure an endless woe forever, stained with sin, they who scorned on earth the glory of the heavenly kingdom.

Then the chosen shall bear before Christ bright treasure, and joy shall live upon the day of doom. They shall know the blessedness of peaceful life with God, which shall be given unto all saints within the heavenly realm. That land shall never come unto an end, but there forevermore, all free of sin, they shall know bliss, praise the Lord of hosts, dear Savior of their life, all wreathed in light, enwrapped in peace, safe from sorrows, glorified with joy, loved of the Lord. Always in bliss forever they shall know the fellowship of angels, and radiant in grace adore the Lord of men. The Father of all hath power and upholdeth the host of the holy. There is the song of angels, the bliss of the blessed; there is the Lord's dear face more radiant than the sun unto all happy souls. There is life without death, a gladsome band of men; youth without age, the glory of the hosts of heaven; health without pangs unto the righteous; rest without toil, the lot of the blessed; day without darkness, bright and filled with glory; bliss without sorrow; love between friends forever without discord; peace without strife for blessed souls in heaven in the company of holy men. There shall be no hunger nor thirst, neither sleep nor heavy sickness, nor burning of the sun, nor cold, nor care. But that blessed band, fairest of hosts, shall know the favor of their King forever and glory with the Lord.

THE DREAM OF THE ROOD

Lo, I will tell the choicest dream,
That came to me in the middle of night
When speaking men were deep in rest.
It seemed that I saw a marvellous tree
Move in the air enwrapped in light,
Brightest of beams. All that beacon was
Wound round with gold; the gems stood
Fair above earth's face, and five there were
Upon the cross-span. All the angels of the Lord beheld
it there,

Fair through creation: no wretch's gallows-tree was that,
But holy spirits watched it there,
Men above earth and all that bright creation.
   Bright was the victory-beam, and I was stained with
      sin,
Wounded with evil. I saw the tree of heaven,
Wrapped round with vestments, shine with joy,
Geared with gold; gems had worthily
Encrusted the tree of the Ruler;
Yet through the gold I might perceive
The scar of ancient combat when long ago it began
To sweat on the right side. I was with sorrow
      troubled;   20
I was afraid of that fair sight. I saw that vivid beam
Alter in vesture and hue; now it was wet with blood,
Soiled with the course of sweat, and now it was geared
      with jewels.
   Yet there I lay for a long while
And watched the sorrowful tree of the Savior,
Until I heard it utter speech;
The best of woods began to say these words:
   "That was long, long ago—but I remember still—
When I was hew'n down at the forest's edge,
Cut from my trunk. Strong foes laid hold on me,   30
Made them a spectacle, bade me lift their felons high;
Men bore me on their shoulders till they set me on a
      hill,
Many foes made me fast there.
                I saw the Lord of mankind
Hasten with courage great to mount on me.
Then I durst not, 'gainst the Almighty's word,
Bend or break, even though I saw
The face of the earth tremble; all those foes
I might have felled, but I stood fast.

The young Savior stripped him then—He that was
    God Almighty—   40
Strong and stout-hearted; he climbed the high gallows-
    tree
Brave in the eyes of many, when He would save man-
    kind.
I trembled when the Man embraced me; yet I dared not
    bow to earth,
Fall to the face of the ground—I must stand fast.
    I was raised a cross; I lifted high the mighty King,
The Lord of heaven; bow down I dared not.
    They pierced me through with dark nails; the scars
        can yet be seen,
Open wounds of hate; yet dared I not scathe any of
    them.
They mocked us both together. I was all dewed with
    blood
That came from the Man's side when He sent forth his
    ghost.   50
    Much I endured upon that hill
Of cruel fate; I saw the God of hosts
Stretched on a cross; darkness had
Covered with clouds the body of the Lord,
The bright glory; a shadow went forth,
Wan under the clouds. All creation wept,
Spoke of the King's fall; Christ was on the cross.
    But eager ones came from afar
To the Ætheling; I beheld all that.
I was sore distressed with sorrow, but I bowed to the
    hands of the men,   60
Humble with great zeal. Then they took Almighty
    God,
Lifted Him from that bitter torment; the warriors left
    me there

To stand bedewed with blood; I was wounded with
    arrows.
They laid Him there, limb-weary, stood at His body's
    head;
There they looked on the Lord of heaven; and He rested
    there awhile,
Tired from that great battle. Then they built for him
    a tomb,
Men in the sight of His slayers; they carved it out of
    shining stone,
And laid therein the Lord of victories. They raised
    their dirge for Him,
Sad in the eventide, when they must depart,
Weary, from their great lord; there He stayed, alone. 70
    Dripping there, a goodly while
We stood in our stations, after the wail of the warriors
    arose.
The body grew cold, the soul's fair dwelling-place.
                Then men began to fell us
All to earth—that was a grisly fate!
They buried us deep in a pit. But the thanes of the
    Lord,
Friends, found me; (they raised me up from earth),
Geared me with gold and silver.
    Now hast thou heard, man dear to me,
How I withstood the work of evil men,   80
Sore sorrow. Now the time is come
That in my worship wide and far
Men on the earth, and all the bright creation
Kneel to this beacon. On me the Son of God
Once suffered; wherefor in glory now
I tower under heaven, and I may save
Any of them that are in awe of me.
    Hardest of tortures long ago was I,
To men most hateful, till I showed to them

The rightful way of life. Lo, the Lord of glory 90
Honored me above all trees of the wood, He, the Lord
        of heaven,
Just as He, Almighty God, set his mother, Mary's self,
Over all womankind.
        Now do I bid thee, hero beloved,
That thou shalt tell this dream to men:
Proclaim in words it is the tree of glory
On which Almighty God once suffered
For mankind's many sins
And Adam's deed of old.
        Death there He tasted; but the Lord rose again 100
With his great might to help mankind.
He ascended into heaven; here He shall come again
Into this world to seek mankind,
The Lord Himself on the day of doom,
Almighty God and His angels with Him.
And He will judge, that has the power of judgment,
Each one by his deserts, earlier here
Earned in this fleeting life.
No man may then be unafraid
Because of the word that the Lord will say: 110
He will ask of the many where the man may be
Who for the Lord's name bitter death would taste
As He did once upon the tree;
But they will be afraid, and scarcely know
What they shall say to Christ.
There need not then be any man afraid
Who bears in his breast this brightest beacon,
But through the Rood shall seek the kingdom
From the ways of earth, each soul
That hopes to dwell with the Lord." 120
        Then, blithe-hearted, I prayed to that tree,
With fervent zeal, there where I was alone,
Without companion; and my soul

Was eager for its journey; long had it waited,
A long, weary time. Now is it my life's hope
That I may seek the victory-beam, alone,
More often than all other men worthily worship it;
My desire for this is great within my heart, and my
    help
Comes from the cross. I have not many
Powerful friends on earth, but they have hence de-
    parted,   130
Gone from the joy of the world to seek the King of
    glory;
Now live they in heaven with the High-Father,
They dwell in glory; and I look each day
For the cross of the Lord that I saw here on earth
To take me from this fleeting life
And bring me where there is great bliss,
Joy in heaven, where the folk of the Lord
Sit at the feast, where is joy everlasting;
And there it will set me where I may thereafter
Dwell in glory, well share in the joy of the saints. 140
May the Lord be my friend, He who here on earth
    suffered
For the sins of men on the gallows-tree;
He brought us salvation, and gave to us life,
A home in the heavens.   Hope came again
With blessing and bliss to the sufferers in flames.
The Son was triumphant upon that journey,
Successful and mighty, He came with a throng,
A host of spirits into God's kingdom,
Ruler almighty—to the joy of the angels,   150
And all those saints who already in heaven
Were dwelling in glory, when their Ruler came,
When Almighty God came to His home.

                        (8th century?)

THE ANGLO-SAXON CHRONICLE

A.D. 1. Octavianus reigned fifty-six years; and in the forty-second year of his reign Christ was born.

A.D. 2. The three astrologers came from the eastern parts in order that they might worship Christ. And the children were slain at Bethlehem, in persecution of Christ by Herod.

A.D. 3. This year died Herod, having stabbed himself, and Archelaus, his son, succeeded to the government. And the child Christ was brought back again from Egypt.

A.D. 4. 5.

A.D. 6. From the beginning of the world to this year, five thousand and two hundred years were gone by.

A.D. 7-10.

A.D. 11. This year Herod, the son of Antipater, obtained the government of Judea.

A.D. 12. Philip and Herod divided Lysia (between them), and Judea they divided into tetrarchies.

A.D. 12. This year Judea was divided into four tetrarchies.

A.D. 13-15.

A.D. 16. This year Tiberius succeeded to the empire.

A.D. 17-25.

A.D. 26. This year Pilate began to rule over the Jews.

A.D. 27-29.

A.D. 30. This year Christ was baptized; and he converted Peter and Andrew, and James and John and Philip, and the twelve apostles.

A.D. 31. 32.

A.D. 33. This year Christ was crucified; being from

the beginning of the world about five thousand two hundred and twenty-six years.

A.D. 30. This year St. Paul was converted, and St. Stephen stoned.

A.D. 35. This year the blessed apostle Peter established a bishop's see in the city of Antioch.

A.D. 36. 37.

A.D. 38. This year Pilate slew himself with his own hand.

A.D. 39. This year Caius obtained the empire.

A.D. 40. Matthew, in Judea, began to write his gospel.

A.D. 41-44.

A.D. 45. This year the blessed apostle Peter established a bishop's see in Rome. This year James, the brother of John, was slain by Herod.

A.D. 46. This year Herod died; he who slew James, one year before his own death.

A.D. 46. This year the emperor Claudius came to Britain, and subdued a large part of the island; and he also added the island of Orkney to the dominion of the Romans.

A.D. 47. This year Claudius, second of the Roman kings, sought the land of Britain, and brought under his power the greater part of the island, and also subjected the Orkney Islands to the dominion of the Romans. This war he effected in the fourth year of his reign; and in the same year was the great famine in Syria, which was foretold in the Acts of the Apostles through Agabus the prophet. Then Nero succeeded to the empire after Claudius: he nearly lost the island of Britain through his cowardice. Mark the Evangelist begins to write the gospel in Egypt.

A.D. 448. This year John the Baptist revealed his head to two monks who came from the east to offer up their prayers at Jerusalem, on the spot which was formerly Herod's residence.

A.D. 449. This year Martianus and Valentinus succeeded to the empire, and reigned seven years. And in their days Hengist and Horsa, invited by Vortigern king of the Britons, landed in Britain on the shore which is called Wippidsfleet; at first in aid of the Britons, but afterwards they fought against them. King Vortigern gave them land in the south-east of this country, on condition that they should fight against the Picts. Then they fought against the Picts and had the victory wheresoever they came. They then sent to the Angles; desired a larger force to be sent, and caused them to be told the worthlessness of the Britons, and the excellencies of the land. Then they soon sent thither a larger force in aid of the others. At that time there came men from three tribes in Germany; from the Old Saxons, from the Angles, from the Jutes. From the Jutes came the Kentishmen and the Wightwarians, that is, the tribe which now dwells in Wight, and that race among the West Saxons which is still called the race of Jutes. From the Old Saxons came the men of Essex and Sussex and Wessex. From Anglia, which has ever since remained waste betwixt the Jutes and Saxons, came the men of East Anglia, Middle Anglia, Mercia, and all Northumbria. Their leaders were brothers, Hengist and Horsa: they were the sons of Wihtgils; Wihtgils son of Witta, Witta of Wecta, Wecta of Woden: from this Woden sprang all our royal families, and those of the Southumbrians also.

A.D. 565. This year Ethelbert succeeded to the kingdom of the Kentishmen, and held it fifty-three years. In his days the holy pope Gregory sent us baptism, that was in the two and thirtieth year of his reign: and

Columba, a mass-priest, came to the Picts, and converted them to the faith of Christ; they are dwellers by the northern mountains. And their king gave him the island which is called Ii (Iona): therein are five hides of land, as men say. There Columba built a monastery, and he was abbot there thirty-seven years, and there he died when he was seventy-two years old. His successors still have the place. The Southern Picts had been baptized long before: Bishop Ninia, who had been instructed at Rome, had preached baptism to them, (his church and his monastery are at Whitherne, consecrated in the name of St. Martin: there he resteth, with many holy men). Now in Ii there must ever be an abbot, and not a bishop; and all the Scottish bishops ought to be subject to him, because Columba was an abbot and not a bishop.

A.D. 806. This year the moon was eclipsed on the Kalends of September: and Eardulf, king of the Northumbrians, was driven from his kingdom; and Eanbert, bishop of Hexham, died. Also in the same year, on the 2d before the Nones of June, a cross appeared in the moon on a Wednesday at dawn; and afterwards in this year, on the third before the Kalends of September, a wonderful circle was seen about the sun.

A.D. 855. This year the heathen men, for the first time, remained over winter in Sheppey: and the same year king Ethelwulf gave by charter the tenth part of his land throughout his realm for the glory of God and his own eternal salvation. And the same year he went to Rome in great state, and dwelt there twelve months, and then returned homewards. And then Charles, king of the Franks, gave him his daughter to wife; and after that he came to his people and they were glad of it. And about two years after he came from

France he died, and his body lies at Winchester. And he reigned eighteen years and a half.

A.D. 871. Then Alfred, the son of Ethelwulf, his brother, succeeded to the kingdom of the West Saxons. And about one month after this, king Alfred with a small band fought against the whole army at Wilton, and put them to flight for a good part of the day; but the Danes had possession of the place of carnage. And this year nine general battles were fought against the army in the kingdom south of the Thames, besides which Alfred the king's brother, and single ealdormen, and king's thanes oftentimes made incursions on them which were not counted; and within the year nine earls and one king were slain. And that year the West Saxons made peace with the army.

A.D. 897. After this, in the summer of this year, the army broke up, some for East Anglia, some for Northumbria; and they who were moneyless procured themselves ships there, and went southwards over sea to the Seine. Thanks be to God, the army had not utterly broken down the English nation; but during the three years it was much more broken down by the mortality among cattle and among men, and most of all by this, that many of the most eminent king's thanes in the land died during the three years; some of whom were: Swithulf, bishop of Rochester, and Ceolmund, ealdorman of Kent, and Bertulf, ealdorman of Essex, and Wulfred, ealdorman of Hampshire, and Ealhard, bishop of Dorchester, and Eadulf, the king's thane in Sussex, and Bernwulf, the governor of Winchester, and Eadulf, the king's horse-thane, and many also besides these, though I have named the most distinguished. That same year the armies from among the East Anglians and from among the Northumbrians harassed the land of the West Saxons, chiefly on the south coast, by predatory bands; most of all by their esks, which they had built many years before. Then king Alfred commanded long ships to be built to oppose the esks; they were full-nigh twice as long as the others; some had sixty oars, and some had more; they were both swifter and steadier, and also higher than the others. They were shapen neither like the Frisian nor the Danish, but so as it seemed to him they would be most efficient. Then some time in the same year, there came six ships to the Isle of Wight, and there did much harm, as well as in Devon, and elsewhere on the sea-coast. Then the king commanded nine of the new ships to go thither, and they obstructed their passage from the port towards the outer sea. Then went they with three of their ships out against them; and three lay in the upper part of the port in the dry; for the men were gone ashore. Then took they two of the three ships at the outer part of the port, and killed the men, and the other ship escaped; in that also the men were killed except five; they got away because the other ships were aground. They also were aground very disadvantageously: three lay aground on that side of the deep on which the Danish ships were aground, and all the rest upon the other side, so that no one of them could get to the others. But when the water had ebbed many furlongs from the ships, then the Danishmen went from their three ships to the other three which were left by the tide on their side, and then they there fought against them. There was slain Lucumon, the king's reeve, and Wulfheard, the Frisian, and Ebb, the Frisian, and Ethelere, the Frisian, and Ethelferth, the king's neat-herd, and of all the men, Frisians and English, seventy-two; and of the Danishmen, one hundred and twenty. Then, however, the flood-tide came to the Danish ships before the Christians could shove theirs off, and they therefore rowed them out: nevertheless, they were damaged to such a degree that they could not row round the Sussex land; and there the sea cast two of them on shore, and the men were led to the king at Winchester; and he commanded them to be there hanged, and the men who were in the single ship came to East Anglia, sorely wounded. That same summer no less than twenty ships, with their crews, wholly perished upon the south coast. That same year died Wulfric, the king's horse-thane; he was also "Wealhreeve."

A.D. 901. This year died ALFRED, the son of Ethelwulf, six days before the mass of All Saints. He was king over the whole English nation, except that part which was under the dominion of the Danes; and he held the kingdom one year and a half less than thirty years. And then Edward, his son, succeeded to the kingdom. Then Ethelwald, the ætheling, his uncle's son, seized the castle at Wimborne and that at Twineham, without leave of the king and of his wise men. Then rode the king with his forces until he encamped at Badbury, near Wimborne; and Ethelwald sat within the vill, with the men who had submitted to him; and he had obstructed all the approaches towards him, and said that he would do one of two things—or there live, or there lie. But notwithstanding that, he stole away by night, and sought the army in Northumbria; and they received him for their king, and became obedient to him. And the king commanded that he should be ridden after; but they were unable to overtake him. They then beset the woman whom he had before taken, without the king's leave, and against the bishop's command; for she had previously been consecrated a nun. And in this same year Ethelred, who was ealdorman of Devonshire, died, four weeks before king Alfred.

THE BATTLE OF BRUNANBURH

A.D. 937. ATHELSTAN King,
    Lord among Earls,
    Bracelet-bestower and
    Baron of Barons,
    He with his brother,
    Edmund Atheling,
    Gaining a lifelong
    Glory in battle,
    Slew with the sword-edge
    There by Brunanburh,   10
    Brake the shield-wall,
    Hewed the linden-wood,
    Hacked the battle-shield,
    Sons of Edward with hammered brands.

    Theirs was a greatness
    Got from their grandsires—
    Theirs that so often in
    Strife with their enemies
    Struck for their hoards and their hearths and
        their homes.

    Bowed the spoiler,   20
    Bent the Scotsman,
    Fell the ship-crews
    Doomed to the death.
    All the field with blood of the fighters
    Flowed, from when first the great
    Sun-star of morning-tide,
    Lamp of the Lord God
    Lord everlasting,

Glode over earth till the glorious creature
Sank to his setting.   30

There lay many a man
Marred by the javelin,
Men of the Northland
Shot over shield.
There was the Scotsman
Weary of war.

We, the West Saxons,
Long as the daylight
-Lasted, in companies
Troubled the track of the host that we hated. 40
Grimly with swords that were sharp from the
     grindstone,
Fiercely we hacked at the flyers before us.

Mighty the Mercian,
Hard was his hand-play,
Sparing not any of
Those that with Anlaf,
Warriors over the
Weltering waters
Borne in the bark's-bosom,
Drew to this island—   50
Doomed to the death.

Five young kings put asleep by the sword-
     stroke,
Seven strong earls of the army of Anlaf
Fell on the war-field, numberless numbers,
Shipmen and Scotsmen.

Then the Norse leader,
Dire was his need of it,
Few were his following,
Fled to his war-ship;
Fleeted his vessel to sea with the king in it, 60
Saving his life on the fallow flood.

Also the crafty one,
Constantinus,
Crept to his North again,
Hoar-headed hero!
Slender warrant had
He to be proud of
The welcome of war-knives—
He that was reft of his
Folk and his friends that had   70
Fallen in conflict,
Leaving his son too
Lost in the carnage,
Mangled to morsels,
A youngster in war!

Slender reason had
He to be glad of
The clash of the war-glaive—
Traitor and trickster
And spurner of treaties—   80
He nor had Anlaf
With armies so broken
A reason for bragging
That they had the better
In perils of battle
On places of slaughter—
The struggle of standards,
The rush of the javelins,

The crash of the charges,
The wielding of weapons—   90
The play that they played with
The children of Edward.

Then with their nailed prows
Parted the Norsemen, a
Blood-reddened relic of
Javelins over
The jarring breaker, the deep-sea billow,
Shaping their way toward Dyflen again,
Shamed in their souls.

Also the brethren,   100
King and Atheling,
Each in his glory,
Went to his own in his own West Saxonland,
Glad of the war.

Many a carcase they left to be carrion,
Many a livid one, many a sallow-skin—
Left for the white-tailed eagle to tear it, and
Left for the horny-nibbed raven to rend it, and
Gave to the garbaging war-hawk to gorge it,
      and
That gray beast, the wolf of the weald.   110

Never had huger
Slaughter of heroes
Slain by the sword-edge—
Such as old writers
Have writ of in histories—
Hapt in this isle, since
Up from the East hither
Saxon and Angle from

Over the broad billow
Broke into Britain with   120
Haughty war-workers who
Harried the Welshman, when
Earls that were lured by the
Hunger of glory gat
Hold of the land.

A.D. 1066. In this year was consecrated the minster at Westminster, on Childer-mass-day. And King Edward died, on the eve of Twelfth Day; and he was buried on Twelfth Day, within the newly consecrated church at Westminster. And Harold the earl succeeded to the kingdom of England, even as the king had granted it to him, and men also had chosen him thereto; and he was crowned as king on Twelfth Day. And that same year that he became king, he went out with a fleet against William; [1] and of the while, came Tosty the earl into Humber with sixty ships. Edwin the earl came with a land-force and drove him out; and the boatmen forsook him. And he went to Scotland with twelve vessels; and Harold, the king of Norway, met him with three hundred ships, and Tosty submitted to him; and they both went into Humber, until they came to York. And Morcar the earl, and Edwin the earl fought against them; and the king of the Norwegians had the victory. And it was made known to King Harold how it there was done, and had happened; and he came there with a great army of English men, and met him at Stanfordbridge, and slew him and the earl Tosty, and boldly overcame all the army. And the while, William the earl landed at Hastings, on St. Michael's Day: and Harold came from the north, and fought against him before all his army had come up: and

[1] Earl of Normandy.

there he fell, and his two brothers, Girth and Leofwin; and William subdued this land. And he came to Westminster, and archbishop Aldred consecrated him king, and men paid him tribute, and delivered him hostages, and afterwards bought their land.

A.D. 1154. This year king Stephen died, and he was buried with his wife and his son at Faversham; they had built that monastery. When the king died the earl was beyond sea, and no man durst do other than good for very dread of him. When he came to England he was received with much honor, and was consecrated king at London on the Sunday before Christmas, and he held a great court there: and on the same day that Martin, abbot of Peterborough, should have gone thither he sickened, and he died on the 4th before the Nones of January. And that day the monks chose another abbot from among themselves. He is named William de Walteville, a good clerk, and a good man, and well beloved of the king and of all good people: and they buried the abbot honorably in the church, and soon afterwards the abbot elect and the monks went to the king at Oxford, and the king gave him the abbacy, and he departed soon afterwards to Peterborough, where he remained with the abbot before he came home. And the king was received at Peterborough with great respect, and in full procession; so he was also at Ramsey, at Thorney, and at . . . and Spalding, and. . . .

ALFRED (849-901)

PREFACE TO THE PASTORAL CARE

KING ALFRED bids greet Bishop Werfrith with his words lovingly and friendlily; and I bid it be known to thee that it has come very often to my mind what wise

men there formerly were throughout England, both of
the sacred and of the secular; and how happy times
then were throughout England; and how the kings who
ruled over the nation in those days obeyed God and
his messengers; and how they maintained peace, moral-
ity, and order within their borders, and also increased
their territory abroad; and how they flourished both in
war and in wisdom; and also how eager the sacred
orders were both for teaching and for learning, and for
all the duties which they owed to God; and how foreigners sought wisdom and teaching in this land, and
how we should now be obliged to get them from abroad
if we were to have them. So complete was this decline in England that there were very few on this
side of the Humber who could understand their books
of service in English, or translate a letter from Latin
into English; and I think that there were not many
beyond the Humber. There were so few of them that
I cannot call to mind one of them south of the Thames,
when I came to the throne. To God Almighty be thanks
that we have a number of teachers now. And for that
reason I command thee to do as I believe thou art willing, to free thyself from worldly affairs as often as
thou canst, that thou mayest use the wisdom which God
has granted thee wherever thou canst. Think what
punishments would come to us because of this world,
if we neither loved wisdom ourselves nor let other men
get it: the name only we should love in being called
Christian, and very few of the practices.

When I brought all this to mind, I remembered also
that I saw, before it had all been harried and burned,
how the churches throughout England were filled with
treasures and books, and a great multitude of God's
servants, too; but they had very little benefit of the
books, because they could not at all understand them,

inasmuch as they were not written in their own language. Just as though they had said, "Our elders, who formerly held these places, loved wisdom, and through it they acquired wealth, and left it to us. Herein we can yet see their footprints, but we cannot follow them, and for that reason we have lost both the wealth and the wisdom, because we would not whole-heartedly follow their tracks."

When I brought all this to mind, then I wondered much that the good, wise men who formerly were throughout England and who had fully learned all the books, had not at all wished to translate them into their own language. But again I soon answered myself and said: "They did not think that men should ever be so thoughtless, and learning decline so; on purpose they neglected it, and wished that the wisdom in this land would be the greater as we learned more languages."

Then I recalled how the law was first known in the Hebrew language, and again, when the Greeks had learned it, they turned the whole of it into their own language, and all other books, too. And again the Romans, likewise, when they had learned them, turned all by wise translators into their own language. And all other Christian nations, too, turned a part of them into their own language. Therefore it seems better to me, if it seems so to you, that we also should translate some books most necessary for all men to know into the language which we all know, and to do as we very easily may, with God's grace, and if we have peace, namely, that all the young men now in England of free men, of those who are wealthy enough to devote themselves to it, be set to learning as long as they are incapable of any other employment, until the time that they can read English writing well; and afterwards still more teach those in the Latin language who are to be taught more, and whom we will advance to a higher office.

When I called to mind how the knowledge of the Latin language formerly had declined throughout England, and yet many could read English writing, I began among other various and manifold cares of this kingdom to turn into English the book that is called in Latin *Pastoralis,* and in English *Shepherd's Book,* sometimes word for word, sometimes sense for sense, as I had learned it from Plegmund, my archbishop, and from Asser, my bishop, and from Grimbald, my mass-priest, and from John, my mass-priest. And after I had learned it as best as I could understand it, and as I could most intelligibly render it, I translated it into English; and I will send one to every bishopric in my kingdom; and in each there is a bookmark worth thirty mancuses.[1] And I order in God's name that no man remove the bookmark from the book, or the book from the monastery. It is unknown how long there will be such learned bishops as now, thanks to God, there are well-nigh everywhere. Therefore I desire the books to be always in their places unless the bishop wish to have them with him, or they be lent out anywhere, or anybody copy from them.

THE VOYAGES OF OHTHERE AND WULFSTAN

Ohthere told his lord, Alfred the king, that he of all the Northmen lived farthest to the north. He said that he lived in the land to the north by the West Sea. He said, though, that the land stretched still farther north from there; but it was all waste, except in a few places here and there where Finns dwelt for hunting in winter and in summer for fishing in the sea. He said that

[1] A *mancus* is worth the eighth of a pound.

once he wanted to find out how far the land extended to the northward and whether any man lived to the north of that waste. So he voyaged due north along the coast, kept all the way the waste land to starboard and the open sea on the larboard for three days. Then he was as far north as the whalers ever go. Thereupon he still went due north as far as he could sail in another three days. There the land curved to the east, or the sea in on that land, he did not know which; but he knew that there he waited for a wind from the west or somewhat from the north, and then sailed along the shore easterly as far as he could in four days' sailing. There he had to wait for a wind from due north, for there the land curved due south, or the sea in on that land, he did not know which. Thence he sailed along the coast due south as far as he was able by five days' sailing. At that point there was a large river running into the land. Then they turned up into this river, for they dared not sail beyond this river because of enemies, for the land was all inhabited on the other side of the river. He had not met with any inhabited land since he voyaged from his own home; but all the way was waste land on the starboard, except for fishermen and fowlers and hunters, and they were all Finns; and the open sea was always on the larboard. The Permians had very well cultivated their land; but they dared not go in there. The land of the Terfinns was all waste, except where hunters lived, or fishermen, or fowlers.

Many stories the Permians told him both about their own land and about the lands which were about them; but he knew not the truth of it, because he did not see it himself. The Finns and the Permians, it seemed to him, spoke nearly alike. In addition to seeing the country he went thither for walruses especially, for they have very fine bone in their teeth—they brought some teeth to the king—and their hides are very good for ship-ropes. The whale is much smaller than other whales; it is not more than seven ells long; but in his own country is the best whaling—they are eight and forty ells long, and the largest are fifty ells. He said that he was one of six who killed sixty of these in two days.

He was a very wealthy man in such things as make up their wealth, that is, in wild beasts. He still had, when he visited the king, six hundred tame deer unsold. These deer they call reindeer; six were decoy deer, which are very valuable among the Finns, for with them they capture the wild reindeer. He was among the first men in the country, though he had not more than twenty horned cattle and twenty sheep and twenty swine, and the little that he ploughed he ploughed with horses. But their income is mainly in the tribute which the Finns give them. That tribute consists of animal skins, feathers, and whale bone, and ship-ropes which are made of whale and seal hide. Each one pays in proportion to his means; the richest must pay fifteen marten skins, and five of reindeer, one bear skin, and ten measures of feathers, a bear or otterskin kirtle, and two ship-ropes, each sixty ells long, one made of whale's hide, the other of seal.

He said that the country of the Northmen was very long and very narrow. All that his man can use either for grazing or ploughing lies along the coast, and that is very rocky in some places, and wild moors lie to the east and along the inhabited land. On these moors dwell the Finns. And the inhabited land is broadest to the east, and the further north the narrower it is. Eastward it may be sixty miles broad, or a little broader; and midway thirty or more; and northward, he said, where it was the narrowest, it might be three miles broad to the moor. Furthermore, the moor is so broad in certain places that a man would take two weeks in crossing it, and in some places so broad that a man could cross it in six days.

Then along the land to the southward, on the other side of the moor, is Sweden, as far as the land to the northward, and along the northern land, the country of the Cwens. The Cwens at times harry the Northmen over the moor, at times the Northmen harry them. And there are very large fresh lakes beyond the moors; the Cwens carry their boats over land to the lakes, and from there harry the Northmen; they have very small boats and very light——.

WULFSTAN'S VOYAGE

Esthonia is very large and there are very many towns there, and in every town is a king. And there is very much honey, and fishing. The king and the richest men drink mare's milk, but the poor people and the slaves drink mead. There is much strife between them. And there is no ale brewed among the Esthonians, but there is mead enough.

There is a custom among the Esthonians, that when a man dies he lies in his house unburnt with his relatives and friends for a month, sometimes two; and the kings and the other high-born men as much longer as they have the more possessions; sometimes half a year they are unburnt, lying above earth in their houses. And all the while that the body is within there must be drinking and playing until the day that they burn it. On the very day on which they are to bear him to the pyre, they divide his property, whatever is left after the drinking and the playing, into five or six shares, sometimes more, according to the extent of his property. Then they place the largest share about a mile from the town, then the second, then the third, until it is all placed within the one mile; and the smallest share must be nearest the town in which the dead man lies. Then there must be gathered together all the men in the country who have the swiftest horses, some five or six miles from the property. Then they all run toward the property; then comes the man who has the swiftest horse to the first and largest share, and so one after another, until it is all taken; and he who runs to the property nearest the town takes the least share. And then each one rides his way with his property, and he may keep it all; and for that reason swift horses are excessively dear there. And when his property is all spent, they bear him out and burn him with his weapons and garments. Generally they spend all his wealth, since the dead man lies for so long in the house and they place his property along the way, which the strangers race for and take.

And it is also a custom among the Esthonians that men of every tribe must be burned, and if any man finds a bone unburned, they shall pay dearly for it. And there is among the Esthonians one tribe that is able to cause cold; and the dead men lie so long and do not decay because they produce this cold on them. And if a man sets two vats full of ale or of water, they make them both freeze over, in summer just the same as in winter.

ÆLFRIC (c.955-c.1020)

THE ASSUMPTION OF SAINT JOHN THE APOSTLE

JOHN THE EVANGELIST, Christ's darling, was on this

day through God's visitation, taken to the joy of the kingdom of heaven. He was the son of Christ's maternal aunt, and he loved him particularly, not so much for the kinship as for the purity of his uncorrected chastity. He was in chastity chosen to God, and he ever continued in undefiled chastity. It is read in historic narratives that he would marry, and Christ was invited to his nuptials. Then it befell that at the nuptials wine was wanting. Jesus then bade the serving men fill six stone vessels with pure water, and he with his blessing turned the water to noble wine. This is the first miracle that he openly wrought in his state of man. Now John was so stimulated by that miracle that he forthwith left his bride in maidenhood, and ever afterwards followed the Lord, and was by him inwardly beloved, because he had withdrawn himself from fleshly lusts. Verily to this beloved disciple Jesus entrusted his mother, when, suspended on the cross, he redeemed mankind, that his pure life might take care of the pure virgin Mary, and that she might continue ministering to her sister's son.

Some time after Christ's ascension to heaven, a cruel emperor reigned in the Roman empire after Nero, who was called Domitian, a persecutor of the Christians. He commanded a vat to be filled with boiling oil, and the great evangelist to be thrust therein; but he, through God's protection, went uninjured from that hot bath. Afterwards, when the cruel one might not suppress the preaching of the blessed apostle, he sent him into exile to an island that is called Patmos, that he there, through sharpness of hunger, might perish. But the Almighty Savior did not leave his beloved apostle to neglect, but revealed to him in that exile the revelation of things to come, concerning which he wrote the book which is called *Apocalypse;* and the cruel

Domitian was slain in the same year by the hand of his senators, and they all unanimously resolved that all his decrees should be annulled. Then was Nerva, a very honorable man, chosen for emperor. With his consent the apostle returned with great worship, he who with contumely had been sent into banishment. Men and women ran to meet him, rejoicing and saying, "Blessed is he who cometh in the name of God."

As the apostle John was entering the city of Ephesus, there was borne toward him the corpse of a widow to be buried; her name was Drusiana. She was of great faith, and gave much in alms, and the poor, whom she bountifully fed, sad, with weeping, followed the corpse. Then the apostle bade them set down the bier, and said, "My Lord, Jesus Christ! Raise thee, Drusiana; arise and return home, and prepare food for us in thy house." Drusiana then arose as if from sleep awakened, and mindful of the apostle's command, returned home.

On the second day the apostle going into the street observed where a philosopher was accompanying two brothers who had turned all their parents' treasure into precious gems and would crush them in the sight of all the people as a spectacle, in contempt, as it were, of worldly riches. It was common at that time for those who would sedulously learn philosophy to change their property for gems, and break them in pieces; or for a wedge of gold, and throw it into the sea; lest the contemplation of those riches should hinder them at their study. Then the apostle called the philosopher Graton to him, and said, "It is foolish that any one should despise worldly riches for praise of men, and be condemned at God's doom. Vain is the medicine that cannot heal the sick; as also is vain the doctrine that healeth not the sins and vices of the soul. Verily, my teacher, Christ, enjoined a youth who desired eternal life, in these words, That he should sell all his wealth, and distribute the value to the poor, if he would be perfect; and he should afterwards have his treasure in heaven, and, in addition thereto, eternal life." The philosopher Graton answered him, "These jewels are crushed for idle vaunt; but if thy teacher is the true God, join the fragments to soundness, that their value may benefit the poor." John then gathered the fragments of the jewels, and looked to heaven, thus saying, "Lord Jesus, to thee no thing is difficult; thou didst restore this crushed world for thy faithful, through sign of the holy rood; restore now these precious gems, by thine angels' hands, that these ignorant men may acknowledge thy powers, and in thee believe." Lo, then suddenly the gems became sound, so that even no sign of their former broken condition was seen. Then the philosopher Graton, together with the youths, fell forthwith at the feet of John, believing in God. The apostle baptized him with all his family, and he began openly to preach God's faith. The two brothers, Atticus and Eugenius, gave their gems, and distributed all their wealth to the poor, and followed the apostle, and a great multitude of believers also joined themselves to him.

Then on a certain time the apostle came to the city of Pergamus, where the before-mentioned youths formerly dwelt, and saw their servants decorated with fine linen, and shining in worldly splendor. Then were they pierced through with the devil's darts, and sad in mind, that they in poverty should go with one miserable cloak, and their servants be shining in worldly splendor. Then perceived the apostle the diabolical wiles, and said, "I see that your mind and your countenance are changed, because ye have distributed your riches to the poor and followed my Lord's doctrine: go now therefore to the wood, and hew a burthen of rods, and bring them to me." They did as he had commanded, and he in God's name blessed the green rods, and they were turned to red gold. Again the apostle said, "Go now to the sea-strand, and fetch me pebble-stones." They did so, and John by God's majesty blessed them, and they were turned to precious gems. Then said the apostle, "Go to the smithy, and try this gold and these gems." They went, and came again, thus saying, "All the gold-smiths say that they have never before seen such pure and such red gold: also the jewellers say that they have never before met with such precious gems." Then said the apostle to them, "Take this gold and these gems, and go and buy landed property, seeing that ye have lost heavenly riches. Buy yourselves purple kirtles, that ye for a little while may shine as the rose, that ye may speedily fade. Be flourishing and rich for a season, that ye may be poor for ever. What, may not the Almighty Ruler so act that he make his servants power-ful before the world, abounding in wealth, and incom-parably to shine? But he has placed warfare for the believing souls, that they may believe in order to possess the eternal riches, they who for his name despise tem-porary possessions. Ye healed the sick in the name of Jesus, ye drove out devils, ye gave sight to the blind, and cured every disease. Behold, now this gift is with-drawn from you, and ye are become poor wretches, ye who were great and strong. The devils stood in so great awe of you, that at your behest they forsook the possessed demoniacs; now ye yourselves dread devils. The heavenly possessions are common to us all. Naked we were born, and naked we depart. The brightness of the sun, and the light of the moon, and of all the stars are common to the high and the low. Rain-showers and the church-door, baptism and forgiveness of sins, par-taking of the housel and God's visitation are common

to all, poor and rich: but the unhappy covetous wishes
to have more than suffices him, though he enjoys not
freedom from care in his abundance. The covetous
hath one body and divers garments; he hath one belly
and a thousand men's sustenance; but that which he,
through the vice of avarice, cannot give to any order,
he hoardeth, and knoweth not for whom, as the prophet
said, 'Vainly is every man troubled who hoardeth, and
knoweth not for whom he gathereth.' Verily he is not
lord of those possessions, when he cannot distribute
them, but he is the slave of those possessions, when he
wholly serveth them; and in addition thereto, diseases
of his body increase, so that he may not enjoy food
or drink. He cares night and day that his money be
preserved; he attends greedily to his gain, his rent, his
buildings; he bereaves the indigent, he follows his lusts
and his pleasure; then suddenly departs he from this
world, naked and charged with crimes, bearing with
him his sins alone; therefore shall he suffer punishment
everlasting."

Behold, while the apostle was speaking this lecture,
a certain widow bare her son to be buried, who had
been married thirty days before. The afflicted mother,
together with the mourners, wailing prostrated herself
at the holy apostle's feet, praying that he would, in
God's name, rear up her son, as he did the widow Drusiana. John then, pitying the grief of the mother and
the mourners, prostrated his body on the earth, in long
prayer, and at length rising up, again with upraised
hands prayed a long time. Having done thus thrice,
he bade them unwrap the corpse of the youth, and said,
"O thou youth, who through thy flesh's lust hast early
lost thy soul; O thou youth, thou knewest not thy Creator; thou knewest not the Savior of men; thou knewest
not the true friend, and hast therefore fallen on the

worst enemy. Now I have shed my tears, and earnestly
prayed for thy sensuality, that thou mayest from death
arise, and to these two brothers, Atticus and Eugenius,
declare how great glory they have lost, and what punishment they have earned." On this the youth Stacteus
arose, and fell at the feet of John, and began to chide
the brothers who had been perverted, thus saying, "I
saw the angels who had charge of you sadly weeping,
and the accursed fiend rejoicing in your destruction.
For you was the kingdom of heaven ready, and shining
structures filled with repasts, and with eternal light:
these ye have lost through heedlessness, and have got
for yourselves dark dwellings filled with serpents, and
with crackling flames, full of unspeakable torments and
horrible stenches; in which groaning and howling cease
not day nor night: pray, therefore, with inward heart,
this apostle of God, your teacher, that he raise you from
eternal perdition, as he hath raised me from death, and
that he your souls, which are now blotted from the living
book, lead back to God's grace and mercy."

The youth then, Stacteus, who had risen from death,
together with the brothers, prostrated himself in the
footsteps of John, and the people with them, all unanimously praying that he would intercede with God for
them. The apostle then commanded the two brothers
that they for thirty days in penitence should sacrifice
to God by penance, and in that space should earnestly
pray that the golden rods might be turned again to their
former nature, and the gems to their worthlessness.
After thirty days' space, when they could not by their
prayers restore the gold and the gems to their nature,
they came with weeping to the apostle, thus saying,
"Ever hast thou taught mercy, and that one should have
mercy on another; and if one have mercy on another,
how much more will God show mercy to and pity men,

his handiwork! The sin which we have committed with covetous eyes, we now with weeping eyes repent." Then answered the apostle, "Bear the rods to the wood, and the stones to the sea-strand: they shall be restored to their nature." When they had done this they again received God's grace, so that they drove out devils, and healed the blind and the sick, and performed many miracles, in the Lord's name, as they before had done.

The apostle then converted to God all the country of Asia, which is accounted the half part of the world; and wrote the fourth book of Christ, which treats most of Christ's divinity. The other three evangelists, Matthew, Mark, Luke, wrote rather of Christ's human state. Then there sprung up heretics in God's church, who said that Christ was not before he was born of Mary. Thereupon all the diocesan bishops besought the holy apostle to compose the fourth book, and extinguish the audacity of the heretics. John then ordered a general fast of three days; and after the fast he was so greatly filled with the spirit of God, that he excelled all God's angels and all creatures with his exalted mind, and began the evangelical memorial with these words, "In principio erat verbum," etc., that is in English, "In the beginning was the word, and the word was with God, and the word was God; this was in the beginning with God; all things are made through him, and without him nothing is created." And so forth, in all the evangelical memorial, he made known many things concerning Christ's divinity, how he eternally without beginning was begotten of his Father, and reigneth with him in unity of the Holy Ghost, ever without end. He wrote few things of his human nature, because the three other evangelists had composed their books abundantly concerning that.

It happened at a certain time, that the idolaters, who

were yet unbelieving, said that they would force the apostle to their heathenship: whereupon the apostle said to the idolaters, "Go all together to God's church, and call all of you to your gods that, through their might, the church may fall down; then will I turn to your heathenship. But if the power of your god may not cast down the holy church, I will cast down your temple, through the might of the Almighty God, and I will crush your idol; and it shall then seem right that ye cease from your error, and believe in the true God, who alone is Almighty." The idolaters assented to this proposal, and John with kind words exhorted the people to go out from the devil's temple; and with clear voice cried before them all, "In the name of God let this temple fall down with all the idols that dwell within it, that this multitude may know that this idolatry is the worship of the devil." Behold then, the temple fell suddenly to the ground, with all its idols turned to dust. On that same day twelve thousand heathens were turned to belief in Christ, and hallowed with baptism.

But the chief idolater still refused with great perverseness, and said that he would not believe unless John drank poison, and through God's might overcame the deadly drink. Then said the apostle, "Though thou give me poison, through God's name it shall not hurt me." Then said the idolater Aristodemus, "Thou shalt first see another drink it, and instantly die, that so at least thy heart may fear the death-bearing drink." John answered him, "If thou wilt believe in God, I will fearless receive this drink." Then Aristodemus went to the prefect, and took from his prison two thieves, and gave them the poison before all the people, in the presence of John; and they immediately after the drink died. Then the idolater gave the venomous drink also to the apostle, and he having armed his mouth and all his body with the sign of the rood, and exorcised the poison in God's name, with bold heart drank it all. Aristodemus then and the people beheld the apostle three hours of the day, and saw him having a glad countenance, without paleness and fear: and they all cried, "There is one true God, whom John worshippeth." Then said the idolater to the apostle, "Yet I doubt; but if thou, in the name of thy God, wilt raise up these dead thieves, then will my heart be cleansed from every doubt." Then said John, "Aristodemus, take my tunic, and lay it on the corpses of the dead men, and say, 'The apostle of Jesus Christ hath sent me to you, that ye in his name may arise from death, and that every man may know that death and life minister to my Savior.'" He then, at the apostle's command, bare his tunic, and laid it on the two dead ones, and they forthwith rose up whole. When the idolater saw that, he prostrated himself at the feet of John, and then went to the prefect, and announced to him those miracles with a loud voice. Then they both sought the apostle, praying for his compassion: whereupon the apostle enjoined them a fast of seven days, and afterwards baptized them; and after their baptism they cast down all their idols, and with the aid of their kinsmen, and with all art, raised a great church to God in honor of the apostle.

When the apostle was ninety-nine years old the Lord Christ appeared to him with the other apostles, whom he had taken from this life, and said, "John, come to me; it is time that thou with thy brethren shouldst feast at my banquet." John then arose, and went towards Jesus. But He said to him, "Lo, on Sunday, the day of my resurrection, thou shalt come to me": and after those words the Lord returned to heaven. The apostle greatly rejoiced in that promise, and at sunrise early rising came to the church, and from cock-crowing until the third hour, taught God's law, and sang mass to them, and said that the Savior had called him to heaven on that day. He then ordered his grave to be dug opposite the altar, and the dust to be removed; and he went quick and whole into his grave, and with outstretched hands cried to God, "Lord Christ, I thank thee that thou hast invited me to thy banquet: thou knowest that with all my heart I have desired thee. Oft have I prayed thee that I might go to thee, but thou saidst that I should abide, that I might gain more people to thee. Thou hast preserved my body against every pollution, and thou hast ever illumined my soul, and hast nowhere forsaken me. Thou hast set in my mouth the word of thy truth, and I have written down the lore which I heard from thy mouth, and the wonders which I saw thee work. Now I commit to thee, Lord! thy children, those which thy church, maiden and mother, through water and the Holy Ghost have gained to thee. Receive me to my brothers with whom thou camest and invitedst me. Open towards me the gate of life, that the princes of darkness may not find me. Thou art Christ, Son of the living God, who, at thy Father's behest, hast saved the world, and hast sent us the Holy Ghost. Thee we praise and thank for thy manifold benefits throughout the world eternal. Amen."

After this prayer a heavenly light appeared above the apostle, within the grave, shining for an hour so bright that no man's sight might look on the rays of light; and with that light he gave up his spirit to the Lord, who had invited him to his kingdom. He departed as joyfully from the pain of death, from this present life, as he was exempt from bodily defilement. Verily his grave was afterwards found filled with manna. Manna the heavenly meat was called which for forty years fed the people of Israel in the wilderness. Now this food was found in the grave of John, and nothing else, and the meat is growing in it to this present day. Many miracles have there been manifested, and sick healed and released from all calamities through the apostle's intercession. This hath the Lord Christ granted unto him, to whom is glory and honor with the Father and the Holy Ghost, ever without end. Amen.

WULFSTAN'S ADDRESS TO THE ENGLISH

Beloved brethren, know the truth: this world is in haste, and nears its end; and so, in the world, ever the later is the worse, and because of men's sins it must needs from day to day grow very evil e'er Antichrist shall come; yea, truly, then will it be dreadful and terrible all over the earth.

Know too, for a truth, that for many years now the devil has led this people too far astray, and there is little faith among men for all their fair speaking; too much has unrighteousness ruled the land, and never have many men considered a remedy with the zeal they should; but every day man adds evil to evil and works iniquity and all manner of injustice too widely among this people. And so, because of this we have suffered many losses and indignities; and if we are to look for any relief then must we deserve it of God better than we have done e'er this. We have greatly deserved and merited that evil which lies over us, and with even greater deserving we must obtain the cure from God, if henceforth things are to be better. For lo, we know full well that a great breach needs mighty mending and a great fire no little water, if a man shall think to quench that fire. And great is the need of every man that henceforth he observe God's law with diligence, better than he did before, and fulfil God's commandments with righteousness.

Among the heathen peoples a man dares not withhold little or much of that ordained for the worship of the idols: but we too often everywhere withhold the rights of God. Among the heathen a man dare not injure any of those things, within or without, that are brought to the idols and ordained for sacrifice: but we have clean despoiled God's house, inside and out. And too, the servants of God are everywhere deprived of honor and protection; and some men say that no one dare in any wise ill-treat the servants of idols among the heathen, as men now do too widely to the servants of God, where Christians should keep God's law and protect God's servants.

I speak truly, there is need for a remedy, for the rights of God have too long been growing less on every side in this land, and the laws of the folk have deteriorated entirely too much since Eadgar [1] died, and the sanctuaries are too widely unprotected, and the houses of God are clean despoiled of their old rights and stripped within of everything seemly, and holy orders have now long been despised; too many a widow has been unrighteously forced to take a husband, and too many lowly, humble, poor men are sorely betrayed and cruelly ensnared, in benefit and sustenance, in property and possessions, all too often; and undeservedly they are sold far from this country into the power of strangers; and for a little theft the child in the cradle is made a slave with cruel injustice, throughout this people. Free-right is taken away, thrall-right is restricted and alms-right is diminished. Free men may not rule themselves, nor go where they will, nor use their property as they desire; thralls may not have

that which they have got for their own through hard
toil, nor what good men have given them for the grace
of God and for God's love have given as alms-gifts; but
each alms-right that a man should give for God's grace
with right zeal is made smaller or withheld. For unrighteousness is too generally common to man, and un-
lawfulness is dear, and, to speak quickly, God's laws
are hateful and his teaching is despised; and for this
we suffer many indignities through God's anger, as
everyone knows, and the loss will be common to all this
people, though men will not believe it, unless God shall
save.

For it is clear and plain to us all that before this we
have more often gone astray than done well, and for
this our people is constantly disturbed. This long time
nothing has prospered at home or abroad, but on every
side there have been frequent wasting and famine,
burning and bloodshed; stealing and murder, plague
and pestilence, murrain and disease, slander and hate
and the stealing of thieves have sorely distressed us, and
heavy taxes have weighed upon us, and bad weather
has blighted our crops. Because in this land, it would
seem, now for many years have been great unrighteousness and fickle faith between men everywhere. Many
a time kinsman has defended kinsman no more than a
stranger, nor father his son, nor, sometimes, son his
own father, nor one brother the other. Not one of us
has ordered his life as he should, neither men in holy
orders according to their regulations, nor laymen according to the law; but we have followed our desires
according to our own dictates, and we have held neither
the teaching nor the law of God or men as we should.
No man has purposed honestly towards another as
rightly as he should, but almost everyone has betrayed
and injured others in word and deed; and how wickedly

has nearly everyone stabbed his neighbor in the back with shameful scandal and calumnies: worse if he might.

For here in our land are great infidelities towards God and mankind, and too, in our land many are traitors to their lords in various ways. And the greatest of all treasons in the world is that a man should betray the soul of his lord, and there is also a very great treachery in the world—that a man should deprive his lord of his life or drive him living from his land; and both of these have been done in this land. Eadweard [2] men betrayed and afterward killed, and Æthelred [3] men drove out of his country. And too many sponsors and godchildren have been killed widely throughout this people, and all too many innocent men have been ruined. And too many holy places have been destroyed because in the past certain men have been lodged there who should not have been if men showed reverence for the sanctuary of God. And too many Christian folk are now all the time sold out of this land; and all that is hateful to God, if you will believe me.

And we also know well where this sad thing has come to pass, that a father has sold his son for a price, and a son his mother, and one brother another into the power of strangers out of this land; and all these are monstrous and frightful deeds, as who will may understand. And yet it is much more than this that afflicts this people. Many are forsworn and liars, and pledges are broken often and commonly; and it is clear that in this land the wrath of God lies heavily upon us, let him understand who can.

And oh! what greater shame can come to man through God's wrath than often befalls us for our proper deserts? For if a thrall run away from his lord, and turn from Christendom to the pirates (the Danes), and

it afterwards comes to pass that thane and thrall meet
in the clash of weapons, if the thrall foully kill the
thane then the thane shall lie without wergild for his
kinsmen, but if the thane foully kill the thrall whom
he once owned he shall pay thanegild.[4] Debasing laws
and shameful tribute are, through God's wrath, common
with us, as who will may understand, and many calamities befall this people constantly. For a long time
now nothing has thriven at home or abroad, but there
has been devastation and hate constantly on every side,
and long have the English been without victory and too
sorely disheartened by God's anger, and the sea-pirates
have been so strong, with God's permission, that often
in battle one of them has put to flight ten of us, and
two have routed twenty, and sometimes more, all for
our sins. And often a thrall will bind fast the thane
who was his master, and force him to thralldom through
God's wrath. Alas for the degradation and the public
shame that the English now have all through God's
wrath! Often two or three vikings will drive a multitude of Christian men from sea to sea out of this
country enslaved together, to the public shame of us all,
if we really knew anything or would understand aught
aright. But all this dishonor that we so often endure
we requite with honor to them that shame us: we constantly reward them and they oppress us every day.
They harry and burn, plunder and rob, and carry off to
their ships; and lo! is there anything in all these calamities clear and manifest except God's wrath?

Nor is it a wonder that we are in trouble, for we
know very well that for many years now men have not
often recked what they wrought in word or deed; but
this people, as it seems, has been very evil, through
manifold sins and many misdeeds, through murder and
crime, through avarice and greed, through stealing and

robbery, through the betrayal of men and heathen vices, through plots and treacheries, through law-breaking and sedition, through kinsmen's attacks on kinsmen and through murders, through violations of religious orders and adulteries, through incests and through various fornications. And therefore, as we said before, through breaking of oaths and through breaking of pledges and various treacheries far and wide, more than should be are ruined and forsworn and breaches of festival and fasting are common. And here on earth God's adversaries abound, degenerate apostates, foes to the church, and grim persecutors of the people, all too many of them, proud despisers of holy law and Christian customs, and foolish deriders everywhere among the people of the things that God's servant decrees, and chiefest, of the things that most clearly belong with right to God's law.

And therefore has it come about that men far and wide are more ashamed of their good deeds than of their evil ones; because too often men scorn good deeds with derision and revile God-fearing men all too much, and especially men despise and greet too often with evil those who love the right and have in any measure the fear of God. And because men so do that they despise all that they should praise, and loathe what they should love, because of this they bring all too many to evil thoughts and unrighteous deeds, so that they are not ashamed, even though they sin greatly and altogether offend against God; but for empty insults they are ashamed to amend their misdeeds as the books teach, like fools who because of their life of pride will not save themselves while they yet may.

Too many in this land are living in grievous impunity in sin. Here are, as we said before, manslayers and kin-slayers and priest-slayers and haters of monasteries

and traitors and open apostates, and here are perjurers and murderers and vow-breakers and law-breakers
and men who have sinned grievously through incest and
various fornications, and here are harlots and murder-
esses of children and many foul adulterers, and here
are witches and sorceresses, and here are plundering
and robberies and world-spoilers and thieves and in-
jurers of the people and traitors and breakers of treaty
and, to speak shortly, unnumbered kinds of all manner
of crime and misdeeds.

And this shames us not, but we are ashamed to begin
a reform, as the books teach, and that is clearly seen
in this miserable, sinful land. Let each man earnestly
consider himself, and let him not delay too long in God's
name. Let us do as is needful for us, save ourselves
as we surely may, lest we perish all together.

Once there was among the Britons a wise man, named
Gildas,[5] who wrote about their evil deeds, how they out-
raged God so excessively with their sins that at last he let
an English army win their land and entirely destroy the
British host. And that happened, as he said, through
the learned breaking the rules of their orders and the
unlettered breaking the law, through the plundering of
the rich and through greed for ill-gotten gains, through
the bad laws of the people and through unjust decisions, through the sloth and folly of the bishops, and
through the wicked cowardice of the servants of God,
who too often kept silence concerning the truth, and
mumbled to themselves when they should have cried
out because of the foul wantonness of the people; and
through gluttony and manifold sins they lost their country, and themselves perished.

But let us do as is needful for us, and take warning
by all this; and what I say is truth, that we know of
some worse deeds among the English than we have heard

of among the early Britons; and we have great need to take thought and to make intercession zealously with God's self. And let us do as is needful for us, turn toward the right, and in some measure forsake unrighteousness and most earnestly amend those things wherein we earlier offended. Let us creep to Christ, and call on Him often with trembling heart, and deserve His mercy; and let us love God and follow God's laws, and perform with zeal what we promised when we received baptism or what they promised who were our sponsors at baptism. And let us order our words and our works aright and earnestly cleanse our inward thoughts, and carefully hold to oath and pledge, and have some truth between us without evil practice, and let us often think on that great judgment that we all shall come to, and save ourselves with zeal from the welling fire of hell-torment, and earn for ourselves the glory and joy that God has prepared for them who work His will on earth. O God our help! Amen.

MIDDLE ENGLISH
LITERATURE

LAYAMON

ARTHUR'S LAST BATTLE

From *Brut*

THEN came there on a time a valiant man riding, and brought news to Arthur the king from Modred, his sister's son. To Arthur he was welcome, because Arthur thought that he brought messages most pleasing. Arthur lay the night long and spoke with the young knight; but the latter would never tell him truthfully how it fared. On the morrow when it was day and warriors began to stir, Arthur arose and stretched his arms; he arose and sat down as though he were exceeding sick. Then asked him a fair knight, "Lord, how didst thou fare last night?" Arthur then answered— his mind was uneasy—"Last night in my sleep, as I lay in my chamber, a dream came to me; therefore I am full sorry. I dreamed that men raised me up in a hall; the hall I began to bestride, as though I would ride. All the lands that I possessed, all I there surveyed. And Gawain sat before me; my sword he bore in his hand. Then Modred advanced there with innumerable folk. He bore in his hand a battle-axe strong. He began to hew most stoutly, and he hewed the posts that held up the hall. Then I saw Guinevere also, dearest of women to me; all the great hall with her hand she drew down. The hall began to fall, and I fell to the ground, so that my right arm broke. Then said Modred, "Have that!" Down fell the hall, and

Gawain began to fall, and fell on the earth. Both his arms broke. And I seized my dear sword with my left hand and smote off Modred's head so that it rolled on the field. And I cut the queen all into pieces with my dear sword, and afterward I set her down in a black pit. And all my good people took to flight, so that I knew not under Christ where they had fled. But I stood upon a woodland and I there began to wander far over the moors. There I saw vultures and horrible birds. Then came a golden lion over the down, a beast most gracious, that our Lord made. The lion ran toward me and seized me by the middle and began to move and went to the sea. I saw the waves drive in the sea there, and the lion went into the flood with me. When we came into the sea, the waves snatched her from me. Came a fish and brought me to land. Then was I all wet, and weary from sorrow, and sick. When I awoke, I began to quake exceedingly; I began to tremble as though I were on fire. And so I have all night long thought much of my dream, for I knew with certainty that my bliss had gone; forever in my life I must endure sorrow. Alas, that I have not here Guinevere my queen!"

Then answered the knight: "Lord, thou art wrong; men should never interpret a dream with sorrow. Thou art the greatest man that reigneth on land, and the wisest of all that live under heaven. If it had happened—and our Lord will not have it so—that Modred, thy sister's son, had taken thy queen, and set all thy royal land in his own hand, which thou grantedst him when thou didst think of going to Rome; and had he done all this with his treachery, thou mightest yet avenge thee worthily with weapons, and again hold thy land and govern thy people, and fell thine enemies, who did evil to thee, and slay them all utterly, that there remain not one."

Arthur then answered, noblest of all kings, "As long as is time itself, I never thought that Modred, my relative, dearest of men to me, would ever betray me for all my realm, nor Guinevere, my queen, weaken in thought; would it not begin, for any worldly man!"

At once the knight answered, "I tell thee the truth, dear king, for I am thine underling. Thus has Modred done: thy queen he has taken, and thy fair land set in his own hand. He is king and she is queen. Of thy coming they have no thought, for they think never in truth that thou shalt come again from Rome. I am thine own man and saw this treachery, and I have come to thee, thyself, to tell thee the truth. My head be my pledge that I have told thee truth, without lying, of thy beloved queen and of Modred, thy sister's son, how he has wrested Britain from thee."

Then sat they all silent in Arthur's hall; then was there sorrow with the good king; then were the British men for that reason most downcast. Then after a while voices broke out; afar men might hear the noise of the Britons, and began to tell in many a speech how they would destroy Modred and the queen, and wipe out all the people who held with Modred.

Arthur then called, most gracious of all Britons, "Sit ye quietly, knights in hall, and I will tell you strange news. Now tomorrow, when it is day, and the Lord sends it, forth I shall march toward Britain, and Modred I will slay and burn the queen. And I will destroy all who are pleased with the treachery. And here I will leave the dearest to me of men, Howell, my dear kinsman, highest of my kin; and half my army I will leave in this country to hold all this realm which I have in my hand. And when these things are finished, I shall come back to Rome and yield my fair land to Gawain my kinsman, and then I will carry out my threat, by my bare life: all my enemies shall make the fated journey!"

Then up stood Gawain, who was Arthur's kinsman, and spoke—the earl was wroth:— "Almighty God, ruler of judgment, guardian of earth, why has it happened that my brother Modred has committed this sin? Today I forsake him here before this people, and I will destroy him, with the Lord's will. I myself will hang him, highest of all villains; the queen, by God's law, I shall tear in pieces with horses. For may I never be merry while I live until I have avenged my uncle with the best!"

The Britons answered with bold voice: "All our weapons are ready; tomorrow we shall march!"

On the morrow, when it was day, and the Lord sent it, Arthur went forth with his noble folk; half he it left, and half he it led forth. Through the land he marched until he came to Whitsand; ships he had soon, many and well equipped. But for a fortnight the army lay there, awaiting the weather, deprived of wind.

Now there was a certain wicked knight in Arthur's army; as soon as he heard Modred doomed to death, he took his servant quickly and sent to this land, and sent word to Guinevere to tell how it had happened, and how Arthur was on the march with a great army, and how he would take on, and how he would act. The queen came to Modred, dearest to her of men, and gave him tidings of Arthur the king, how he would take on, and how he would act. Modred took his messengers and sent to the land of the Saxons for Childrich—the king was very powerful—and bade him come to Britain; he should have possession of it. Modred bade Childrich, the strong and the powerful, to send messengers afar to the four quarters of the land of the Saxons, and command all the knights they could find to come soon to this kingdom; and he would give Childrich part of his kingdom, all beyond the Humber, because he should help him to battle against his uncle, Arthur the king.

Childrich advanced soon into Britain. When Modred had assembled his army, then were there numbered sixty thousand valiant warriors of heathen folk, when they had come thither for Arthur's harm, and to help Modred, most knavish of men. When the army was assembled of each tribe, then were there a hundred thousand in a mass, heathen and Christian, with Modred the king.

Arthur lay at Whitsand; a fortnight seemed too long to him; and Modred knew all that Arthur intended to do there; each day came messengers to him from the king's army. Then it happened on a time that much rain began to fall, and the wind began to turn, and blew from the east. And Arthur embarked with all his army and commanded his seamen to bring him to Romney, where he thought to come up into this land. When he came to the haven, Modred was there before him. As the day began to light they began to fight, all the long day; many a man lay there dead. Some fought on land, some by the strand; some hurled spears from out the ships. Gawain went before and cleared the way, and slew there soon eleven thanes. He slew Childrich's son; he had come there with his father. The sun went to rest. Woe was then to the men. Gawain was slain there and deprived of his life through a Saxon earl— sorry be his soul! Then was Arthur sad and sorrowful in his heart therefore, and these words he spoke, most powerful of all Britons: "Now I have lost my dear followers. I knew by my dream what sorrow had been allotted me. Slain is Angel the king, who was my own darling, and Gawain, my sister's son—woe is me that I was born man. Up now from ship at once, my valiant knights!"

As he spoke sixty thousand good fighters turned to the fight, and broke Modred's ranks, and he himself was almost taken. Modred began to flee; and his people to follow after. They fled like fiends; the fields even trembled; the stones babbled with the blood-streams. Then would the fight have been quite finished but the night came too soon; if night had not come on they would all have been slain. The night separated them over grassland and over downs. And Modred came so far forth that he was at London. The citizens heard how it all had fared, and refused him entrance, and all his folk. Modred then went toward Winchester and they received him with all his men. And Arthur followed with all his might until he came to Winchester with a huge army, and besieged the city. And Modred therein abode.

When Modred saw that Arthur was so near, often he thought of what he should do. Then on the same night he ordered all his knights to go out of the city with their weapons, and said that he would fight a battle there. He promised the citizens free law for ever provided they would help him in his need.

When it was daylight their battle-array was ready. Arthur saw that; the king was wroth. He had trumpets blown and men summoned to battle. He ordered all his thanes and his noble knights to join battle together and slay his enemies and destroy the city and hang the citizenry. They marched together and sternly fought. Modred then thought what he might do, and he did there as he did elsewhere, treachery with the most. Ever he acted wickedly; he betrayed his companions before Winchester, and had his dearest knights called to him at once, and his dearest friends all, all of his people, and stole away from the fight—the fiend have him!—and let the good folk perish there, utterly. They fought all day; they thought that their lord there lay and was by them in their great need. Then took he the way that led toward Hampton, and went toward the haven—most wicked of men—and took all the ships of any value that were there, and all the steersmen for the need of the ships; and journeyed into Cornwall, most wretched of kings in those days. And Arthur besieged Winchester right closely, and slew all the people—there was sorrow enough—the young and the old, all he slew. When the folk was all dead, the town burned up, then he had the walls smashed to bits. Then there came to pass what Merlin had formerly said: "Wretched shalt thou be, Winchester! The earth shall swallow thee!" Thus spoke Merlin, who was a great prophet.

The queen lay at York; never was she so sad; that was Guinevere the queen, fairest of women. She heard true words said, how often Modred fled, and how Arthur pursued him. Woe was to her the while that she was alive. Out of York she went by night, and drew toward Cærleon, as quickly as she could. There she brought by night two of her knights; and men covered her head with a holy veil, and she was there a nun, saddest of women. Then men knew not of the queen where she had gone, and not for many years after did man truly know whether she were dead or how she had gone away, or whether she herself was drowned in the water.

Modred was in Cornwall and gathered many knights. To Ireland he sent speedily his messengers; to the land of the Saxons he sent speedily his messengers; to Scotland he sent speedily his messengers; he ordered them all to come at once who would have land or silver or gold or possessions or land; in each way he himself warned every man—so doth each wise man upon whom need cometh.

Arthur heard, angriest of kings, that Modred was in Cornwall with a huge army, and would wait there until Arthur approached. Arthur sent messengers over all his kingdom, and commanded all who were alive in the land to come, since to fight and to bear arms was good, and whoso refused whom the king commanded, the king would consume in the land, utterly. Innumerable folk came toward the army, on horse and on foot, like the falling rain.

Arthur marched to Cornwall with a huge army. Modred heard of that, and advanced toward him with innumerable folk—many were doomed. By the Tamar they came together, the place called Camelford; ever more the very word shall last. And at Camelford were gathered sixty thousand, and more thousands too. Modred was their leader.

Then thither went Arthur, the mighty, riding, with innumerable folk—doomed though they were. By the Tamar they met; raised their standards; marched together; drew their long swords, and hacked at the helmets. Fire sprang out; spears were shattered; shields began to break; shafts broke in pieces. There fought innumerable folk together. Tamar was in flood with unmeasured blood. There could no man in the fight know any warrior, neither who did worse nor who did better, so confused was the battle. For each slew forthright, were he servant, were he knight. Then was Modred slain and deprived of his life, and all his knights were slain in the fight. There were slain all the bold, Arthur's warriors, high and low, and all the Britons of Arthur's board, and all his followers of many kingdoms. And Arthur was grievously wounded with a broad battle-spear; fifteen fearful wounds he had; in the smallest one might thrust two gloves. Then no more remained in the fight of two hundred thousand men who lay there hewn in pieces, except Arthur the king alone, and two of his knights.

Arthur was sorely wounded. Then there came to him a youth who was one of his kin; he was Cador's son, the earl of Cornwall; Constantine the youth was called, and he was dear to the king. Arthur, as he lay on the ground, looked at him, and said these words with heavy heart: "Constantine, thou art welcome; thou wert Cador's son. I bequeath thee here my kingdom, and guard thou my Britons—ever unto thy life's end, and maintain all the laws that have stood in my days, and all the good laws that stood in Uther's day. And I will fare to Avalon, to the fairest of all maidens—to Argante the queen, an elf most beautiful, and she shall make all my wounds sound, make me whole with healing draughts. And afterwards I shall come to my kingdom, and dwell with the Britons in great bliss."

Even as he spoke there came from the sea a short boat, urged on by the waves, and two women therein, wondrously formed. And they took Arthur anon, and bore him quickly and laid him softly down, and departed.

Then did it come to pass what Merlin had formerly said, that great sadness would come from Arthur's departure. The Britons believe yet that he is alive and dwells in Avalon with the fairest of all elves; and the Britons ever expect that Arthur will return. Was never the man born, chosen ever by any lady, that truly knows how to tell more of Arthur. But formerly there was a sage called Merlin; he said—his sayings were true—that Arthur should yet come to help the English.

c. 1205.

BESTIARY

The Lion's Nature

The lion stands on a hill. And when he hears man hunting, or by the smell in his nose scents him near, by whatever way he wishes he goes down to the valley. All his footsteps he fills after him; he drags dust with his tail as he steps down, either dust or dew, so that he cannot be found. He pushes on down to his den, where he will hide himself.

Another habit he has. When he is born, the lion lies still, does not stir out of sleep, until the sun has shone three times about him. Then his father arouses him with the noise that he makes.

The lion has a third habit: when he lies down to sleep he never closes the lids of his eyes.

Signification

High indeed is that hill, the kingdom of heaven. Our Lord is the lion who dwells there above. Just how it pleased him to light on earth may devil never know, be he ever so keen a hunter, how he came down, and how he took up his dwelling in that sweet maiden, Mary by name, who bore him as man.

When our Lord was dead, and buried as he wished, in a stone he lay still until the third day came. His father helped him so that he arose then from the dead to preserve us for life. He waked according to his will, as a shepherd for his flock. He is the shepherd, we are sheep. He will shield us if we hearken to his word and never go astray.

THE WHALE'S NATURE

The whale is a fish, the greatest that is in the water. This you would say if you saw it when it floated, that it is an island that rests on the strand. This fish is huge, and when he is hungry he gapes wide. Out of his throat he sends a breath, the sweetest thing on earth. Therefore other fish draw near him; when they feel it they are happy. They come and hover in his mouth; of his trickery they know nothing. This whale then closes his jaws, these fish he sucks in. The small he will thus deceive; the great he may not seize.

This fish lives on the bottom of the sea and lives there ever hale and sound until the time comes that a storm stirs up the sea, when summer and winter fight. He may not live down there, so troubled is the bottom of the sea; and he cannot live there at that time. But he rises up and lies still. While the weather is so ill to the ships that are driven on the sea, loath is death and dear is life. They look about and see this fish—an island they think it is. Therefore they are very glad and with their might they draw toward it, fasten the ship and all climb up. They begin to make a bright fire from stone and steel and tinder on this wonder, and warm themselves and eat and drink. The fire he feels and makes them sink, for soon he dives down to the bottom. He destroys them all without a wound.

SIGNIFICATION

This devil is great with will and might, such as witches have in their power. He causes men to hunger and be thirsty, and to have many other sinful lusts. He draws men to him with his breath; whoso follows

him finds disgrace. They are the ones of little faith;
the great he may not draw to him. The great, I mean
the steadfast in right belief regarding body and spirit.
Whoever listens to devil's lore in the end shall sorely
rue. Whoever fastens his hope on him shall follow him
to dim hell.

c. 1225 (?)

SIR JOHN MANDEVILLE (d. 1372?)

THE VOYAGE AND TRAVEL

FROM THE PROLOGUE—ON HIMSELF

I, JOHN MANDEVILLE, knight, albeit I be not worthy,
that was born in England in the town of Saint Albans,
passed the sea, in the year of our Lord Jesus Christ
1322, on Saint Michael's Day; and have been a long
time over the sea, and have seen and gone through many
diverse lands and many provinces and kingdoms and
isles, and have passed through Tartary, Persia, Armenia the little and the great; through Lybia, Chaldea,
and a great part of Ethiopia; through the land of the
Amazons, India the less and the more, a great part;
and throughout many other isles that are about India,
where dwell many diverse folks of diverse manners and
laws, and of diverse shapes of men. Of which lands and
isles I shall speak more plainly hereafter. And I shall
describe to you some part of the things that are there,
when time shall be after it may best come to my mind,
and especially for them that will and are in purpose
to visit the holy city of Jerusalem, and the holy places
thereabout. And I shall tell the way, that they may
keep to it thither. For I have often times passed and

ridden over the way with good company of many lords; God be thanked!

And you shall understand that I have put this book out of Latin into French, and translated it again out of French into English, that every man of my nation may understand it. But lords and knights and other noble and worthy men who know Latin but little and have been beyond the sea know and understand, if I err in describing, for forgetting, or else, that they may redress it and amend it. For things passed out of long time from a man's mind or from his sight turn soon into forgetting, because the mind of man may not be comprehended or withholden, for the frailty of mankind.

(Having described to the reader the way from England to Constantinople, and various places in the Holy Land, the author calls the attention of the reader to various marvels.)

THE DRY TREE

And two miles from Hebron is the grave of Lot, that was Abraham's brother. And a little from Hebron is the Mount of Mambre, of the which the valley taketh its name. And there is a tree of oak that the Saracens call *dirp*, that is of Abraham's time, the which men call the *dry tree*. And they say that it hath been there since the beginning of the world, and was some time green and bore leaves, unto the time that our Lord died on the Cross, and then it dried; and so did all the trees that were then in the world. And some say, by their prophecies, that a lord and prince of the west side of the world shall win the Land of Promise, that is the Holy Land, with help of Christian men; and he shall have sung a mass under that tree, and then the tree shall wax green and bear both fruit and leaves. And through that miracle many Saracens and Jews shall be turned to Christian faith. And therefore they do great worship thereto, and keep it full busily. And albeit so, that it be dry, nevertheless it beareth great virtue; for certainly he that hath a tittle thereof upon him, it healeth him of the falling evil, and his horse shall not be afoundered. And many other virtues it hath, wherefore men hold it full precious.

THE FIELD ENFLOWERED

From Hebron men go to Bethlehem in half a day, for it is but five miles. Bethlehem is a little city, long and narrow and well walled, and on each side enclosed with good ditches.—And toward the east end of the city is a full fair church and a gracious; and it hath many towers, pinnacles, and corners, full strong and curiously made, and within that church are forty-four pillars of marble, great and fair. And between the city and the church is the Field Enflowered. For a fair maiden was blamed with wrong and slandered—for which cause she was doomed to the death, and to be burned in that place, to which she was led. And as the fire began to burn about her she made her prayers to our Lord, that as she truly was not guilty of that sin he would help her, and make it known to all men of his merciful grace. And when she had thus said, she entered into the fire; and at once was the fire quenched and out. And the brands that were burning became red roses; and the brands that were not kindled became white roses. And these were the first rosebushes and roses, both white and red, that ever any man saw. And thus was this maiden saved by the grace of God. And therefore is that field called the Field of God Enflowered, for it was full of roses.

The Dead Sea

And from Jericho, a three mile, is the Dead Sea. The water of that sea is full bitter and salt, and if the earth were made moist and wet with that water it would never bear fruit. And the earth and the land change often their color. And it casteth out of the water a thing that men call asphalt; also great pieces, as the greatness of a horse, every day and on all sides.—It is called the Dead Sea, for it runneth not, but is ever immovable. And neither man, beast, nor anything that beareth life in him may die in that Sea; and that hath been proved many times by men who deserved to die, who had been cast therein, and left therein three days or four, and they could never die therein; for it receiveth nothing within itself that beareth life. And no man drinketh of the water for bitterness. And if a man cast iron therein it will float above. And if men cast a feather therein, it will sink to the bottom; and these things are against nature. And also the cities that were lost, because of sin. And there beside grow trees that bear full fair apples, and fair of color to behold; but whoso breaketh them or cutteth them in two, he shall find within them coals and cinders, in token that, by the wrath of God, the cities and the land were burned and sunk into hell.

On Diamonds

And in the land of Macedonia men find diamonds also. But the best and most precious are in India. And men find many times hard diamonds in a mass that cometh out of gold, when men purify it and refine it from the mine; men break that mass into small pieces. And some times it happeneth that men find some as great as peas, and some less; and they are as hard as those of India. And albeit that men find good diamonds in India, nevertheless men find them more commonly upon the rocks in the sea and upon hills where the mine of gold is. And they grow many of them together, one little, another great. And there are some of the greatness of a bean, and some as great as a hazel nut. And they are square and pointed of their own nature, both above and beneath, without working of man's hand. And they grow together, male and female. And they are nourished with the dew of heaven. And they conceive and bring forth small children, who multiply and grow all the year. I have often times proved that if a man keep them with a little of the rock and wet them with May dew very often, they will grow every year, and the small will wax great. For just as the fine pearl congealeth and waxeth great of the dew of heaven, right so doth the very diamond; and just as the pearl of its own nature taketh roundness, right so the diamond, by virtue of God, taketh squareness. And men should carry the diamond on their left side; for it is of greater virtue then than on the right side. For the strength of their growing is toward the north, that is the left side of the world; and the left part of man is when he turneth his face to the east. And if you like to know the virtues of the diamonds (as men may find in the *Lapidary,* which many men know not at all) I shall tell you, as they beyond the sea say and affirm, from whom come all science and philosophy. He that beareth the diamond upon him, it giveth him hardness and manhood, and it keepeth the limbs of his body whole. It giveth him victory over his enemies, in play and in war, if his cause be rightful. And it keepeth him that beareth it in good wit, and it keepeth him from strife and riot, from sorrows and enchantments and from phantasies and illusions of wicked spirits. And if any cursed witch or enchanter would bewitch him that beareth the diamond, all that sorrow and mischance shall turn to himself, through virtue of that stone. And also no wild beast dare assail the man that beareth it on him. Also the diamond should be given freely, without coveting and without begging, and then it is of greater virtue. And it maketh a man stronger and more sad against his enemies. And it healeth him that is lunatic, and him that the Fiend pursueth or travaileth. And if venom or poison be brought into the presence of the diamond, at once it beginneth to wax moist and to sweeten———.

OF THE PEPPER TREES IN THE ORIENT

And you shall understand that the pepper groweth in manner as doth a wild vine that is planted fast by the trees of that wood for to sustain it by, as doth the vine. And the fruit thereof hangeth in the manner of raisins. And the tree is so thickly laden that it seemeth that it would break. And when it is ripe it is all green as though it were ivy berries. And then men cut them, as men do vines, and then they put them upon an oven, and there they wax black and crisp. And there are three manners of pepper, all upon one tree: long pepper, black pepper, and white pepper. The long pepper men call *sorbotyn;* and the black pepper is called *fulfulle,* and the white pepper is called *bano.* The long pepper cometh first, when the leaf beginneth to come, and it is like the flowers of the hazel that come before the leaf and hang low. And after cometh the black with the leaf in the manner of clusters of raisins, all green; and when men have gathered it, then come the white, which is somewhat less than the black; and of that men bring but little into this country, for they beyond withholden it for themselves, for it is more attempered by nature than is the black. In that country are many kinds of serpents and other vermin, for the great heat of the sun and of the pepper. And some men say that when they will gather the pepper, they make a fire and burn about to make the serpents to flee. But save their grace of all that say so! For if they burned about the trees that bear, the pepper should be burned, and it would dry up all the virtue, as of any other thing; and then they would do themselves much harm, and they could never quench the fire. But thus they do: they anoint their hands and their feet with a juice made of snails and of other things made therefore, of which the serpents and the venomous beasts hate and dread the savor; and that maketh them flee before them because of the smell, and then they gather it safely enough.

SIR GAWAIN AND THE GREEN KNIGHT

I

AFTER the siege and the assault of Troy, when that burg was destroyed and burnt to ashes, and the traitor tried for his treason, the noble Æneas and his kin sailed forth to become princes and patrons of well-nigh all the Western Isles. Thus Romulus built Rome (and gave to the city his own name, which it bears even to this day); and Ticius turned him to Tuscany; and Langobard raised him up dwellings in Lombardy; and Felix Brutus sailed far over the French flood, and founded the kingdom of Britain, wherein have been war and waste and wonder, and bliss and bale, ofttimes since.

And in that kingdom of Britain have been wrought more gallant deeds than in any other; but of all British kings Arthur was the most valiant, as I have heard tell; therefore will I set forth a wondrous adventure that fell out in his time. And if ye will listen to me, but for a little while, I will tell it even as it stands in story stiff and strong, fixed in the letter, as it hath long been known in the land.

King Arthur lay at Camelot upon a Christmas-tide, with many a gallant lord and lovely lady, and all the noble brotherhood of the Round Table. There they held rich revels with gay talk and jest; one while they would ride forth to joust and tourney, and again back to the court to make carols; for there was the feast holden fifteen days with all the mirth that men could devise, song and glee, glorious to hear, in the daytime, and dancing at night. Halls and chambers were crowded with noble guests, the bravest of knights and the loveliest of ladies, and Arthur himself was the comeliest king that ever held a court. For all this fair folk were in their youth, the fairest and most fortunate under heaven, and the king himself of such fame that it were hard now to name so valiant a hero.

Now the New Year had but newly come in, and on that day a double portion was served on the high table to all the noble guests, and thither came the king with all his knights, when the service in the chapel had been sung to an end. And they greeted each other for the New Year, and gave rich gifts, the one to the other (and they that received them were not wroth, that may ye well believe!), and the maidens laughed and made mirth till it was time to get them to meat. Then they washed and sat them down to the feasting in fitting rank and order, and Guinevere the queen, gaily clad, sat on the high daïs. Silken was her seat, with a fair canopy over her head, of rich tapestries of Tars, embroidered, and studded with costly gems; fair she was to look upon, with her shining gray eyes, a fairer woman might no man boast himself of having seen.

But Arthur would not eat till all were served, so full of joy and gladness was he, even as a child; he liked not either to lie long, or to sit long at meat, so worked upon him his young blood and his wild brain. And another custom he had also, that came of his nobility, that he would never eat upon an high day till he had been advised of some knightly deed, or some strange and marvelous tale, of his ancestors, or of arms, or of other ventures. Or till some stranger knight should seek of him leave to joust with one of the Round Table, that they might set their lives in jeopardy, one against another, as fortune might favor them. Such was the king's custom when he sat in hall at each high feast with his noble knights; therefore on that New Year tide, he abode, fair of face, on the throne, and made much mirth withal.

Thus the king sat before the high tables, and spake of many things; and there good Sir Gawain was seated by Guinevere the queen, and on her other side sat Agravain, à la dure main; both were the king's sister's sons and full gallant knights. And at the end of the table was Bishop Bawdewyn, and Ywain, King Urien's son, sat at the other side alone. These were worthily served on the daïs, and at the lower tables sat many valiant knights. Then they bare the first course with the blast of trumpets and waving of banners, with the sound of drums and pipes, of song and lute, that many a heart was uplifted at the melody. Many were the dainties, and rare the meats; so great was the plenty they might scarce find room on the board to set on the dishes. Each helped himself as he liked best, and to each two were twelve dishes, with great plenty of beer and wine.

Now I will say no more of the service, but that ye

may know there was no lack, for there drew near a
venture that the folk might well have left their labor
to gaze upon. As the sound of the music ceased, and the
first course had been fitly served, there came in at the
hall door one terrible to behold, of stature greater than
any on earth; from neck to loin so strong and thickly
made, and with limbs so long and so great that he
seemed even as a giant. And yet he was but a man, only
the mightiest that might mount a steed; broad of chest
and shoulders and slender of waist, and all his features
of like fashion; but men marveled much at his color, for
he rode even as a knight, yet was green all over.

For he was clad all in green, with a straight coat, and
a mantle above; all decked and lined with fur was the
cloth and the hood that was thrown back from his locks
and lay on his shoulders. Hose had he of the same
green, and spurs of bright gold with silken fastenings
richly worked; and all his vesture was verily green.
Around his waist and his saddle were bands with fair
stones set upon silken work, 'twere too long to tell of
all the trifles that were embroidered thereon—birds and
insects in gay gauds of green and gold. All the trappings of his steed were of metal of like enamel, even
the stirrups that he stood in stained of the same, and
stirrups and saddle-bows alike gleamed and shone with
green stones. Even the steed on which he rode was of
the same hue, a green horse, great and strong, and hard
to hold, with broidered bridle, meet for the rider.

The knight was thus gaily dressed in green, his hair
falling around his shoulders; on his breast hung a beard,
as thick and green as a bush, and the beard and the
hair of his head were clipped all round above his elbows.
The lower part of his sleeves was fastened with clasps
in the same wise as a king's mantle. The horse's mane
was crisp and plaited with many a knot folded in with

gold thread about the fair green, here a twist of the hair, here another of gold. The tail was twined in like manner, and both were bound about with a band of bright green set with many a precious stone; then they were tied aloft in a cunning knot, whereon rang many bells of burnished gold. Such a steed might no other ride, nor had such ever been looked upon in that hall ere that time; and all who saw that knight spake and said that a man might scarce abide his stroke.

The knight bore no helm nor hauberk, neither gorget nor breast-plate, neither shaft nor buckler to smite nor to shield, but in one hand he had a holly-bough, that is greenest when the groves are bare, and in his other an axe, huge and uncomely, a cruel weapon in fashion, if one would picture it. The head was an ell-yard long, the metal all of green steel and gold, the blade burnished bright, with a broad edge, as well shapen to shear as a sharp razor. The steel was set into a strong staff, all bound round with iron, even to the end, and engraved with green in cunning work. A lace was twined about it, that looped at the head, and all adown the handle it was clasped with tassels on buttons of bright green richly broidered.

The knight rideth through the entrance of the hall, driving straight to the high daïs, and greeted no man, but looked ever upwards; and the first words he spake were, "Where is the ruler of this folk? I would gladly look upon that hero, and have speech with him." He cast his eyes on the knights, and mustered them up and down, striving ever to see who of them was of most renown.

Then was there great gazing to behold that chief, for each man marveled what it might mean that a knight and his steed should have even such a hue as the green grass; and that seemed even greener than green enamel on bright gold. All looked on him as he stood, and drew near unto him, wondering greatly what he might be; for many marvels had they seen, but none such as this, and phantasm and faërie did the folk deem it. Therefore were the gallant knights slow to answer, and gazed astounded, and sat stone still in a deep silence through that goodly hall, as if a slumber were fallen upon them. I deem it was not all for doubt, but some for courtesy that they might give ear unto his errand.

Then Arthur beheld this adventurer before his high daïs, and knightly he greeted him, for fearful was he never. "Sir," he said, "thou art welcome to this place —lord of this hall am I, and men call me Arthur. Light thee down, and tarry awhile, and what thy will is, that shall we learn after."

"Nay," quoth the stranger, "so help me he that sitteth on high, 'twas not mine errand to tarry any while in this dwelling; but the praise of this thy folk and thy city is lifted up on high, and thy warriors are holden for the best and the most valiant of those who ride mail-clad to the fight. The wisest and the worthiest of this world are they, and well proven in all knightly sports. And here, as I have heard tell, is fairest courtesy; therefore have I come hither as at this time. Ye may be sure by the branch that I bear here that I come in peace, seeking no strife. For had I willed to journey in warlike guise I have at home both hauberk and helm, shield and shining spear, and other weapons to mine hand, but since I seek no war, my raiment is that of peace. But if thou be as bold as all men tell, thou wilt freely grant me the boon I ask."

And Arthur answered, "Sir Knight, if thou cravest battle here thou shalt not fail for lack of a foe."

And the knight answered, "Nay, I ask no fight; in faith here on the benches are but beardless children;

were I clad in armor on my steed there is no man here
might match me. Therefore I ask in this court but a
Christmas jest, for that it is Yule-tide, and New Year,
and there are here many fain for sport. If any one in
this hall holds himself so hardy, so bold both of blood
and brain, as to dare strike me one stroke for another, I
will give him as a gift this axe, which is heavy enough,
in sooth, to handle as he may list, and I will abide the
first blow, unarmed as I sit. If any knight be so bold
as to prove my words, let him come swiftly to me here,
and take this weapon; I quit claim to it, he may keep it
as his own, and I will abide his stroke, firm on the floor.
Then shalt thou give me the right to deal him another,
the respite of a year and a day shall he have. Now
haste, and let see whether any here dare say aught."

Now if the knights had been astounded at the first,
yet stiller were they all, high and low, when they had
heard his words. The knight on his steed straightened
himself in the saddle, and rolled his eyes fiercely round
the hall; red they gleamed under his green and bushy
brows. He frowned and twisted his beard, waiting to
see who should rise, and when none answered he cried
aloud in mockery, "What, is this Arthur's hall, and these
the knights whose renown hath run through many
realms? Where are now your pride and your conquests,
your wrath, and anger, and mighty words? Now are the
praise and the renown of the Round Table overthrown
by one man's speech, since all keep silence for dread
ere ever they have seen a blow!"

With that he laughed so loudly that the blood rushed
to the king's fair face for very shame; he waxed wroth,
as did all his knights, and sprang to his feet, and drew
near to the stranger and said, "Now by heaven, foolish
is thy asking, and thy folly shall find its fitting answer.
I know no man aghast as thy great words. Give me

here thine axe and I shall grant thee the boon thou hast asked." Lightly he sprang to him and caught at his hand, and the knight, fierce of aspect, lighted down from his charger.

Then Arthur took the axe and gripped the haft, and swung it round, ready to strike. And the knight stood before him, taller by the head than any in the hall; he stood, and stroked his beard, and drew down his coat, no more dismayed for the king's threats than if one had brought him a drink of wine.

Then Gawain, who sat by the queen, leaned forward to the king and spake, "I beseech ye, my lord, let this venture be mine. Would ye but bid me rise from this seat, and stand by your side, so that my liege lady thought it not ill, then would I come to your counsel before this goodly court. For I think it not seemly when such challenges be made in your hall that ye yourself should undertake it, while there are many bold knights who sit beside ye, none are there, methinks, of readier will under heaven, or more valiant in open field. I am the weakest, I wot, and the feeblest of wit, and it will be the less loss of my life if ye seek sooth. For save that ye are mine uncle, naught is there in me to praise, no virtue is there in my body save your blood, and since this challenge is such folly that it beseems ye not to take it, and I have asked it from ye first, let it fall to me, and if I bear myself ungallantly, then let all this court blame me."

Then they all spake with one voice that the king should leave this venture and grant it to Gawain.

Then Arthur commanded the knight to rise, and he rose up quickly and knelt down before the king, and caught hold of the weapon; and the king loosed his hold of it, and lifted up his hand, and gave him his blessing, and bade him be strong both of heart and hand. "Keep thee well, nephew," quoth Arthur, "that thou give him but the one blow, and if thou redest him rightly I trow thou shalt well abide the stroke he may give thee after."

Gawain stepped to the stranger, axe in hand, and he, never fearing, awaited his coming. Then the Green Knight spake to Sir Gawain, "Make we our covenant ere we go further. First, I ask thee, knight, what is thy name? Tell me truly, that I may know thee."

"In faith," quoth the good knight, "Gawain am I, who give thee this buffet, let what may come of it; and at this time twelvemonth will I take another at thine hand with whatsoever weapon thou wilt, and none other."

Then the other answered again, "Sir Gawain, so may I thrive as I am fain to take this buffet at thine hand," and he quoth further, "Sir Gawain, it liketh me well that I shall take at thy fist that which I have asked here, and thou hast readily and truly rehearsed all the covenant that I asked of the king, save that thou shalt swear me, by thy troth, to seek me thyself wherever thou hopest that I may be found, and win thee such reward as thou dealest me to-day, before this folk."

"Where shall I seek thee?" quoth Gawain. "Where is thy place? By him that made me, I wot never where thou dwellest, nor know I thee, knight, thy court, nor thy name. But teach me truly all that pertaineth thereto, and tell me thy name, and I shall use all my wit to win my way thither, and that I swear thee for sooth, and by my sure troth."

"That is enough in the New Year, it needs no more," quoth the Green Knight to the gallant Gawain, "if I tell thee truly when I have taken the blow, and thou hast smitten me; then will I teach thee of my house and home, and mine own name, then mayest thou ask thy road and keep covenant. And if I waste no words then farest thou the better, for thou canst dwell in thy land, and seek no further. But take now thy toll, and let see how thou strikest."

"Gladly will I," quoth Gawain, handling his axe.

Then the Green Knight swiftly made him ready, he bowed down his head, and laid his long locks on the crown that his bare neck might be seen. Gawain gripped his axe and raised it on high, the left foot he set forward on the floor, and let the blow fall lightly on the bare neck. The sharp edge of the blade sundered the bones, smote through the neck, and clave it in two, so that the edge of the steel bit on the ground, and the fair head fell to the earth that many struck it with their feet as it rolled forth. The blood spurted forth, and glistened on the green raiment, but the knight neither faltered nor fell; he started forward with out-stretched hand, and caught the head, and lifted it up; then he turned to his steed, and took hold of the bridle, set his foot in the stirrup, and mounted. His head he held by the hair, in his hand. Then he seated himself in his saddle as if naught ailed him, and he were not headless. He turned his steed about, the grim corpse bleeding freely the while, and they who looked upon him doubted them much for the covenant.

For he held up the head in his hand, and turned the face towards them that sat on the high daïs, and it lifted up the eyelids and looked upon them and spake as ye shall hear. "Look, Gawain, that thou art ready to go as thou hast promised, and seek loyally till thou find me, even as thou hast sworn in this hall in the hearing of these knights. Come thou, I charge thee, to the Green Chapel; such a stroke as thou hast dealt thou hast deserved, and it shall be promptly paid thee on New Year's morn. Many men know me as the knight of the Green Chapel, and if thou askest, thou shalt not fail to find me. Therefore it behooves thee to come, or to yield thee as recreant."

With that he turned his bridle, and galloped out at the hall door, his head in his hands, so that the sparks flew from beneath his horse's hoofs. Whither he went none knew, no more than they wist whence he had come; and the king and Gawain they gazed and laughed, for in sooth this had proved a greater marvel than any they had known aforetime.

Though Arthur the king was astonished at his heart, yet he let no sign of it be seen, but spake in courteous wise to the fair queen: "Dear lady, be not dismayed, such craft is well suited to Christmas-tide when we seek jesting, laughter, and song, and fair carols of knights and ladies. But now I may well get me to meat, for I have seen a marvel I may not forget." Then he looked on Sir Gawain, and said gaily, "Now, fair nephew, hang up thine axe, since it has hewn enough," and they hung it on the dossal above the daïs, where all men might look on it for a marvel, and by its true token tell of the wonder. Then the twain sat them down together, the king and the good knight, and men served them with a double portion, as was the share of the noblest, with all manner of meat and of minstrelsy. And they spent that day in gladness, but Sir Gawain must well bethink him of the heavy venture to which he had set his hand.

II

This beginning of adventures had Arthur at the New Year; for he yearned to hear gallant tales, though his words were few when he sat at the feast. But now had they stern work on hand. Gawain was glad to begin the jest in the hall, but ye need have no marvel if the end be heavy. For though a man be merry in mind when he has well drunk, yet a year runs full swiftly, and the beginning but rarely matches the end.

For Yule was now over-past, and the year after, each season in its turn following the other. For after Christmas comes crabbed Lent, that will have fish for flesh and simpler cheer. But then the weather of the world chides with winter; the cold withdraws itself, the clouds uplift, and the rain falls in warm showers on the fair plains. Then the flowers come forth, meadows and grove are clad in green, the birds make ready to build, and sing sweetly for solace of the soft summer that follows thereafter. The blossoms bud and blow in the hedgerows rich and rank, and noble notes enough are heard in the fair woods.

After the season of summer, with the soft winds, when zephyr breathes lightly on seeds and herbs, joyous indeed is the growth that waxes thereout when the dew drips from the leaves beneath the blissful glance of the bright sun. But then comes harvest and hardens the grain, warning it to wax ripe ere the winter. The drought drives the dust on high, flying over the face of the land; the angry wind of the welkin wrestles with the sun; the leaves fall from the trees and light upon the ground, and all brown are the groves that but now were green, and ripe is the fruit that once was flower. So the year passes into many yesterdays, and winter comes again, as it needs no sage to tell us.

When the Michaelmas moon was come in with warnings of winter, Sir Gawain bethought him full oft of his perilous journey. Yet till All Hallows Day he lingered with Arthur, and on that day they made a great feast for the hero's sake, with much revel and richness of the Round Table. Courteous knights and comely ladies, all were in sorrow for the love of that knight, and though they spake no word of it, many were joyless for his sake.

And after meat, sadly Sir Gawain turned to his uncle, and spake of his journey, and said, "Liege lord of my life, leave from you I crave. Ye know well how the matter stands without more words; to-morrow am I bound to set forth in search of the Green Knight."

Then came together all the noblest knights, Ywain and Erec, and many another. Sir Dodinel le Sauvage, the Duke of Clarence, Launcelot and Lionel, and Lucan the Good, Sir Bors and Bedivere, valiant knights both, and many another hero, with Sir Mador de la Porte, and they all drew near, heavy at heart, to take counsel with Sir Gawain. Much sorrow and weeping was there in the hall to think that so worthy a knight as Gawain should wend his way to seek a deadly blow, and should no more wield his sword in fight. But the knight made ever good cheer, and said, "Nay, wherefore should I shrink? What may a man do but prove his fate?"

He dwelt there all that day, and on the morn he arose and asked betimes for his armor; and they brought it unto him on this wise: first, a rich carpet was stretched on the floor (and brightly did the gold gear glitter upon it), then the knight stepped upon it, and handled the steel; clad he was in a doublet of silk, with a close hood, lined fairly throughout. Then they set the steel shoes upon his feet, and wrapped his legs with greaves, with polished knee-caps, fastened with knots of gold. Then they cased his thighs in cuisses closed with thongs, and brought him the byrnie of bright steel rings sewn upon a fair stuff. Well burnished braces they set on each arm with good elbow-pieces, and gloves of mail, and all the goodly gear that should shield him in his need. And they cast over all a rich surcoat, and set the golden spurs on his heels, and girt him with a trusty sword fastened with a silken bawdrick. When he was thus clad his harness was costly, for the least loop or latchet gleamed with gold. So armed as he was he hearkened Mass and made his offering at the high altar. Then he came to the king, and the knights of his court, and courteously took leave of lords and ladies, and they kissed him, and commended him to Christ.

With that was Gringalet ready, girt with a saddle that gleamed gaily with many golden fringes, enriched and decked anew for the venture. The bridle was all barred about with bright gold buttons, and all the covertures and trappings of the steed, the crupper and the rich skirts, accorded with the saddle; spread fair with the rich red gold that glittered and gleamed in the rays of the sun.

Then the knight called for his helmet, which was well lined throughout, and set it high on his head, and hasped it behind. He wore a light kerchief over the ventail, that was broidered and studded with fair gems on a broad silken ribbon, with birds of gay color, and many a turtle and true-lover's knot interlaced thickly, even as many a maiden had wrought diligently for seven winters long. But the circlet which crowned his helmet was yet more precious, being adorned with a device in diamonds. Then they brought him his shield, which was of bright red, with the pentangle painted thereon in gleaming gold. And why that noble prince bare the pentangle I am minded to tell you, though my tale tarry thereby. It is a sign that Solomon set ere-while, as betokening truth; for it is a figure with five points and each line overlaps the other, and nowhere hath it beginning or end, so that in English it is called "the endless knot." And therefore was it well suiting to this knight and to his arms, since Gawain was faithful in five and five-fold, for pure was he as gold, void of all villainy and endowed with all virtues. Therefore he bare the pentangle on shield and surcoat as truest of heroes and gentlest of knights.

For first he was faultless in his five senses; and his five fingers never failed him; and all his trust upon earth was in the five wounds that Christ bare on the cross, as the Creed tells. And wherever this knight found himself in stress of battle he deemed well that he drew his strength from the five joys which the Queen of Heaven had of her Child. And for this cause did he bear an image of Our Lady on the one half of his shield, that whenever he looked upon it he might not lack for aid. And the fifth five that the hero used were frankness and fellowship above all, purity and courtesy that never failed him, and compassion that surpasses all; and in these five virtues was that hero wrapped and clothed. And all these, five-fold, were linked one in the other, so that they had no end, and were fixed on five points that never failed, neither at any side were they joined or sundered, nor could ye find beginning or end. And therefore on his shield was the knot shapen, red-gold upon red, which is the pure pentangle. Now was Sir Gawain ready, and he took his lance in hand, and bade them all farewell, he deemed it had been for ever.

Then he smote the steed with his spurs, and sprang on his way, so that sparks flew from the stones after him. All that saw him were grieved at heart, and said one to the other, "By Christ, 'tis great pity that one of such noble life should be lost! I' faith, 'twere not easy to find his equal upon earth. The king had done better to have wrought more warily. Yonder knight should have been made a duke; a gallant leader of men is he, and such a fate had beseemed him better than to be hewn in pieces at the will of an elfish man, for mere pride. Who ever knew a king to take such counsel as to risk his knights on a Christmas jest?" Many were the tears that flowed from their eyes when that goodly knight rode from the hall. He made no delaying, but went his way swiftly, and rode many a wild road, as I heard say in the book.

So rode Sir Gawain through the realm of Logres, on an errand that he held for no jest. Often he lay companionless at night, and must lack the fare that he liked. No comrade had he save his steed, and none save God with whom to take counsel. At length he drew nigh to North Wales, and left the isles of Anglesey on his left hand, crossing over the fords by the foreland over at Holyhead, till he came into the wilderness of Wirral, where but few dwell who love God and man of true heart. And ever he asked, as he fared, of all whom he met, if they had heard any tidings of a Green Knight in the country thereabout, or of a Green Chapel? And all answered him, Nay, never in their lives had they seen any man of such a hue. And the knight wended his way by many a strange road and many a rugged path, and the fashion of his countenance changed full often ere he saw the Green Chapel.

Many a cliff did he climb in that unknown land, where afar from his friends he rode as a stranger. Never did he come to a stream or a ford but he found a foe before him, and that one so marvelous, so foul and fell, that it behooved him to fight. So many wonders did that knight behold, that it were too long to tell the tenth part of them. Sometimes he fought with dragons and wolves; sometimes with wild men that dwelt in the rocks; another while with bulls, and bears, and wild boars, or with giants of the high moorland that drew near to him. Had he not been a doughty knight, enduring, and of well-proved valor, and a servant of God, doubtless he had been slain, for he was oft in danger of death. Yet he cared not so much for the strife; what he deemed worse was when the cold clear water was shed from the clouds, and froze ere it fell on the fallow ground. More nights than enough he slept in his harness on the bare rocks, near slain with the sleet, while the stream leapt bubbling from the crest of the hills, and hung in hard icicles over his head.

Thus in peril and pain, and many a hardship, the knight rode alone till Christmas Eve, and in that tide he made his prayer to the Blessed Virgin that she would guide his steps and lead him to some dwelling. On that morning he rode by a hill, and came into a thick forest, wild and drear; on each side were high hills, and thick woods below them of great hoar oaks, a hundred together, of hazel and hawthorn with their trailing boughs intertwined, and rough ragged moss spreading everywhere. On the bare twigs the birds chirped piteously, for pain of the cold. The knight upon Gringalet rode lonely beneath them, through marsh and mire, much troubled at heart lest he should fail to see the service of the Lord, who on that self-same night was born of a maiden for the cure of our grief; and therefore he said, sighing, "I beseech thee, Lord, and Mary thy gentle Mother, for some shelter where I may hear Mass, and thy matins at morn. This I ask meekly, and thereto I pray my Paternoster, Ave, and Credo." Thus he rode praying, and lamenting his misdeeds, and he crossed himself, and said, "May the Cross of Christ speed me."

Now that knight had crossed himself but thrice ere he was aware in the wood of a dwelling within a moat, above a lawn, on a mound surrounded by many mighty trees that stood round the moat. 'Twas the fairest castle that ever a knight owned; built in a meadow with a park all about it, and a spiked palisade, closely driven, that enclosed the trees for more than two miles. The knight was ware of the hold from the side, as it shone through the oaks. Then he lifted off his helmet, and thanked Christ and Saint Julian that they had courteously granted his prayer, and hearkened to his cry. "Now," quoth the knight, "I beseech ye, grant me fair hostel." Then he pricked Gringalet with his golden spurs, and rode gaily towards the great gate, and came swiftly to the bridge end.

The bridge was drawn up and the gates close shut; the walls were strong and thick, so that they might fear no tempest. The knight on his charger abode on the bank of the deep double ditch that surrounded the castle. The walls were set deep in the water, and rose aloft to a wondrous height; they were of hard hewn stone up to the corbels, which were adorned beneath the battlements with fair carvings, and turrets set in between with many a loophole; a better barbican Sir Gawain had never looked upon. And within he beheld the high wall, with its tower and many windows with carven cornices, and chalk-white chimneys on the turreted roofs that shone fair in the sun. And everywhere, thickly scattered on the castle battlements, were pinnacles, so many that it seemed as if it were all wrought out of paper, so white was it.

The knight on his steed deemed it fair enough, if he might come to be sheltered within it to lodge there while that the holy-day lasted. He called aloud, and soon there came a porter of kindly countenance, who stood on the wall and greeted this knight and asked his errand.

"Good sir," quoth Gawain, "wilt thou go mine errand to the high lord of the castle, and crave for me lodging?"

"Yea, by Saint Peter," quoth the porter. "In sooth

I trow that ye be welcome to dwell here so long as it may like ye."

Then he went, and came again swiftly, and many folk with him to receive the knight. They let down the great drawbridge, and came forth and knelt on their knees on the cold earth to give him worthy welcome. They held wide open the great gates, and courteously he bade them rise, and rode over the bridge. Then men came to him and held his stirrup while he dismounted, and took and stabled his steed. There came down knights and squires to bring the guest with joy to the hall. When he raised his helmet there were many to take it from his hand, fain to serve him, and they took from him sword and shield.

Sir Gawain gave good greeting to the noble and the mighty men who came to do him honor. Clad in his shining armor they led him to the hall, where a great fire burnt brightly on the floor; and the lord of the household came forth from his chamber to meet the hero fitly. He spake to the knight, and said: "Ye are welcome to do here as it likes ye. All that is here is your own to have at your will and disposal."

"Gramercy!" quoth Gawain, "may Christ requite ye."

As friends that were fain each embraced the other; and Gawain looked on the knight who greeted him so kindly, and thought 'twas a bold warrior that owned that burg.

Of mighty stature he was, and of high age; broad and flowing was his beard, and of a bright hue. He was stalwart of limb, and strong in his stride, his face fiery red, and his speech free: in sooth he seemed one well fitted to be a leader of valiant men.

Then the lord led Sir Gawain to a chamber, and commanded folk to wait upon him, and at his bidding there came men enough who brought the guest to a fair bower. The bedding was noble, with curtains of pure silk wrought with gold, and wondrous coverings of fair cloth all embroidered. The curtains ran on ropes with rings of red gold, and the walls were hung with carpets of Orient, and the same spread on the floor. There with mirthful speeches they took from the guest his byrnie and all his shining armor, and brought him rich robes of the choicest in its stead. They were long and flowing, and became him well, and when he was clad in them all who looked on the hero thought that surely God had never made a fairer knight: he seemed as if he might be a prince without peer in the field where men strive in battle.

Then before the hearth-place, whereon the fire burned, they made ready a chair for Gawain, hung about with cloth and fair cushions; and there they cast around him a mantle of brown samite, richly embroidered and furred within with costly skins of ermine, with a hood of the same, and he seated himself in that rich seat, and warmed himself at the fire, and was cheered at heart. And while he sat thus, the serving men set up a table on trestles, and covered it with a fair white cloth, and set thereon salt-cellar, and napkin, and silver spoons; and the knight washed at his will, and set him down to meat.

The folk served him courteously with many dishes seasoned of the best, a double portion. All kinds of fish were there, some baked in bread, some broiled on the embers, some sodden, some stewed and savored with spices, with all sorts of cunning devices to his taste. And often he called it a feast, when they spake gaily to him all together, and said, "Now take ye this penance, and it shall be for your amendment." Much mirth thereof did Sir Gawain make.

Then they questioned that prince courteously of

whence he came; and he told them that he was of the court of Arthur, who is the rich royal king of the Round Table, and that it was Gawain himself who was within their walls, and would keep Christmas with them, as the chance had fallen out. And when the lord of the castle heard those tidings he laughed aloud for gladness, and all men in that keep were joyful that they should be in the company of him to whom belonged all fame, and valor, and courtesy, and whose honor was praised above that of all men on earth. Each said softly to his fellow, "Now shall we see courteous bearing, and the manner of speech befitting courts. What charm lieth in gentle speech shall we learn without asking, since here we have welcomed the fine father of courtesy. God has surely shown us his grace since he sends us such a guest as Gawain! When men shall sit and sing, blithe for Christ's birth, this knight shall bring us to the knowledge of fair manners, and it may be that hearing him we may learn the cunning speech of love."

By the time the knight had risen from dinner it was near nightfall. Then chaplains took their way to the chapel, and rang loudly, even as they should, for the solemn evensong of the high feast. Thither went the lord, and the lady also, and entered with her maidens into a comely closet, and thither also went Gawain. Then the lord took him by the sleeve and led him to a seat, and called him by his name, and told him he was of all men in the world the most welcome. And Sir Gawain thanked him truly, and each kissed the other, and they sat gravely together throughout the service.

Then was the lady fain to look upon that knight; and she came forth from her closet with many fair maidens. The fairest of ladies was she in face, and figure, and coloring, fairer even than Guinevere, so the knight thought. She came through the chancel to greet the hero; another lady held her by the left hand, older than she, and seemingly of high estate, with many nobles about her. But unlike to look upon were those ladies, for if the younger were fair, the elder was yellow. Rich red were the cheeks of the one, rough and wrinkled those of the other; the kerchiefs of the one were broidered with many glistening pearls, her throat and neck bare, and whiter than the snow that lies on the hills; the neck of the other was swathed in a gorget, with a white wimple over her black chin. Her forehead was wrapped in silk with many folds, worked with knots, so that naught of her was seen save her black brows, her eyes, her nose, and her lips, and those were bleared, and ill to look upon. A worshipful lady in sooth one might call her! In figure was she short and broad, and thickly made—far fairer to behold was she whom she led by the hand.

When Gawain beheld that fair lady, who looked at him graciously, with leave of the lord he went towards them, and, bowing low, he greeted the elder, but the younger and fairer he took lightly in his arms, and kissed her courteously, and greeted her in knightly wise. Then she hailed him as friend, and he quickly prayed to be counted as her servant, if she so willed. Then they took him between them, and talking, led him to the chamber, to the hearth, and bade them bring spices, and they brought them in plenty with the good wine that was wont to be drunk at such seasons. Then the lord sprang to his feet and bade them make merry, and took off his hood, and hung it on a spear, and bade him win the worship thereof who should make most mirth that Christmas-tide. "And I shall try, by my faith, to fool it with the best, by the help of my friends, ere I lose my raiment." Thus with gay words the lord made trial to gladden Gawain with jests that night, till it was time to bid them light the tapers, and Sir Gawain took leave of them and gat him to rest.

In the morn when all men call to mind how Christ our Lord was born on earth to die for us, there is joy, for his sake, in all dwellings of the world; and so was there here on that day. For high feast was held, with many dainties and cunningly cooked messes. On the daïs sat gallant men, clad in their best. The ancient dame sat on the high seat, with the lord of the castle beside her. Gawain and the fair lady sat together, even in the midst of the board when the feast was served; and so throughout all the hall each sat in his degree, and was served in order. There was meat, there was mirth, there was much joy, so that to tell thereof would take me too long, though peradventure I might strive to declare it. But Gawain and that fair lady had much joy of each other's company through her sweet words and courteous converse. And there was music made before each prince, trumpets and drums, and merry pipings; each man hearkened his minstrel, and they too hearkened theirs.

So they held high feast that day and the next, and the third day thereafter, and the joy on Saint John's Day was fair to hearken, for 'twas the last of the feast and the guests would depart in the gray of the morning. Therefore they awoke early, and drank wine, and danced fair carols, and at last, when it was late, each man took his leave to wend early on his way. Gawain would bid his host farewell, but the lord took him by the hand, and led him to his own chamber beside the hearth, and there he thanked him for the favor he had shown him in honoring his dwelling at that high season, and gladdening his castle with his fair countenance. "I wis, sir, that while I live I shall be held the worthier that Gawain has been my guest at God's own feast."

"Gramercy, sir," quoth Gawain, "in good faith, all the honor is yours, may the High King give it you, and I am but at your will to work your behest, inasmuch as I am beholden to you in great and small by rights."

Then the lord did his best to persuade the knight to tarry with him, but Gawain answered that he might in no wise do so. Then the host asked him courteously what stern behest had driven him at the holy season from the king's court, to fare all alone, ere yet the feast was ended.

"Forsooth," quoth the knight, "ye say but the truth: 'tis a high quest and a pressing that hath brought me afield, for I am summoned myself to a certain place, and I know not whither in the world I may wend to find it; so help me Christ, I would give all the kingdom of Logres an I might find it by New Year's morn. Therefore, sir, I make request of you that ye tell me truly if ye ever heard word of the Green Chapel, where it may be found, and the Green Knight that keeps it. For I am pledged by solemn compact sworn between us to meet that knight at the New Year if so I were on life; and of that same New Year it wants but little— I' faith, I would look on that hero more joyfully than on any other fair sight! Therefore, by your will, it behooves me to leave you, for I have but barely three days, and I would as fain fall dead as fail of mine errand."

Then the lord quoth, laughing, "Now must ye needs stay, for I will show you your goal, the Green Chapel, ere your term be at an end, have ye no fear! But ye can take your ease, friend, in your bed, till the fourth day, and go forth on the first of the year and come to that place at mid-morn to do as ye will. Dwell here till New Year's Day, and then rise and set forth, and ye shall be set in the way; 'tis not two miles hence."

Then was Gawain glad, and he laughed gaily. "Now

I thank you for this above all else. Now my quest is achieved, I will dwell here at your will, and otherwise do as ye shall ask."

Then the lord took him, and set him beside him, and bade the ladies be fetched for their greater pleasure, tho' between themselves they had solace. The lord, for gladness, made merry jest, even as one who wist not what to do for joy; and he cried aloud to the knight, "Ye have promised to do the thing I bid ye: will ye hold to this behest, here, at once?"

"Yea, forsooth," said that true knight, "while I abide in your burg I am bound by your behest."

"Ye have traveled from far," said the host, "and since then ye have waked with me, ye are not well refreshed by rest and sleep, as I know. Ye shall therefore abide in your chamber, and lie at your ease to-morrow at Mass-tide, and go to meat when ye will with my wife, who shall sit with you, and comfort you with her company till I return; and I shall rise early and go forth to the chase." And Gawain agreed to all this courteously.

"Sir knight," quoth the host, "we will make a covenant. Whatsoever I win in the wood shall be yours, and whatever may fall to your share, that shall ye exchange for it. Let us swear, friend, to make this exchange, however our hap may be, for worse or for better."

"I grant ye your will," quoth Gawain the good; "if ye list so to do, it liketh me well."

"Bring hither the wine-cup, the bargain is made," so said the lord of that castle. They laughed each one, and drank of the wine, and made merry, these lords and ladies, as it pleased them. Then with gay talk and merry jest they rose, and stood, and spoke softly, and kissed courteously, and took leave of each other. With burning torches, and many a serving-man, was each led to his couch; yet ere they gat them to bed the old lord oft repeated their covenant, for he knew well how to make sport.

III

Full early, ere daylight, the folk rose up; the guests who would depart called their grooms, and they made them ready, and saddled the steeds, tightened up the girths, and trussed up their mails. The knights, all arrayed for riding, leapt up lightly, and took their bridles, and each rode his way as pleased him best.

The lord of the land was not the last. Ready for the chase, with many of his men, he ate a sop hastily when he had heard Mass, and then with blast of the bugle fared forth to the field. He and his nobles were to horse ere daylight glimmered upon the earth.

Then the huntsmen coupled their hounds, unclosed the kennel door, and called them out. They blew three blasts gaily on the bugles, the hounds bayed fiercely, and they that would go a-hunting checked and chastised them. A hundred hunters there were of the best, so I have heard tell. Then the trackers gat them to the trysting-place and uncoupled the hounds, and the forest rang again with their gay blasts.

At the first sound of the hunt the game quaked for fear, and fled, trembling, along the vale. They betook them to the heights, but the liers in wait turned them back with loud cries; the harts they let pass them, and the stags with their spreading antlers, for the lord had forbidden they they should be slain, but the hinds and the does they turned back, and drave down into the valleys. Then might ye see much shooting of arrows. As the deer fled under the boughs a broad whistling shaft smote and wounded each sorely, so that, wounded and bleeding, they fell, dying on the banks. The hounds followed swiftly on their tracks, and hunters, blowing the horn, sped after them with ringing shouts as if the cliffs burst asunder. What game escaped those that shot was run down at the outer ring. Thus were they driven on the hills, and harassed at the waters, so well did the men know their work, and the greyhounds were so great and swift that they ran them down as fast as the hunters could slay them. Thus the lord passed the day in mirth and joyfulness, even to nightfall.

So the lord roamed the woods, and Gawain, that good knight, lay ever a-bed, curtained about, under the costly coverlet, while the daylight gleamed on the walls. And as he lay half slumbering, he heard a little sound at the door, and he raised his head, and caught back a corner of the curtain, and waited to see what it might be. It was the lovely lady, the lord's wife; she shut the door softly behind her, and turned towards the bed; and Gawain was shamed, laid him down softly and made as if he slept. And she came lightly to the bedside, within the curtain, and sat herself down beside him, to wait till he wakened. The knight lay there awhile, and marveled within himself what her coming might betoken; and he said to himself, " 'Twere more seemly if I asked her what hath brought her hither." Then he made feint to waken, and turned towards her, and opened his eyes as one astonished, and crossed himself; and she looked on him laughing, with her cheeks red and white, lovely to behold, and small smiling lips.

"Good morrow, Sir Gawain," said that fair lady; "ye are but a careless sleeper, since one can enter thus. Now are ye taken unawares, and lest ye escape me I shall bind you in your bed; of that be ye assured!" Laughing, she spake these words.

"Good morrow, fair lady," quoth Gawain blithely. "I will do your will, as it likes me well. For I yield me readily, and pray your grace, and that is best, by my faith, since I needs must do so." Thus he jested again, laughing. "But an ye would, fair lady, grant me this grace that ye pray your prisoner to rise. I would get me from bed, and array me better, then could I talk with ye in more comfort."

"Nay, forsooth, fair sir," quoth the lady, "ye shall not rise, I will rede ye better. I shall keep ye here, since ye can do no other, and talk with my knight whom I have captured. For I know well that ye are Sir Gawain, whom all the world worships, wheresoever ye may ride. Your honor and your courtesy are praised by lords and ladies, by all who live. Now ye are here and we are alone, my lord and his men are afield; the serving men in their beds, and my maidens also, and the door shut upon us. And since in this hour I have him that all men love, I shall use my time well with speech, while it lasts. Ye are welcome to my company, for it behooves me in sooth to be your servant."

"In good faith," quoth Gawain, "I think me that I am not he of whom ye speak, for unworthy am I of such service as ye here proffer. In sooth, I were glad if I might set myself by word or service to your pleasure; a pure joy would it be to me!"

"In good faith, Sir Gawain," quoth the gay lady, "the praise and the prowess that pleases all ladies I lack them not, nor hold them light; yet are there ladies enough who would liever now have the knight in their hold, as I have ye here, to dally with your courteous words, to bring them comfort and to ease their cares, than much of the treasure and the gold that are theirs.

And now, through the grace of Him who upholds the heavens, I have wholly in my power that which they all desire!"

Thus the lady, fair to look upon, made him great cheer, and Sir Gawain, with modest words, answered her again: "Madam," he quoth, "may Mary requite ye, for in good faith I have found in ye a noble frankness. Much courtesy have other folk shown me, but the honor they have done me is naught to the worship of yourself, who knoweth but good."

"By Mary," quoth the lady, "I think otherwise; for were I worth all the women alive, and had I the wealth of the world in my hand, and might choose me a lord to my liking, then, for all that I have seen in ye, Sir Knight, of beauty and courtesy and blithe semblance, and for all that I have hearkened and hold for true, there should be no knight on earth to be chosen before ye."

"Well I wot," quoth Sir Gawain, "that ye have chosen a better; but I am proud that ye should so prize me, and as your servant do I hold ye my sovereign, and your knight am I, and may Christ reward ye."

So they talked of many matters till mid-morn was past, and ever the lady made as though she loved him, and the knight turned her speech aside. For though she were the brightest of maidens, yet had he forborne to show her love for the danger that awaited him and the blow that must be given without delay.

Then the lady prayed her leave from him, and he granted it readily. And she gave him good-day, with laughing glance, but he must needs marvel at her words:

"Now He that speeds fair speech reward ye this disport; but that ye be Gawain my mind misdoubts me greatly."

"Wherefore?" quoth the knight quickly, fearing lest he had lacked in some courtesy.

And the lady spake: "So true a knight as Gawain is holden, and one so perfect in courtesy, would never have tarried so long with a lady but he would of his courtesy have craved a kiss at parting."

Then quoth Gawain, "I wot I will do even as it may please ye, and kiss at your commandment, as a true knight should who forbears to ask for fear of displeasure."

At that she came near and bent down and kissed the knight, and each commended the other to Christ, and she went forth from the chamber softly.

Then Sir Gawain rose and called his chamberlain and chose his garments, and when he was ready he gat him forth to Mass, and then went to meat, and made merry all day till the rising of the moon, and never had a knight fairer lodging than had he with those two noble ladies, the elder and the younger.

And ever the lord of the land chased the hinds through holt and heath till eventide, and then with much blowing of bugles and baying of hounds they bore the game homeward; and by the time daylight was done all the folk had returned to that fair castle. And when the lord and Sir Gawain met together, then were they both well pleased. The lord commanded them all to assemble in the great hall, and the ladies to descend with their maidens, and there, before them all, he bade the men fetch in the spoil of the day's hunting, and he called unto Gawain, and counted the tale of the beasts, and showed them unto him, and said, "What think ye of this game, Sir Knight? Have I deserved of ye thanks for my woodcraft?"

"Yea, I wis," quoth the other, "here is the fairest spoil I have seen this seven year in the winter season."

"And all this do I give ye, Gawain," quoth the host, "for by accord of covenant ye may claim it as your own."

"That in sooth," quoth the other, "I grant you that same; and I have fairly won this within walls, and with as good will do I yield it to ye." With that he clasped his hands round the lord's neck and kissed him as courteously as he might. "Take ye here my spoils, no more have I won; ye should have it freely, though it were greater than this."

" 'Tis good," said the host, "gramercy thereof. Yet were I fain to know where ye won this same favor, and if it were by your own wit?"

"Nay," answered Gawain, "that was not in the bond. Ask me no more: ye have taken what was yours by right, be content with that."

They laughed and jested together, and sat them down to supper, where they were served with many dainties; and after supper they sat by the hearth, and wine was served out to them; and oft in their jesting they promised to observe on the morrow the same covenant that they had made before and whatever chance might betide, to exchange their spoil, be it much or little, when they met at night. Thus they renewed their bargain before the whole court, and then the night-drink was served, and each courteously took leave of the other and gat him to bed.

By the time the cock had crowed thrice the lord of the castle had left his bed; Mass was sung and meat fitly served. The folk were forth to the wood ere the day broke, with hound and horn they rode over the plain, and uncoupled their dogs among the thorns. Soon they struck on the scent, and the hunt cheered on the hounds who were first to seize it, urging them with shouts. The others hastened to the cry, forty at once, and there rose such a clamor from the pack that the rocks rang again. The huntsmen spurred them on with shouting and blasts of the horn; and the hounds drew together to a thicket betwixt the water and a high crag in the cliff beneath the hillside. There where the rough rock fell ruggedly they, the huntsmen, fared to the finding, and cast about round the hill and the thicket behind them. The knights wist well what beast was within, and would drive him forth with the bloodhounds. And as they beat the bushes, suddenly over the beaters there rushed forth a wondrous great and fierce boar; long since had he left the herd to roam by himself. Grunting, he cast many to the ground, and fled forth at his best speed, without more mischief. The men hallooed loudly and cried, "Hay! Hay!" and blew the horns to urge on the hounds, and rode swiftly after the boar. Many a time did he turn to bay and tare the hounds, and they yelped, and howled shrilly. Then the men made ready their arrows and shot at him, but the points were turned on his thick hide, and the barbs would not bite upon him, for the shafts shivered in pieces, and the head but leapt again wherever it hit.

But when the boar felt the stroke of the arrows he waxed mad with rage, and turned on the hunters and tare many, so that, affrightened, they fled before him. But the lord on a swift steed pursued him, blowing his bugle; as a gallant knight he rode through the woodland chasing the boar till the sun grew low.

So did the hunters this day, while Sir Gawain lay in his bed lapped in rich gear; and the lady forgat not to salute him, for early was she at his side, to cheer his mood.

She came to the bedside and looked on the knight,

and Gawain gave her fit greeting, and she greeted him again with ready words, and sat her by his side and laughed, and with a sweet look she spake to him:

"Sir, if ye be Gawain, I think it a wonder that ye be so stern and cold, and care not for the courtesies of friendship, but if one teach ye to know them ye cast the lesson out of your mind. Ye have soon forgotten what I taught ye yesterday, by all the truest tokens that I knew!"

"What is that?" quoth the knight. "I trow I know not. If it be sooth that ye say, then is the blame mine own."

"But I taught ye of kissing," quoth the fair lady. "Wherever a fair countenance is shown him, it behooves a courteous knight quickly to claim a kiss."

"Nay, my dear," said Sir Gawain, "cease that speech; that durst I not do lest I were denied, for if I were forbidden I wot I were wrong did I further entreat."

"I' faith," quoth the lady merrily, "ye may not be forbid, ye are strong enough to constrain by strength an ye will, were any so discourteous as to give ye denial."

"Yea, by heaven," said Gawain, "ye speak well; but threats profit little in the land where I dwell, and so with a gift that is given not of good will! I am at your commandment to kiss when ye like, to take or to leave as ye list."

Then the lady bent her down and kissed him courteously.

And as they spake together she said, "I would learn somewhat from ye, and ye would not be wroth, for young ye are and fair, and so courteous and knightly as ye are known to be, the head of all chivalry, and versed in all wisdom of love and war—'tis ever told of true knights how they adventured their lives for their

true love, and endured hardships for her favors, and
avenged her with valor, and eased her sorrows, and
brought joy to her bower; and ye are the fairest knight
of your time, and your fame and your honor are everywhere, yet I have sat by ye here twice, and never a word
have I heard of love! Ye who are so courteous and
skilled in such love ought surely to teach one so young
and unskilled some little craft of true love! Why are
ye so unlearned who art otherwise so famous? Or is it
that ye deemed me unworthy to hearken to your teaching? For shame, Sir Knight! I come hither alone and
sit at your side to learn of ye some skill; teach me of
your wit, while my lord is from home."

"In good faith," quoth Gawain, "great is my joy and
my profit that so fair a lady as ye are should deign to
come hither, and trouble ye with so poor a man, and
make sport with your knight with kindly countenance,
it pleaseth me much. But that I, in my turn, should
take it upon me to tell of love and such like matters to
ye who know more by half, or a hundred fold, of such
craft than I do, or ever shall in all my lifetime, by my
troth 'twere folly indeed! I will work your will to the
best of my might as I am bounden, and evermore will I
be your servant, so help me Christ!"

Then often with guile she questioned that knight that
she might win him to woo her, but he defended himself
so fairly that none might in any wise blame him, and
naught but bliss and harmless jesting was there between
them. They laughed and talked together till at last she
kissed him, and craved her leave of him, and went her
way.

Then the knight rose and went forth to Mass, and
afterward dinner was served and he sat and spake with
the ladies all day. But the lord of the castle rode ever
over the land chasing the wild boar, that fled through

the thickets, slaying the best of his hounds and breaking their backs in sunder; till at last he was so weary he might run no longer, but made for a hole in a mound by a rock. He got the mound at his back and faced the hounds, whetting his white tusks and foaming at the mouth. The huntsmen stood aloof, fearing to draw nigh him; so many of them had been already wounded that they were loath to be torn with his tusks, so fierce he was and mad with rage. At length the lord himself came up, and saw the beast at bay, and the men standing aloof. Then quickly he sprang to the ground and drew out a bright blade, and waded through the stream to the boar.

When the beast was aware of the knight with weapon in hand, he set up his bristles and snorted loudly, and many feared for their lord lest he should be slain. Then the boar leapt upon the knight so that beast and man were one atop of the other in the water; but the boar had the worst of it, for the man had marked, even as he sprang, and set the point of his brand to the beast's chest, and drove it up to the hilt, so that the heart was split in twain, and the boar fell snarling, and was swept down by the water to where a hundred hounds seized on him, and the men drew him to shore for the dogs to slay.

Then was there loud blowing of horns and baying of hounds, the huntsmen smote off the boar's head, and hung the carcass by the four feet to a stout pole, and so went on their way homewards. The head they bore before the lord himself, who had slain the beast at the ford by force of his strong hand.

It seemed him o'er long ere he saw Sir Gawain in the hall, and he called, and the guest came to take that which fell to his share. And when he saw Gawain the lord laughed aloud, and bade them call the ladies and the household together, and he showed them the game, and told them the tale, how they hunted the wild boar through the woods, and of his length and breadth and height; and Sir Gawain commended his deeds and praised him for his valor, well proven, for so mighty a beast had he never seen before.

Then they handled the huge head, and the lord said aloud, "Now, Gawain, this game is your own by sure covenant, as ye right well know."

" 'Tis sooth," quoted the knight, "and as truly will I give ye all I have gained." He took the host round the neck, and kissed him courteously twice. "Now are we quits," he said, "this eventide, of all the covenants that we made since I came hither."

And the lord answered, "By Saint Giles, ye are the best I know; ye will be rich in a short space if ye drive such bargains!"

Then they set up the tables on trestles, and covered them with fair cloths, and lit waxen tapers on the walls. The knights sat and were served in the hall, and much game and glee was there round the hearth, with many songs, both at supper and after; song of Christmas, and new carols, with all the mirth one may think of. And ever that lovely lady sat by the knight, and with still stolen looks made such feint of pleasing him, that Gawain marveled much, and was wroth with himself, but he could not for his courtesy return her fair glances, but dealt with her cunningly, however she might strive to wrest the thing.

When they had tarried in the hall so long as it seemed them good, they turned to the inner chamber and the wide hearth-place, and there they drank wine, and the host proffered to renew the covenant for New Year's Eve; but the knight craved leave to depart on the morrow, for it was nigh to the term when he must fulfil his pledge. But the lord would withhold him from so doing, and prayed him to tarry, and said,

"As I am a true knight I swear my troth that ye shall come to the Green Chapel to achieve your task on New Year's morn, long before prime. Therefore abide ye in your bed, and I will hunt in this wood, and hold ye to the covenant to exchange with me against all the spoil I may bring hither. For twice have I tried ye, and found ye true, and the morrow shall be the third time and the best. Make we merry now while we may, and think on joy, for misfortune may take a man whensoever it wills."

Then Gawain granted his request, and they brought them drink, and they gat them with lights to bed.

Sir Gawain lay and slept softly, but the lord, who was keen on woodcraft, was afoot early. After Mass he and his men ate a morsel, and he asked for his steed; all the knights who should ride with him were already mounted before the hall gates.

'Twas a fair frosty morning, for the sun rose red in ruddy vapor, and the welkin was clear of clouds. The hunters scattered them by a forest side, and the rocks rang again with the blast of their horns. Some came on the scent of a fox, and a hound gave tongue; the huntsmen shouted, and the pack followed in a crowd on the trail. The fox ran before them, and when they saw him they pursued him with noise and much shouting, and he wound and turned through many a thick grove, often cowering and hearkening in a hedge. At last by a little ditch he leapt out of a spinney, stole away slily by a copse path, and so out of the wood and away from the hounds. But he went, ere he wist, to a chosen tryst, and three started forth on him at once, so he must needs double back, and betake him to the wood again.

Then was it joyful to hearken to the hounds; when

all the pack had met together and had sight of their game they made as loud a din as if all the lofty cliffs had fallen clattering together. The huntsmen shouted and threatened, and followed close upon him so that he might scarce escape, but Reynard was wily, and he turned and doubled upon them, and led the lord and his men over the hills, now on the slopes, now in the vales, while the knight at home slept through the cold morning beneath his costly curtains.

But the fair lady of the castle rose betimes, and clad herself in a rich mantle that reached even to the ground, left her throat and her fair neck bare, and was bordered and lined with costly furs. On her head she wore no golden circlet, but a network of precious stones, that gleamed and shone through her tresses in clusters of twenty together. Thus she came into the chamber, closed the door after her, and set open a window, and called to him gaily, "Sir Knight, how may ye sleep? The morning is so fair."

Sir Gawain was deep in slumber, and in his dream he vexed him much for the destiny that should befall him on the morrow, when he should meet the knight at the Green Chapel, and abide his blow; but when the lady spake he heard her, and came to himself, and roused from his dream and answered swiftly. The lady came laughing, and kissed him courteously, and he welcomed her fittingly with a cheerful countenance. He saw her so glorious and gaily dressed, so faultless of features and complexion, that it warmed his heart to look upon her.

They spake to each other smiling, and all was bliss and good cheer between them. They exchanged fair words, and much happiness was therein, yet was there a gulf between them, and she might win no more of her knight, for that gallant prince watched well his words—he would neither take her love, nor frankly refuse it.

He cared for his courtesy, lest he be deemed churlish, and yet more for his honor lest he be traitor to his host. "God forbid," quoth he to himself, "that it should so befall." Thus with courteous words did he set aside all the special speeches that came from her lips.

Then spake the lady to the knight, "Ye deserve blame if ye hold not that lady who sits beside ye above all else in the world, if ye have not already a love whom ye hold dearer, and like better, and have sworn such firm faith to that lady that ye care not to loose it—and that am I now fain to believe. And now I pray ye straitly that ye tell me that in truth, and hide it not."

And the knight answered, "By Saint John," (and he smiled as he spake) "no such love have I, nor do I think to have yet awhile."

"That is the worst word I may hear," quoth the lady, "but in sooth I have mine answer; kiss me now courteously, and I will go hence; I can but mourn as a maiden that loves much."

Sighing, she stooped down and kissed him, and then she rose up and spake as she stood, "Now, dear, at our parting do me this grace: give me some gift, if it were but thy glove, that I may bethink me of my knight, and lessen my mourning."

"Now, I wis," quoth the knight, "I would that I had here the most precious thing that I possess on earth that I might leave ye as love-token, great or small, for ye have deserved forsooth more reward than I might give ye. But it is not to your honor to have at this time a glove for reward as gift from Gawain, and I am here on a strange errand, and have no man with me, nor mails with goodly things—that mislikes me much, lady, at this time; but each man must fare as he is taken, if for sorrow and ill."

"Nay, knight highly honored," quoth that lovesome

lady, "though I have naught of yours, yet shall ye have somewhat of mine." With that she reached him a ring of red gold with a sparkling stone therein, that shone even as the sun (wit ye well, it was worth many marks); but the knight refused it, and spake readily,

"I will take no gift, lady, at this time. I have none to give, and none will I take."

She prayed him to take it, but he refused her prayer, and sware in sooth that he would not have it.

The lady was sorely vexed, and said, "If ye refuse my ring as too costly, that ye will not be so highly beholden to me, I will give you my girdle as a lesser gift." With that she loosened a lace that was fastened at her side, knit upon her kirtle under her mantle. It was wrought of green silk, and gold, only braided by the fingers, and that she offered to the knight, and besought him though it were of little worth that he would take it, and he said nay, he would touch neither gold nor gear ere God give him grace to achieve the adventure for which he had come hither. "And therefore, I pray ye, displease ye not, and ask me no longer, for I may not grant it. I am dearly beholden to ye for the favor ye have shown me, and ever, in heat and cold, will I be your true servant."

"Now," said the lady, "ye refuse this silk, for it is simple in itself, and so it seems, indeed; lo, it is small to look upon and less in cost, but whoso knew the virtue that is knit therein he would, peradventure, value it more highly. For whatever knight is girded with this green lace, while he bears it knotted about him there is no man under heaven can overcome him, for he may not be slain for any magic on earth."

Then Gawain bethought him, and it came into his heart that this were a jewel for the jeopardy that awaited him when he came to the Green Chapel to seek the return blow—could he so order it that he should escape unslain, 'twere a craft worth trying. Then he bare with her chiding, and let her say her say, and she pressed the girdle on him and prayed him to take it, and he granted her prayer, and she gave it him with good will, and besought him for her sake never to reveal it but to hide it loyally from her lord; and the knight agreed that never should any man know it, save they two alone. He thanked her often and heartily, and she kissed him for the third time.

Then she took her leave of him, and when she was gone Sir Gawain rose, and clad him in rich attire, and took the girdle, and knotted it round him, and hid it beneath his robes. Then he took his way to the chapel, and sought out a priest privily and prayed him to teach him better how his soul might be saved when he should go hence; and there he shrived him, and showed his misdeeds, both great and small, and besought mercy and craved absolution; and the priest assoiled him, and set him as clean as if doomsday had been on the morrow. And afterwards Sir Gawain made him merry with the ladies, with carols, and all kinds of joy, as never he did but that one day, even to nightfall; and all the men marveled at him, and said that never since he came thither had he been so merry.

Meanwhile the lord of the castle was abroad chasing the fox; awhile he lost him, and as he rode through a spinney he heard the hounds near at hand, and Reynard came creeping through a thick grove, with all the pack at his heels. Then the lord drew out his shining brand, and cast it at the beast, and the fox swerved aside for the sharp edge, and would have doubled back, but a hound was on him ere he might turn, and right before the horse's feet they all fell on him, and worried him fiercely, snarling the while.

Then the lord leapt from his saddle, and caught the fox from the jaws, and held it aloft over his head, and hallooed loudly, and many brave hounds bayed as they beheld it; and the hunters hied them thither, blowing their horns; all that bare bugles blew them at once, and all the others shouted. 'Twas the merriest meeting that ever men heard, the clamor that was raised at the death of the fox. They rewarded the hounds, stroking them and rubbing their heads, and took Reynard and stripped him of his coat; then blowing their horns, they turned them homewards, for it was nigh nightfall.

The lord was gladsome at his return, and found a bright fire on the hearth, and the knight beside it, the good Sir Gawain, who was in joyous mood for the pleasure he had had with the ladies. He wore a robe of blue, that reached even to the ground, and a surcoat richly furred, that became him well. A hood like to the surcoat fell on his shoulders, and all alike were done about with fur. He met the host in the midst of the floor, and jesting, he greeted him, and said, "Now shall I be first to fulfil our covenant which we made together when there was no lack of wine." Then he embraced the knight, and kissed him thrice, as solemnly as he might.

"Of a sooth," quoth the other, "ye have good luck in the matter of this covenant, if ye made a good exchange!"

"Yet, it matters naught of the exchange," quoth Gawain, "since what I owe is swiftly paid."

"Marry," said the other, "mine is behind, for I have hunted all this day, and naught have I got but this foul foxskin, and that is but poor payment for three such kisses as ye have here given me."

"Enough," quoth Sir Gawain, "I thank ye, by the Rood."

Then the lord told them of his hunting, and how the fox had been slain.

With mirth and minstrelsy, and dainties at their will, they made them as merry as a folk well might till 'twas time for them to sever, for at last they must needs betake them to their beds. Then the knight took his leave of the lord, and thanked him fairly.

"For the fair sojourn that I have had here at this high feast may the High King give ye honor. I give ye myself, as one of your servants, if ye so like; for I must needs, as you know, go hence with the morn, and ye will give me, as ye promised, a guide to show me the way to the Green Chapel, an God will suffer me on New Year's Day to deal the doom of my weird."

"By my faith," quoth the host, "all that ever I promised, that shall I keep with good will." Then he gave him a servant to set him in the way, and lead him by the downs, that he should have no need to ford the stream, and should fare by the shortest road through the groves; and Gawain thanked the lord for the honor done him. Then he would take leave of the ladies, and courteously he kissed them, and spake, praying them to receive his thanks, and they made like reply; then with many sighs they commended him to Christ, and he departed courteously from that fold. Each man that he met he thanked him for his service and his solace, and the pains he had been at to do his will; and each found it as hard to part from the knight as if he had ever dwelt with him.

Then they led him with torches to his chamber, and brought him to his bed to rest. That he slept soundly I may not say, for the morrow gave him much to think on. Let him rest awhile, for he was near that which he sought, and if ye will but listen to me I will tell ye how it fared with him thereafter.

IV

Now the New Year drew nigh, and the night passed, and the day chased the darkness, as is God's will; but wild weather wakened therewith. The clouds cast the cold to the earth, with enough of the north to slay them that lacked clothing. The snow drave smartly, and the whistling wind blew from the heights, and made great drifts in the valleys. The knight, lying in his bed, listened, for though his eyes were shut, he might sleep but little, and hearkened every cock that crew.

He arose ere the day broke, by the light of a lamp that burned in his chamber, and called to his chamberlain, bidding him bring his armor and saddle his steed. The other gat him up, and fetched his garments, and robed Sir Gawain.

First he clad him in his clothes to keep off the cold, and then in his harness, which was well and fairly kept. Both hauberk and plates were well burnished, the rings of the rich byrnie freed from rust, and all as fresh as at first, so that the knight was fain to thank them. Then he did on each piece, and bade them bring his steed, while he put the fairest raiment on himself; his coat with its fair cognizance, adorned with precious stones upon velvet, with broidered seams, and all furred within with costly skins. And he left not the lace, the lady's gift, that Gawain forgot not, for his own good. When he had girded on his sword he wrapped the gift twice about him, swathed around his waist. The girdle of green silk set gaily and well upon the royal red cloth, rich to behold, but the knight ware it not for pride of the pendants, polished though they were with fair gold that gleamed brightly on the ends, but to save himself from sword and knife, when it behooved him to abide his hurt without question. With that the hero went forth, and thanked that kindly folk full often.

Then was Gringalet ready, that was great and strong, and had been well cared for and tended in every wise; in fair condition was that proud steed, and fit for a journey. Then Gawain went to him, and looked on his coat, and said by his sooth, "There is a folk in this place that thinketh on honor; much joy may they have, and the lord who maintains them, and may all good betide that lovely lady all her life long. Since they for charity cherish a guest, and hold honor in their hands, may he who holds the heaven on high requite them, and also ye all. And if I might live anywhile on earth, I would give ye full reward, readily, if so I might." Then he set foot in the stirrup and bestrode his steed, and his squire gave him his shield, which he laid on his shoulder. Then he smote Gringalet with his golden spurs, and the steed pranced on the stones and would stand no longer.

By that his man was mounted, who bare his spear and lance, and Gawain quoth, "I commend this castle to Christ, may he give it ever good fortune." Then the drawbridge was let down, and the broad gates unbarred and opened on both sides; the knight crossed himself, and passed through the gateway, and praised the porter, who knelt before the prince, and gave him good-day, and commended him to God. Thus the knight went on his way with the one man who should guide him to that dread place where he should receive rueful payment.

The two went by hedges where the boughs were bare, and climbed the cliffs where the cold clings. Naught fell from the heavens, but 'twas ill beneath them; mist brooded over the moor and hung on the mountains; each hill had a cap, a great cloak, of mist. The streams foamed and bubbled between their banks, dashing sparkling on the shores where they shelved downwards. Rugged and dangerous was the way through the woods, till it was time for the sun-rising. Then were they on a high hill; the snow lay white beside them, and the man who rode with Gawain drew rein by his master.

"Sir," he said, "I have brought ye hither, and now ye are not far from the place that ye have sought so specially. But I will tell ye for sooth, since I know ye well, and ye are such a knight as I well love, would ye follow my counsel ye would fare the better. The place whither ye go is accounted full perilous, for he who liveth in that waste is the worst on earth, for he is strong and fierce, and loveth to deal mighty blows; taller he is than any man on earth, and greater of frame than any four in Arthur's court, or in any other. And this is his custom at the Green Chapel: there may no man pass by that place, however proud his arms, but he does him to death by force of his hand, for he is a discourteous knight, and shows no mercy. Be he churl or chaplain who rides by that chapel, monk or mass-priest, or any man else, he thinks it as pleasant to slay them as to pass alive himself. Therefore, I tell ye, as sooth as ye sit in saddle, if ye come there and that knight know it, ye shall be slain, though ye had twenty lives; trow me that truly! He has dwelt here full long and seen many a combat; ye may not defend ye against his blows. Therefore, good Sir Gawain, let the man be, and get ye away some other road; for God's sake seek ye another land, and there may Christ speed ye! And I will hie me home again, and I promise ye further that I will swear by God and the saints, or any other oath ye please, that I will keep counsel faithfully, and never let any wit the tale that ye fled for fear of any man."

"Gramercy," quoth Gawain, but ill-pleased. "Good

fortune be his who wishes me good, and that thou wouldst keep faith with me I will believe; but didst thou keep it never so truly, an I passed here and fled for fear as thou sayest, then were I a coward knight, and might not be held guiltless. So I will to the chapel let chance what may, and talk with that man, even as I may list, whether for weal or for woe as fate may have it. Fierce though he may be in fight, yet God knoweth well how to save his servants."

"Well," quoth the other, "now that ye have said so much that ye will take your own harm on yourself, and ye be pleased to lose your life, I will neither let nor keep ye. Have here your helm and the spear in your hand, and ride down this same road beside the rock till ye come to the bottom of the valley, and there look a little to the left hand, and ye shall see in that vale the chapel, and the grim man who keeps it. Now fare ye well, noble Gawain; for all the gold on earth I would not go with ye nor bear ye fellowship one step further." With that the man turned his bridle into the wood, smote the horse with his spurs as hard as he could, and galloped off, leaving the knight alone.

Quoth Gawain, "I will neither greet nor moan, but commend myself to God, and yield me to his will."

Then the knight spurred Gringalet, and rode adown the path close in by a bank beside a grove. So he rode through the rough thicket, right into the dale, and there he halted, for it seemed him wild enough. No sign of a chapel could he see, but high and burnt banks on either side and rough rugged crags with great stones above. An ill-looking place he thought it.

Then he drew in his horse and looked round to seek the chapel, but he saw none and thought it strange. Then he saw as it were a mound on a level space of land by a bank beside the stream where it ran swiftly; the water bubbled within as if boiling. The knight turned his steed to the mound, and lighted down and tied the rein to the branch of a linden; and he turned to the mound and walked round it, questioning with himself what it might be. It had a hole at the end and at either side, and was overgrown with clumps of grass, and it was hollow within as an old cave or the crevice of a crag; he knew not what it might be.

"Ah," quoth Gawain, "can this be the Green Chapel? Here might the devil say his matins at midnight! Now I wis there is wizardry here. 'Tis an ugly oratory, all overgrown with grass, and 'twould well beseem that fellow in green to say his devotions on devil's wise. Now feel I in five wits, 'tis the foul fiend himself who hath set me this tryst, to destroy me here! This is a chapel of mischance: ill-luck betide it, 'tis the cursedest kirk that ever I came in!"

Helmet on head and lance in hand, he came up to the rough dwelling, when he heard over the high hill beyond the brook, as it were in a bank, a wondrous fierce noise, that rang in the cliff as if it would cleave asunder. 'Twas as if one ground a scythe on a grindstone, it whirred and whetted like water on a mill-wheel and rushed and rang, terrible to hear.

"By God," quoth Gawain, "I trow that gear is preparing for the knight who will meet me here. Alas! naught may help me, yet should my life be forfeit, I fear not a jot!" With that he called aloud, "Who waiteth in this place to give me tryst? Now is Gawain come hither: if any man will aught of him let him hasten hither now or never."

"Stay," quoth one on the bank above his head, "and ye shall speedily have that which I promised ye." Yet for a while the noise of whetting went on ere he appeared, and then he came forth from a cave in the crag

with a fell weapon, a Danish axe newly dight, wherewith to deal the blow. An evil head it had, four feet
large, no less, sharply ground, and bound to the handle
by the lace that gleamed brightly. And the knight himself was all green as before, face and foot, locks and
beard, but now he was afoot. When he came to the
water he would not wade it, but sprang over with the
pole of his axe, and strode boldly over the bent that was
white with snow.

Sir Gawain went to meet him, but he made no low
bow. The other said, "Now, fair sir, one may trust thee
to keep tryst. Thou art welcome, Gawain, to my place.
Thou hast timed thy coming as befits a true man. Thou
knowest the covenant set between us: at this time twelve
months agone thou didst take that which fell to thee,
and I at this New Year will readily requite thee. We
are in this valley, verily alone; here are no knights to
sever us, do what we will. Have off thy helm from
thine head, and have here thy pay; make me no more
talking than I did then when thou didst strike off my
head with one blow."

"Nay," quoth Gawain, "by God that gave me life,
I shall make no moan whatever befall me, but make
thou ready for the blow and I shall stand still and say
never a word to thee, do as thou wilt."

With that he bent his head and showed his neck all
bare, and made as if he had no fear, for he would not
be thought adread.

Then the Green Knight made him ready, and grasped
his grim weapon to smite Gawain. With all his force he
bore it aloft with a mighty feint of slaying him: had
it fallen as straight as he aimed he who was ever
doughty of deed had been slain by the blow. But
Gawain swerved aside as the axe came gliding down to
slay him as he stood, and shrank a little with the shoul-

ders, for the sharp iron. The other heaved up the blade and rebuked the prince with many proud words:

"Thou art not Gawain," he said, "who is held so valiant, that never feared he man by hill or vale, but thou shrinkest for fear ere thou feelest hurt. Such cowardice did I never hear of Gawain! Neither did *I* flinch from thy blow, or make strife in King Arthur's hall. My head fell to my feet, and yet I fled not; but thou didst wax faint of heart ere any harm befell. Wherefore must I be deemed the braver knight."

Quoth Gawain, "I shrank once, but so will I no more; though an my head fall on the stones I cannot replace it. But haste, Sir Knight, by thy faith, and bring me to the point, deal me my destiny, and do it out of hand, for I will stand thee a stroke and move no more till thine axe have hit me—my troth on it."

"Have at thee, then," quoth the other, and heaved aloft the axe with fierce mien, as if he were mad. He struck at him fiercely but wounded him not, withholding his hand ere it might strike him.

Gawain abode the stroke, and flinched in no limb, but stood still as a stone or the stump of a tree that is fast rooted in the rocky ground with a hundred roots.

Then spake gaily the man in green, "So now thou hast thine heart whole it behooves me to smite. Hold aside thy hood that Arthur gave thee, and keep thy neck thus bent lest it cover it again."

Then Gawain said angrily, "Why talk on thus? Thou dost threaten too long. I hope thy heart misgives thee."

"For sooth," quoth the other, "so fiercely thou speakest I will no longer let thine errand wait its reward." Then he braced himself to strike, frowning with lips and brow, 'twas no marvel that it pleased but ill him who hoped for no rescue. He lifted the axe lightly and let it fall with the edge of the blade on the bare neck.

Though he struck swiftly, it hurt him no more than on the one side where it severed the skin. The sharp blade cut into the flesh so that the blood ran over his shoulder to the ground. And when the knight saw the blood staining the snow, he sprang forth, swift-foot, more than a spear's length, seized his helmet and set it on his head, cast his shield over his shoulder, drew out his bright sword, and spake boldly (never since he was born was he half so blithe), "Stop, Sir Knight, bid me no more blows. I have stood a stroke here without flinching, and if thou give me another, I shall requite thee, and give thee as good again. By the covenant made betwixt us in Arthur's hall but one blow falls to me here. Halt, therefore."

Then the Green Knight drew off from him and leaned on his axe, setting the shaft on the ground, and looked on Gawain as he stood all armed and faced him fearlessly—at heart it pleased him well. Then he spake merrily in a loud voice, and said to the knight, "Bold sir, be not so fierce; no man here hath done thee wrong, nor will do, save by covenant, as we made at Arthur's court. I promised thee a blow and thou hast it—hold thyself well paid! I release thee of all other claims. If I had been so minded I might perchance have given thee a rougher buffet. First I menaced thee with a feigned one, and hurt thee not for the covenant that we made in the first night, and which thou didst hold truly. All the gain didst thou give me as a true man should. The other feint I proffered thee for the morrow: my fair wife kissed thee, and thou didst give me her kisses—for both those days I gave thee two blows without scathe—true man, true return. But the third time thou didst fail, and therefore hadst thou that blow. For 'tis *my* weed thou wearest, that same woven girdle, my own wife wrought it, that do I wot for sooth. Now know I well thy kisses, and thy conversation, and the wooing of my wife, for 'twas mine own doing. I sent her to try thee, and in sooth I think thou art the most faultless knight that ever trod earth. As a pearl among white peas is of more worth than they, so is Gawain, i' faith, by other knights. But thou didst lack a little, Sir Knight, and wast wanting in loyalty, yet that was for no evil work, nor for wooing neither, but because thou lovedst thy life—therefore I blame thee the less."

Then the other stood a great while, still sorely angered and vexed within himself; all the blood flew to his face, and he shrank for shame as the Green Knight spake; and the first words he said were, "Cursed be ye, cowardice and covetousness, for in ye is the destruction of virtue." Then he loosed the girdle, and gave it to the knight. "Lo, take there the falsity, may foul befall it! For fear of thy blow cowardice bade me make friends with covetousness and forsake the customs of largess and loyalty, which befit all knights. Now am I faulty and false and have been afeared: from treachery and untruth come sorrow and care. I avow to thee, Sir Knight, that I have ill done; do then thy will. I shall be more wary hereafter."

Then the other laughed and said gaily, "I wot I am whole of the hurt I had, and thou hast made such free confession of thy misdeeds, and hast so borne the penance of mine axe edge, that I hold thee absolved from that sin, and purged as clean as if thou hadst never sinned since thou wast born. And this girdle that is wrought with gold and green, like my raiment, do I give thee, Sir Gawain, that thou mayest think upon this chance when thou goest forth among princes of renown, and keep this for a token of the adventure of the Green Chapel, as it chanced between chivalrous knights. And thou shalt come again with me to my dwelling and pass the rest of this feast in gladness." Then the lord laid hold of him, and said, "I wot we shall soon make peace with my wife, who was thy bitter enemy."

"Nay, forsooth," said Sir Gawain, and seized his helmet and took it off swiftly, and thanked the knight: "I have fared ill, may bliss betide thee, and may He who rules all things reward thee swiftly. Commend me to that courteous lady, thy fair wife, and to the other my honored ladies, who have beguiled their knight with skilful craft. But 'tis no marvel if one be made a fool and brought to sorrow by women's wiles, for so was Adam beguiled by one, and Solomon by many, and Samson all too soon, for Delilah dealt him his doom; and David thereafter was wedded with Bathsheba, which brought him much sorrow—if one might love a woman and believe her not, 'twere great gain! And since all they were beguiled by women, methinks 'tis the less blame to me that I was misled! But as for thy girdle, that will I take with good will, not for gain of the gold, nor for samite, nor silk, nor the costly pendants, neither for weal nor for worship, but in sign of my frailty. I shall look upon it when I ride in renown and remind myself of the fault and faintness of the flesh; and so when pride uplifts me for prowess of arms, the sight of this lace shall humble my heart. But one thing would I pray, if it displease thee not: since thou art lord of yonder land wherein I have dwelt, tell me what thy rightful name may be, and I will ask no more."

"That will I truly," quoth the other. "Bernlak de Hautdesert am I called in this land. Morgain le Fay dwelleth in mine house, and through knowledge of clerkly craft hath she taken many. For long time was she the mistress of Merlin, who knew well all you knights of the court. Morgain the goddess is she called therefore, and there is none so haughty but she can

bring him low. She sent me in this guise to yon fair hall
to test the truth of the renown that is spread abroad of
the valor of the Round Table. She taught me this marvel
to betray your wits, to vex Guinevere and fright her to
death by the man who spake with his head in his hand
at the high table. That is she who is at home, that
ancient lady, she is even thine aunt, Arthur's half-sister,
the daughter of the Duchess of Tintagel, who afterward
married King Uther. Therefore I bid thee, knight, come
to thine aunt, and make merry in thine house; my folk
love thee, and I wish thee as well as any man on earth,
by my faith, for thy true dealing."

But Sir Gawain said nay, he would in no wise do so;
so they embraced and kissed, and commended each other
to the Prince of Paradise, and parted right there, on
the cold ground. Gawain on his steed rode swiftly to
the king's hall, and the Green Knight got him whither-
soever he would.

Sir Gawain, who had thus won grace of his life, rode
through wild ways on Gringalet; oft he lodged in a
house, and oft without, and many adventures did he have
and came off victor full often, as at this time I cannot
relate in tale. The hurt that he had in his neck was
healed, he bare the shining girdle as a baldric bound by
his side, and made fast with a knot 'neath his left arm,
in token that he was taken in a fault—and thus he came
in safety again to the court.

Then joy awakened in that dwelling when the king
knew that the good Sir Gawain was come, for he deemed
it gain. King Arthur kissed the knight, and the queen
also, and many valiant knights sought to embrace him.
They asked him how he had fared, and he told them all
that had chanced to him—the adventure of the chapel,
the fashion of the knight, the love of the lady—at last of
the lace. He showed them the wound in the neck which

he won for his disloyalty at the hand of the knight; the blood flew to his face for shame as he told the tale.

"Lo, lady," he quoth, and handled the lace, "this is the bond of the blame that I bear in my neck, this is the harm and the loss I have suffered, the cowardice and covetousness in which I was caught, the token of my covenant in which I was taken. And I must needs wear it so long as I live, for none may hide his harm, but undone it may not be, for if it hath clung to thee once, it may never be severed."

Then the king comforted the knight, and the court laughed loudly at the tale, and all made accord that the lords and the ladies who belonged to the Round Table, each hero among them, should wear bound about him a baldric of bright green for the sake of Sir Gawain. And to this was agreed all the honor of the Round Table, and he who ware it was honored the more thereafter, as it is testified in the book of romance. That in Arthur's days this adventure befell, the book of Brutus bears witness. For since that bold knight came hither first, and the siege and the assault were ceased at Troy, I wis

Many a venture herebefore
Hath fallen such as this:
May He that bare the crown of thorn
Bring us unto His bliss.

Amen.

PEARL

The "Pearl," by an unknown author, is the out-standing elegiac poem in Middle English. It is possibly the lament of a father for his dead child.

The translation, in which most of the theological discussion has been omitted, is by S. Weir Mitchell.

I

PEARL, for a prince's pleasance fair enow,
Right cleanly housed in gold so clear,
No orient pearl I dare avow
Was ever yet her precious peer.
So rounded, in such rare array,
So small, of smoothen comeliness,
I judged her of all jewels gay
As singly set in singleness.
Lost in mine arbour,—woe is me!
'Neath earth she with grass o'ergrown,   10
I mourn love's sweet anxiety
That spotless pearl had made my own.

II

There have I tarried ofttimes where below
It left my sight, to seek again the joy
That once was wont to scatter all my woe,
And lift my life above the world's annoy.
About my heart do ceaseless sorrows throng,
That constant grief must ever constant be—
Yet, thought I, never was so sweet a song
As the still hours thither brought to me.   20

Ah me! what thoughts are mine! I sit and dream
Of those fair colours clad, alas! in clay.
O earth! why hast thou marred this tender theme—
My spotless pearl, that was mine own alway?

III

What lavish fragrance here is spread
By herb and flower, newly won!
Of blossoms white and blue and red,
No gayer rise to greet the sun.
Here nor fruit nor flower may fade,
Where passed my pearl to night of ground;　30
From dead grain cometh fruitful blade,
Else never wheat had harvest found.
Ever 't is good that good doth bring,
Such seemly seed it faileth not;
Here ever-fragrant flowers shall spring
O'er thee, my pearl without a spot.

IV

That place I sweeten with gentle rhyme,
I came to, where was my arbour green,
In the high season of August time,
When corn is cut with the sickle keen.　40
Where pearl lay under the grassy mead,
Shadowed it was with leafage green,
Gillyflower, ginger, and gromwell seed,
And peonies powdered all between.
Fair and seemly the sight was seen,
Fairer fragrance earth knoweth not;
Worthily won it was, I ween,
Of pearl, the precious, without a spot.

V

I gazed, my hands together pressed,
For, chilled with care and sorrow caught, 50
My heart beat wildly in my breast,
Though reason sager counsel taught.
I wept my pearl in earthly cell,
And timid reason fought with doubt;
Though Christ did comfort me full well,
Weak will with woe me cast about.
Such soothing scents the air did fill
That, lulled on this rose-peopled plot,
By sleep o'ercome, I rested still
Above my pearl without a spot. 60

VI

Thence sped my spirit far through space,
My body tranced upon the ground,
My soul's quick ghost by God's sure grace
Adventuring where be marvels found.
I wist not where on earth that place
With cloven cliffs, so high and sheer,
But toward a wood I set my face,
Borne whither radiant rocks appear.
Their light more golden than the sun,
A gleaming glory glinted thence: 70
Was never web of mortals spun
So wondrous fair to mortal sense.

VII

The hill-sides there were brightly crowned
With crystal cliffs so clear of kind,

And wood-sides, set with boles around,
Shone blue as is the blue of Inde.
On every branch, with light between,
The leaves of quivering silver hung;
Through gleaming glades with shimmering sheen
The light fell glistering them among.   80
The gravel rolled upon the shore
Was precious pearls of Orient.
The sun's bright beams were pale before
That sight so fair of wonderment.

VIII

My spirit there forgot its woe,
So wondrous were those charmèd hills.
Rare flavoured fruits thereon did grow,
Fit food to cure all human ills.
In fair accord the birds flew by,
Like wingèd flames, both great and small,   90
Nor cittern string nor minstrelsy
Might hope to match their joyous call:
For when the air their red wings beat,
Full choir sang they rapturously.
No greater joy a man could greet
Than this to hear, and that to see.

IX

Past all that eye of man has seen,
Past any wealth of words he hath,
The beauty of those wood-ways green,
The witchery of that wooing path.   100
Still on I pressed, as one who goes
Companioned by a joyous mood,
Through deepening dells where richly rose

Fair flowers by winsome breezes wooed.
Hedge-rows and marsh where wild fowl breed
I saw, and lo! a golden band—
A wonder that did all exceed—
A sunlit river cleft the strand.

x

O marvellous river, broad and deep,
With banks that beam with beryl bright!   110
As music sweet the waters sweep,
Or gently murmur low and light.
From darkened depths shone jewels fine,
As gleams through glowing glass the light,
As quivering stars in the welkin shine,
When tired men sleep of a winter night.
Each little stone that stream below
Was emerald green, or sapphire gent;
From them the light did leap and glow,
To daze a man with wonderment.   120

XI

Wondrous glamour of down and vale,
Wood and water and noble plain,
Did build me bliss and made me hale,
Routed sorrow and cured my pain.
Low bowed beside the stream I strayed,
With breed of joys my mind was glad;
The more I walked by mere and glade,
More strength of joy my spirit had.
Fortune fares where likes she still,
Sends she solace or evil sore,   130
The wight on whom she works her will
Hath ever of either more and more.

XII

More and more, and yet far more,
I longed to see beyond the strand;
For if 't was fair on the nearer shore,
More lovelike was that farther land.
I stayed my steps,—I stood at gaze,
To find a ford I sought,—alas!
Beside the strand, as in a maze,
I won not any way to pass. 140
Though peril in my path might stand,
I recked not, where such treasures were;
But fresh delights were nigh at hand,
That did my wondering spirit stir.

XIII

What wonder more did daunt my sight?
I saw beyond that mystic mere
A shining cliff of crystal bright,
With royal rays, as morning clear.
At foot there sat a little maid—
A maid of grace, and debonair; 150
In glistening white was she arrayed,
Well known long ere I saw her there.
More radiant than refinèd gold,
She stood in sunshine on the shore.
Long did my sight that vision hold,
And more I knew her, more and more.

XIV

Long feasted I on her dear face,
The lissome curves her figure wore,

Until the gladness of her grace
My heart's guest was as ne'er before.   160
Her gentle name I fain had called,
But stayed was I with wonderment,
So strange the place I stood appalled,
My eager gaze upon her bent.
Then turned on me her visage fair,—
As ivory white the face she wore.
Heart-struck was I to see her there,
And still I loved her more and more.

XV

Yearning had I by dread opposed.
I stood full still, I durst not call,   170
With eyes wide open and mouth full closed,
Like to a well-trained hawk in hall.
Hope had I for my soul's behoof;
Fear had I it might thus befall,
That she I longed for might stay aloof,
Or pass forever beyond recall.
Lo! uprose that child of grace,
Slender, small, and seemly slight,—
Rose right royal with lifted face,
A precious maid, with pearls bedight.   180

XVI

When, fresh as dewy fleur-de-lys,
Adown the bank she moved toward me,
High fortuned he on earth that sees
Such peerless pearls of empery.
As white as snow her amice gleams,
Her waist a lustrous broidery
Of pearls a man might see in dreams,

But never else on earth could see.
Full ample hung her sleeves, I ween;
Twain braided they with pearlës bright. 190
Her kirtle green alike was seen,
With pearls of price around bedight.

XVII

A crown did wear that maiden girl
Of margerys, and none other stone.
High pinnacled, of clear white pearl,
It glowed with flowers wrought thereon.
Her head no other gem did grace;
Her hair half hid her neck from view.
In statelihood of mighty place
She stood more white than whale tooth's hue. 200
Her loosened locks, that gold exceed,
Flowed wandering, o'er her shoulders curled;
Though dark their gold, they scarce did need
For contrast fair her robe impearled.

XVIII

Bravely broidered was every hem,
On sleeve and vest fair broidery lay
Of white pearls and no other gem,
And glossy shone her white array.
A wonder pearl without a taint
Lay moon-white where her bodice met; 210
Soul of man might falter and faint
Ere mind of man its price could set.
Tongue of man might ne'er be sure
With fitting words to tell aright
How spotless white and virgin pure
Was that rare pearl, my soul's delight.

xix

Decked with pearls, that precious piece
Of Heaven's make came down the strand;
My grief won wings of glad release
When that I saw her nearer stand.   220
None else of kin were dear as she,
And joyful then was my surprise
When seemed it she would speak to me,
And courteous bowed in woman wise.
She doffed her crown of jewels bright,
With low obeisance bending blithe.
Leave to answer that pearl of light
Made worth it well to be alive.

xx

'O Pearl, so gay with pearls,' quoth I,—
'O Pearl that in my loneliness   230
Art yearned for when at night I lie
Sole comrade of my own distress,—
Since over thee the grasses twine,
No love to mine with love replies.
May liking, love, and joy be thine,—
The strifeless bourne of Paradise.
Such weird as brought thee hither here,
With plight of sorrow hath me undone;
Now are we twayned that were so dear,
And in love's life were but as one.'   240

xxi

High crowned with pearls of Orient,
Looked up at me with fair blue eyes

That gracious maid with grave intent,
And sober spake in courtly wise:
'Sir, the tale is by half mistold
To say thy pearl is all perdue,
That a comely coffer in guard doth hold,
In flowered gardens, gay to view,
Where she may ever dwell and play,
Where sin nor sorrow come never near.   250
Safe should such treasury seem alway
If thou didst love thy jewel dear.

xxii

'Gentle Sir,' said the maiden gem,
'Why do men jest? Distraught ye be.
Three words hast said, and all of them
Forsooth are folly,—yea, all the three.
Thou knowest not what thy words may mean;
Quick words thy tardy wits outfly.
Dost surely think that I here am seen
Because thou seest with mortal eye.   260
Thou sayest, too, that thou, alas!
May bide with me in this domain.
The way this stream to freely pass
No living wight may know to gain.

xxiii

'Small praise that man would have of me
That trusts the wisdom of the eye.
Much to be blamed and graceless he
That thinks the Lord could speak a lie,—
Our Lord who promised thy life to raise,
Though fortune bid thy body die!   270
Ye read his words in crooked ways

To trust alone what sees the eye:
And that is a fault of haughtiness
Doth ill a righteous man beseem,
To trow no tale has worthiness
Unless his reason so may deem.

xxiv

'Think now thyself **if it be well**
Of God such words as thine to say.
Dost think in this fair land to dwell?
Methinks 't were better his leave to pray: 280
And yet might fail thine eager quest.
Ere thou shalt pass that watery way
Thou first must find another rest,
And cold must lie thy corse in clay;
For it was marred in Paradise,
Where our yore-father wrought it loss,—
Through dreary death thy journey lies
Ere God will give thee leave to cross.

xxv

'Thou thinkest sorrow is naught but dole.
Why dost thou make this vain pretence?   290
For lesser loss the wailing soul
May lose far more than he laments.
Shouldst rather hold thee blessed by it,
And love thy God in weal and woe,
For anger helpeth thee no whit,
And man must bear what all must know.
Though thou shouldst prance as any doe,
And fret and chafe in mad unrest,
Thou canst not any further go,—
Abide thou must what He thinks best.'   300

xxvi

Then spake I to that demoiselle—
'Let not my Lord be wroth with me.
As from a spring quick waters well,
Leaps forth my speech so wild and free.
My lonely heart is sorrow-scarred,
In misericorde of Christ I rest,
Rebuke me not with words so hard,
Forlorn am I, adored and best.
Thy kindly comfort me afford
With piteous thinking upon this—   310
Of care and me ye made accord
Who once were ground of all my bliss.

xxvii

'Thou hast been both my bale and bliss,
But greater is the bale I moan.
On every field my pearl I miss,
I wist not where my pearl has flown.
With clearer sight is sorrow eased.
Ere parting came we were at one.
Forbid it, God, we be displeased,
Though met we not beneath the sun.   320
Though tender sweet thy courtesy,
I am but earth, my joy is gone;
Gone every hope of help for me
Save mercy of Christ, Marie, and John.

xxviii

'I see thee with thy comrade, joy.
Ah, think of me when thou art glad;

Sad hours my ageing life annoy,
A lonely man bereft and sad.
But now, within thy presence here
I fain would bide, and patient wait   330
That ye may tell—ah, pearl most dear—
What life ye have both early and late.
Full glad am I that thy estate
Is changed to worship and to weal;
Where thou hast passed to lofty state—
There lies the only joy I feel.'

xxix

'To know if here the life is led
Be glad, will that thy grief assuage.
Thou knowest when thy pearl lay dead
Full young was I, of tender age.   340
Lo! I am bride of Christ the Lamb!
Through sacred Godhead wedded sure;
A crownèd queen of bliss I am,
Through days that shall for aye endure.
Who have his love do hold in fee
This heritage. I am his alone;
His priceless glory is to me
The source of every joy I own.'

xxx

'Ah, Pearl of bliss, can this be true?
Let not my error bid me rue.   350
Art thou the Queen of heaven's blue
That all the world does honour to?
Art her we worship, the spring of grace,
Who bare a Child of virgin flower?
Ah, none can take her crown and place,

That pass her not in worth and power.
For singleness of gentillesse
We call her phenix of Araby,—
The bird none match in stateliness,
Like to that Queen of Courtesy.'   360

xxxi

'Ay, Queen of Courtesy!' she said;
And lowly knelt and hid her face.
'Matchless mother and merriest maid!
Blest beginner of all our grace.'
Then rose she up and 'gan to speak,
And looked at me across the space.
'Though many find what here they seek,
None here may take another's place.
The heavens do her empire make,
Of earth and hell the Queen is she;   370
Her heritage may no one take,
For she is Queen of Courtesy.'

xxxii

'Yea, courtesy, I well believe,
And charity do here belong.
Let not my words thy goodness grieve—
To me thy speech still seemeth wrong.
Thyself to set so high in heaven
As queen to make of one so young—
What honour more might him be given
That in the world by grief was wrung,   380
And bought his bliss by years of bale—
Yea, lived in penance wearily?
No lesser honour him could fail
Than King be crowned by courtesy.

XXXIII

'Such courtesy too free appears,
If that be sooth which thou dost say.
On earth were thine but two brief years,
Never couldst thou God please or pray,
Knew never neither pater nor creed,—
But queen outright on thy death day,—   390
I may not trow it, so God me speed,
That God should rule so wrong a way.
Countess or demoiselle, par ma fay,
Were fair to be in heaven's estate,
Or else a lady of less array,—
But queen! it were too high a fate.'

XXXIV

'His goodness hath nor mete nor bound,'
Said then to me this worthsome wight;
'For all is truth where he is found,
Nought can he do but that is right.   400
This Matthew doth for thee express,
Writ clear in gospel sooth aright,
Ensampled plain for easy guess,
A parable of heavenly light.'
'My realm,' saith Christ, 'is like, on high,
A lord's that had a vineyard fair,
When lo! the vintage time was nigh,
And men must to his vines repair.

XXXV

'Right well his men the season know,
So up full early that lord arose   410

To send them where his vines did grow,
And unto some did there propose
A penny a day to be their gain.
With this accord forthwith they go,
And toil and labour with honest pain,
And prune and carry, go to and fro.
At noon this lord the market seeks,
And finds men standing idle here.
"Why stand ye idle?" thus he speaks
"Now know ye not the time of year?"   420

XXXVI

‹ "We hither came ere day begun,"
This was their answer, one and all.
"Here have we stood since rose the sun,
And no man yet on us doth call."
"Go to my vineyard, work aright,
And rest ye sure," that lord did say,
"What wages fair ye earn by night,
In very sooth I will surely pay."
Into his vines they went and wrought,
The while he came, and came again,   430
And new men into his vineyard brought,
Until the day was on the wane.

XXXVII

‘At close of day, at evensong,
An hour before the sun had fled,
He saw their idle men and strong,
And unto them he gently said:
"Why stand ye idle all day long?"
"No man," they said, "has come to hire."
"Go to my vines, ye yeomen strong,

And work your best, as I desire." 440
Soon the world grew dusk and gray,
The sun went down, it waxèd late;
He summoned them to take their pay—
The hour had come for which they wait.

XXXVIII

'That lord well knew the time of day,
And bade his steward pay them all.
"Give every man his proper pay;
And that no blame on me may fall,
Set ye all of them in a row,
And give alike a penny to each. 450
Begin with him that stands most low,
Until the first his wage shall reach."
Thereon the first did quick complain:
"My lord, we toiled full long and sore;
These last have had but little pain,
Our wage should justly be far more."

XXXIX

'Then said this lord, "In sooth, I try
To use mine own as seemeth meet.
Why turn on me an evil eye,
Who justice seek and no man cheat?" 460
Quoth Christ, "I now do thus decree,
The first shall be the last, and those
Who latest came the first shall be,—
Of many called but few be chose."
Thus do poor men win their way,
Though late they come and low their state;
If brief has been their labour day,
The more of grace doth them await.

XL

'More bliss have I, and joy herein
Of ladyship, and life's delight,   470
Than all the men on earth might win
If all they sought were theirs by right.
Although the night was nigh at hand
When came I to the vines at even,
Among the first God bade me stand,
And fullest wage to me was given.
Yet others waited there in vain,
Who toiled and sweated long of yore,
And still no wage repaid their pain,
And may not for a year or more.'   480

XLI

The Lamb's delight none doubted there.
Though seemed he hurt and wounded sore,
Yet glorious glad his glances were,
And nought of pain his semblance bore.
I looked among his radiant host,
Quick with eternal life,—and lo!
I saw my pearlës gentle ghost,
I loved and lost so long ago.
Lord! much of mirth that maiden made
Among her peers, so pure and white   490
I yearned to cross—all unafraid,
So longed my love—so dear the sight.

XLII

Delight held captive eye and ear;
My mortal mind toward madness drave,

I would be there where stayed my dear,
Beyond that river's mystic wave.
Methought that none would do so ill
As me to halt, if now I tried;
And if at start none checked my will,
Fain would I venture though I died. 500
Anon, from bold resolve I fell
When I would take that peril's chance;
In that rash mood I dare not dwell—
Not so my Prince's fair pleasance.

XLIII

It pleased not God that I come near,
Or think to cross that guarding mere,
Aghast I stood, alone with fear—
Alone, and she no longer here.
For, as I stood beside the stream,
I wakened in that arbour's shade. 510
Gone was the gladness of my dream!
My head was on that hillock laid
Where over her the roses grow.
Heartsore I lay upon the sod,
And to myself I murmured low:
'Blest be my maid in care of God.'

XLIV

So hard it was to drift away
From that fair region all too soon,
From sights so gallant, blithe and gay,
That weak with hurt I seemed to swoon, 520
And ruefully my head I bowed.
'O Pearl,' said I, 'of rare renown!

O, news of joy!' I cried aloud,
'In this glad vision sent me down.
And if thy tale in sooth be so,
And thou art clad in joy's delight,
Well am I in this home of woe,
Since thou hast pleased the Prince's sight.'

XLV

If to God's pleasure I had but bent,
And craved no more than man is given,   530
And held me humble, with this content,
As prayed that pearl in goodness thriven,—
Then by God's grace I were less amiss,
More mysteries my soul had won;
But man doth have more greed of bliss
Than life may give ere life be done.
Therefore too soon my joy was riven,
And I exiled from realms eterne.
Lord! mad are they with thee have striven,
For what doth not thy pleasure earn!   540

XLVI

To win the Prince's love aright
For Christen men is an easy end.
Yea, I have found him, by day and night,
A God, a Lord, full firm a friend.
Befell me this on that mound's green sod,—
For sorrow of Pearl there lay I prone,
And this my jewel gave o'er to God,
In Christ's dear blessing and eke mine own.
Christ, that in form of bread and wine,
The priest doth show, wherein God grants   550

To us his servants here a sign
That we be pearls of his pleasance.

c. 1375

THE VISION OF WILLIAM CONCERNING PIERS PLOWMAN

THE FIELD FULL OF FOLK

In a summer season when the sun was softest,
Shrouded in a smock, in shepherd's clothing,
In the habit of a hermit of unholy living,
I went through this world to witness wonders.
On a May morning on a Malvern hillside
I saw strange sights like scenes of Faerie.
I was weary of wandering and went to rest
By the bank of a brook in a broad meadow.
As I lay and leaned and looked on the water
I slumbered and slept, so sweetly it murmured.   **10**
  Then I met with marvelous visions.
I was in a wilderness; where, I knew not.
I looked up at the East at the high sun,
And saw a tower on a toft artfully fashioned.
A deep dale was beneath with a dungeon in it,
And deep ditches and dark, dreadful to see.
  A fair field full of folk I found between them,
With all manner of men, the meanest and the richest,
Working and wandering as the world demanded.
Some put them to the plow and practiced hardship   **20**
In setting and sowing and seldom had leisure;
They won what wasters consumed in gluttony.
Some practiced pride and quaint behavior,
And came disguised in clothes and features.
Prayer and penance prevailed with many.
For the love of our Lord they lived in strictness,

To have bliss hereafter and heavenly riches.
Hermits and anchorites held to their dwellings,
Gave up the course of country roving
And all lusty living that delights the body.   30
Some turned to trade; they tried barter;
And seemed in our sight to succeed better.
Some men were mirthful, learned minstrelcies,
And got gold as gleemen—a guiltless practice.
Yet jesters and janglers, Judas' children,
Feigned idle fancies and wore fool's clothing,
But had wit if they wished to work as others.
What Paul has preached I proffer without glossing:
Qui loquitur turpiloquium,[1] is Lucifer's servant.
    Bidders and beggars ride about the country   40
With bread to the brim in their bags and bellies;
They feign that they are famished and fight in the
    ale-house.
God wot, they go in gluttony to their chambers
And rise with ribaldry, like Robert's children.
Sleep and sloth pursue them always.
    Pilgrims and palmers were plighted together
To seek Saint James and saints in Rome.
They went on their way with many wise stories,
And had leave to lie for a lifetime after.
I saw some who said that they sought for relics;   50
In each tale that they told their tongue would always
Speak more than was so, it seemed to my thinking.
    A host of hermits with hooked staves
Went to Walsingham with their wenches behind them.
These great lubbers and long, who were loath to labor,
Clothed themselves in copes to be distinguished from
    others,
And robed themselves as hermits to roam at their leisure.
There I found friars of all the four orders,

[1] He who speaks slander.

Who preached to the people for the profit of their
    bellies,
And glossed the gospel to their own good pleasure; 60
They coveted their copes, and construed it to their
    liking.
Many master-brothers may clothe themselves to their
    fancy,
For their money and their merchandise multiply to-
    gether.
Since charity has turned chapman to shrive lords and
    ladies,
Strange sights have been seen in a few short years.
Unless they and Holychurch hold closer together
The worst misery of man will mount up quickly.

    There a pardoner preached as priest of the parish,
And brought out a bull with a bishop's signet
Said that he himself might assoil all men   70
Of all falsehood in fasting and vows that were broken.
Common folk confided in him and liked his preaching,
And crept up on cowed knees and kissed his pardons.
He abused them with brevets and blinded their eye-
    sight;
His devil's devises drew rings and brooches.
They gave their gold to keep gluttons,
And believed in liars and lovers of lechery.
If the bishop were blessed and worth both his ears
His seal would not be sent to deceive the people.
But the power of the bishop is not this preacher's
    license,   80
For the parish priest and the pardoner share the profits
    together
Which the poor of the parish would have if these were
    honest.

    Because parishes were poor since the pestilence season,
Parsons and parish priests petitioned the bishops

For a license to leave and live in London
And sing there for simony, for silver is sweet.
   Bishops and bachelors, both masters and doctors,
Who have cures under Christ and are crowned with the
     tonsure,
In sign of their service to shrive the parish,
To pray and preach and give the poor nourishment, 90
Lodge in London in Lent and the long year after;
Some are counting coins in the king's chamber,
Or in exchequer and chancery challenging his debts
From wards and wardmotes, waifs and strays.
Some serve as servants to lords and ladies
And sit in the seats of steward and butler.
They hear mass and matins, and many of their hours
Are done without devotion. There is danger that at
     last
Christ in his consistory will curse many.

THE CONFESSION OF SLOTH

   THEN Sloth came all beslobbered, with slime on his
     eyelids;
"I must sit," he said, "or else I shall slumber.
I cannot stand or stoop, and want a stool for kneeling.
If I were brought to bed, unless my buttocks made me,
No ringing should make me rise till I was ripe for
     dinner."
   He began *benedicite* with a belch and beat his fore-
     head,
And roared and raved and snored for a conclusion.
"Awake! awake! wretch," cried Repentance, "make
     ready for shriving."
"If I should die to-day I should never do it.
I cannot say *pater noster* perfectly, as the priest sings
   it.   10

I know rhymes of Robin Hood and Randolph Earl of
    Chester,
But of our Lord or of our Lady I have learned nothing.
I have made forty vows and forgotten them on the
    morrow.
I never performed the penance as the priest commanded,
Nor was sorry for my sins as a man should be.
And if I pray at my beads, unless Wrath bids me,
What I tell with my tongue is two miles from my
    meaning.
I am occupied each day, on holy days and all days,
With idle tales at ale, or at other times in churches.
Rarely do I remember God's pain and passion.   20
    I never visit the feeble nor the fettered men in prison.
I had rather hear ribaldry or a summer game of cob-
    blers,
Or lies to laugh at and belie my neighbor,
Than all that the four evangelists have ever written.
Vigils and fasting days slip unheeded.
I lie abed in Lent with my lemman beside me,
And when matins and mass are over I go to my friars.
If I reach to *ite missa est*[1] I have done my duty.
Sometimes I am not shriven, unless sickness force me,
More than twice in two years, and then I do it by guess
    work.   30
    I have been priest and parson for the past thirty
    winters,
Yet I know neither the scales nor the singing nor the
    Saints' Legends.
I can find an hare afield or frighten him from his furrow
Better than read *beatus vir*[2] or *beati omnes*,[3]
Construe their clauses and instruct my parishoners.
I can hold love-days and hear a reve's reckoning,

---

[1] The concluding words of the mass.
[2] Psalms, i or cxii.   [3] Psalms, cxxviii.

But I cannot construe a line in the Canons or Decretals.
 If I beg or borrow and it be not tallied
I forget it as quickly; men can ask me
Six times or seven and I will swear to the falsehood. 40
So I trouble true men twenty times over.
 The salary of my servants is seldom even.
I answer angrily when the accounts are reckoned,
And my workman's wages are wrath and cursing.
If any man does me a favour or helps me in trouble,
I answer courtesy with unkindness, and cannot under-
    stand it.
I have now and I have ever had a hawk's manners.
I am not lured with love where nothing lies in the fingers.
 Sixty times I, Sloth, have since forgotten
The kindness that fellow Christians have granted to
    me. 50
Sometimes I spill—in speech or silence—
Both flesh and fish and many other victuals,
Bread and ale, butter, milk and cheeses,
All slobbered in my service till they may serve no man.
 I was a roamer in my youth and reckless in study,
And ever since have been a beggar from foul slothful-
    ness:
Heu mihi! quia sterilem vitam duxi juvenilem!" [1]
 "Do you repent," said Repentance,—but the wretch
    was swooning,
Till Vigilate, the watcher, threw water on his forehead,
And flung it in his face, and vehemently addressed
    him, 60
And cried, "Beware of Desperation, that betrays many!
Say, 'I am sorry for my sins,' say it and believe it,
Beat your breast and beseech Him to have mercy;
For there is no guilt so great that His goodness is not
    greater."

[1] Woe is me that I led such an unprofitable life in my youth.

Then Sloth sat up and so crossed himself quickly,
And made a vow before God: "For my foul living
Every Sunday this seven years, unless sickness keep
    me,
I will go down before day-break to the dear chapel,
And hear matins and mass, like a monk in his cloister.
No ale after meat shall hold me absent   70
Till I have heard evensong, I vow by the rood-tree."

PIERS THE PLOWMAN'S PARDON

"PIERS," said a priest, "give me your pardon quickly.
I shall translate the text and turn it into English."
    Piers opened his pardon at the priest's bidding.
I was behind them both and beheld all the charter.
All lay in two lines, and not a leaf further.
The witness was Truth; and it was written thus:
    Et qui bona egerunt, ibunt in vitam eternam.
    Qui vero mala, in ignem eternum.[1]
"Peter," said the priest, "there is no pardon in it,
But do well and have well, and God shall have your
    soul,   10
And do evil and have evil, and you may hope only
That after your death day the devil shall take you."
    Then Piers in pure wrath pulled it to pieces,
And said: *"Si ambulavero in medio umbræ mortis, non
    timebo mala, quoniam tu mecum es.*[2]
I shall stop my sowing," said Piers, "and cease from
    such hard labor,
Nor be so busy now about my comfort.
Prayers and penance shall be my plow hereafter.
I shall weep when I should sleep, though wheat bread
    fail me.

[1] And they whose works are good shall pass into life eternal, but
they whose works are evil into fire everlasting.
[2] Psalms, xxiii, 4.

The prophet ate bread in penance and in sorrow.
The psalter says that so did many others.   20
He who loves God loyally has livelihood easily.
    Fuerunt mihi lacrimae meæ panes die ac nocte.[1]
And unless Luke lie, birds teach us the lesson
Not to be too busy about the world's pleasures.
Ne soliciti sitis, he says in the gospel,
And gives us guidance in governing ourselves rightly.
Who finds the fowls their food in winter?
They have no garner to go to, but God provisions them."
    "What," said the priest to Perkin, "Peter, bless
        me,
You are lettered a little; where did you learn read-
        ing?"   30
"Abstinence, the abbess," said Piers, "taught the
        A. B. C. to me,
And Conscience came forward and declared much fur-
        ther."
    "If you were a priest, Piers," he said, "you might
        preach at your liking,
And be a doctor in divinity, with *Dixit insipiens.*"
"Rude rogue," said Piers, "you have read little in the
        Bible.
You have seldom seen Solomon's proverbs:
    Ejice derisores et jurgia cum eis, ne crescant,"[2] etc.
The priest and Perkin opposed each other,
And at their wrangling I awoke and saw the world
        about me,
And the sun sailing in the southern heaven.   40
Meatless and moneyless on the Malvern hillsides
I went on my way, wondering at the vision.
    Often has this vision forced me to wonder
If what I saw asleep were so indeed.
I pondered pensively on Piers the Plowman;

[1] Psalms, xlii. 3.   [2] Proverbs, xxii, 10.

On what a pardon Piers had for all peoples' comfort,
And how the priest impugned it with two pert words.
I am a doubter of dreams, for they deceive men often.
Cato and the Canonists counsel us never
To seek assurance in dreams, for *sompnia ne cures*.[1]   50
But a book of the Bible bears witness.

c. 1376

GEOFFREY CHAUCER (1340?-1400)

THE CANTERBURY TALES

The Prologue

Whan that Aprille with his shoures sote [2]
The droghte of Marche hath perced to the rote,
And bathed every veyne in swich [3] licour,
Of which vertu [4] engendred is the flour;
Whan Zephirus eek with his swete breeth
Inspired hath in every holt [5] and heeth
The tendre croppes, and the yonge sonne
Hath in the Ram his halfe cours y-ronne,[6]
And smale fowles maken melodye
That slepen al the night with open yë,   10
(So priketh hem nature in hir corages):[7]
Than longen folk to goon on pilgrimages
(And palmers for to seken straunge strondes)
To ferne halwes,[8] couthe [9] in sondry londes;
And specially, from every shires ende
Of Engelond, to Caunterbury they wende,
The holy blisful martir [10] for to seke,
That hem hath holpen, whan that they were seke.

[1] Pay no heed to dreams   [2] sweet   [3] such   [4] by virtue of
which   [5] wood   [6] i.e. in mid-April   [7] hearts   [8] distant saints
[9] known   [10] St. Thomas à Becket

Bifel that, in that seson on a day,
In Southwerk at the Tabard as I lay   20
Redy to wenden on my pilgrimage
To Caunterbury with ful devout corage,
At night was come in-to that hostelrye
Wel nyne and twenty in a companye,
Of sondry folk, by aventure y-falle [1]
In felawshipe, and pilgrims were they alle,
That toward Caunterbury wolden ryde;
The chambres and the stables weren wyde,
And wel we weren esed atte beste.[2]
And shortly, whan the sonne was to reste,   30
So hadde I spoken with hem everichon,
That I was of hir felawshipe anon,
And made forward [3] erly for to ryse,
To take our wey, ther as I yow devyse.

But natheles, whyl I have tyme and space,
Er that I ferther in this tale pace,
Me thinketh it acordaunt to resoun,
To telle yow al the condicioun
Of ech of hem, so as it semed me,
And whiche they weren, and of what degree;   40
And eek in what array that they were inne:
And at a knight than wol I first biginne.

A KNIGHT ther was, and that a worthy man,
That fro the tyme that he first bigan
To ryden out, he loved chivalrye,
Trouthe and honour, fredom and curteisye.
Ful worthy was he in his lordes werre,
And thereto hadde he riden (no man ferre)[4]
As wel in Cristendom as hethenesse,
And ever honoured for his worthinesse.   50

At Alisaundre he was, whan it was wonne;
Ful ofte tyme he hadde the bord bigonne [5]

---

[1] by chance fallen   [2] entertained in the best manner   [3] agreement   [4] farther   [5] sat at the head of the table

Aboven alle naciouns in Pruce.[1]
In Lettow [2] hadde he reysed [3] and in Ruce,
No Cristen man so ofte of his degree.
In Gernade [4] at the sege eek hadde he be
Of Algezir, and riden in Belmarye.[5]
At Lyeys [6] was he, and at Satalye,[7]
Whan they were wonne; and in the Grete See [8]
At many a noble aryve [9] hadde he be.   60
At mortal batailles hadde he been fiftene,
And foughten for our feith at Tramissene [10]
In listes thryes, and ay slayn his fo.
This ilke worthy knight had been also
Somtyme with the lord of Palatye,[11]
Ageyn [12] another hethen in Turkye:
And evermore he hadde a sovereyn prys.[13]
And though that he were worthy, he was wys,
And of his port as meke as is a mayde.
He never yet no vileinye ne sayde   70
In al his lyf, un-to no maner wight.
He was a verray parfit gentil knight.
But for to tellen yow of his array,
His hors were gode, but he was nat gay.
Of fustian [14] he wered a gipoun [15]
Al bismotered [16] with his habergeoun;[17]
For he was late y-come from his viage,[18]
And wente for to doon his pilgrimage.
    With him ther was his sone, a yong SQUYER,
A lovyere, and a lusty bacheler,   80
With lokkes crulle,[19] as they were leyd in presse.
Of twenty yeer of age he was, I gesse.

---

[1] Prussia   [2] Lithuania   [3] made an expedition   [4] Granada
[5] in northern Africa   [6] in Armenia   [7] in Asia Minor   [8] Mediterranean   [9] landing   [10] in northern Africa   [11] in Asia Minor
[12] against   [13] excellent reputation   [14] coarse cloth   [15] doublet
[16] stained   [17] coat-of-mail   [18] voyage   [19] curly

Of his stature he was of evene [1] lengthe,
And wonderly deliver,[2] and greet of strengthe.
And he had been somtyme in chivachye,[3]
In Flaundres, in Artoys, and Picardye,
And born him wel, as of so litel space,
In hope to stonden in his lady grace.
Embrouded was he, as it were a mede [4]
Al ful of fresshe floures, whyte and rede.   90
Singinge he was, or floytinge,[5] al the day;
He was as fresh as is the month of May.
Short was his goune, with sleves longe and wyde.
Wel coude he sitte on hors, and faire ryde.
He coude songes make and wel endyte,
Juste [6] and eek daunce, and wel purtreye and wryte.
So hote he lovede, that by nightertale [7]
He sleep namore than dooth a nightingale.
Curteys he was, lowly, and servisable,
And carf [8] biforn his fader at the table.   100
     A YEMAN [9] hadde he, and servaunts namo
At that tyme, for him liste ryde so;
And he was clad in cote and hood of grene;
A sheef of pecok-arwes brighte and kene
Under his belt he bar ful thriftily;
(Wel coude he dresse his takel [10] yemanly:
His arwes drouped noght with fetheres lowe),
And in his hand he bar a mighty bowe.
A not-heed [11] hadde he, with a broun visage.
Of wode-craft wel coude [12] he al the usage.   110
Upon his arm he bar a gay bracer,[13]
And by his syde a swerd and a bokeler,
And on that other syde a gay daggere,
Harneised [14] wel, and sharp as point of spere;

---

[1] average   [2] active   [3] military expeditions   [4] meadow   [5] fluting   [6] joust   [7] at night   [8] carved   [9] yeoman   [10] take care of his weapons   [11] cropped head   [12] knew   [13] guard   [14] equipped

A Cristofre [1] on his brest of silver shene. [2]
An horn he bar, the bawdrik was of grene;
A forster [3] was he, soothly, as I gesse.
    Ther was also a Nonne, a PRIORESSE,
That of hir smyling was ful simple and coy
Hir gretteste ooth was but by sëynt Loy;   120
And she was cleped madame Eglentyne.
Ful wel she song the service divyne,
Entuned in hir nose ful semely;
And Frensh she spak ful faire and fetisly, [4]
After the scole of Stratford atte Bowe, [5]
For Frensh of Paris was to hir unknowe.
At mete wel y-taught was she with-alle;
She leet no morsel from hir lippes falle,
Ne wette hir fingres in hir sauce depe.
Wel coude she carie a morsel, and wel kepe,   130
That no drope ne fille up-on her brest.
In curteisye was set full muche hir lest. [6]
Hir over lippe wyped she so clene,
That in hir coppe was no ferthing [7] sene
Of grece, whan she dronken hadde hir draughte.
Ful semely after hir mete she raughte, [8]
And sikerly she was of great disport, [9]
And ful plesaunt, and amiable of port,
And peyned hir to countrefete chere [10]
Of court, and been estatlich of manere,   140
And to ben holden digne [11] of reverence.
But, for to speken of hir conscience,
She was so charitable and so pitous,
She wolde wepe, if that she sawe a mous
Caught in a trappe, if it were deed or bledde.
Of smale houndes had she, that she fedde

---

[1] image of Saint Christopher (patron saint of travelers)   [2] bright
[3] forester   [4] elegantly   [5] a convent-school near London   [6] desire
[7] smallest bit   [8] reached   [9] good-nature   [10] manners   [11] worthy

With rosted flesh, or milk and wastelbreed.[1]
But sore weep she if oon of hem were deed,
Or if men smoot it with a yerde smerte:[2]
And al was conscience and tendre herte.   150
Ful semely hir wimpel pinched[3] was;
Hir nose tretys;[4] hir eyen greye as glas;
Hir mouth ful smal, and ther-to softe and reed;
But sikerly she hadde a fair forheed;
It was almost a spanne brood, I trowe;
For, hardily,[5] she was nat undergrowe.
Ful fetis[6] was hir cloke, as I was war.
Of smal coral aboute hir arm she bar
A peire[7] of bedes, gauded al with grene;[8]
And ther-on heng a broche of gold ful shene,   160
On which ther was first write a crowned A,
And after, *Amor vincit omnia.*[9]

  Another NONNE with hir hadde she,
That was hir chapeleyne, and PREESTES THREE.

  A MONK ther was, a fair for the maistrye,[10]
An out-rydere,[11] that lovede venerye;[12]
A manly man, to been an abbot able.
Ful many a deyntee hors hadde he in stable:
And, whan he rood, men mighte his brydel here
Ginglen in a whistling wind as clere,   170
And eek as loude as dooth the chapel-belle
Ther as this lord was keper of the celle.[13]
The reule of seint Maure or of seint Beneit,[14]
By-cause that it was old and som-del streit,[15]
This ilke monk leet olde thinges pace,[16]

---

[1] fine bread   [2] with a stick smartly   [3] pleated   [4] well formed
[5] certainly   [6] handsome   [7] string   [8] furnished with green beads
[9] Love conquers all   [10] a very fine fellow   [11] inspector (of equipment of monasteries)   [12] hunting   [13] subordinate monastery
[14] the regulations of the Benedictines   [15] somewhat strict   [16] go

And held after the newe world the space.
He yaf nat of that text a pulled [1] hen,
That seith, that hunters been nat holy men;
Ne that a monk, whan he is cloisterlees,
Is lykned til a fish that is waterlees;   180
This is to seyn, a monk out of his cloistre.
But thilke text held he nat worth an oistre;
And I seyde, his opinioun was good.
What sholde he studie, and make himselven wood,[2]
Upon a book in cloistre alway to poure,
Or swinken [3] with his handes, and laboure,
As Austin [4] bit? [5] How shal the world be served?
Lat Austin have his swink to him reserved.
Therfore he was a pricasour [6] aright;
Grehoundes he hadde, as swifte as fowel in flight;   190
Of priking [7] and of hunting for the hare
Was al his lust, for no cost wolde he spare.
I seigh [8] his sleves purfiled [9] at the hond
With grys,[10] and that the fyneste of a lond;
And, for to festne his hood under his chin,
He hadde of gold y-wroght [11] a curious pin:
A love-knotte in the gretter ende ther was.
His heed was balled [12] that shoon as any glas,
And eek his face, as he had been anoint.
He was a lord ful fat and in good point; [13]   200
His even stepe,[14] and rollinge in his heed,
That stemed [15] as a forneys of a leed; [16]
His botes [17] souple, his hors in greet estat.
Now certeinly he was a fair prelat;
He was nat pale as a for-pyned [18] goost.

---

[1] plucked   [2] crazy   [3] labor   [4] Saint Augustine   [5] commands
[6] hard rider   [7] riding   [8] saw   [9] trimmed   [10] fur   [11] fashioned   [12] bald   [13] condition   [14] bright   [15] glowed   [16] fire under a cauldron   [17] boots   [18] wasted away

A fat swan loved he best of any roost.
His palfrey was as broun as is a berye.
   A Frere ther was, a wantown and a merye,
A limitour,[1] a ful solempne man.
In alle the ordres foure [2] is noon that can [3]   210
So muche of daliaunce and fair langage.
He hadde maad ful many a mariage
Of yonge wommen, at his owne cost.
Un-to his ordre he was a noble post.[4]
Ful wel biloved and famulier was he
With frankeleyns [5] over-al in his contree,
And eek with worthy wommen of the toun:
For he had power of confessioun,
As seyde him-self, more than a curat,
For of his ordre he was licentiat.   220
Ful swetely herde he confessioun,
And plesaunt was his absolucioun;
He was an esy man to yeve penaunce
Ther as he wiste to han [6] a good pitaunce;
For unto a povre ordre for to yive
Is signe that a man is wel y-shrive.
For if he yaf, he dorste make avaunt,[7]
He wiste that a man was repentaunt.
For many a man so hard is of his herte,
He may nat wepe al-thogh him sore smerte.   230
Therfore, in stede of weping and preyeres,
Men moot [8] yeve silver to the povre freres.
His tipet was ay farsed [9] ful of knyves
And pinnes, for to yeven faire wyves.
And certeinly he hadde a mery note;
Wel coude he singe and pleyen on a rote.[10]
Of yeddinges [11] he bar utterly the prys.

---

[1] a friar licensed to beg   [2] the four monastic orders: Augustinian, Franciscan, Dominican, Carmelite   [3] knows   [4] pillar   [5] country gentlemen   [6] knew he should have   [7] boast   [8] should   [9] stuffed   [10] fiddle   [11] songs

His nekke whyt was as the flour-de-lys;
Ther-to he strong was as a champioun.
He knew the tavernes wel in every toun, 240
And everich hostiler and tappestere
Bet [1] than a lazar [2] or a beggestere; [3]
For un-to swich a worthy man as he
Acorded nat,[4] as by his facultee,[5]
To have with seke lazars aqueyntaunce.
It is nat honest, it may nat avaunce
For to delen with no swich poraille,[6]
But al with riche and sellers of vitaille.
And over-al, ther as profit sholde aryse,
Curteys he was, and lowly of servyse. 250
Ther nas no man no-wher so vertuous.
He was the beste begger in his hous;
For thogh a widwe hadde noght a sho,[7]
So plesaunt was his *"In principio,"* [8]
Yet wolde he have a ferthing, er he wente.
His purchas [9] was wel bettre than his rente.[10]
And rage he coude, as it were right a whelpe.
In love-dayes [11] ther coude he muchel helpe.
For there he was nat lyk a cloisterer,
With a thredbar cope, as is a povre scoler, 260
But he was lyk a maister or a pope.
Of double worsted was his semi-cope,[12]
That rounded as a belle out of the presse.[13]
Somewhat he lipsed, for his wantownesse,
To make his English swete up-on his tongue;
And in his harping, whan that he had songe,
His eyen twinkled in his heed aright,
As doon the sterres in the frosty night.
This worthy limitour was cleped Huberd.

---

[1] better　　[2] leper　　[3] beggar woman　　[4] it was not fitting
[5] importance　　[6] poor people　　[7] shoe　　[8] the beginning of the gospel of Saint John　　[9] proceeds of his begging　　[10] regular income
[11] days for settling disputes　　[12] short cape　　[13] clothes press

A MARCHANT was ther with a forked berd,   270
In mottelee,[1] and hye on horse he sat,
Up-on his heed a Flaundrish bever hat;
His botes clasped faire and fetisly.
His resons he spak ful solempnely,
Souninge [2] always th'encrees of his winning.
He wolde the see were kept for any thing [3]
Bitwixe Middleburgh [4] and Orewelle.[5]
Wel coude he in eschaunge [6] sheeldes [7] selle.
This worthy man ful wel his wit bisette;[8]
Ther wiste no wight that he was in dette,   280
So estatly was he of his governaunce,[9]
With his bargaynes, and with his chevisaunce.[10]
For sothe he was a worthy man with-alle,
But sooth to seyn, I noot how men him calle.

A CLERK ther was of Oxenford also,
That un-to logik hadde longe y-go.
As lene was his hors as is a rake,
And he nas nat right fat, I undertake;
But loked holwe, and ther-to soberly.
Ful thredbar was his overest courtepy;[11]   290
For he had geten him yet no benefyce,
Ne was so worldly for to have offyce.
For him was lever [12] have at his beddes heed
Twenty bokes, clad in blak or reed,
Of Aristotle and his philosophye,
Than robes riche, or fithele,[13] or gay sautrye.[14]
But al be that he was a philosophre,
Yet hadde he but litel gold in cofre;[15]
But al that he mighte of his freendes hente,[16]
On bokes and on lerning he it spente,   300

---

[1] cloth of a mixed color   [2] concerning   [3] guarded at all costs
[4] in Holland   [5] in England   [6] exchange   [7] shields, French coins
[8] employed   [9] management   [10] dealings   [11] overcoat   [12] would
rather   [13] fiddle   [14] psaltery (musical instrument)   [15] i.e. he
did not understand alchemy   [16] get

And bisily gan for the soules preye
Of hem that yaf him wher-with to scoleye.[1]
Of studie took he most cure [2] and most hede.
Noght o word spak he more than was nede,
And that was seyd in forme and reverence,
And short and quik, and ful of hy sentence.[3]
Souninge in [4] moral vertu was his speche,
And gladly wolde he lerne, and gladly teche.

A SERGEANT OF THE LAWE, war [5] and wys,
That often hadde been at the parvys,[6]   310
Ther was also, ful riche of excellence.
Discreet he was, and of greet reverence:
He semed swich, his wordes weren so wyse.
Justyce he was ful often in assyse,
By patente, and by pleyn commissioun;
For his science, and for his heigh renoun
Of fees and robes hadde he many oon.
So greet a purchasour [7] was no-wher noon.
Al was fee simple to him in effect,
His purchasing mighte nat been infect.[8]   320
No-wher so bisy a man as he ther nas,
And yet he semed bisier than he was,
In termes [9] hadd he caas [10] and domes [11] alle,
That from the tyme of king William were falle.
Therto he coude endyte, and make a thing,
Ther coude no wight pinche at his wryting;
And every statut coude he pleyn by rote.[12]
He rood but hoomly in a medlee cote
Girt with a ceint [13] of silk, with barres smale;
Of his array telle I no lenger tale.   330

A FRANKELEYN [14] was in his companye;
Whyt was his berd, as is the dayesye.

---

[1] go to school   [2] care   [3] maxims   [4] conducing to   [5] cautious
[6] the church porch (of St. Paul's where lawyers met)   [7] conveyancer
[8] invalidated   [9] verbatim   [10] cases   [11] decisions   [12] fully by
heart   [13] girdle   [14] land owner

Of his complexioun he was sangwyn.
Wel loved he by the morwe a sop in wyn.[1]
To liven in delyt was ever his wone,[2]
For he was Epicurus owne sone,
That heeld opinioun, that pleyn delyt
Was verraily felicitee parfyt.
An housholdere, and that a greet, was he;
Seint Julian[3] he was in his contree.   340
His breed, his ale, was alwey after oon,[4]
A bettre envyned[5] man was no-wher noon.
With-oute bake mete was never his hous,
Of fish and flesh, and that so plentevous,
It snewed[6] in his hous of mete and drinke,
Of alle deyntees that men coude thinke.
After the sondry sesons of the yeer,
So chaunged he his mete and his soper.
Ful many a fat partrich hadde he in mewe,[7]
And many a breem[8] and many a luce[9] in stewe.[10]   350
Wo was his cook, but-if his sauce were
Poynaunt and sharp, and redy al his gere.
His table dormant[11] in his halle alway
Stood redy covered al the longe day.
At sessiouns ther was he lord and sire;
Ful ofte tyme he was knight of the shire.
An anlas[12] and a gipser[13] al of silk
Heng at his girdel, whyt as morne milk.
A shirreve hadde he been, and a countour;[14]
Was no-wher such a worthy vavasour.[15]   360
   An HABERDASSHER and a CARPENTER,
A WEBBE,[16] a DYERE, and a TAPICER[17]
Were with us eek,[18] clothed in o[19] liveree,

---

[1] wine   [2] habit   [3] patron saint of hospitality   [4] the same
quality   [5] provided with wine   [6] snowed   [7] coop   [8] a kind
of fish   [9] pike   [10] fish-pond   [11] permanent table   [12] dagger
[13] purse   [14] auditor   [15] landed gentleman   [16] weaver   [17] upholsterer   [18] also   [19] one

Of a solempne and greet fraternitee.
Ful fresh and newe hir gere apyked [1] was;
Hir knyves were y-chaped [2] noght with bras,
But al with silver, wroght ful clene and weel,
Hir girdles and hir pouches every-deel.[3]
Wel semed ech of hem a fair burgeys,
To sitten in a yeldhalle [4] on a deys.[5]   370
Everich, for the wisdom that he can,
Was shaply for to been an alderman.
For catel [6] hadde they y-nogh and rente,
And eek hir wyves wolde it wel assente;
And elles certein were they to blame.
It is ful fair to been y-clept *"ma dame,"*
And goon to vigilyës al bifore,
And have a mantel royalliche y-bore.

A Cook they haddē with hem for the nones
To boille the chiknes with the marybones,   380
And poudre-marchant tart,[7] and galingale.[8]
Wel coude he knowe a draughte of London ale.
He coude roste, and sethe, and broille, and frye,
Maken mortreux,[9] and wel bake a pye.
But greet harm was it, as it thoughte me,
That on his shine a mormal [10] hadde he;
For blankmanger,[11] that made he with the beste.

A Shipman was ther, woning fer by weste:
For aught I woot, he was of Dertemouthe.
He rood up-on a rouncy,[12] as he couthe,[13]   390
In a gowne of falding [14] to the knee.
A daggere hanging on a laas [15] hadde he
Aboute his nekke under his arm adoun.
The hote somer had maad his hewe al broun;
And, certainly, he was a good felawe.

[1] trimmed   [2] mounted   [3] every bit   [4] guild-hall   [5] dais
[6] property   [7] sharp flavoring powder   [8] a spice   [9] stews
[10] sore   [11] chicken compote   [12] nag   [13] as well as he knew how
[14] coarse cloth   [15] cord

Ful many a draughte of wyn had he y-drawe
From Burdeux-ward, whyl that the chapman sleep.
Of nyce conscience took he no keep.
If that he faught, and hadde the hyer hond,
By water he sente hem hoom to every land.[1]   400
But of his craft to rekene wel his tydes,
His stremes [2] and his daungers him bisydes,
His herberwe [3] and his mone, his lodemenage,[4]
Ther nas noon swich from Hulle to Cartage.[5]
Hardy he was, and wys to undertake;
With many a tempest hadde his berd been shake.
He knew wel alle the havenes, as they were,
From Gootlond [6] to the cape of Finistere,
And every cryke in Britayne and in Spayne;
His barge y-cleped was the Maudelayne.   410

With us ther was a Doctour of Phisyk,
In al this world ne was ther noon him lyk
To speke of phisik and of surgerye;
For he was grounded in astronomye.
He kepte his pacient a ful greet del
In houres,[7] by his magik naturel.
Wel coude he fortunen the ascendent
Of his images [8] for his pacient.
He knew the cause of everich maladye,
Were it of hoot or cold, or moiste, or drye,   420
And where engendred, and of what humour;
He was a verrey parfit practisour.
The cause y-knowe, and of his harm the rote,
Anon he yaf the seke man his bote.[9]
Ful redy hadde he his apothecaries,
To sende him drogges and his letuaries,[10]

---

[1] he made them walk the plank   [2] currents   [3] harborage   [4] pilot-
age   [5] Carthaginia in Spain   [6] Gottland in the Baltic   [7] he
watched for the favorable star of his patient   [8] he knew by the
stars the exact moment for devising images   [9] remedy   [10] syrups

For ech of hem made other for to winne;
Hir frendschipe nas nat newe to biginne.
Wel knew he th' olde Esculapius,
And Deiscorides, and eek Rufus,   430
Old Ypocras, Haly, and Galien;
Serapion, Razis, and Avicen;
Averrois, Damascien, and Constantyn;
Bernard, and Gatesden, and Gilbertyn.[1]
Of his diete mesurable was he,
For it was of no superfluitee,
But of greet norissing and digestible.
His studie was but litel on the bible.
In sangwin [2] and in pers [3] he clad was al,
Lyned with taffata and with sendal;[4]   440
And yet he was but esy of dispence;[5]
He kepte that he wan in pestilence.
For gold in phisik is a cordial,
Therfore he lovede gold in special.

A good WYF was ther of bisyde BATHE,
But she was som-del [6] deef, and that was scathe.[7]
Of clooth-making she hadde swiche an haunt,[8]
She passed hem of Ypres and of Gaunt.
In al the parisshe wyf ne was ther noon
That to th' offring bifore hir sholde goon;   450
And if ther dide, certeyn, so wrooth was she,
That she was out of alle charitee.
Hir coverchiefs ful fyne were of ground;[9]
I dorste swere they weyeden ten pound
That on a Sonday were upon hir heed.
Hir hosen weren of fyn scarlet reed,
Ful streite y-teyd, and shoos ful moiste and newe.
Bold was hir face, and fair, and reed of hewe.

---

[1] medical authorities   [2] red   [3] blue   [4] thin silk   [5] careful
about spending   [6] somewhat   [7] a pity   [8] skill   [9] fine texture

She was a worthy womman al hir lyve.
Housbondes at chirche-dore she hadde fyve, 460
Withouten [1] other companye in youthe;
But therof nedeth nat to speke as nouthe.[2]
And thryes hadde she been at Jerusalem;
She hadde passed many a straunge streem;
At Rome she hadde been, and at Boloigne,
In Galice at seint Jame, and at Coloigne.
She coude muche of wandring by the weye:
Gat-tothed [3] was she, soothly for to seye.
Up-on an amblere [4] esily she sat,
Y-wimpled [5] wel, and on hir heed an hat 470
As brood as is a bokeler or a targe;
A foot-mantel aboute hir hipes large,
And on hir feet a paire of spores sharpe.
In felawschip wel coude she laughe and carpe.[6]
Of remedyes of love she knew perchaunce,
For she coude of that art the olde daunce.

A good man was ther of religioun,
And was a povre PERSOUN [7] of a toun;
But riche he was of holy thoght and werk.
He was also a lerned man, a clerk, 480
That Cristes gospel trewely wolde preche;
His parisshens [8] devoutly wolde he teche.
Benigne he was, and wonder diligent,
And in adversitee ful pacient;
And swich he was y-preved ofte sythes.[9]
Ful looth were him to cursen for his tythes,
But rather wolde he yeven, out of doute,
Un-to his povre parisshens aboute
Of his offring, and eek of his substaunce.
He coude in litel thing han suffisaunce. 490

[1] besides   [2] at present   [3] with teeth far apart   [4] ambling nag
[5] with a pleated head covering   [6] talk   [7] parson   [8] parishioners
[9] times

Wyd was his parisshe, and houses fer a-sonder,
But he ne lafte nat, for reyn ne thonder,
In siknes nor in meschief,[1] to visyte
The ferreste in his parisshe, muche and lyte,[2]
Up-on his feet, and in his hand a staf.
This noble ensample to his sheep he yaf,
That first he wroghte, and afterward he taughte;
Out of the gospel he tho wordes caughte;
And this figure he added eek ther-to,
That if gold ruste, what shal iren do?   500
For if a preest be foul, on whom we truste,
No wonder is a lewed[3] man to ruste;
And shame it is, if a preest take keep,[4]
A shiten shepherde and a clene sheep.
Wel oghte a preest ensample for to yive,
By his clennesse, how that his sheep shold live.
He sette nat his benefice to hyre,
And leet his sheep encombred in the myre,
And ran to London, un-to sëynt Poules,
To seken him a chaunterie for soules,[5]   510
Or with a bretherhed to been withholde;
But dwelte at hoom, and kepte wel his folde,
So that the wolf ne made it nat miscarie;
He was a shepherde and no mercenarie.
And though he holy were, and vertuous,
He was to sinful man nat despitous,
Ne of his speche daungerous[6] ne digne,[7]
But in his teching discreet and benigne.
To drawen folk to heven by fairnesse
By good ensample, was his bisinesse: 520
But it were any persone obstinat,
What-so he were, of heigh or lowe estat,
Him wolde he snibben[8] sharply for the nones.

---

[1] trouble   [2] great and small   [3] lay   [4] should reflect   [5] to
seek easier work in saying masses for the dead   [6] overbearing
[7] scornful   [8] reprove

A bettre preest, I trowe that nowher noon is.
He wayted after no pompe and reverence,
Ne maked him a spyced[1] conscience,
But Cristes lore, and his apostles twelve,
He taughte, and first he folwed it himselve.

With him ther was a PLOWMAN, was his brother,
That hadde y-lad of dong ful many a fother,[2]   530
A trewe swinker[3] and a good was he,
Livinge in pees and parfit charitee.
God loved he best with al his hole herte
At alle tymes, thogh him gamed or smerte,[4]
And thanne his neighebour right as himselve.
He wolde thresshe, and ther-to dyke and delve,
For Cristes sake, for every povre wight,
Withouten hyre, if it lay in his might.
His tythes payed he ful faire and wel,
Bothe of his propre swink and his catel.   540
In a tabard[5] he rood upon a mere.

Ther was also a Reve[6] and a Millere,
A Somnour[7] and a Pardoner[8] also,
A Maunciple,[9] and my-self; ther were namo.

The MILLER was a stout carl, for the nones,
Ful big he was of braun, and eek of bones;
That proved wel,[10] for over-al ther he cam,
At wrastling he wolde have alwey the ram,[11]
He was short-sholdred, brood, a thikke knarre,[12]
Ther nas no dore that he nolde heve[13] of harre,[14]   550
Or breke it, at a renning, with his heed.
His berd as any sowe or fox was reed,
And ther-to brood, as though it were a spade.
Up-on the cop[15] right of his nose he hade

---

[1] over-scrupulous   [2] load   [3] laborer   [4] whether he were gay or sad   [5] sleeveless jerkin   [6] bailiff   [7] summoner for the ecclesiastical courts   [8] pedlar of papal indulgences   [9] steward of a college   [10] was clearly proved   [11] i.e. the prize   [12] sturdy fellow   [13] lift   [14] hinge   [15] tip

A werte, and ther-on stood a tuft of heres,
Reed as the bristles of a sowes eres;
His nose-thirles¹ blake were and wyde.
A swerd and bokeler bar he by his syde;
His mouth as greet was as a greet forneys.
He was a janglere² and a goliardeys,³ 560
And that was most of sinne and harlotryes.⁴
Wel coude he stelen corn, and tollen thryes;⁵
And yet he hadde a thombe of gold, pardee.
A whyt cote and a blew hood wered he.
A baggepype wel coude he blowe and sowne,
And ther-with-al he broghte us out of towne.

A gentil MAUNCIPLE was ther of a temple,⁶
Of which achatours⁷ mighte take exemple
For to be wyse in bying of vitaille
For whether that he payde, or took by taille,⁸ 570
Algate he wayted so in his achat,⁹
That he was ay biforn and in good stat.
Now is nat that of God a ful fair grace,
That swich a lewed mannes wit shal pace
The wisdom of an heep of lerned men?
Of maistres hadde he mo than thryes ten,
That were of lawe expert and curious;
Of which ther were a doseyn in that hous
Worthy to been stiwardes of rente and lond
Of any lord that is in Engelond, 580
To make him live by his propre good,
In honour dettelees, but he were wood,¹⁰
Or live as scarsly as him list desire;
And able for to helpen al a shire
In any cas that mighte falle or happe;
And yit this maunciple sette hir aller cappe.¹¹

---

¹ nostrils ² an idler talker ³ coarse jester ⁴ ribaldries
⁵ take triple toll ⁶ one of the Inns of Court ⁷ buyers ⁸ on
credit ⁹ he always attended so well to his purchase ¹⁰ unless he
were crazy ¹¹ made fools of them all

The REVE was a sclendre colerik man,
His berd was shave as ny as ever he can.
His heer was by his eres round y-shorn.
His top was dokked lyk a preest biforn,[1]   590
Ful longe were his legges, and ful lene,
Y-lyk a staf, ther was no calf y-sene.
Wel coude he kepe a gerner [2] and a binne;
Ther was noon auditour coude on him winne.
Wel wiste he, by the droghte, and by the reyn,
The yelding of his seed, and of his greyn.
His lordes sheep, his neet,[3] his dayerye,
His swyn, his hors, his stoor,[4] and his pultrye,
Was hoolly in this reves governing,
And by his covenaunt yaf the rekening,   600
Sin that his lord was twenty yeer of age;
Ther coude no man bringe him in arrerage.[5]
Ther nas baillif, ne herde,[6] ne other hyne,[7]
That he ne knew his sleighte and his covyne;[8]
They were adrad of him, as of the deeth.
His woning [9] was ful fair up-on an heeth,
With grene treës shadwed was his place.
He coude bettre than his lord purchace.
Ful riche he was astored prively,
His lord wel coude he plesen subtilly,   610
To yeve and lene him of his owne good,
And have a thank, and yet a cote and hood.
In youthe he lerned hadde a good mister;[10]
He was a wel good wrighte, a carpenter.
This reve sat up-on a ful good stot,[11]
That was al pomely [12] grey, and highte Scot.
A long surcote of pers up-on he hade,

---

[1] his hair was cut short in front like a priest's   [2] granary   [3] cattle
[4] stock   [5] catch him in arrears   [6] herdsman   [7] laborer   [8] trickery   [9] house   [10] trade   [11] horse   [12] dappled

And by his syde he bar a rusty blade.
Of Northfolk was this reve, of which I telle,
Bisyde a toun men clepen Baldeswelle.   620
Tukked he was, as is a frere, aboute,
And ever he rood the hindreste of our route.

A SOMNOUR was ther with us in that place,
That hadde a fyr-reed cherubinnes face,
For sawcefleem [1] he was, with eyen narwe.[2]
As hoot he was, and lecherous, as a sparwe;
With scalled [3] browes blake, and piled [4] berd;
Of his visage children were aferd.
Ther nas quik-silver, litarge, ne brimstoon,
Boras, ceruce, ne oille of tartre noon,   630
Ne oynement that wolde clense and byte,
That him mighte helpen of his whelkes [5] whyte,
Nor of the knobbes sitting on his chekes.
Wel loved he garleek, oynons, and eek lekes,
And for to drinken strong wyn, reed as blood.
Than wolde he speke, and crye as he were wood.
And whan that he wel dronken hadde the wyn,
Than wolde he speke no word but Latyn.
A fewe termes hadde he, two or three,
That he had lerned out of som decree;   640
No wonder is, he herde it al the day;
And eek ye knowen wel, how that a jay
Can clepen "Watte," [6] as well as can the pope.
But who-so coude in other thing him grope,[7]
Thanne hadde he spent al his philosophye;
Ay "Questio quid iuris" wolde he crye.
He was a gentil harlot [8] and a kinde;
A bettre felawe sholde men noght finde.
He wolde suffre, for a quart of wyn,
A good felawe to have his concubyn   650

---

[1] pimpled   [2] close together   [3] scabby   [4] sparse   [5] pimples
[6] can cry "Wat."   [7] test   [8] rascal

A twelf-month, and excuse him atte fulle:
Ful prively a finch eek coude he pulle.[1]
And if he fond o-wher a good felawe,
He wolde techen him to have non awe,
In swich cas, of the erchedeknes curs,
But-if a mannes soule were in his purs;
For in his purs he sholde y-punisshed be.
"Purs is the erchedeknes helle," seyde he.
But wel I woot he lyed right in dede;
Of cursing oghte ech gilty man him drede—   660
For curs wol slee, right as assoilling[2] saveth—
And also war him[3] of a *significavit*.[4]
In daunger[5] hadde he at his owne gyse[6]
The yonge girles[7] of the diocyse,
And knew hir counseil, and was al hir reed.
A gerland hadde he set up-on his heed,
As greet as it were for an ale-stake;[8]
A bokeler hadde he maad him of a cake.

With him ther rood a gentil PARDONER
Of Rouncival, his freend and his compeer,   670
That streight was comen fro the court of Rome.
Ful loude he song, "Com hider, love, to me."
This somnour bar to him a stif burdoun,[9]
Was never trompe of half so greet a soun.
This pardoner hadde heer as yelow as wex,
But smothe it heng, as dooth a strike of flex;
By ounces[10] henge his lokkes that he hadde,
And ther-with he his shuldres overspradde;
But thinne it lay, by colpons[11] oon and oon;
But hood, for jolitee, ne wered he noon,   680
For it was trussed up in his walet.
Him thoughte, he rood al of the newe jet;[12]

---

[1] fleece a simple-minded person   [2] absolution   [3] let him beware
[4] writ of excommunication   [5] in his power   [6] way   [7] persons
[8] sign of an ale-house   [9] strong accompaniment   [10] small
strands   [11] shreds   [12] fashion

Dischevele, save his cappe, he rood al bare.
Swiche glaringe eyen hadde he as an hare.
A vernicle [1] hadde he sowed on his cappe.
His walet lay biforn him in his lappe,
Bret-ful [2] of pardoun come from Rome al hoot.
A voys he hadde as smal as hath a goot.
No berd hadd he, ne never sholde have,
As smothe it was as it were late y-shave; 690
I trowe he were a gelding or a mare.
But of his craft, fro Berwik into Ware,
Ne was ther swich another pardoner.
For in his male [3] he hadde a pilwe-beer,[4]
Which that, he seyde, was our lady [5] veyl:
He seyde, he hadde a gobet of the seyl
That seynt Peter hadde, whan that he wente
Up-on the see, til Jesu Crist him hente.
He hadde a croys of latoun,[6] ful of stones,
And in a glas he hadde pigges bones. 700
But with thise relikes, whan that he fond
A povre person dwelling up-on lond,
Up-on a day he gat him more moneye
Than that the person gat in monthes tweye.
And thus, with feyned flaterye and japes,[7]
He made the person and the peple his apes.
But trewely to tellen, atte laste,
He was in chirche a noble ecclesiaste.
Wel coude he rede a lessoun or a storie,
But alderbest [8] he song an offertorie; 710
For wel he wiste, whan that song was songe,
He moste preche, and wel affyle [9] his tonge,
To winne silver, as he ful wel coude;
Therefore he song so meriely and loude.

---

[1] a St. Veronica handkerchief, showing the face of Christ [2] brimful [3] wallet [4] pillow-case [5] the Virgin's [6] a kind of brass [7] tricks [8] best of all [9] smooth

Now have I told you shortly, in a clause,
Th'estat, th'array, the nombre, and eek the cause
Why that assembled was this companye
In Southwerk, at this gentil hostelrye,
That highte the Tabard, faste by the Belle.
But now is tyme to yow for to telle   720
How that we baren us that ilke night,
Whan we were in that hostelrye alight.
And after wol I telle of our viage,
And al the remenaunt of our pilgrimage.
But first I pray yow, of your curteisye,
That ye n'arette it nat my vileinye,[1]
Thogh that I pleynly speke in this matere,
To telle yow hir wordes and hir chere [2]
Ne thogh I speke hir wordes properly.
For this ye knowen al-so wel as I,   730
Who-so shal telle a tale after a man,
He moot reherce, as ny as ever he can,
Everich a word, if it be in his charge,
Al speke he never so rudeliche and large;[3]
Or elles he moot telle his tale untrewe
Or feyne thing, or finde wordes newe.
He may nat spare, al-thogh he were his brother;
He moot as wel seye o word as another.
Crist spak him-self ful brode in holy writ,
And wel ye woot, no vileinye is it.   740
Eek Plato seith, who-so that can him rede,
The wordes mote be cosin to the dede.
Also I prey yow to foryeve it me,
Al have I nat set folk in hir degree
Here in this tale, as that they sholde stonde;
My wit is short, ye may wel understonde.

Greet chere made our hoste us everichon,
And to the soper sette us anon;

[1] that you do not ascribe it to my bad manners   [2] behavior
[3] coarsely

And served us with vitaille at the beste.
Strong was the wyn, and wel to drinke us leste.[1]   750
A semely man our hoste was with-alle
For to han been a marshal in an halle;
A large man he was with eyen stepe,[2]
A fairer burgeys is ther noon in Chepe:
Bold of his speche, and wys, and wel y-taught,
And of manhod him lakkede right naught.
Eek therto he was right a mery man,
And after soper pleyen he bigan,
And spak of mirthe amonges othere thinges,
Whan that we hadde maad our rekeninges;   760
And seyde thus: "Now, lordinges, trewely,
Ye been to me right welcome hertely:
For by my trouthe, if that I shal nat lye,
I ne saugh this yeer so mery a companye
At ones in this herberwe[3] as is now.
Fayn wolde I doon yow mirthe, wiste I how.
And of a mirthe I am right now bithoght,
To doon yow ese, and it shal coste noght.

Ye goon to Caunterbury; God yow spede,
The blisful martir quyte yow your mede.[4]   770
And wel I woot, as ye goon by the weye,
Ye shapen yow to talen[5] and to pleye;
For trewely, confort ne mirthe is noon
To ryde by the weye doumb as a stoon;
And therfore wol I maken yow disport,
As I seyde erst,[6] and doon yow som confort.
And if yow lyketh alle, by oon assent,
Now for to stonden at my jugement,
And for to werken as I shal yow seye,
To-morwe, whan ye ryden by the weye,   780
Now, by my fader soule, that is deed,

---

[1] we were pleased   [2] glittering   [3] inn   [4] reward you   [5] tell
stories   [6] earlier

But ye be merye, I wol yeve yow myn heed.
Hold up your hond, withouten more speche."

Our counseil was nat longe for to seche;[1]
Us thoughte it was noght worth to make it wys,[2]
And graunted him withouten more avys,
And bad him seye his verdit, as him leste.

"Lordinges," quod he, "now herkneth for the beste;
But tak it not, I prey yow, in desdeyn;
This is the poynt, to speken short and pleyn,   790
That ech of yow, to shorte with your weye,
In this viage, shal telle tales tweye,
To Caunterbury-ward, I mene it so,
And hom-ward he shal tellen othere two,
Of aventures that whylom han bifalle.
And which of yow that bereth him best of alle,
That is to seyn, that telleth in this cas
Tales of best sentence and most solas,[3]
Shal have a soper at our aller cost[4]
Here in this place, sitting by this post,   800
Whan that we come agayn fro Caunterbury.
And for to make yow the more mery,
I wol my-selven gladly with yow ryde,
Right at myn owne cost, and be your gyde.
And who-so wol my judgement withseye[5]
Shal paye all that we spenden by the weye.
And if ye vouche-sauf that it be so,
Tel me anon, with-outen wordes mo,[6]
And I wol erly shape me[7] therfore."

This thing was graunted, and our othes swore   810
With ful glad herte, and preyden him also
That he wold vouche-sauf for to do so,
And that he wolde been our governour,

---

[1] it did not take us long to come to an agreement   [2] to deliberate
about it   [3] most edifying and pleasing   [4] at our common expense
[5] dispute   [6] more   [7] prepare myself

And of our tales juge and reportour
And sette a soper at a certeyn prys;
And we wold reuled been at his devys,
In heigh and lowe; and thus, by oon assent,
We been acorded to his jugement.
And ther-up-on the wyn was fet [1] anon;
We dronken, and to reste wente echon,   820
With-outen any lenger taryinge.

A-morwe, whan that day bigan to springe,
Up roos our host, and was our aller cok,[2]
And gadrede us togidre, alle in a flok,
And forth we riden, a litel more than pas,[3]
Un-to the watering of seint Thomas.
And there our host bigan his hors areste,
And seyde; "Lordinges, herkneth, if yow leste.
Ye woot your forward,[4] and I it yow recorde.
If even-song and morwe-song acorde,[5]   830
Lat see now who shal telle the firste tale.
As ever mote I drinke wyn or ale,
Who-so be rebel to my jugement
Shal paye for al that by the weye is spent.
Now draweth cut, er that we ferrer twinne;[6]
He which that hath the shortest shal biginne.
"Sire knight," quod he, "my maister and my lord,
Now draweth cut, for that is myn acord.
Cometh neer," quod he, "my lady prioresse;
And ye, sir clerk, lat be your shamfastnesse,   840
Ne studieth noght; ley hond to, every man."

Anon to drawen every wight bigan,
And shortly for to tellen, as it was,
Were it by aventure,[7] or sort,[8] or cas,[9]
The sothe [10] is this, the cut fil to the knight,

---

[1] fetched   [2] the cock who aroused us all   [3] a little faster than
a walk   [4] agreement   [5] if you feel the same now as you did last
night   [6] go   [7] accident   [8] destiny   [9] chance   [10] truth

Of which ful blythe and glad was every wight;
And telle he moste his tale, as was resoun,
By forward and by composicioun,[1]
As ye han hard; what nedeth wordes mo?
And whan this gode man saugh it was so,   850
As he that wys was and obedient
To kepe his forward by his free assent,
He seyde: "Sin I shal beginne the game,
What, welcome be the cut, a Goddes name!
Now lat us ryde, and herkneth what I seye."
    And with that word we riden forth our weye;
And he bigan with right a mery chere
His tale anon, and seyde in this manere.
                Here endeth the prolog of this book

The Nun's Priest's Tale

*Here biginneth the Nonne Preestes Tale of the Cok and
Hen, Chauntecleer and Pertelote.*

A povre widwe, somdel stape [2] in age,
Was whylom dwelling in a narwe cotage,
Bisyde a grove, stonding in a dale.
This widwe, of which I telle yow my tale,
Sin thilke day that she was last a wyf,
In pacience ladde a ful simple lyf,
For litel was hir catel [3] and hir rente;
By housbondrye,[4] of such as God hir sente,
She fond [5] hir-self, and eek hir doghtren two.
Three large sowes hadde she, and namo,   10
Three kyn, and eek a sheep that highte [6] Malle,
Ful sooty was hir bour,[7] and eek hir halle,
In which she eet ful many a sclendre meel.

---

[1] compact   [2] advanced   [3] property   [4] economy   [5] provided
for   [6] was called   [7] bed-chamber

Of poynaunt sauce hir neded never a deel.
No deyntee morsel passed thurgh hir throte;
Hir dyete was accordant to [1] hir cote.
Repleccioun ne made hir never syk;
Attempree [2] dyete was al hir phisyk,
And exercyse, and hertes suffisaunce. [3]
The goute lette [4] hir no-thing [5] for to daunce,   20
N'apoplexye shonte [6] nat hir heed;
No wyn ne drank she, neither whyt ne reed;
Hir bord was served most with whyt and blak,
Milk and broun breed, in which she fond no lak,
Seynd [7] bacoun, and somtyme an ey [8] or tweye,
For she was as it were a maner deye. [9]

A yerd she hadde, enclosed al aboute
With stikkes, and a drye dich with-oute,
In which she hadde a cok, hight Chauntecleer,
In al the land of crowing nas [10] his peer.   30
His vois was merier than the mery orgon
On messe-dayes that in the chirche gon;
Wel sikerer [11] was his crowing in his logge,
Than is a clokke, or an abbey orlogge. [12]
By nature knew he ech ascencioun
Of equinoxial in thilke toun;
For whan degrees fiftene were ascended, [13]
Thanne crew he, that it mighte nat ben amended.
His comb was redder than the fyn coral,
And batailed, as it were a castel-wal.   40
His bile was blak, and as the jeet [14] it shoon;
Lyk asur were his legges, and his toon;
His nayles whytter than the lilie flour,
And lyk the burned gold was his colour.
This gentil cok hadde in his governaunce

[1] in keeping with   [2] temperate   [3] contentment   [4] hindered
[5] not at all   [6] injured   [7] broiled   [8] egg   [9] dairy woman
[10] was not   [11] more reliable   [12] clock   [13] every hour   [14] jet

Sevene hennes, for to doon al his plesaunce,
Whiche were his sustres and his paramours,
And wonder lyk to him, as of colours.
Of whiche the faireste hewed on hir throte
Was cleped faire damoysele Pertelote.　　　　　50
Curteys she was, discreet, and debonaire,
And compaignable, and bar hir-self so faire,
Sin thilke day that she was seven night old,
That trewely she hath the herte in hold
Of Chauntecleer loken [1] in every lith; [2]
He loved hir so, that wel was him therwith.
But such a joye was it to here hem singe,
Whan that the brighte sonne gan to springe,
In swete accord, "my lief is faren [3] in londe."
For thilke tyme, as I have understonde,　　　　　60
Bestes and briddes coude speke and singe.

And so bifel, that in a daweninge,
As Chauntecleer among his wyves alle
Sat on his perche, that was in the halle,
And next him sat this faire Pertelote,
This Chauntecleer gan gronen in his throte,
As man that in his dreem is drecched [4] sore.
And whan that Pertelote thus herde him rore,
She was agast, and seyde, "O herte dere,
What eyleth yow, to grone in this manere?　　　　　70
Ye been a verray sleper, fy for shame!"
And he answerde and seyde thus, "madame,
I pray yow, that ye take it nat a-grief:
By god, me mette [5] I was in swich meschief
Right now, that yet myn herte is sore afright.
Now god," quod he, "my swevene [6] recche [7] aright,
And keep my body out of foul prisoun!
Me mette, how that I romed up and doun

---

[1] locked　　[2] limb　　[3] gone　　[4] troubled　　[5] I dreamed　　[6] dream
[7] interpret

Withinne our yerde, wher-as I saugh a beste,
Was lyk an hound, and wolde han maad areste   80
Upon my body, and wolde han had me deed.
His colour was bitwixe yelwe and reed;
And tipped was his tail, and bothe his eres,
With blak, unlyk the remenant of his heres;
His snowte smal, with glowinge eyen tweye.
Yet of his look for fere almost I deye;
This caused me my groning, doutelees."

"Avoy!" quod she, "fy on yow, hertelees!
Allas!" quod she, "for, by that god above,
Now han ye lost myn herte and al my love;   90
I can nat love a coward, by my feith.
For certes, what so any womman seith,
We alle desyren, if it mighte be,
To han housbondes hardy, wyse, and free,[1]
And secree, and no nigard, ne no fool,
Ne him that is agast of every tool,[2]
Ne noon avauntour,[3] by that god above!
How dorste ye seyn for shame unto your love,
That any thing mighte make yow aferd?
Have ye no mannes herte, and han a berd?   100
Allas! and conne ye been agast of swevenis?
No-thing, god wot, but vanitee,[4] in sweven is.
Swevenes engendren of[5] replecciouns,[6]
And ofte of fume,[7] and of complecciouns,[8]
Whan humours been to habundant in a wight.
Certes this dreem, which ye han met to-night,
Cometh of the grete superfluitee
Of youre rede colera,[9] pardee,
Which causeth folk to dreden in here dremes
Of arwes, and of fyr with rede lemes,[10]   110

[1] generous   [2] weapon   [3] boaster   [4] emptiness   [5] are caused by   [6] overeating   [7] gas on the stomach   [8] temperament   [9] red bile   [10] flames

Of grete bestes, that they wol hem byte,
Of contek,[1] and of whelpes grete and lyte;
Right as the humour of malencolye [2]
Causeth ful many a man, in sleep, to crye,
For fere of blake beres, or boles [3] blake,
Or elles, blake develes wole hem take.
Of othere humours coude I telle also,
That werken many a man in sleep ful wo;
But I wol passe as lightly as I can.

Lo Catoun, which that was so wys a man,   120
Seyde he nat thus, ne do no fors [4] of dremes?
Now, sire," quod she, "whan we flee fro the bemes,
For Goddes love, as tak som laxatyf;
Up peril of my soule, and of my lyf,
I counseille yow the beste, I wol nat lye,
That bothe of colere and of malencolye
Ye purge yow; and for ye shul nat tarie,
Though in this toun is noon apotecarie,
I shall my-self to herbes techen yow,
That shul ben for your hele, and for your prow; [5]   130
And in our yerd tho herbes shal I finde,
The whiche han of hir propretee, by kinde,[6]
To purgen yow binethe, and eek above.
Forget not this, for goddes owene love!
Ye been ful colerik of compleccioun.
Ware the sonne in his ascencioun
Ne fynde yow nat repleet of humours hote;
And if it do, I dar wel leye a grote,
That ye shul have a fevere terciane,
Or an agu, that may be youre bane.   140
A day or two ye shul have digestyves
Of wormes, er ye take your laxatyves,
Of lauriol, centaure, and fumetere,
Or elles of ellebor, that groweth there,

Of catapuce, or of gaytres beryis,
Of erbe yve,[1] growing in our yerd, that mery is;
Pekke hem up right as they growe, and ete hem in.
Be mery, housbond, for your fader kin!
Dredeth no dreem; I can say yow namore."

    "Madame," quod he, *"graunt mercy* [2] of your
        lore.   150
But nathelees, as touching daun Catoun,
That hath of wisdom such a greet renoun,
Though that he bad no dremes for to drede,
By god, men may in olde bokes rede
Of many a man, more of auctoritee
Than ever Catoun was, so mote I thee,[3]
That al the revers seyn of his sentence,
And han wel founden by experience,
That dremes ben significaciouns,
As wel of joye as tribulaciouns   160
That folk enduren in this lyf present.
Ther nedeth make of this noon argument;
The verray preve [4] sheweth it in dede.

    Oon of the gretteste auctours that men rede
Seith thus, that whylom two felawes wente
On pilgrimage, in a ful good entente;
And happed so, thay come into a toun,
Wher-as ther was swich congregacioun
Of peple, and eek so streit of herbergage [5]
That they ne founde as muche as o cotage   170
In which they bothe mighte y-logged be.
Wherfor thay mosten, of necessitee,
As for that night, departen compaignye;
And ech of hem goth to his hostelrye,
And took his logging as it wolde falle.
That oon of hem was logged in a stalle,

----

[1] medicinal herbs   [2] many thanks   [3] prosper   [4] proof   [5] limited in its lodgings

Fer in a yerd, with oxen of the plough;
That other man was logged wel y-nough,
As was his aventure, or his fortune,
That us governeth alle as in commune. 180

And so bifel, that, longe er it were day,
This man mette in his bed, ther-as he lay,
How that his felawe gan up-on him calle,
And seyde, 'allas! for in an oxes stalle
This night I shal be mordred ther I lye.
Now help me, dere brother, er I dye;
In alle haste com to me,' he sayde.
This man out of his sleep for fere abrayde;[1]
But whan that he was wakned of his sleep,
He turned him, and took of this no keep;[2] 190
Him thoughte his dreem nas but a vanitee.
Thus twyës in his sleping dremed he.
And atte thridde tyme yet his felawe
Cam, as him thoughte, and seide, 'I am now slawe;
Bihold my blody woundes, depe and wyde!
Arys up erly in the morwe-tyde,
And at the west gate of the toun,' quod he,
'A carte ful of dong ther shaltow see,
In which my body is hid ful prively;
Do thilke carte aresten boldely. 200
My gold caused my mordre, sooth to sayn';
And tolde him every poynt how he was slayn,
With a ful pitous face, pale of hewe.
And truste wel, his dreem he fond ful trewe;
For on the morwe, as sone as it was day,
To his felawes in he took the way;
And whan that he came to this oxes stalle,
After his felawe he bigan to calle.

The hostiler answered him anon,
And seyde, 'sire, your felawe is agon, 210
As sone as day he wente out of the toun.'

---

[1] started   [2] thought

This man gan fallen in suspecioun,
Remembring on his dremes that he mette,
And forth he goth, no lenger wolde he lette,[1]
Unto the west gate of the toun, and fond
A dong-carte, as it were to donge lond,
That was arrayed in the same wyse
As ye han herd the dede man devyse;
And with an hardy herte he gan to crye
Vengeaunce and justice of this felonye:—   220
'My felawe mordred is this same night,
And in this carte he lyth gapinge upright.
I crye out on the ministres,' quod he,
'That sholden kepe and reulen this citee;
Harrow! allas! her lyth my felawe slayn!'
What sholde I more un-to this tale sayn?
The peple out-sterte, and caste the cart to grounde,
And in the middel of the dong they founde
The dede man, that mordred was al newe.

O blisful god, that art so just and trewe!   230
Lo, how that thou biwreyest [2] mordre alway!
Mordre wol out, that see we day by day.
Mordre is so wlatsom [3] and abhominable
To god, that is so just and resonable,
That he ne wol nat suffre it heled [4] be;
Though it abyde a yeer, or two, or three,
Mordre wol out, this my conclusioun.
And right anoon, ministres of that toun
Han hent the carter, and so sore him pyned,[5]
And eek the hostiler so sore engyned,[6]   240
That thay biknewe [7] hir wikkednesse anoon,
And were an-hanged by the nekke-boon.

Here may men seen that dremes been to drede.
And certes, in the same book I rede,

[1] delay   [2] revealed   [3] heinous   [4] concealed   [5] tortured
[6] racked   [7] confessed

Right in the nexte chapitre after this,
(I gabbe [1] nat, so have I joye or blis,)
Two men that wolde han passed over see,
For certeyn cause, in-to a fer contree,
If that the wind ne hadde been contrarie,
That made hem in a citee for to tarie,   250
That stood ful mery upon an haven-syde.
But on a day, agayn the even-tyde,
The wind gan chaunge, and blew right as hem leste.
Jolif and glad they wente un-to hir reste,
And casten hem [2] ful erly for to saille;
But to that oo [3] man fil a greet mervaille.
That oon of hem, in sleping as he lay,
Him mette a wonder dreem, agayn the day;
Him thoughte a man stood by his beddes syde,
And him comaunded, that he sholde abyde,   260
And seyde him thus, 'if thou to-morwe wende,
Thou shalt be dreynt; [4] my tale is at an ende.'
He wook, and tolde his felawe what he mette,
And preyde him his viage for to lette;
As for that day, he preyde him to abyde.
His felawe, that lay by his beddes syde,
Gan for to laughe, and scorned him ful faste.
'No dreem,' quod he, 'may so myn herte agaste,
That I wol lette for to do my thinges.
I sette not a straw by thy dreminges,   270
For swevenes been but vanitees and japes. [5]
Men dreme al-day of owles or of apes,
And eke of many a mase [6] therwithal;
Men dreme of thing that never was ne shal.
But sith I see that thou wolt heer abyde,
And thus for-sleuthen [7] wilfully thy tyde,
God wot it reweth me, [8] and have good day.'

[1] lie   [2] they planned   [3] one   [4] drowned   [5] jests   [6] bewilderment   [7] waste   [8] I am sorry

And thus he took his leve, and wente his way.
But er that he hadde halfe his cours y-seyled,
Noot I nat why, ne what mischaunce it eyled,   280
But casuelly [1] the shippes botme rente,
And ship and man under the water wente
In sighte of othere shippes it byside,
That with hem seyled at the same tyde.
And therfor, faire Pertelote so dere,
By swiche ensamples olde maistow [2] lere,
That no man sholde been to recchelees
Of dremes, for I sey thee, doutelees,
That many a dreem ful sore is for to drede.

Lo, in the lyf of seint Kenelm, I rede,   290
That was Kenulphus sone, the noble king
Of Mercenrike,[3] how Kenelm mette a thing;
A lyte er [4] he was mordred, on a day,
His mordre in his avisioun he say.[5]
His norice [6] him expouned every del
His sweven, and bad him for to kepe him wel
For [7] traisoun; but he nas but seven yeer old,
And therfore litel tale hath he told
Of any dreem, so holy was his herte.
By god, I hadde lever than my sherte   300
That ye had rad his legende, as have I.
Dame Pertelote, I sey yow trewely,
Macrobeus, that writ th'avisioun
In Affrike of the worthy Cipioun,
Affermeth dremes, and seith that they been
Warning of thinges that men after seen.

And forther-more, I pray yow loketh wel
In th'olde testament, of Daniel,
If he held dremes any vanitee.
Reed eek of Joseph, and ther shul ye see   310

---

[1] accidentally   [2] mayest thou   [3] Mercia   [4] a little while before   [5] saw   [6] nurse   [7] for fear of

Wher dremes ben somtyme (I sey nat alle)
Warning of thinges that shul after falle.
Loke of Egipt the king, daun [1] Pharao,
His bakere and his boteler also,
Wher they ne felte noon effect in dremes.
Who-so wol seken actes of sondry remes,[2]
May rede of dremes many a wonder thing.

Lo Cresus, which that was of Lyde [3] king,
Mette he nat that he sat upon a tree,
Which signified he sholde anhanged be? 320
Lo heer Andromacha, Ectores wyf,
That day that Ector sholde lese [4] his lyf,
She dremed on the same night biforn,
How that the lyf of Ector sholde be lorn,
If thilke day he wente in-to bataille;
She warned him, but it mighte nat availle;
He wente for to fighte nathelees,
But he was slayn anoon of Achilles.
But thilke tale is al to long to telle,
And eek it is ny [5] day, I may nat dwelle. 330
Shortly I seye, as for conclusioun,
That I shal han of this avisioun
Adversitee; and I seye forther-more,
That I ne telle of laxatyves no store,[6]
For they ben venimous, I woot it wel;
I hem defye, I love hem never a del.[7]

Now let us speke of mirthe, and stinte [8] al this;
Madame Pertelote, so have I blis,
Of o thing god hath sent me large grace;
For whan I see the beautee of your face, 340
Ye ben so scarlet-reed about your yën,
It maketh al my drede for to dyen;
For, also siker [9] as In principio,

[1] lord　[2] realms　[3] Lydia　[4] lose　[5] almost　[6] have no
faith in　[7] never a bit　[8] cease　[9] just as sure

Mulier est hominis confusio; [1]
Madame, the sentence [2] of this Latin is—
Womman is mannes joye and al his blis.
For whan I fele a-night your softe syde,
Al-be-it that I may nat on you ryde,
For that our perche is maad so narwe, alas!
I am so ful of joye and of solas   350
That I defye bothe sweven and dreem."
And with that word he fley doun fro the beem,
For it was day, and eek his hennes alle;
And with a chuk he gan hem for to calle,
For he had founde a corn, lay in the yerd.
Royal he was, he was namore aferd;
He fethered Pertelote twenty tyme,
And trad as ofte, er that it was pryme.
He loketh as it were a grim leoun;
And on his toos he rometh up and doun,   360
Him deyned not to sette his foot to grounde.
He chukketh, whan he hath a corn y-founde,
And to him rennen thanne his wyves alle.
Thus royal, as a prince is in his halle,
Leve I this Chauntecleer in his pasture;
And after wol I telle his aventure.

Whan that the month in which the world bigan,
That highte March, whan god first maked man,
Was complet, and passed were also,
Sin March bigan, thritty dayes and two,   370
Bifel that Chauntecleer, in al his pryde,
His seven wyves walking by his syde,
Caste up his eyen to the brighte sonne,
That in the signe of Taurus hadde y-ronne
Twenty degrees and oon, and somewhat more;

---

[1] "Woman is man's undoing." Chauntecleer translates it incorrectly on purpose. [2] meaning

And knew by kynde,[1] and by noon other lore,[2]
That it was pryme,[3] and crew with blisful stevene.[4]
"The sonne," he sayde, "is clomben up on hevene
Fourty degrees and oon, and more, y-wis.[5]
Madame Pertelote, my worldes blis,   380
Herkneth thise blisful briddes how they singe,
And see the fresshe floures how they springe;
Ful is myn herte of revel and solas."
But sodeinly him fil a sorweful cas;[6]
For ever the latter ende of joye is wo.
God woot that worldly joye is sone ago;[7]
And if a rethor [8] coude faire endyte,
He in a cronique saufly [9] mighte it wryte,
As for a sovereyn notabilitee.[10]
Now every wys man, lat him herkne me;   390
This storie is al-so trewe, I undertake,
As is the book of Launcelot de Lake,
That wommen holde in ful gret reverence.
Now wol I torne agayn to my sentence.

  A col-fox,[11] ful of sly iniquitee,
That in the grove hadde woned [12] yeres three,
By heigh imaginacioun forn-cast,[13]
The same night thurgh-out the hegges [14] brast [15]
Into the yerd, ther Chauntecleer the faire
Was wont, and eek his wyves, to repaire;   400
And in a bed of wortes [16] stille he lay,
Til it was passed undern [17] of the day,
Wayting his tyme on Chauntecleer to falle,
As gladly doon thise homicydes alle,
That in awayt liggen [18] to mordre men.
O false mordrer, lurking in thy den!

---

[1] nature   [2] no other teaching   [3] nine o'clock   [4] voice   [5] certainly   [6] a sad accident befell him   [7] gone   [8] rhetorician   [9] safely   [10] wonder   [11] black fox   [12] lived   [13] destined by God   [14] hedges   [15] burst   [16] herbs   [17] middle of the forenoon   [18] lie

O newe Scariot, newe Genilon![1]
False dissimilour,[2] O Greek Sinon,
That broghtest Troye al outrely[3] to sorwe!
O Chauntecleer, acursed be that morwe, 410
That thou into that yerd flough fro the bemes!
Thou were ful wel y-warned by thy dremes,
That thilke day was perilous to thee.
But what that god forwoot mot nedes be,[4]
After the opinioun of certeyn clerkis.
Witnesse on him,[5] that any perfit clerk is,
That in scole is gret altercacioun
In this matere, and greet disputisoun,
And hath ben of an hundred thousand men.
But I ne can not bulte it to the bren,[6] 420
As can the holy doctour Augustyn,
Or Boëce,[7] or the bishop Bradwardyn,[8]
Whether that goddes worthy forwiting
Streyneth[9] me nedely[10] for to doon a thing,
(Nedely clepe I simple necessitee);
Or elles, if free choys be graunted me
To do that same thing, or do it noght,
Though god forwoot it, er that it was wroght;
Or if his witing streyneth nevere a del
But by necessitee condicionel. 430
I wol not han to do of swich matere;
My tale is of a cok, as ye may here,
That took his counseil of his wyf, with sorwe,
To walken in the yerd upon that morwe
That he had met the dreem, that I yow tolde.
Wommennes counseils been ful ofte colde;[11]
Wommannes counseil broghte us first to wo,

---

[1] Ganelon, traitor in the *Song of Roland* [2] dissembler [3] completely [4] what God foreknows must be [5] let him be a witness [6] sift the matter [7] Boethius [8] fourteenth century English theologian [9] constrains [10] necessity [11] harmful

And made Adam fro paradys to go,
Ther-as he was ful mery, and wel at ese.—
But for I noot, to whom it mighte displese,   440
If I counseil of wommen wolde blame,
Passe over, for I seyde it in my game.[1]
Rede auctours,[2] wher they trete of swich matere,
And what thay seyn of wommen ye may here.
Thise been the cokkes wordes, and nat myne;
I can noon harm of no womman divyne.—

Faire in the sond, to bathe hir merily,
Lyth Pertelote, and alle hir sustres by,
Agayn the sonne; and Chauntecleer so free
Song merier than the mermayde in the see;   450
For Phisiologus[3] seith sikerly,
How that they singen wel and merily.
And so bifel that, as he caste his yë,
Among the wortes, on a boterflye,
He was war of this fox that lay ful lowe.
No-thing ne liste him thanne for to crowe,[4]
But cryde anon, "cok, cok," and up he sterte,
As man that was affrayed in his herte.
For naturelly a beest desyreth flee
Fro his contrarie, if he may it see,   460
Though he never erst[5] had seyn it with his yë.

This Chauntecleer, whan he gan him espye,
He wolde han fled, but that the fox anon
Seyde, "Gentil sire, allas! wher wol ye gon?
Be ye affrayed of me that am your freend?
Now certes, I were worse than a feend,
If I to yow wolde harm or vileinye.
I am nat come your counseil[6] for t'espye;[7]
But trewely, the cause of my cominge
Was only for to herkne how that ye singe.   470

[1] in sport   [2] authors   [3] a book of animal fables   [4] Then he did not at all want to crow   [5] before   [6] secrets   [7] spy out

For trewely ye have as mery a stevene[1]
As eny aungel hath, that is in hevene;
Therwith ye han in musik more felinge
Than hadde Boëce, or any that can singe.
My lord your fader (god his soule blesse!)
And eek your moder, of hir gentilesse,
Han in myn hous y-been, to my gret ese;
And certes, sire, ful fayn wolde I yow plese.
But for men speke of singing, I wol saye,
So mote I brouke[2] wel myn eyen tweye,   480
Save yow, I herde never man so singe,
As dide your fader in the morweninge;
Certes, it was of herte, al that he song.
And for to make his voys the more strong,
He wolde so peyne him, that with bothe his yën
He moste winke, so loude he wolde cryen,
And stonden on his tiptoon ther-with-al,
And strecche forth his nekke long and smal.
And eek he was of swich discrecioun,
That ther nas no man in no regioun   490
That him in song or wisdom mighte passe.
I have wel rad in daun Burnel the Asse,[3]
Among his vers, how that ther was a cok,
For that a preestes sone yaf him a knok
Upon his leg, whyl he was yong and nyce,
He made him for to lese[4] his benefyce.
But certeyn, ther nis no comparisoun
Bitwix the wisdom and discrecioun
Of youre fader, and of his subtiltee.
Now singeth, sire, for seinte Charitee,   500
Let see, conne ye your fader countrefete?'[5]
This Chauntecleer his winges gan to bete,

---

[1] voice   [2] have the use of   [3] a twelfth century Latin satirical
poem   [4] lose   [5] imitate

As man that coude his tresoun nat espye,
So was he ravisshed with his flaterye.
    Allas! ye lordes, many a fals flatour
Is in your courtes, and many a losengeour,[1]
That plesen yow wel more, by my feith,
Than he that soothfastnesse[2] unto yow seith.
Redeth Ecclesiaste of flaterye;
Beth[3] war, ye lordes, of hir trecherye.   510
    This Chauntecleer stood hye up-on his toos,
Strecching his nekke, and heeld his eyen cloos,
And gan to crowe loude for the nones;[4]
And daun Russel the fox sterte up at ones,
And by the gargat[5] hente Chauntecleer,
And on his bak toward the wode him beer,
For yet ne was ther no man that him sewed.[6]
O destinee, that mayst nat been eschewed![7]
Allas, that Chauntecleer fleigh fro the bemes!
Allas, his wyf ne roghte nat[8] of dremes!   520
And on a Friday fil al this meschaunce.
O Venus, that art goddesse of pleasaunce,
Sin that thy servant was this Chauntecleer,
And in thy service dide al his poweer,
More for delyt, than world to multiplye,
Why woldestow[9] suffre him on thy day to dye?
O Gaufred,[10] dere mayster soverayn,
That, whan thy worthy king Richard was slayn
With shot, compleynedest his deth so sore,
Why ne hadde I[11] now thy sentence and thy lore,   530
The Friday for to chyde, as diden ye?
(For on a Friday soothly slayn was he.)
Than wolde I shewe yow how that I coude pleyne[12]
For Chauntecleres drede, and for his peyne.

---

[1] deceiver   [2] truth   [3] be   [4] for the nonce   [5] throat   [6] pursued   [7] avoided   [8] paid no attention to   [9] wouldst thou
[10] Geoffrey of Vinsauf, who wrote in Latin a treatise on the art of poetry containing a lament for Richard I   [11] had I not   [12] lament

Certes, swich cry ne lamentacioun
Was never of ladies maad, whan Ilioun
Was wonne, and Pirrus with his streite swerd,
Whan he hadde hent [1] king Priam by the berd,
And slayn him (as saith us *Eneydos*),
As maden alle the hennes in the clos,   540
Whan they had seyn of Chauntecleer the sighte.
But sovereynly dame Pertelote shrighte,
Ful louder than dide Hasdrubales wyf,
Whan that hir housbond hadde lost his lyf,
And that the Romayns hadde brend [2] Cartage;
She was so ful of torment and of rage,
That wilfully into the fyr she sterte, [3]
And brende hir-selven with a stedfast herte.
O woful hennes, right so cryden ye,
As, whan that Nero brende the citee   550
Of Rome, cryden senatoures wyves,
For that hir housbondes losten alle hir lyves;
Withouten gilt this Nero hath hem slayn.
Now wol I torne to my tale agayn:—

This sely [4] widwe, and eek [5] hir doghtres two,
Herden thise hennes crye and maken wo,
And out at dores sterten they anoon,
And syen the fox toward the grove goon,
And bar upon his bak the cok away;
And cryden, "Out! harrow! and weylaway!   560
Ha, ha, the fox!" and after him they ran,
And eek with staves many another man;
Ran Colle our dogge, and Talbot, and Gerland,
And Malkin, with a distaf in hir hand;
Ran cow and calf, and eek the verray hogges
So were they fered for [6] berking of the dogges
And shouting of the men and wimmen eke,

---

[1] seized   [2] burned   [3] leaped   [4] luckless   [5] also   [6] frightened by

They ronne so, hem thoughte hir herte breke.
They yelleden as feendes doon in helle;
The dokes cryden as [1] men wolde hem quelle; [2]   570
The gees for fere flowen over the trees;
Out of the hyve cam the swarm of bees;
So hideous was the noyse, a! *benedicite!*
Certes, he Jakke Straw,[3] and his meynee,[4]
Ne made never shoutes half so shrille,
Whan that they wolden any Fleming [5] kille,
As thilke day was maad upon the fox.
Of bras thay broghten bemes,[6] and of box,[7]
Of horn, of boon, in whiche they blewe and pouped,
And therwithal thay shryked and they houped;   580
It semed as that heven sholde falle.
Now, gode men, I pray yow herkneth alle!

Lo, how fortune turneth sodeinly
The hope and pryde eek of hir enemy!
This cok, that lay upon the foxes bak,
In al his drede, un-to the fox he spak,
And seyde, "sire, if that I were as ye,
Yet sholde I seyn (as wis [8] god helpe me),
Turneth agayn, ye proude cherles alle!
A verray pestilence up-on yow falle!   590
Now am I come un-to this wodes syde,
Maugree [9] your heed, the cok shal heer abyde;
I wol him ete in feith, and that anon."—
The fox answerde, "in feith, it shal be don,"—
And as he spak that word, al sodeinly
This cok brak from his mouth deliverly,[10]
And heighe up-on a tree he fleigh anon.
And whan the fox saugh that he was y-gon,
"Allas!" quod he, "O Chauntecleer, allas!

---

[1] as if   [2] kill   [3] leader of the Peasants' Revolt of 1381   [4] company   [5] Many Flemings were London tradesmen.   [6] trumpets   [7] box-wood   [8] surely   [9] in spite of   [10] nimbly

I have to yow," quod he, "y-doon trespas,   600
In-as-muche as I maked yow aferd,
Whan I yow hente, and broghte out of the yerd;
But, sire, I dide it in no wikke [1] entente;
Com doun, and I shal telle yow what I mente.
I shal seye sooth to yow, god help me so."
"Nay than," quod he, "I shrewe [2] us bothe two,
And first I shrewe my-self, bothe blood and bones,
If thou bigyle me ofter than ones.
Thou shalt na-more, thurgh thy flaterye,
Do me to singe and winke with myn yë.   610
For he that winketh, whan he sholde see,
Al wilfully, god lat him never thee !" [3]
"Nay," quod the fox, "but god yeve him meschaunce,
That is so undiscreet of governaunce,
That jangleth [4] whan he sholde holde his pees."

Lo, swich it is for to be recchelees, [5]
And necligent, and truste on flaterye.
But ye that holden this tale a folye,
As of a fox, or of a cok and hen,
Taketh the moralitee, good men.   620
For seint Paul seith, that al that writen is,
To our doctryne [6] it is y-write, y-wis.
Taketh the fruyt, and lat the chaf be stille.

Now, gode god, if that it be thy wille,
As seith my lord, so make us alle good men;
And bringe us to his heighe blisse. Amen.

Here is ended the Nonne Preestes Tale.

[1] wicked   [2] curse   [3] prosper   [4] talks   [5] careless   [6] for our
teaching

The Prologue of the Pardoner's Tale

Here folweth the Prologe of the Pardoners Tale

Radix malorum est Cupiditas: Ad Thimotheum, sexto.

"Lordings," quod he, "in chirches whan I preche,
I peyne me to han an hauteyn speche,[1]
And ringe it out as round as gooth a belle,
For I can al by rote[2] that I telle.
My theme is alwey oon, and ever was—
'Radix malorum est Cupiditas.'[3]
  First I pronounce whennes that I come,
And than my bulles shewe I, alle and somme.
Our lige lordes seel on my patente,[4]
That shewe I first, my body to warente,   10
That no man be so bold, ne preest ne clerk,
Me to destourbe of Cristes holy werk;
And after that than telle I forth my tales,
Bulles of popes and of cardinales,
Of patriarkes, and bishoppes I shewe;
And in Latyn I speke a wordes fewe,
To saffron with my predicacioun,[5]
And for to stire men to devocioun.
Than shewe I forth my longe cristal stones,
Y-crammed ful of cloutes and of bones;   20
Reliks been they, as wenen they echoon.[6]
Than have I in latoun[7] a sholder-boon
Which that was of an holy Jewes shepe.
'Good men,' seye I, 'take of my wordes kepe;[8]
If that this boon be wasshe in any welle,

---

[1] I am careful to speak in a dignified manner   [2] know all by heart   [3] "For the love of money is the root of all evil" (1 Timothy 6.10)   [4] letter of authority   [5] to flavor my preaching   [6] each one   [7] latten, a metal resembling brass   [8] heed

If cow, or calf, or sheep, or oxe swelle
That any worm [1] hath ete, or worm y-stonge,
Tak water of that welle, and wash his tonge,
And it is hool anon; and forthermore,
Of pokkes and of scabbe, and every sore   30
Shal every sheep be hool, that of this welle
Drinketh a draughte; tak kepe eek what I telle.
If that the good-man, that the bestes oweth, [2]
Wol every wike, [3] er that the cok him croweth,
Fastinge, drinken of this welle a draughte,
As thilke holy Jewe our eldres taughte,
His bestes and his stoor shal multiplye.
And, sirs, also it heleth jalousye;
For, though a man be falle in jalous rage,
Let maken with this water his potage,   40
And never shal he more his wyf mistriste,
Though he the sooth of hir defaute wiste;
Al had she taken preestes two or three.

Heer is a miteyn eek, that ye may see.
He that his hond wol putte in this miteyn,
He shal have multiplying of his greyn,
Whan he hath sowen, be it whete or otes,
So that he offre pens, or elles grotes.

Good men and wommen, o thing warne I yow,
If any wight be in this chirche now,   50
That hath doon sinne horrible, that he
Dar nat, for shame, of it y-shriven be,
Or any womman, be she yong or old,
That hath y-maad hir housbond cokewold, [4]
Swich folk shul have no power ne no grace
To offren to my reliks in this place.
And who-so findeth him out of swich blame,
He wol com up and offre in goddes name,

[1] snake   [2] owns   [3] week   [4] who has disgraced her husband

And I assoille [1] him by the auctoritee
Which that by bulle y-graunted was to me.'   60
   By this gaude [2] have I wonne, yeer by yeer,
An hundred mark sith I was Pardoner.
I stonde lyk a clerk in my pulpet,
And whan the lewed [3] peple is doun y-set,
I preche, so as ye han herd bifore,
And telle an hundred false japes more.
Than peyne I me to strecche forth the nekke,
And est and west upon the peple I bekke, [4]
As doth a dowve sitting on a berne.
Myn hondes and my tonge goon so yerne, [5]   70
That it is joye to see my bisinesse.
Of avaryce and of swich cursednesse
Is al my preching, for to make hem free
To yeve her pens, and namely [6] un-to me.
For my entente is nat but for to winne,
And no-thing for correccioun of sinne.
I rekke never, whan that they ben beried,
Though that her soules goon a-blake-beried! [7]
For certes, many a predicacioun
Comth ofte tyme of yvel entencioun;   80
Som for plesaunce of folk and flaterye,
To been avaunced by ipocrisye,
And som for veyne glorie, and som for hate.
For, whan I dar non other weyes debate, [8]
Than wol I stinge him with my tonge smerte
In preching, so that he shal nat asterte [9]
To been defamed falsly, if that he
Hath trespased to my brethren or to me.
For, though I telle noght his propre name,
Men shal wel knowe that it is the same   90

---

[1] absolve   [2] trick   [3] ignorant   [4] nod   [5] quickly   [6] particularly   [7] go blackberrying   [8] quarrel   [9] escape

By signes and by othere circumstances.
Thus quyte I folk that doon us displesances;
Thus spitte I out my venim under hewe
Of holynesse, to seme holy and trewe.

But shortly myn entente I wol devyse;
I preche of no-thing but for coveityse.
Therfor my theme is yet, and ever was—
'*Radix malorum est cupiditas.*'
Thus can I preche agayn that same vyce
Which that I use, and that is avaryce.   100
But, though my-self be gilty in that sinne
Yet can I maken other folk to twinne [1]
From avaryce, and sore to repente.
But that is nat my principal entente.
I preche no-thing but for coveityse;
Of this matere it oughte y-nogh suffyse.

Than telle I hem ensamples many oon
Of olde stories, longe tyme agoon:
For lewed peple loven tales olde;
Swich thinges can they wel reporte and holde.   110
What? trowe ye, the whyles I may preche,
And winne gold and silver for I teche,
That I wol live in povert wilfully?
Nay, nay, I thoghte it never trewely!
For I wol preche and begge in sondry londes;
I wol not do no labour with myn hondes,
Ne make baskettes, and live therby,
Because I wol nat beggen ydelly.
I wol non of the apostles counterfete;[2]
I wol have money, wolle, chese, and whete,   120
Al were it yeven of the povrest page,
Or of the povrest widwe in a village,
Al sholde hir children sterve for famyne.
Nay! I wol drinke licour of the vyne,

---

[1] separate   [2] imitate

And have a joly wenche in every toun.
But herkneth, lordings, in conclusioun;
Your lyking is that I shal telle a tale.
Now, have I dronke a draughte of corny ale,
By god, I hope I shal yow telle a thing
That shal, by resoun, been at your lyking. 130
For, though myself be a ful vicious man,
A moral tale yet I yow telle can,
Which I am wont to preche, for to winne.
How holde your pees, my tale I wol beginne."

THE PARDONER'S TALE

Here biginneth the Pardoners Tale

In Flaundres whylom was a companye
Of yonge folk, that haunteden [1] folye,
As ryot, hasard, stewes,[2] and tavernes,
Wher-as, with harpes, lutes, and giternes,
They daunce and pleye at dees bothe day and night,
And ete also and drinken over hir might,
Thurgh which they doon the devel sacrifyse
With-in that develes temple, in cursed wyse,
By superfluitee abhominable;
Hir othes been so grete and so dampnable, 10
That it is grisly for to here hem swere;
Our blissed lordes body they to-tere;[3]
Hem thoughte Jewes rente him noght y-nough;
And ech of hem at otheres sinne lough.
And right anon than comen tombesteres[4]
Fetys[5] and smale, and yonge fruytesteres,[6]
Singers with harpes, baudes, wafereres,[7]

---

[1] indulged in   [2] brothels   [3] They tear Christ's body to pieces, i.e. they swear by the various parts of it.   [4] girl acrobats   [5] well formed   [6] girl fruit-sellers   [7] cake vendors

Whiche been the verray develes officeres
To kindle and blowe the fyr of lecherye,
That is annexed un-to glotonye;   20
The holy writ take I to my witnesse,
That luxurie is in wyn and dronkenesse.

Lo, how that dronken Loth, unkindely,[1]
Lay by his doghtres two, unwitingly;
So dronke he was, he niste what he wroghte.

Herodes (who-so wel the stories soghte),
Whan he of wyn was replet at his feste,
Right at his owene table he yaf his heste [2]
To sleen the Baptist John ful giltelees.

Senek seith eek a good word douteles;   30
He seith, he can no difference finde
Bitwix a man that is out of his minde
And a man which that is dronkelewe,[3]
But that woodnesse, y-fallen in a shrewe,[4]
Persevereth lenger than doth dronkenesse.

O glotonye, ful of cursednesse,
O cause first of our confusioun,
O original of our dampnacioun,
Til Crist had boght us with his blood agayn!
Lo, how dere, shortly for to sayn,   40
Aboght was thilke cursed vileinye;
Corrupt was all this world for glotonye!

Adam our fader, and his wyf also,
Fro Paradys to labour and to wo
Were driven for that vyce, it is no drede; [5]
For whyl that Adam fasted, as I rede,
He was in Paradys; and whan that he
Eet of the fruyt defended [6] on the tree,
Anon he was out-cast to wo and peyne.
O glotonye, on thee wel oghte us pleyne! [7]   50

[1] unnaturally   [2] command   [3] drunken   [4] madness, when it
comes upon a wicked man   [5] without doubt   [6] forbidden   [7] indeed of thee we should complain

O, wiste a man how many maladyes
Folwen of excesse and of glotonyes,
He wolde been the more mesurable [1]
Of his diete, sittinge at his table.
Allas! the shorte throte, the tendre mouth,
Maketh that, Est and West, and North and South,
In erthe, in eir, in water men to-swinke [2]
To gete a glotoun deyntee mete and drinke!
Of this matere, o Paul, wel canstow trete,
"Mete un-to wombe,[3] and wombe eek un-to mete,   60
Shal god destroyen bothe," as Paulus seith.
Allas! a foul thing it is, by my feith,
To seye this word, and fouler is the dede,
Whan man so drinketh of the whyte and rede,
That of his throte he maketh his privee,
Thurgh thilke cursed superfluitee.

The apostel weping seith ful pitously,
"Ther walken many of whiche yow told have I,
I seye it now weping with pitous voys,
That they been enemys of Cristes croys,   70
Of whiche the ende is deeth, wombe is her god."
O wombe! O bely! O stinking cod,[4]
Fulfild of donge and of corrupcioun!
At either ende of thee foul is the soun.
How greet labour and cost is thee to finde! [5]
Thise cokes, how they stampe, and streyne,[6] and grinde,
And turnen substance in-to accident,[7]
To fulfille al thy likerous talent! [8]
Out of the harde bones knokke they
The mary,[9] for they caste noght a-wey   80
That may go thurgh the golet softe and swote; [10]

---

[1] temperate   [2] labor hard   [3] belly   [4] bag   [5] provide for
[6] labor   [7] "Substance" in scholastic philosophy means essential
nature contrasted with the "accidents" of shape, smell, color, etc.
[8] over-dainty taste   [9] marrow   [10] sweetly

Of spicerye, of leef, and bark, and rote
Shal been his sauce y-maked by delyt,
To make him yet a newer appetyt.
But certes, he that haunteth swich delyces
Is deed, whyl that he liveth in tho vyces.

A lecherous thing is wyn, and dronkenesse
Is ful of stryving and of wrecchednesse.
O dronke man, disfigured is thy face,
Sour is thy breeth, foul artow to embrace,   90
And thurgh thy dronke nose semeth the soun
As though thou seydest ay "Sampsoun, Sampsoun";
And yet, god wot, Sampsoun drank never no wyn.
Thou fallest, as it were a stiked swyn;
Thy tonge is lost, and al thyn honest cure; [1]
For dronkenesse is verray sepulture
Of mannes wit and his discrecioun.
In whom that drinke hath dominacioun,
He can no conseil kepe, it is no drede. [2]
Now kepe yow fro the whyte and fro the rede,   100
And namely fro the whyte wyn of Lepe, [3]
That is to selle in Fish-strete or in Chepe. [4]
This wyn of Spayne crepeth subtilly
In othere wynes, growing faste by,
Of which ther ryseth swich fumositee, [5]
That whan a man hath dronken draughtes three,
And weneth that he be at hoom in Chepe,
He is in Spayne, right at the toune of Lepe,
Nat at the Rochel, ne at Burdeux toun;
And thanne wol he seye, "Sampsoun, Sampsoun."   110

But herkneth, lordings, o word, I yow preye,
That alle the sovereyn actes, dar I seye,
Of victories in th'olde testament,
Thurgh verray god, that is omnipotent,

[1] care for a good name   [2] doubt   [3] a town in Spain   [4] Cheapside in London   [5] fumes

Were doon in abstinence and in preyere;
Loketh the Bible, and ther ye may it lere.
  Loke, Attila, the grete conquerour,
Deyde in his sleep, with shame and dishonour,
Bledinge ay at his nose in dronkenesse;
A capitayn sholde live in sobrenesse.   **120**
And over [1] al this, avyseth yow right wel
What was comaunded un-to Lamuel—
Nat Samuel, but Lamuel, seye I—
Redeth the Bible, and finde it expresly
Of wyn-yeving to hem that han justyse.
Na-more of this, for it may wel suffyse.
  And now that I have spoke of glotonye,
Now wol I yow defenden hasardrye.[2]
Hasard is verray moder of lesinges,[3]
And of deceite, and cursed forsweringes,   **130**
Blaspheme of Crist, manslaughtre, and wast also
Of catel [4] and of tyme; and forthermo,
It is repreve [5] and contrarie of honour
For to ben holde a commune hasardour.
And ever the hyër he is of estaat,
The more is he holden desolaat.
If that a prince useth hasardrye,
In alle governaunce and policye
He is, as by commune opinioun,
Y-holde the lasse in reputacioun.   **140**
  Stilbon, that was a wys embassadour,
Was sent to Corinthe, in ful greet honour,
Fro Lacidomie, to make hir alliaunce.
And whan he cam, him happede, par chaunce,
That alle the grettest that were of that lond,
Pleyinge atte hasard he hem fond.
For which, as sone as it mighte be,
He stal him hoom agayn to his contree,

[1] in addition to   [2] forbid gambling   [3] lies   [4] property   [5] reproach

And seyde, "ther wol I nat lese my name;
N' I wol nat take on me so greet defame, 150
Yow for to allye un-to none hasardours.
Sendeth othere wyse embassadours;
For, by my trouthe, me were lever dye,[1]
Than I yow sholde to hasardours allye.
For ye that been so glorious in honours
Shul nat allyen yow with hasardours
As by my wil, ne as by my tretee."
This wyse philosophre thus seyde he.

Loke eek that, to the king Demetrius
The king of Parthes, as the book seith us, 160
Sente him a paire of dees[2] of gold in scorn,
For he hadde used hasard ther-biforn;
For which he heeld his glorie or his renoun
At no value or reputacioun.
Lordes may finden other maner pley
Honeste y-nough to dryve the day awey.

Now wol I speke of othes false and grete
A word or two, as olde bokes trete.
Gret swering is a thing abhominable,
And false swering is yet more reprevable. 170
The heighe god forbad swering at al,
Witnesse on Mathew; but in special
Of swering seith the holy Jeremye,
"Thou shalt seye sooth thyn othes, and nat lye,
And swere in dome, and eek in rightwisnesse;"
But ydel swering is a cursednesse.
Bihold and see, that in the firste table
Of heighe goddes hestes honurable,
How that the seconde heste of him is this—
"Tak nat my name in ydel or amis." 180
Lo, rather he forbedeth swich swering
Than homicyde or many a cursed thing;

[1] I should rather die [2] dice

I seye that, as by ordre, thus it stondeth;
This knowen, that his hestes understondeth,
How that the second heste of god is that.
And forther over, I wol thee telle al plat,[1]
That vengeance shal nat parten from his hous,
That of his othes is to outrageous.
"By goddes precious herte, and by his nayles,
And by the blode of Crist, that it is in Hayles,[2]   190
Seven is my chaunce, and thyn is cink and treye;[3]
By goddes armes, if thou falsly pleye,
This dagger shal thurgh-out thyn herte go"—
This fruyt cometh of the bicched bones[4] two,
Forswering, ire, falsnesse, homicyde.
Now, for the love of Crist that for us dyde,
Leveth your othes, bothe grete and smale;
But, sirs, now wol I telle forth my tale.

This ryotoures three, of which I telle,
Longe erst er pryme[5] rong of any belle,   200
Were set hem in a taverne for to drinke;
And as they satte, they herde a belle clinke
Biforn a cors, was caried to his grave;
That oon of hem gan callen to his knave,[6]
"Go bet,"[7] quod he, "and axe redily,
What cors is this that passeth heer forby;
And look that thou reporte his name wel."

"Sir," quod this boy, "it nedeth never-a-del.
It was me told, er ye cam heer, two houres;
He was, pardee, an old felawe of youres;   210
And sodeynly he was y-slayn to-night,[8]
For-dronke,[9] as he sat on his bench upright;
Ther cam a privee theef, men clepeth Deeth,

---

[1] and furthermore I tell you plainly   [2] an abbey in Gloucester-
shire   [3] five and three   [4] cursed bones (dice)   [5] nine in the
morning   [6] servant   [7] quickly   [8] last night   [9] dead drunk

That in this contree al the peple sleeth,
And with his spere he smoot his herte a-two,
And wente his wey with-outen wordes mo.
He hath a thousand slayn this pestilence:
And, maister, er ye come in his presence,
Me thinketh that it were necessarie
For to be war of swich an adversarie: 220
Beth redy for to mete him evermore.
Thus taughte me my dame, I sey na-more."
"By seinte Marie," seyde this taverner,
"The child seith sooth, for he hath slayn this yeer,
Henne [1] over a myle, with-in a greet village,
Both man and womman, child and hyne,[2] and page.
I trowe his habitacioun be there;
To been avysed greet wisdom it were,
Er that he dide a man a dishonour."
"Ye, goddes armes," quod this ryotour,   230
"Is it swich peril with him for to mete?
I shal him seke by wey and eek by strete,
I make avow to goddes digne bones!
Herkneth, felawes, we three been al ones;
Lat ech of us holde up his hond til other,
And ech of us bicomen otheres brother,
And we wol sleen this false traytour Deeth;
He shal be slayn, which that so many sleeth,
By goddes dignitee, er it be night."

Togidres han thise three her trouthes plight,   240
To live and dyen ech of hem for other,
As though he were his owene y-boren brother.
And up they sterte al dronken, in this rage,
And forth they goon towardes that village,
Of which the taverner had spoke biforn,
And many a grisly ooth than han they sworn,

1 hence   2 servant

And Cristes blessed body they to-rente—
"Deeth shal be deed, if that they may him hente."
　　Whan they han goon nat fully half a myle,
Right as they wolde han troden over a style,　　　　　250
An old man and a povre with hem mette.
This olde man ful mekely hem grette,[1]
And seyde thus, "now, lordes, god yow see!"[2]
　　The proudest of thise ryotoures three
Answerde agayn, "what? carl,[3] with sory grace,
Why artow al forwrapped[4] save thy face?
Why livestow so longe in so greet age?"
　　This olde man gan loke in his visage,
And seyde thus, "for I ne can nat finde
A man, though that I walked-in-to Inde,　　　　　260
Neither in citee nor in no village,
That wolde chaunge his youthe for myn age;
And therfore moot I han myn age stille,
As longe time as it is goddes wille.
　　Ne deeth, allas! ne wol nat han my lyf;
Thus walke I, lyk a restelees caityf,[5]
And on the ground, which is my modres gate,
I knokke with my staf, bothe erly and late,
And seye, 'leve moder, leet me in!
Lo, how I vanish, flesh, and blood, and skin!　　　　　270
Allas! whan shul my bones been at reste?
Moder, with yow wolde I chaunge my cheste,
That in my chambre longe tyme hath be,
Ye! for an heyre clout to wrappe me!'[6]
But yet to me she wol nat do that grace,
For which full pale and welked[7] is my face.
　　But, sirs, to yow it is no curteisye
To speken to an old man vileinye,

---

[1] greeted　　[2] God protect you　　[3] fellow　　[4] wrapped up　　[5] wretch
[6] I would exchange my money chest for a hair-cloth shroud to wrap about me　　[7] withered

But he trespasse in worde, or elles in dede.
In holy writ ye may your-self wel rede, 280
"Agayns [1] an old man, hoor upon his heed,
Ye sholde aryse; wherefore I yeve yow reed, [2]
Ne dooth un-to an old man noon harm now,
Na-more than ye wolde men dide to yow
In age, if that ye so longe abyde;
And god be with yow, wher ye go [3] or ryde.
I moot go thider as I have to go."

   "Nay, olde cherl, by god, thou shalt nat so,"
Seyde this other hasardour anon;
"Thou partest nat so lightly, by seint John! 290
Thou spak right now of thilke traitour Deeth,
That in this contree alle our frendes sleeth.
Have heer my trouthe, as thou are his aspye, [4]
Tel wher he is, or thou shalt it abye, [5]
By god, and by the holy sacrament!
For soothly thou art oon of his assent,
To sleen us yonge folk, thou false theef!"

   "Now, sirs," quod he, "if that yow be so leef [6]
To finde Deeth, turne up this croked wey,
For in that grove I lafte him, by my fey, 300
Under a tree, and ther he wol abyde;
Nat for your boost he wol him no-thing hyde.
See ye that ook? right ther ye shul him finde.
God save yow, that boghte agayn mankinde,
And yow amende!"—thus seyde this olde man.
And everich of thise ryotoures ran,
Til he cam to that tree, and ther they founde
Of florins fyne of golde y-coyned rounde
Wel ny an eighte busshels, as hem thoughte.
No lenger thanne after Deeth they soughte, 310
But ech of hem so glad was of that sighte,
For that the florins been so faire and brighte,

---

[1] in the presence of   [2] advice   [3] walk   [4] spy   [5] be sorry
anxious

That doun they sette hem by this precious hord.
The worste of hem he spake the firste word.

"Brethren," quod he, "tak kepe what I seye;
My wit is greet, though that I bourde [1] and pleye.
This tresor hath fortune un-to us yiven,
In mirthe and jolitee our lyf to liven,
And lightly as it comth, so wol we spende.
Ey! goddes precious dignitee! who wende [2]   320
To-day, that we sholde han so fair a grace?
But mighte this gold be caried fro this place
Hoom to myn hous, or elles un-to youres—
For wel ye woot that al this gold is oures—
Than were we in heigh felicitee.
But trewely, by daye it may nat be;
Men wolde seyn that we were theves stronge.
And for our owene tresor doon us honge. [3]
This tresor moste y-caried be by nighte
As wysly and as slyly as it mighte.   330
Wherfore I rede that cut among us alle
Be drawe, and lat see wher the cut wol falle;
And he that hath the cut with herte blythe
Shal renne to the toune, and that ful swythe, [4]
And bringe us breed and wyn ful prively.
And two of us shul kepen subtilly
This tresor wel; and, if he wol nat tarie,
Whan it is night, we wol this tresor carie
By oon assent, wher-as us thinketh best."
That oon of hem the cut broughte in his fest,   340
And bad hem drawe, and loke wher it wol falle;
And it fil on the yongeste of hem alle;
And forth toward the toun he wente anon.
And al-so sone as that he was gon,
That oon of hem spak thus un-to that other,
"Thou knowest wel thou art my sworne brother,

    [1] joke   [2] thought   [3] have us hanged   [4] quickly

Thy profit wol I telle thee anon.
Thou woost wel that our felawe is agon;
And heer is gold, and that ful greet plentee,
That shal departed been among us three.   350
But natheles, if I can shape it so
That it departed were among us two,
Hadde I nat doon a freendes torn to thee?"

That other answerde, "I noot how that may be;
He woot how that the gold is with us tweye,
What shal we doon, what shal we to him seye?"

"Shal it be conseil?"[1] seyde the firste shrewe,[2]
"And I shal tellen thee, in wordes fewe,
What we shal doon, and bringe it wel aboute."

"I graunte," quod that other, "out of doute,   360
That, by my trouthe, I wol thee nat biwreye."[3]

"Now," quod the firste, "thou woodst wel we be
        tweye,
And two of us shul strenger be than oon.
Look whan that he is set, and right anoon
Arys, as though thou woldest with him pleye;
And I shal ryve him thurgh the sydes tweye
Whyl that thou strogelest with him as in game,
And with thy dagger look thou do the same;
And than shal al this gold departed be,
My dere freend, bitwixen me and thee;   370
Than may we bothe our lustes al fulfille,
And pleye at dees right at our owene wille."
And thus acorded been thise shrewes tweye
To sleen the thridde, as ye han herd me seye.

This yongest, which that wente un-to the toun,
Ful ofte in herte he rolleth up and doun
The beautee of thise florins newe and brighte.
"O lord!" quod he, "if so were that I mighte
Have al this tresor to my-self allone,

<hr>

[1] secret   [2] rascal   [3] betray

Ther is no man that liveth under the trone   380
Of god, that sholde live so mery as I!"
And atte laste the feend, our enemy,
Putte in his thought that he shold poyson beye,[1]
With which he mighte sleen his felawes tweye;
For-why the feend fond him in swich lyvinge,
That he had leve him to sorwe bringe,
For this was outrely [2] his fulle entente
To sleen hem bothe, and never to repente.
And forth he gooth, no lenger wolde he tarie,
Into the toun, un-to a pothecarie,   390
And preyed him, that he him wolde selle
Som poyson, that he mighte his rattes quelle,[3]
And eek ther was a polcat in his hawe,[4]
That, as he seyde, his capouns hadde y-slawe,
And fayn he wolde wreke him, if he mighte,
On vermin, that destroyed him by nighte.

  The pothecarie answerde, "and thou shalt have
A thing that, al-so god my soule save,
In al this world there nis no creature,
That ete or dronke hath of this confiture [5]   400
Noght but the mountance [6] of a corn [7] of whete,
That he ne shal his lyf anon forlete;
Ye, sterve [8] he shal, and that in lasse whyle
Than thou wolt goon a paas [9] nat but a myle;
This poyson is so strong and violent."

  This cursed man hath in his hond y-hent
This poyson in a box, and sith he ran
In-to the nexte strete, un-to a man,
And borwed of him large botels three;
And in the two his poyson poured he;   410
The thridde he kepte clene for his drinke.
For al the night he shoop him for to swinke.[10]

---

[1] buy   [2] entirely   [3] kill   [4] yard   [5] mixture   [6] amount
[7] grain   [8] die   [9] at a foot-pace   [10] planned to work hard

In caryinge of the gold out of that place.
And whan this ryotour, with sory grace,
Had filled with wyn his grete botels three,
To his felawes agayn repaireth he.
　　What nedeth it to sermone of it more?
For right as they had cast his deeth bifore,
Right so they han him slayn, and that anon.
And whan that this was doon, thus spak that oon,　420
"Now lat us sitte and drinke, and make us merie,
And afterward we wol his body berie."
And with that word it happed him, par cas,
To take the botel ther the poyson was,
And drank, and yaf his felawe drinke also,
For which anon they storven [1] bothe two.
　　But, certes, I suppose that Avicen
Wroot never in no canon, ne in no fen, [2]
Mo wonder [3] signes of empoisoning
Than hadde thise wrecches two, er hir ending.　430
Thus ended been thise homicydes two,
And eek the false empoysoner also.

　　O cursed sinne, ful of cursednesse!
O traytours homicyde, o wikkednesse!
O glotonye, luxurie, and hasardrye!
Thou blasphemour of Crist with vileinye
And othes grete, of usage and of pryde!
Allas! mankinde, how may it bityde,
That to thy creatour which that thee wroghte,
And with his precious herte-blood thee boghte,　440
Thou art so fals and so unkinde, allas!
　　Now, goode men, god foryeve yow your trespas,
And ware yow fro [4] the sinne of avaryce.
Myn holy pardoun may yow alle waryce, [5]

---

[1] died　　[2] never wrote in any book or chapter　　[3] more wonderful
[4] beware of　　[5] cure

So that ye offre nobles or sterlinges,[1]
Or elles silver broches, spones, ringes.
Boweth your heed under this holy bulle!
Cometh up, ye wyves, offreth of your wolle!
Your name I entre heer in my rolle anon;
In-to the blisse of hevene shul ye gon; 450
I yow assoile,[2] by myn heigh power,
Yow that wol offre, as clene and eek as cleer
As ye were born; and, lo, sirs, thus I preche.
And Jesu Crist, that is our soules leche,
So graunte yow his pardon to receyve;
For that is best; I wol yow nat deceyve.

But sirs,[3] o word forgat I in my tale,
I have relikes and pardon in my male,[4]
As faire as any man in Engelond,
Whiche were me yeven by the popes hond. 460
If any of yow wol, of devocioun,
Offren, and han myn absolucioun,
Cometh forth anon, and kneleth heer adoun,
And mekely receyveth my pardoun:
Or elles, taketh pardon as ye wende,
Al newe and fresh, at every tounes ende,
So that ye offren alwey newe and newe
Nobles and pens, which that be gode and trewe.
It is an honour to everich that is heer,
That ye mowe have a suffisant pardoneer 470
T'assoille yow, in contree as ye ryde,
For aventures which that may bityde.
Peraventure ther may falle oon or two
Doun of his hors, and breke his nekke atwo.
Look which a seuretee is it to yow alle
That I am in your felaweship y-falle,
That may assoille yow, bothe more and lasse,
Whan that the soule shal fro the body passe.

---

[1] silver coins   [2] absolve   [3] i.e. his fellow-pilgrims   [4] bag

I rede that our hoste heer shal biginne,
For he is most envoluped in sinne. 480
Com forth, sir hoste, and offre first anon,
And thou shalt kisse the reliks everichon,
Ye, for a grote! unbokel anon thy purs."

"Nay, nay," quod he, "than have I Cristes curs!
Lat be," quod he, "it shall nat be, so thee'ch![1]
Thou woldest make me kisse thyn old breech,[2]
And swere it were a relik of a seint."

. . . .

This pardoner answerde nat a word;
So wrooth he was, no word ne wolde he seye.

"Now," quod our host, "I wol no lenger pleye 490
With thee, ne with noon other angry man."
But right anon the worthy Knight bigan,
Whan that he saugh that all the peple lough,
"Na-more of this, for it is right y-nough;
Sir Pardoner, be glad and mery of chere;
And ye, sir host, that been to me so dere,
I prey yow that ye kisse the Pardoner.
And Pardoner, I prey thee, drawe thee neer,
And, as we diden, lat us laughe and pleye."
Anon they kiste, and riden forth hir weye. 500

Here is ended the Pardoners Tale.

TRUTH

Balade de bon conseyl

FLEE fro the prees,[3] and dwelle with sothfastnesse,[4]
Suffyce unto thy good,[5] though hit be smal;
For hord hath hate, and climbing tikelnesse,[6]

---

[1] so may I prosper   [2] breeches   [3] crowd   [4] truth   [5] be content with your property   [6] uncertainty

Prees hath envye, and wele blent overal; [1]
Savour [2] no more than thee bihove shal;
Werk wel thy-self, that other folk canst rede; [3]
And trouthe shal delivere, hit is no drede.

Tempest [4] thee noght al croked to redresse, [5]
In trust of hir that turneth as a bal: [6]
Gret reste [7] stant [8] in litel besinesse;
And eek be war to sporne ageyn an al; [9]
Stryve noght, as doth the crokke with the wal.
Daunte [10] thy-self, that dauntest otheres dede;
And trouthe shal delivere, hit is no drede.

That thee is sent, receyve in buxumnesse, [11]
The wrastling for this worlde axeth a fal.
Her nis non hoom, her nis but wildernesse:
Forth, pilgrim, forth! Forth, beste, out of thy stal!
Know thy contree, look up, thank God of al;
Hold the hye wey, and lat thy gost [12] thee lede: 20
And trouthe shal delivere, hit is no drede.

Envoy

Therfore, thou Vache, [13] leve thyn old wrecchednesse
Unto the worlde; leve now to be thral;
Crye him mercy, that of his hy goodnesse
Made thee of noght, and in especial
Draw unto him, and pray in general
For thee, and eek for other, hevenlich mede; [14]
And trouthe shal delivere, hit is no drede.

Explicit Le bon counseill de G. Chaucer

[1] wealth always blinds   [2] desire   [3] advice   [4] trouble   [5] set straight   [6] i.e. Fortune   [7] leisure   [8] is found in   [9] And also be wary of kicking against an awl   [10] subdue   [11] humility   [12] spirit   [13] Sir Philip la Vache, a friend of Chaucer's   [14] reward

THE COMPLEINT OF CHAUCER TO HIS EMPTY PURSE

To you, my purse, and to non other wight [1]
Compleyne I, for ye be my lady dere!
I am so sory, now that ye be light;
For certes, but ye make me hevy chere,
Me were as leef be leyd up-on my bere; [2]
For whiche un-to your mercy thus I crye:
Beth [3] hevy ageyn, or elles mot I dye!

Now voucheth sauf this day, or [4] hit be night,
That I of you the blisful soun may here,
Or see your colour lyk the sonne bright,   10
That of yelownesse hadde never pere.
Ye be my lyf, ye be myn hertes stere, [5]
Quene of comfort and of good companye:
Beth hevy ageyn, or elles mot I dye!

Now purs, that be to me my lyves light,
And saveour, as doun in this worlde here,
Out of this toune help me through your might,
Sin that ye wole nat been my tresorere;
For I am shave as nye [6] as any frere. [7]
But yit I pray un-to your curtesye: 20
Beth hevy ageyn, or elles mot I dye!

Lenvoy de Chaucer

O conquerour [8] of Brutes [9] Albioun!
Which that by lyne and free eleccioun
Ben verray king, this song to you I sende;

---

[1] creature   [2] bier   [3] be   [4] before   [5] guide   [6] close   [7] friar
[8] Henry IV   [9] Brutus, mythical founder of Albion (Britain)

And ye, that mowen [1] al our harm amende,
Have minde up-on my supplicacioun!

BALLADS

GET UP AND BAR THE DOOR

IT FELL about the Martinmas time,
And a gay time it was then,
When our good wife got puddings to make,
And she's boild them in the pan.

The wind sae cauld blew south and north,
And blew into the door;
Quoth our goodman to our good wife,
"Gae out and bar the door."

"My hand is in my hussyfskap,
Goodman, as ye may see;　　　　　　　　　　　　10
An it shoud nae be barrd this hundred year,
It's no be barrd for me."

They made a paction tween them twa,
They made it firm and sure,
That the first word whaeer shoud speak,
Shoud rise and bar the door.

Then by there came two gentlemen,
At twelve o'clock at night,
And they could neither see house nor hall,
Nor coal nor candle-light.　　　　　　　　　　　20

"Now whether is this a rich man's house,
Or whether is it a poor?"

[1] are able

But neer a word wad ane o them speak,
For barring of the door.

And first they ate the white puddings,
And then they ate the black;
Tho muckle thought the goodwife to hersel,
Yet neer a word she spake.

Then said the one unto the other,
"Here, man, tak ye my knife;   30
Do ye tak aff the auld man's beard,
And I'll kiss the goodwife."

"But there's nae water in the house,
And what shall we do than?"
"What ails thee at the pudding-broo,
That boils into the pan?"

O up then started our goodman,
And angry man was he:
"Will ye kiss my wife before my een,
And sead[1] me wi pudding-bree?"   40

Then up and started our goodwife,
Gied three skips on the floor:
"Goodman, you've spoken the foremost word,
Get up and bar the door."

IONNË ARMSTRONG

THERE dwelt a man in faire Westmerland,
Ionnë Armstrong men did him call,
He had nither lands nor rents coming in,
Yet he kept eight score men in his hall.

[1]Scald

He had horses and harness for them all,
Goodly steeds were all milke-white;
O the golden bands an about their necks,
And their weapons, they were all alike.

Newes then was brought unto the king
That there was sicke a won as hee,   10
That lived lyke a bold outlaw,
And robbed all the north country.

The king he writt an a letter then,
A letter which was large and long;
He signed it with his owne hand,
And he promised to doe him no wrong.

When this letter came Ionnë untill,
His heart it was as blythe as birds on the tree:
"Never was I sent for before any king,
My father, my grandfather, nor none but mee.   20

"And if wee goe the king before,
I would we went most orderly;
Every man of you shall have his scarlet cloak,
Laced with silver laces three.

"Every man of you shall have his velvett coat,
Laced with silver lace so white;
O the golden bands an about your necks,
Black hatts, white feathers, all alyke."

By the morrow morninge at ten of the clock,
Towards Edenburough gon was hee,   30
And with him all his eight score men;
Good lord, it was a goodly sight for to see!

When Ionnë came befower the king,
He fell down on his knee;
"O pardon, my soveraine leige," he said,
"O pardon my eight score men and mee!"

"Thou shalt have no pardon, thou traytor strong,
For thy eight score men nor thee;
For to-morrow morning by ten of the clock,
Both thou and them shall hang on the gallow-tree."   40

But Ionnë looked over his left shoulder,
Good lord, what a grevious look looked hee!
Saying, "Asking grace of a graceless face--
Why there is none for you nor me."

But Ionnë had a bright sword by his side,
And it was made of the mettle so free,
That had not the king stept his foot aside,
He had smitten his head from his faire boddë.

Saying, "Fight on, my merry men all,
And see that none of you be taine;   50
For rather then men shall say we were hanged,
Let them report how we were slaine."

Then, God wott, faire Edenburough rose,
And so besett poore Ionnë rounde,
That fowerscore and tenn of Ionnë's best men
Lay gasping all upon the ground.

Then like a mad man Ionnë laide about,
And like a mad man then fought hee,
Untilc a false Scot came Ionnë behinde,
And runn him through the faire boddee.   60

Saying, "Fight on, my merry men all,
And see that none of you be taine;
For I will stand by and bleed but awhile,
And then will I come and fight againe."

Newes then was brought to young Ionnë Armstrong,
As he stood by his nurses knee,
Who vowed if ere he lived for to be a man,
O the treacherous Scots revenged hee'd be.

EDWARD

'Why dois [1] your brand [2] sae drap wi bluid, [3]
                    Edward, Edward,
Why dois your brand sae drap wi bluid,
    And why sae sad gang [4] yee O?'
'O I hae killed my hauke sae guid,
                    Mither, mither,
O I hae killed my hauke sae guid,
    And I had nae mair [5] bot [6] hee O.'

'Your haukis bluid was nevir sae reid, [7]
                    Edward, Edward,   10
Your haukis bluid was nevir sae reid,
    My deir son I tell thee O.'
'O I hae killed my reid-roan steid,
                    Mither, mither,
O I hae killed my reid-roan steid,
    That erst [8] was sae fair and frie O.'

'Your steid was auld, and ye hae got mair,
                    Edward, Edward,

[1] does   [2] sword   [3] blood   [4] go   [5] more   [6] but   [7] red
[8] once

Your steid was auld, and ye hae got mair,
   Sum other dule [1] ye drie [2] O.'   20
'O I hae killed my fadir deir,
           Mither, mither,
O I hae killed my fadir deir,
   Alas, and wae is mee O!'

'And whatten penance wul ye drie for that,
           Edward, Edward?
And whatten penance will ye drie for that?
   My deir son, now tell me O.'
'Ile set my feit in yonder boat,
           Mither, mither,   30
Ile set my feit in yonder boat,
   And Ile fare ovir the sea O.'

'And what wul ye doe wi your towirs and your ha, [3]
           Edward, Edward?
And what wul you doe wi your towirs and your ha,
   That were sae fair to see O?'
'Ile let thame stand tul they doun fa,
           Mither, mither,
Ile let thame stand tul they doun fa,
   For here nevir mair maun [4] I bee O.'   40

'And what wul ye leive to your bairns and your wife,
           Edward, Edward?
And what wul ye leive to your bairns and your wife,
   Whan ye gang ovir the sea O?'
'The warldis room, late them beg thrae [5] life,
           Mither, mither,
The warldis room, late them beg thrae life,
   For thame nevir mair wul I see O.'

[1] sorrow   [2] suffer   [3] hall   [4] must   [5] through

'And what wul ye leive to your ain [1] mither deir,

Edward, Edward?   50

And what wul ye leive to your ain mither deir?

My deir son, now tell me O.'

'The curse of hell frae me sall [2] ye beir,[3]

Mither, mither,

The curse of hell frae me sall ye beir,

Sic counseils ye gave to me O.'

THE DÆMON LOVER

1. 'O where have you been, my long, long love,
      This long seven years and mair?'
   'O I'm come to seek my former vows
      Ye granted me before.'

2. 'O hold your tongue of your former vows,
      For they will breed sad strife;
   O hold your tongue of your former vows,
      For I am become a wife.'

3. He turned him right and round about,
      And the tear blinded his ee: 10
   'I wad never hae trodden on Irish ground,
      If it had not been for thee.

4. 'I might hae had a king's daughter,
      Far, far beyond the sea;
   I might have had a king's daughter,
      Had it not been for love o thee.'

5. 'If ye might have had a king's daughter,
      Yersel ye had to blame;

¹ own   ² shall   ³ bear

Ye might have had taken the king's daughter,
    For ye kend [1] that I was nane.   20

6. 'If I was to leave my husband dear,
    And my two babes also,
O what have you to take me to,
    If with you I should go?'

7. 'I hae seven ships upon the sea—
    The eighth brought me to land—
With four-and-twenty bold mariners,
    And music on every hand.'

8. She has taken up her two little babes,
    Kissd them baith [2] cheek and chin: 30
'O fair ye weel, my ain two babes,
    For I'll never see you again.'

9. She set her foot upon the ship,
    No mariners could she behold;
But the sails were o the taffetie, [3]
    And the masts o the beaten gold.

10. She had not sailed a league, a league,
    A league but barely three,
When dismal grew his countenance,
    And drumlie [4] grew his ee.   40

11. They had not saild a league, a league,
    A league but barely three,
Until she espied his cloven foot,
    And she wept right bitterlie.

[1] knew   [2] both   [3] fine silk   [4] gloomy

12. 'O hold your tongue of your weeping,' says he,
    'Of your weeping now let me be;
I will shew you how the lilies grow
    On the banks of Italy.'

13. 'O what hills are yon, yon pleasant hills,
    That the sun shines sweetly on?'   50
'O yon are the hills of heaven,' he said,
    'Where you will never win.' [1]

14. 'O whaten a mountain is yon,' she said,
    'All so dreary wi frost and snow?'
'O yon is the mountain of hell,' he cried,
    'Where you and I will go.'

15. He strack [2] the tap-mast wi his hand,
    The fore-mast wi his knee,
And he brake that gallant ship in twain,
    And sank her in the sea.   60

THOMAS RYMER

1. TRUE Thomas lay oer yond grassy bank,
    And he beheld a ladie gay,
A ladie that was brisk and bold,
    Come riding oer the fernie brae.

2. Her skirt was of the grass-green silk,
    Her mantel of the velvet fine,
At ilka tett of her horse's mane
    Hung fifty silver bells and nine.

3. True Thomas he took off his hat
    And bowed him low down till his knee: 10

[1] go   [2] struck

'All hail, thou mighty Queen of Heaven!
　For your peer on earth I never did see.'

4. 'O no, O no, True Thomas,' she says,
　'That name does not belong to me;
I am but the queen of fair Elfland,
　And I'm come here for to visit thee.

. . . .

5. 'But ye maun go wi me now, Thomas,
　True Thomas, ye maun go wi me,
For ye maun serve me seven years,
　Thro weel or wae as may chance to be.'　　20

6. She turned about her milk-white steed,
　And took True Thomas up behind,
And aye wheneer her bridle rang,
　The steed flew swifter than the wind.

7. For forty days and forty nights
　He wade thro red blude to the knee,
And he saw neither sun nor moon,
　But heard the roaring of the sea.

8. O they rade on and further on,
　Until they came to a garden green:　　30
'Light down, light down, ye ladie free,
　Some of that fruit let me pull to thee.'

9. 'O no, O no, True Thomas,' she says,
　'That fruit maun not be touched by thee,
For a' the plagues that are in hell
　Light on the fruit of this countrie.

10. 'But I have a loaf here in my lap,
　Likewise a bottle of claret wine,

And here ere we go farther on,
    We'll rest a while, and ye may dine.'   40

11. When he had eaten and drunk his fill,
    'Lay down your head upon my knee,'
The lady sayd, 'ere we climb yon hill,
    And I will show you fairlies three.

12. 'O see ye not yon narrow road,
    So thick beset wi thorns and briers?
That is the path of righteousness,
    Tho after it but few enquires.

13. 'And see not ye that braid braid road,
    That lies across yon lillie leven?   50
That is the path of wickedness,
    Tho some call it the road to heaven.

14. 'And see ye not that bonny road,
    Which winds about the fernie brae?
That is the road to fair Elfland,
    Where you and I this night maun gae.

15. 'But Thomas, ye maun hold your tongue,
    Whatever ye may hear or see,
For gin ae word you should chance to speak,
    You will neer get back to your ain countrie.'   60

16. He has gotten a coat of the even cloth,
    And a pair of shoes of velvet green,
And till seven years were past and gone
    True Thomas on earth was never seen.

KEMP OWYNE [1]

HER mother died when she was young,
    Which gave her cause to make great moan;
Her father married the warst woman
    That ever lived in Christendom.

She servèd her with foot and hand,
    In every thing that she could dee,[2]
Till once, in an unlucky time,
    She threw her in ower Craigy's sea.[3]

Says, "Lie you there, dove Isabel,
    And all my sorrows lie with thee;   **10**
Till Kemp Owyne come ower the sea,
    And borrow you with kisses three;
Let all the warld do what they will,
    Oh borrowed shall you never be!"

Her breath grew strang, her hair grew lang,
    And twisted thrice about the tree,
And all the people, far and near,
    Thought that a savage beast was she.

These news did come to Kemp Owyne,
    Where he lived, far beyond the sea;   **20**
He hasted him to Craigy's sea,
    And on the savage beast lookd he.

Her breath was strang, her hair was lang,
    And twisted was about the tree,

---

[1] Owain, one of King Arthur's knights   [2] do   [3] probably a
variant for "over a crag of the sea"

And with a swing she came about:
    "Come to Craigy's sea, and kiss with me.

"Here is a royal belt," she cried,
    "That I have found in the green sea;
And while your body it is on,
    Drawn shall your blood never be;   30
But if you touch me, tail or fin,
    I vow my belt your death shall be."

He stepped in, gave her a kiss,
    The royal belt he brought him wi;[1]
Her breath was strang, her hair was lang,
    And twisted twice about the tree,
And with a swing she came about:
    "Come to Craigy's sea, and kiss with me.

"Here is a royal ring," she said,
    "That I have found in the green sea;   40
And while your finger it is on,
    Drawn shall your blood never be;
But if you touch me, tail or fin,
    I swear my ring your death shall be."

He stepped in, gave her a kiss,
    The royal ring he brought him wi;
Her breath was strang, her hair was lang,
    And twisted ance about the tree,
And with a swing she came about:
    "Come to Craigy's sea, and kiss with me.   50

"Here is a royal brand," she said,
    "That I have found in the green sea;
And while your body it is on,
    Drawn shall your blood never be;

[1] with

But if you touch me, tail or fin,
  I swear my brand your death shall be."

He stepped in, gave her a kiss,
  The royal brand he brought him wi;
Her breath was sweet, her hair grew short,
  And twisted nane about the tree,   60
And smilingly she came about,
  As fair a woman as fair could be.

SIR PATRICK SPENCE

THE king sits in Dumferling toune,
  Drinking the blude-reid wine:
"O whar will I get guid sailor,
  To sail this schip of mine?"

Up and spak an eldern knicht,
  Sat at the kings richt kne:
"Sir Patrick Spence is the best sailor,
  That sails upon the se."

The king has written a braid [1] letter,
  And signd it wi his hand,   10
And sent it to Sir Patrick Spence,
  Was walking on the sand.

The first line that Sir Patrick red,
  A loud lauch [2] lauchèd he;
The next line that Sir Patrick red,
  The teir blinded his ee.

"O wha is this has done this deid,
  This ill deid don to me,

---

[1] broad   [2] laugh

To send me out this time o' the yeir,
    To sail upon the se!   20

"Mak hast, mak haste, my mirry men all,
    Our guid schip sails the morne:"
"O say na sae, my master deir,
    For I feir a deadlie storme.

"Late, late yestreen I saw the new moone,
    Wi the auld moone in hir arme,
And I feir, I feir, my deir master,
    That we will cum to harme."

O our Scots nobles wer richt laith[1]
    To weet their crok-heild schoone;   30
Bot lang owre a' the play wer playd,
    Thair hats they swam aboone.

O lang, lang may their ladies sit,
    With thair fans into their hand,
Or eir they se Sir Patrick Spence
    Cum sailing to the land.

O lang, lang may the ladies stand,
    Wi thair gold kems in their hair,
Waiting for thair ain[2] deir lords,
    For they'll se thame na mair.   40

Half owre, half owre to Aberdour,
    It's fiftie fadom deip,
And thair lies guid Sir Patrick Spence,
    Wi the Scots lords at his feit.

[1] loth   [2] own

ROBIN HOOD'S DEATH AND BURIAL

When Robin Hood and Little John
  Down a down a down a down
Went oer yon bank of broom,
  Said Robin Hood bold to Little John,
"We have shot for many a pound."
  Hey, down, a down, a down.

"But I am not able to shoot one shot more,
  My broad arrows will not flee;
But I have a cousin lives down below,
  Please God, she will bleed me." 10

Now Robin he is to fair Kirkly gone,
  As fast as he can win; [1]
But before he came there, as we do hear,
  He was taken very ill.

And when he came to fair Kirkly-hall,
  He knockd all at the ring,
But none was so ready as his cousin herself
  For to let bold Robin in.

"Will you please to sit down, cousin Robin," she said,
  "And drink some beer with me?" 20
"No, I will neither eat nor drink,
  Till I am blooded by thee."

"Well, I have a room, cousin Robin," she said,
  "Which you did never see,
And if you please to walk therein,
  You blooded by me shall be."

[1] go

She took him by the lily-white hand,
   And led him to a private room,
And there she blooded bold Robin Hood,
   While one drop of blood would run down. 30

She blooded him in a vein of the arm,
   And locked him up in the room;
Then did he bleed all the live-long day,
   Until the next day at noon.

He then bethought him of a casement there,
   Thinking for to get down;
But was so weak he could not leap,
   He could not get him down.

He then bethought him of his bugle-horn,
   Which hung low down to his knee; 40
He set his horn unto his mouth,
   And blew out weak blasts three.

Then Little John, when hearing him,
   As he sat under a tree,
"I fear my master is now near dead,
   He blows so wearily."

Then Little John to fair Kirkly is gone,
   As fast as he can dree; [1]
But when he came to Kirkly-hall,
   He broke locks two or three: 50

Until he came bold Robin to see,
   Then he fell on his knee;
"A boon, a boon," cries Little John,
   "Master, I beg of thee."

[1] endure

"What is that boon," said Robin Hood,
  "Little John, [thou] begs of me?"
"It is to burn fair Kirkly-hàll,
  And all their nunnery."

"Now nay, now nay," quoth Robin Hood,
  "That boon I'll not grant thee;   60
I never hurt woman in all my life,
  Nor men in woman's company.

"I never hurt fair maid in all my time,
  Nor at mine end shall it be;
But give me my bent bow in my hand,
  And a broad arrow I'll let flee,
And where this arrow is taken up,
  There shall my grave digged be.

"Lay me a green sod under my head,
  And another at my feet;   70
And lay my bent bow by my side,
  Which was my music sweet;
And make my grave of gravel and green,
  Which is most right and meet.

"Let me have length and breadth enough,
  With a green sod under my head;
That they may say, when I am dead,
  Here lies bold Robin Hood."

These words they readily granted him,
  Which did bold Robin please: 80
And there they buried bold Robin Hood,
  Within the fair Kirkleys.

LYRICS

(*Anonymous*)

CUCKOO SONG

Sumer is icumen in:
   Lhude [1] sing cuccu! [2]
Groweth sed, and bloweth [3] med,[4]
   And springth the wude nu.[5]
       Sing cuccu!

Awe [6] bleteth after lomb;
   Lhouth [7] after calve cu; [8]
Bulluc sterteth, bucke verteth.
   Murie [9] sing cuccu!

Cuccu, cuccu, well singes thu, cuccu: 10
   Ne swike [10] thu naver nu.
Sing cuccu, nu, sing cuccu!
   Sing cuccu, sing cuccu, nu!

               c. 1300.

SPRINGTIME

Lenten [11] ys come with love to toune,
With blosmen and with briddes [12] roune,[13]
   That al this blisse bryngeth;
Dayes-eyes [14] in this dales,
Notes suete [15] of nyhtegales,[16]
   Uch [17] foul song singeth.

---

[1] loudly   [2] cuckoo   [3] blossometh   [4] meadow   [5] now   [6] ewe
[7] loweth   [8] cow   [9] merrily   [10] cease   [11] spring   [12] birds'
[13] whispering   [14] daisies   [15] sweet   [16] nightingales   [17] each

The threstelcoc [1] him threteth [2] oo,[3]
Away is huere [4] wynter wo,
   When woderove [5] springeth;
This foules singeth ferly [6] fele,[7]   10
And wlyteth [8] on huere wynter wele,[9]
   That al the wode ryngeth.

The rose rayleth [10] hir rode,[11]
The leves on the lyhte [12] wode
   Waxen al with wille; [13]
The mone mandeth [14] hire bleo,[15]
The lilie is lossom [16] to seo,
   The fenyl [17] and the fille; [18]
Wowes [19] this wilde drakes;
Miles [20] murgeth [21] huere makes; [22]   20
   Ase strem that striketh [23] stille,
Mody [24] meneth,[25] so doth mo,[26]
Ichot [27] ycham [28] on of tho,[29]
   For love that likes [30] ille.

The mone mandeth hire lyht,
So doth the semly sonne bryht,
   When briddes singeth breme; [31]
Deawes donketh [32] the dounes,
Deores [33] with huere derne [34] rounes,
   Domes [35] forte [36] deme; [37]   30
Wormes woweth under cloude,[38]
Wymmen waxeth wounder proude,
   So wel hit wol hem seme,[39]

[1] male thrush   [2] chides   [3] ever   [4] their   [5] woodruff (an
herb)   [6] wondrously   [7] many   [8] cry   [9] weal   [10] puts on
[11] redness   [12] light   [13] a will   [14] mends   [15] complexion   [16] lovely
[17] fennel   [18] thyme   [19] woo   [20] animals   [21] make merry   [22] mates
[23] flows   [24] The moody one   [25] moaneth   [26] others   [27] I know
[28] I am   [29] those   [30] pleases   [31] loudly   [32] make dank   [33] lovers
[34] secret   [35] fates   [36] to   [37] seal   [38] snakes woo under clod
[39] become

Yef [1] me shal wonte [2] wille of on:
This wunne weole [3] I wole for-gon,
    And wyht in wode be fleme.[4]

c. 1300

A HYMN TO THE VIRGIN

Of on that is so fayr and bright,
    Velut maris stella,
Brighter than the day is light,
    Parens et puella:
Ic [5] crie to the, thou se to me,
Levedy,[6] preye thi sone for me,
    Tam pia,
That ic mote come to the,
    Maria.

Al this world was for-lore,[7]   10
    Eva peccatrice,
Tyl our lord was y-bore
    De te genetrice.
With *ave* it went away,
Thùster [8] nyth [9] and comz the day
    Salutis;
The welle springeth ut [10] of the
    Virtutis.

Levedi, flour of alle thing,
    Rosa sine spina,   20
Thu bere Jhesu, hevene king,
    Gratia divina;
Of alle thu berst the pris,[11]
Levedi, quene of parays [12]

[1] if   [2] lack   [3] this joyful boon   [4] And be a banished wight
in the woods   [5] I   [6] Lady   [7] lost   [8] dark   [9] night   [10] out
[11] prize   [12] paradise

Electa.
Mayde milde, moder *es*
   Effecta.

Of kare conseil thou ert best,
   Felix fecundata,
Of alle wery thou ert rest,   30
   Mater honorata.
Bisek him wiz [1] milde mod,[2]
That for ous alle sad [3] is [4] blod
   In cruce,
That we moten comen til him
   In luce.

Wel he wot [5] he is thi sone.
   Ventre quem portasti;
He wyl nout werne [6] the thi bone,
   Parvum quem lactasti;   40
So hende [7] and so god he his,[8]
He havet [9] brout ous to blis
   Superni,
That havez [9] hi-dut [10] the foule put [11]
   Inferni.

c. 1300

ALYSOUN

Bytuene Mershe and Averil
   When spray beginneth to springe,
The lutel foul hath hire wyl
   On hyre lud [12] to synge;
Ich [13] libbe [14] in love-longinge

---

[1] with   [2] mind   [3] shed   [4] his   [5] knows   [6] refuse   [7] gracious   [8] is   [9] has   [10] concealed   [11] pit   [12] in her language
[13] I   [14] live

For semlokest [1] of alle thynge,
He [2] may me blisse bringe,
Icham [3] in hire baundoun. [4]
    An hendy hap ichabbe yhent, [5]
    Ichot [6] from hevene it is me sent,   10
    From alle wymmen mi love is lent [7]
Ant lyht [8] on Alysoun.

On heu hire her [9] is fayr ynoh,
    Hire browe broune, hire eye blake,
With lossum [10] chere he on me loh; [11]
    With middel [12] smal and wel y-make;
    Bote he me wolle to hire take
    Forte [13] buen [14] hire owen make, [15]
    Longe to lyven ichulle [16] forsake,
And feye [17] fallen adoun.   20
    An hendy hap, etc.

Nihtes when I wende [18] and wake,
    Forthi [19] myn wonges waxeth won; [20]
Levedi, [21] al for thine sake
    Longinge is ylent me on [22]
    In world nis non so wytermon [23]
    That al hire bounte telle con;
    Hire swyre [24] is whittore then the swon,
And feyrest may [25] in toune.
    An hendy hap, etc.   30

Icham for wowyng [26] al forwake, [27]
    Wery so water in wore; [28]

---

[1] the fairest   [2] she   [3] I am   [4] power   [5] A happy lot I have
received   [6] I know   [7] gone   [8] lighted   ['] hair   [10] lovesome
[11] laughed   [12] waist   [13] to   [14] be   [15] mate   [16] I shall   [17] doomed
to death   [18] turn   [19] therefore   [20] cheeks grow wan   [21] lady
[22] has come to me   [23] wise man   [24] neck   [25] maid   [26] wooing
[27] worn with vigils   [28] as water in a weir

Lest eny reve [1] me my make,
  Ichabbe y-yernèd yore.[2]
  Betere is tholien whyle sore [3]
  Then mournen evermore.
  Geynes [4] under gore,[5]
Herkne to my roun.[6]
  An hendy hap, etc.

c. 1300

A PLEA FOR PITY

WITH longyng I am lad,
On molde [7] I waxe mad,
  A maide marreth me;
I grede,[8] I grone, un-glad,
For selden I am sad [9]
  That semly forte se;
  Levedi, thou rewe me!
To routhe thou havest me rad; [10]
Be bote of that I bad,[11]
  My lyf is long on the.   **10**

Levedy of alle londe,
Les [12] me out of bonde,
  Broht icham in wo;
Have resting on honde,
And sent thou me thi sonde,[13]
  Sone, er thou me slo; [14]
  My reste is with the ro: [15]
Thah men to me han onde,[16]
To love nuly [17] noht wonde,[18]
  Ne lete for non of tho.[19]   **20**

---

[1] deprive   [2] for a long time   [3] It is better to bear pain awhile
[4] comeliest   [5] attire   [6] tale   [7] earth   [8] cry out   [9] satisfied
[10] advised   [11] asked   [12] loose   [13] message   [14] slayest   [15] roe
[16] jealousy   [17] will I not   [18] fear   [19] Nor cease for any of them

Levedi, with al my miht
My love is on the liht,
   To menske [1] when I may;
Thou rew and red [2] me ryht,
To dethe thou havest me diht, [3]
   I deye longe er my day;
   Thou leve [4] upon my lay.
Treuthe ichave the plyht,
To don that ich have hyht, [5]
   Whil mi lif leste may.   30

Lylie-whyt hue is,
Hire rode [6] so rose on rys, [7]
   That reveth [8] me mi rest.
Wymmon war [9] and wys,
Of prude hue bereth the pris, [10]
   Burde [11] on of the best;
   This wommon woneth [12] by west,
Brihtest under bys; [13]
Hevene I tolde [14] al his
   That o nyht were hire gest.   40

                                          c. 1300

THE *QUEM-QUÆRITIS* TROPE

DE RESURRECTIONE DOMINI

Int [errogatio] :
   Quem quæritis in sepulchro, [o] Christicolæ?
R [esponsio] :
   Jesum Nazarenum crucifixum, o cœlicolæ.
[Angeli:]
   Non est hic; surrexit, sicut prædixerat.
   Ite, nuntiate quia surrexit de sepulchro.

---

[1] honor   [2] teach   [3] prepared   [4] believe   [5] promised   [6] complexion   [7] stalk   [8] deprives   [9] careful   [10] prize   [11] lady   [12] lives   [13] purple   [14] should consider

OF THE LORD'S RESURRECTION

Question [of the angels]:
Whom seek ye in the sepulchre, O followers of Christ?

Answer [of the Marys]:
*Jesus of Nazareth, which was crucified, O celestial
ones.*

[The angels:]
*He is not here; he is risen, just as he foretold.
Go, announce that he is risen from the sepulchre.*

9th c.

SEPULCHRUM

[Easter.]

WHILE the third lesson is being chanted, let four
brethren vest themselves; of whom let one, vested in an
alb, enter as if to take part in the service, and let him
without being observed approach the place of the sepulchre, and there, holding a palm in his hand, let him
sit down quietly. While the third responsory is being
sung, let the remaining three follow, all of them vested
in copes, and carrying in their hands censers filled with
incense; and slowly, in the manner of seeking something,
let them come before the place of the sepulchre. These
things are done in imitation of the angel seated in the
monument, and of the women coming with spices to
anoint the body of Jesus. When therefore that one
seated shall see the three, as if straying about and seeking something, approach him, let him begin in a dulcet
voice of medium pitch to sing:

Whom seek ye in the sepulchre, O followers of Christ?

When he has sung this to the end, let the three respond in unison:

> *Jesus of Nazareth, which was crucified, O celestial one.*

To whom that one:

> *He is not here; he is risen, just as he foretold.*
> *Go, announce that he is risen from the dead.*

At the word of this command let those three turn themselves to the choir, saying:

> *Alleluia! The Lord is risen to-day,*
> *The strong lion, the Christ, the Son of God.*
> *Give thanks to God, huzza!*

This said, let the former, again seating himself, as if recalling them, sing the anthem:

> *Come, and see the place where the Lord was laid.*
> *Alleluia! Alleluia!*

And saying this, let him rise, and let him lift the veil and show them the place bare of the cross, but only the cloths laid there with which the cross was wrapped. Seeing which, let them set down the censers which they carried into the same sepulchre, and let them take up the cloth and spread it out before the eyes of the clergy; and, as if making known that the Lord had risen and was not now therein wrapped, let them sing this anthem:

> *The Lord is risen from the sepulchre,*
> *Who for us hung upon the cross.*

And let them place the cloth upon the altar. The anthem being ended, let the Prior, rejoicing with them at the triumph of our King, in that, having conquered death, he arose, begin the hymn:

We praise thee, O God.

This begun, all the bells chime out together.

c. 970

THE SHEPHERDS

[*At one end of the pageant, the open fields where the thrce Shepherds tend their sheep; at the other end, the home of Mak and his wife Gill.   Enter the First Shepherd, half frozen with the cold.*]

1. PASTOR.   Lord, what these weders ar cold!   And I
      am yll happyd.[1]
I am nere-hande dold,[2] so long haue I nappyd.
My legys thay fold, my fyngers ar chappyd;
It is not as I wold, for I am al lappyd
   In sorrow.
In stormes and tempest,
Now in the eest, now in the west,
Wo is hym has neuer rest
   Myd-day nor morrow!

Bot we sely [3] shepardes that walkys on the moore,   10
In fayth, we are nere-handys outt of the doore!
No wonder, as it standys, if we be poore,
For the tylthe of oure landys lyys falow as the floore,
   As ye ken.
We ar so hamyd,[4]

   ᶜ clothed   [2] nearly numb   [3] poor   [4] crippled

Fox-taxed, and ramyd,[1]
We ar mayde hand-tamyd
   With thyse gentlery men.

Thus thay refe [2] vs oure reste —Oure Lady theym
       wary![3]
These men that ar lord-fest [4] thay cause the ploghe
      tary.   20
That, men say, is for the best; we fynde it contrary.
Thus ar husbandys opprest in po[i]nte to myscary
   On lyfe.
Thus hold thay vs hunder;
Thus thay bryng vs in blonder!
It were greatte wonder
   And euer shuld we thryfe.

Ther shall com a swane as prowde as a po,[5]
He must borow my wane,[6] my ploghe also;
Then I am full fane to graunt or he go.   30
Thus lyf we in payne, anger, and wo,
   By nyght and day.
He must haue if he langyd,
If I shud forgang [7] it.
I were better be hangyd
   Then oones say hym nay.

For may he gett a paynt slefe,[8] or a broche, now on
      dayes,
Wo is hym that hym grefe or onys agane says!
Dar noman hym reprefe what mastry he mays.
And yit may noman lefe [9] oone word that he says,   40
   No letter.
He can make purveance,

---

[1] over-taxed and crushed   [2] rob   [3] curse   [4] bound to a lord
[5] peacock   [6] wagon   [7] have to do without it   [8] embroidered
sleeve   [9] believe

With boste and bragance;
And all is thrugh mantenance
  Of men that are gretter.

It dos me good, as I walk thus by myn oone,
Of this warld for to talk in maner of mone.
To my shepe wyll I stalk and herkyn anone;
Ther abyde on a balk,[1] or sytt on a stone,
  Full soyne.[2]   50
For I trowe, perde,
Trew men if thay be,
We gett more compane
  Or it be noyne.[3]

[*Enter the Second Shepherd. He does not see the
  First Shepherd.*]

II. PASTOR. Benste[4] and Dominus! What may this
        bemeyne?
Why fares this warld thus? Oft haue we not sene!
Lord, thyse weders are spytus,[5] and the winds full
        kene;
And the frostys so hydus thay water myn eeyne;
  No ly.
Now in dry, now in wete,
Now in snaw, now in slete,   60
When my shone freys to my fete,
  It is not all esy.

Bot, as far as I ken, or yit as I go,
We sely wedmen dre[6] mekyll wo;
We haue sorow then and then, it fallys oft so.
Sely Capyle, oure hen, both to and fro
  She kakyls;
Bot begyn she to crok,

---

[1] ridge [2] soon [3] noon [4] Benedicite [5] spiteful [6] suffer

To groyne or [to clo]k,   **70**
Wo is hym oure cok,
   For he is in the shekyls.[1]

These men that ar wed haue not all thare wyll.
When they ar full hard sted,[2] thay sygh full styll.
God wayte [3] thay ar led full hard and full yll;
In bower nor in bed thay say noght thertll.[4]
   This tyde,
My parte haue I fun—
I know my lesson!—
Who is hym that is bun,[5]   **80**
   For he must abyde.

Bot now late in oure lyfys—a meruell to me,
That I thynk my hart ryfys [6] sich wonders to see,
What that destany dryfys, it shuld so be!—
Som men wyll have two wyfys, and som men thre
   In store.
Som ar wo that has any!
Bot so far can I,—
Wo is hym that has many,
   For he felys sore.   **90**

[Addressing the audience.]

Bot, yong men, of wowyng, for God that you boght,
Be well war of wedyng, and thynk in youre thoght,
"Had I wyst" is a thyng it seruys of noght.
Mekyll [7] styll mowrnyng has wedyng home broght,
   And grefys,
With many a sharp showre:
For thou may cach in an **owre**

[1] shackles   [2] situated   [3] knows   [4] thereto   [5] bound   [6] breaks
[7] much

That shall savour fulle sowre
    As long as thou lyffys.

For, as euer red I pystyll,[1] I haue oone to my fere,[2] 100
As sharp as a thystyll, as rugh as a brere;
She is browyd lyke a brystyll, with a sowre-loten
    chere [3];
Had she oones wett hyr whystyll, she couth syng full
    clere
    Hyr Pater Noster.
She is as greatt as a whall;
She has a galon of gall;
By hym that dyed for vs all,
    I wald I had ryn to I had lost hir!

[*The First Shepherd interrupts him.*]

I. PASTOR.   God! looke ouer the raw![4]
    Full defly [5] ye stand.

II. PASTOR.   Yee, the dewill in thi maw, so tariand![6] 110
Sagh thou awro [7] of Daw?
I. PASTOR.   Yee, on a ley-land [8]
Hard I hym blaw. He commys here at hand
    Not far.
Stand styll.
II. PASTOR. Qwhy?
I. PASTOR.   For he commys, hope I.
II. PASTOR.   He wyll make vs both a ly
    Bot if we be war.[9]

[*Enter the Third Shepherd, a boy.*]

[1] epistle, i.e. in the New Testament   [2] companion   [3] sour face
[4] row   [5] deaf   [6] tarrying   [7] anywhere   [8] unploughed land
[9] wary

III. Pastor.　Crystys crosse me spede, and Sant Nycho-
　　　las!

Ther-of had I nede; it is wars then it was.

Whoso couthe take hede and lett the warld pas,　120

It is euer in drede and brekyll as glas,
　　And slyths.[1]

This warld fowre[2] neuer so,

With meruels mo and mo,

Now in weyll, now in wo,
　　And all thyng wryths.[3]

Was neuer syn Noe floode sich floodys seyn,

Wyndys and ranys so rude, and stormes so keyn!

Som stamerd, some stod in dowte, as I weyn.

Now God turne all to good! I say as I mene,　130
　　For ponder.

These floodys so thay drowne,

Both in feyldys and in towne,

And berys all downe;
　　And that is a wonder.

We that walk on the nyghtys oure catell to kepe,

We se sodan syghtys when othere men slepe. [*Spying
　　the others.*]

Yit me-thynk my hart lyghtys;[4] I se shrewys pepe.

Ye ar two tall wyghtys! I wyll gyf my shepe
　　A turne.　140

Bot full yll haue I ment;

As I walk on this bent,[5]

I may lyghtly repent,
　　My toes if I spurne.

[The other two advance.]

---

[1] slides　　[2] fared　　[3] writhes　　[4] lightens　　[5] bare field

A, sir, God you saue! and master myne!
A drynk fayn wold I haue, and somwhat to dyne.

I. PASTOR.   Crystys curs, my knaue, thou art a ledyr
    hyne! [1]

II. PASTOR.   What! the boy lyst rave!
    Abyde vnto syne [2]
  We haue mayde it.
Yll thryft on thy pate!   **150**
Though the shrew cam late,
Yit is he in state
  To dyne—if he had it.

III. PASTOR. Sich seruandys as I, that swettys and
    swynkys, [3]
Etys oure brede full dry; and that me forthynkys. [4]
We are oft weytt and wery when mastermen wynkys; [5]
Yit commys full lately both dyners and drynkys.
  Bot nately [6]
Both oure dame and oure syre,
When we haue ryn in the myre,   **160**
Thay can nyp [7] at oure hyre,
  And pay vs full lately.

Bot here my trouth, master: for the fayr that ye make,
I shall do thereafter,—wyrk as I take, [8]
I shall do a lytyll, sir, and emang euer lake; [9]
For yit lay my soper neuer on my stomake
  In feyldys.
Whereto shude I threpe? [10]
With my staf can I lepe;
And men say "Lyght chepe [11]   **170**
  Letherly [12] for-yeldys."

---

[1] worthless hind   [2] until after   [3] labor   [4] displeases   [5] sleep
[6] quickly   [7] reduce   [8] receive   [9] play   [10] argue   [11] cheap
bargain   [12] badly

I. PASTOR. Thou were an yll lad to ryde on wowyng
With a man that had bot lytyll of spendyng.

II. PASTOR. Peasse, boy, I bad! No more iangling,
Or I shall make the full rad,[1] by the heuens kyng,
   With thy gawdys.[2]
Wher ar oure shepe, boy, we skorne?

III. PASTOR. Sir, this same day at morne
I thaym left in the corne,
   When thay rang lawdys.[3]   180

They haue pasture good, thay can not go wrong.

I. PASTOR. That is right. By the roode, thyse nyghtys
   are long!
Yit I wold, or we yode,[4] oone gaf vs a song.

II. PASTOR. So I thoght as I stode, to myrth vs emong.

III. PASTOR. I grauntt.

I. PASTOR. Lett me syng the tenory.

II. PASTOR. And I the tryble so hye.

III. PASTOR. Then the meyne fallys to me.
   Lett se how ye chauntt. [*They sing.*]

[*Then Mak enters with a cloak drawn over his tunic.*]

MAK. Now, Lord, for thy naymes sevyn,   190
    that made both moyn and starnes
Well mo then I can meuen,[5] thi will, Lorde, of me
    tharnys.[6]
I am all vneuen; that moves oft my harnes.[7]
Now wold God I were in heuen, for the[re] wepe no
    barnes [8]
   So styll.[9]

I. PASTOR. Who is that pypys so poore?

MAK. Wold God ye wyst how I foore![10]

---

[1] afraid   [2] tricks   [3] lauds, the first of the day hours of the
Church   [4] went   [5] name   [6] lacks   [7] brains   [8] children
[9] continuously   [10] fared

Lo, a man that walkys on the moore,
  And has not all his wyll!

ii. Pastor. Mak, where has thou gon? tell vs tythyng.
iii. Pastor. Is he commen? Then ylkon [1] take hede
    to his thyng.   200

[He takes the cloak from him.]

Mak. What! ich [2] be a yoman, I]ch[tell you, of the
    king;
The self and the same, sond [3] from a greatt lordyng,
  And sich.
Fy on you! Goyth hence!
Out of my presence!
I[ch] must haue reuerence.
  Why, who be ich?

i. Pastor. Why make ye it so qwaynt? [4] Mak, ye do
    wrang.
ii. Pastor. Bot, Mak, lyst ye saynt? [5] I trow that ye
    lang. [6]
iii. Pastor. I trow the shrew can paynt! [7]
    The dewyll myght hym hang!   210
Mak. Ich shall make complaynt, and make you all to
    thwang [8]
  At a worde;
And tell euyn how ye doth.
i. Pastor. Bot, Mak, is that sothe?
Now take outt that sothren tothe, [9]
  And sett in a torde!

ii. Pastor. Mak, the dewill in youre ee!
    A stroke wold I leyne [10] you.

[Strikes him.]

[1] every one   [2] I   [3] messenger   [4] strange   [5] deceive   [6] long
to do so   [7] deceive   [8] be flogged   [9] Mak has been imitating the
Southern dialect.   [10] lend

III. PASTOR.　Mak, know ye not me?　By God, I couthe
　　　　teyn [1] you.

　　　　　　　　　　　　　　　[*Drawing back to strike him.*]

MAK.　God, looke you all thre!　Me thoght I had sene
　　　you.

Ye ar a fare compane.

I. PASTOR.　Can ye now mene [2] you?　　　　　　　　　220

II. PASTOR.　Shrew[d] iape! [3]

Thus late as thou goys,

What wyll men suppos?

And thou has an yll noys [4]

　　Of stelyng of shepe.

MAK.　And I am trew as steyll: all men waytt! [5]

Bot a sekenes I feyll that haldys me full haytt; [6]

My belly farys not weyll, it is out of astate.

III. PASTOR.　Seldom lyys the dewyll dede by the
　　　　gate! [7]

MAK.　Therfor　　　　　　　　　　　　　　　　　230

Full sore am I and yll;

If I stande stone styll,

I ete not an nedyll

　　Thys moneth and more.

I. PASTOR.　How farys thi wyff? by my hoode, how
　　　　farys sho?

MAK.　Lyys walteryng, [8] by the roode, by the fyere, lo!

And a howse full of brude. [9]　She drynkys well, to;

Yll spede othere good that she wyll do

　　Bot so!

Etys as fast as she can;　　　　　　　　　　　　240

And ilk [10] yere that commys to man

She bryngys furth a lakan, [11]—

　　And som yeres two.

---

[1] injure　　[2] behave yourself　　[3] clever joke　　[4] reputation　　[5] know
[6] hot　　[7] path　　[8] rolling about　　[9] children　　[10] every　　[11] baby

Bot were I not more gracyus and rychere be far,
I were eten outt of howse and of harbar.
Yit is she a fowll dowse [1] if ye com nar;
Ther is none that trowse nor knowys a war [2]
  Then ken I.
Now wyll ye se what I profer?
To gyf all in my cofer   250
To-morne at next [3] to offer
  Hyr hed-mas penny. [4]

II. PASTOR. I wote [5] so forwakyd [6] is none in this
     shyre.
I wold slepe, if I takyd les to my hyere.
III. PASTOR. I am cold and nakyd, and wold haue a
     fyere.
I. PASTOR. I am wery, for-rakyd, [7] and run in the myre.
  Wake thou!
II. PASTOR. Nay, I wyll lyg downe by,
For I must slepe, truly.
III. PASTOR. As good a mans son was I   260
  As any of you.

Bot, Mak, com heder! Betwene shall thou lyg lowne.
MAK. Then myght I lett [8] you, bedene, [9] of that ye wold
    rowne, [10]
. . . .
. . . . [11]

        [They lie down.]

  [MAK.] No dred.
Fro my top to my too,
Manus tuas commendo,

---

[1] slut   [2] worse   [3] the following morning   [4] for her funeral
[5] know   [6] worn out   [7] tired   [8] hinder   [9] of course   [10] whisper   [11] a lacuna in the MS.

Poncio Pilato,
   Cryst crosse me spede!

[*Then he rises up, the shepherds being asleep, and says:*]

Now were tyme for a man that lakkys what he wold
To stalk preuely than vnto a fold,   270
And neemly [1] to wyrk than, and be not to bold,
For he might aby [2] the bargan, if it were told,
   At the endyng.
Now were tyme for to reyll; [3]
Bot he nedys good counsell
That fayn wold fare weyll,
   And has bot lytyll spendyng.

[*Pretends to be a magician.*]

Bot abowte you a serkyll [4] as rownde as a moyn, [5]
To I haue done that I wyll, tyll that it be noyn, [6]
That ye lyg stone styll to that I haue doyne.   280
And I shall say thertyll of good wordys a foyne. [7]
   On hight
Ouer youre heydys my hand I lyft:
Outt go youre een! Fordo your syght!—
Bot yit I must make better shyft
   And it be right.

[*The shepherds begin to snore.*]

Lord, what! thay slepe hard! that may ye all here.
Was I neuer a shepard, bot now wyll I lere. [8]
If the flok he skard, yit shall I nyp nere.

[*He approaches the sheep.*]

---

  [1] quickly   [2] pay for   [3] set about it   [4] circle   [5] moon
  [6] noon   [7] few   [8] learn

How! Drawes hederward! Now mendys oure chere 290
  From sorow.
A fatt shepe I dar say!
A good flese dar I lay!
Eft-whyte [1] when I may,
  Bot this will I borow.

[Takes the sheep, and crosses to his home.]

How, Gyll, art thou in? Gett vs som lyght.
Vxor eius. Who makys sich dyn this tyme of the
    nyght?
I am sett for to spyn; I hope not I myght
Ryse a penny to wyn. I shrew them on hight
  So farys!   300
A huswyff that has bene
To be rasyd [2] thus betwene!
Here may no note [3] be sene
  For sich small charys. [4]

Mak. Good wyff, open the hek! [5] Seys thou not what
    I bryng?
Vxor. I may thole [6] the dray the snek. [7] A, com in, my
    swetyng!
Mak. Yee, thou thar not rek [8] of my long standyng.
Vxor. By the nakyd nek art thou lyke for to hyng.
  Mak. Do way!
I am worthy my mete;   310
For in a strate can I gett
More then thay that swynke and swette
  All the long day.

Thus it fell to my lott, Gyll! I had sich grace.

[He shows her the sheep.]

---

[1] pay back   [2] has to be aroused   [3] work   [4] chores   [5] door
[6] allow   [7] draw the latch   [8] you did not think about

Vxor. It were a fowll blott to be hanged for the case.

Mak. I haue skapyd, Ielott, oft as hard a glase.[1]

Vxor. Bot so long goys the pott to the water, men says,
   At last

Comys it home broken.

Mak. Well knowe I the token;   320

Bot let it neuer be spoken,

   Bot com and help fast.

I wold he were slayn; I lyst well ete.

This twelmonthe was I not so fayn of oone shepe mete.

Vxor. Com thay or [2] he be slayn and here the shepe
   blete—

Mak. Then myght I be tane! That were a cold swette!

[*He begins to tremble.*]

  Go spar

The gaytt doore.[3]

Vxor.   Yis, Mak,

For and thay com at thy bak—

Mak. Then myght I by for all the pak!   330

   The dewill of the war!

Vxor. A good bowrde [4] haue I spied,—syn thou can
   none.

Here shall we hym hyde to thay be gone,—

In my credyll abyde,—lett me alone,

And I shall lyg besyde in chylbed, and grone.

   Mak. Thou red! [5]

And I shall say thou was lyght [6]

Of a knaue [7] childe this nyght.

Vxor. Now well is me day bright,

   That euer was I bred!   340

---

[1] blow   [2] before   [3] front door   [4] trick   [5] Get thee ready
[6] delivered   [7] boy child

This is a good gyse [1] and a far cast! [2]
Yit a woman avyse helpys at the last!
I wote neuer who spyse. Agane go thou fast.
Mak. Bot I com or thay ryse, els blawes a cold blast!
 I wyll go slepe.

[Mak returns to the shepherds, and resumes his place.]
Yit slepys all this meneye; [3]
And I shall go stalk preuely,
As it had neuer bene I
 That I caryed thare shepe.

  [The First and Second Shepherds awake.]
I. Pastor. *Resurrex a mortruis!* Haue hald my
  hand.   350
Iudas carnas dominus! I may not well stand:
My foytt slepys, by Ihesus; and I water fastand.
I thoght that we layd vs full nere Yngland.
 II. Pastor. A ye!
Lord, what I haue slept weyll.
As fresh as an eyll,
As lyght I me feyll
 As leyfe on a tre.

  [The Third Shepherd awakes.]
III. Pastor. Benste be here-in! so my body qwakys,
My hart is outt of skyn, what-so it makys. 360
Who makys all this dyn? So my browes blakys. [4]
To the dowore [5] wyll I wyn. [6] Harke, felows, wakys!
 We were fowre:
Se ye awre [7] of Mak now?
I. Pastor. We were vp or thou.
II. Pastor. Man, I gyf God a-vowe,
 Yit yede he nawre. [8]

---

[1] disguise [2] chance [3] company [4] grows black [5] door
  [6] go [7] anything [8] went he nowhere

III. PASTOR. Me thoght he was lapt in a wolfe skyn.

I. PASTOR. So are many hapt now—namely, within.

III. PASTOR. When we had long napt, me thoght with
    a gyn [1]

A fatt shepe he trapt; bot he mayde no dyn.

  II. PASTOR. Be styll!

Thi dreme makys the woode; [2]

It is bot fantom, by the roode.

I. PASTOR. Now God turne all to good,
    If it be his wyll!

           [*They awaken Mak.*]

II. PASTOR. Ryse, Mak! For shame! thou lygys right
    lang.

MAK. Now Crystys holy name be vs emang!

What is this, for Sant Iame? I may not well gang!

I trow I be the same. A! my nek has lygen wrang 380
    Enoghe.

          [*They help him to his feet.*]

Mekill thank! Syn yister euen,

Now, by Sant Strevyn, [3]

I was flayd with a swevyn, [4]
    My hart out of-sloghe. [5]

I thoght Gyll began to crok and trauell full sad,

Welner [6] at the fyrst cok of a yong lad

For to mend oure flok. Then be I neuer glad;

I haue tow on my rok [7] more then euer I had.
    A, my heede! 390

A house full of yong tharnes! [8]

The dewill knok outt thare harnes!

Wo is hym has many barnes,
    And therto lytyll brede!

---

[1] snare   [2] mad   [3] Stephen   [4] dream   [5] that slew my heart
[6] well nigh   [7] distaff   [8] bellies

I must go home, by youre lefe, to Gyll, as I thoght.
I pray you looke my slefe that I steyll noght;
I am loth you to grefe or from you take oght.

[*Mak leaves them.*]

III. PASTOR. Go furth; yll myght thou chefe![1] Now
    wold I we soght,
  This morne,   400
That we had all oure store.
I. PASTOR. Bot I will go before;
Let vs mete.
II. PASTOR. Whore?
  III. PASTOR. At the crokyd thorne.

[*Exeunt.*]

[*Mak arrives at his home.*]

MAK. Vndo this doore! Who is here?
  How long shall I stand?
VXOR EIUS. Who makys sich a bere?[2] Now walk in the
    wenyand![3]
MAK. A, Gyll, what chere? It is I, Mak, youre hus-
    bande.
VXOR. Then may we se here the dewill in a bande,
  Syr Gyle.
Lo, he commys with a lote[4]
As he were holden in the throte.
I may not syt at my note[5]   410
  A hand-lang while.[6]

MAK. Wyll ye here what fare she makys to gett hir a
    glose?[7]
And dos noght bot lakys,[8] and clowse hir toose.[9]

---

[1] prosper   [2] noise   [3] in the waning of the moon (an unlucky
time)   [4] noise (the allusion is to hanging)   [5] work   [6] an instant
[7] excuse   [8] play   [9] scratch her toes

Vxor. Why, who wanders? who wakys? who commys?
    who gose?
Who brewys? who bakys? who makys me thus hose?
  And than,
It is rewthe to beholde,
Now in hote, now in colde,
Full wofull is the householde   420
  That wantys a woman.

Bot what ende has thou mayde with the hyrdys.[1] Mak?
Mak. The last worde that thay sayde, when I turnyd
    my bak,
Thay wold looke that thay hade thare shepe all the
    pak.
I hope thay wyll nott be well payde when thay thare
    shepe lak,
  Perde.
Bot how-so the gam gose,
To me thay wyll suppose,
And make a fowll noyse,
  And cry outt apon me.   430

Bot thou must do as thou hyght.[2]
Vxor.   I accorde me thertyll;
I shall swedyll[3] hym right in my credyll.
If it were a gretter slyght,[4] yit couthe I help tyll.
I wyll lyg downe stright. Com hap[5] me.
Mak.   I wyll.

[*He tucks her in bed.*]
  Vxor. Behynde!
Com Coll and his maroo,[6]
Thay will nyp vs full naroo.

----

[1] shepherds   [2] promised   [3] swaddle   [4] trick   [5] cover me up
[6] mate

Mak. Bot I may cry "Out haroo!"
 The shepe if thay fynde.

Vxor. Harken ay when thay call; thay will com
  onone.   440
Com and make redy all; and syng by thy oone;
Syng lullay thou shall, for I must grone
And cry outt by the wall on Mary and Iohn,
 For sore.
Syng lullay on fast
When thou heris at the last;
And bot I play a fals cast,
 Trust me no more!

[The Shepherds return, and speak at the other end of
the pageant.]

iii. Pastor. A, Coll, good morne! Why slepys thou
  nott?

i. Pastor. Alas, that euer was I borne! we haue a
  fowll blott.   450
A fat wedir [1] haue we lorne.

iii. Pastor.   Mary, Godys forbott!

ii. Pastor. Who shuld do vs that skorne? That were
  a fowll spott.

 i. Pastor. Som shrewe.
I haue soght with my dogys
All Horbery Shrogys,[2]
And of fefteyn hogys
 Fond I bot oone ewe.

iii. Pastor. Now trow [3] me, if ye will; by Sant Thomas
  of Kent,   460
Ayther Mak or Gyll was at that assent.

[1] sheep   [2] Horbury thickets, four miles from Wakefield   [3] believe

I. PASTOR.   Peasse, man! Be still! I sagh when he
 went.
Thou sklanders hym yll. Thou aght to repent
 Goode spede.
II. PASTOR.   Now as euer myght I the,[1]
If I shuld euyn here de,
I wold say it were he
 That dyd that same dede.

III. PASTOR.   Go we theder, I rede,[2] and ryn on oure
 feete.
Shall I neuer ete brede the sothe to I wytt.[3]
I. PASTOR.   Nor drynk in my heede with hym tyll I
 mete.
II. PASTOR.   I wyll rest in no stede tyll that I hym.
 grete,   470
 My brothere.
Oone I will hight:[4]
Tyll I se hym in sight
Shall I neuer slepe one nyght
 Ther I do anothere.

[*As the shepherds approach, Mak's wife begins to
groan, and Mak, sitting by the cradle, to sing a
lullaby.*]

III. PASTOR.   Will ye here how thay hak?[5] Oure syre
 lyst croyne.[6]
I. PASTOR.   Hard I neuer none crak[7] so clere out of
 toyne![8]
Call on hym.
II. PASTOR.   Mak! vndo youre doore soyne.
MAK.   Who is that spak as it were noyne
 On loft?   480

---

[1] thrive [2] advise [3] until I know the truth [4] one thing will
I promise [5] sing [6] croon [7] bawl [8] tune

Who is that, I say?

III. PASTOR. Goode felowse, were it day.

MAK. [*Opening the door.*] As far as ye may,
   Good, spekys soft,

Ouer a seke womans heede that is at maylleasse; [1]
I had leuer be dede or she had any dyseasse [2]

VXOR. Go to an othere stede! I may not well qweasse.[3]
Ich fote that ye trede goys thorow my nese.[4]
   So hee!

I. PASTOR. Tell vs, Mak, if ye may,   490
How fare ye, I say?

MAK. Bot ar ye in this towne to-day?
   Now how fare ye?

Ye haue ryn in the myre, and ar weytt yit.
I shall make you a fyre if ye will syt.
A nores[5] wold I hyre, thynk ye on yit.
Well qwytt is my hyre; my dreme—this is it,
                              [*Points to the cradle.*]
   A seson.
I haue barnes, if ye knew,
Well mo then enewe.   500
Bot we must drynk as we brew,
   And that is bot reson.
I wold ye dynyd or ye yode. Me thynk that ye swette.

II. PASTOR. Nay, nawther mendys oure mode drynke
         nor mette.

MAK. Why, sir, alys you oght bot goode?

III. PASTOR. Yee, oure shepe that we gett
Ar stollyn as thay yode. Oure los is grette.
   MAK. Syrs, drynkys!

---

[1] in discomfort   [2] annoyance   [3] breathe   [4] nose   [5] nurse

Had I bene thore,
Som shuld haue boght it full sore.

I. PASTOR.   Mary, som men trowes that ye wore;   510
  And that vs forthynkys.[1]

I. PASTOR.   Mak, som men trowys that it shuld be ye.
III. PASTOR.   Ayther ye or youre spouse, so say we.
MAK.   Now, if ye haue suspowse [2] to Gill, or to me,
Com and rype oure howse, and then may ye se
  Who had hir.
If I any shepe fott,[3]
Aythor cow or stott,[4]
And Gyll, my wyfe, rose nott
  Here syn she lade hir,   520

As I am true and lele, to God here I pray
That this be the fyrst mele that I shall ete this day.
                              [*Points to the cradle.*]
I. PASTOR.   Mak, as haue I ceyll,[5] avyse the, I say;
He lernyd tymely to steyll that couth not say nay.

     [*The Shepherds begin the search.*]
  VXOR.   I swelt! [6]
Outt, thefys, fro my wonys! [7]
Ye com to rob vs, for the nonys.
MAK.   Here ye not how she gronys?
  Youre hartys shuld melt.

VXOR.   Outt, thefys, fro my barne! Negh hym not
      thor!   530
MAK.   Wyst ye how she had farne,[8] youre hartys wold
      be sore.
Ye do wrang, I you warne, that thus commys before

---

[1] troubles   [2] suspicion   [3] fetched   [4] stoat   [5] bliss   [6] faint
[7] house   [8] labored

To a woman that has farne. Bot I say no more!
   Vxor. A, my medyll!
I pray to God so mylde,
If euer I you begyld,
That I ete this chylde
   That lygys in this credyll.
Mak. Peasse, woman, for Godys payn! and cry not so!
Thou spyllys thy brane, and makys me full wo. 540
ii. Pastor. I trow oure shepe be slayn. What finde
     ye two?
iii. Pastor. All wyrk we in vayn; as well may we go.
   Bot, hatters,[1]
I can fynde no flesh,
Hard nor nesh,[2]
Salt nor fresh,
   Bot two tome[3] platers.

Whik[4] catell bot this, tame nor wylde,
None, as haue I blys, as lowde as he smylde.[5]
   Vxor. No, so God me blys, and gyf me ioy of my
     chylde!
                        550
i. Pastor. We haue merkyd amys; I hold vs begyld.
   ii. Pastor. Syr, don.

          [Addressing Mak at the cradle.]
Syr, Oure Lady hym saue!
Is youre chyld a knaue?
Mak. Any lord myght hym haue,
   This chyld to his son.

When he wakyns he kyppys[6] that ioy is to se.
iii. Pastor. In good tyme to hys hyppys[7] and in
     cele![8]

  [1] plague take it   [2] soft   [3] empty   [4] living   [5] smelled
  [5] snatches   [7] hips   [8] happiness

Bot who was his gossyppys [1] so sone rede?

MAK. So fare fall thare lyppys!

I. PASTOR. [*Aside.*] Hark now, a le! [2]   560

  MAK. So God thaym thank,

Parkyn, and Gybon Waller, I say,

And gentill Iohn Horne, in good fay,

He made all the garray, [3]

  With the greatt shank.

II. PASTOR. Mak, freyndys will we be, ffor we ar all
    oone.

MAK. We! now I hald for me, for mendys [4] gett I none.

Fare-well all thre! All glad were ye gone!

      [*Exeunt the shepherds.*]

III. PASTOR. Fare wordys may ther be, bot luf is ther
    none

  This yere.   570

I. PASTOR. Gaf ye the chyld any-thyng?

II. PASTOR. I trow, not oone farthyng!

III. PASTOR. Fast agane will I flyng;

  Abyde ye me there.

      [*The Third Shepherd returns.*]

Mak, take it to no grefe, if I com to thi barne.

MAK. Nay, thou dos me greatt reprefe, and fowll has
    thou farne.

III. PASTOR. The child will it not grefe, that lytyll day-
    starne. [5]

Mak, with youre leyfe, let me gyf youre barne

  Bot sex pence.

MAK. Nay, do way! He slepys.

III. PASTOR. Me thynk he pepys.   580

MAK. When he wakyns he wepys!

  I pray you go hence!

[1] god-parents   [2] lie   [3] commotion   [4] amends   [5] day-star

III. Pastor. Gyf me lefe hym to kys, and lyft vp the
   clowtt.[1]

[Lifts the cloth, thinks the baby deformed.]
What the dewill is this? he has a long snowte!

*[The other shepherds, pressing forward, look at the
baby.]*
I. Pastor. He is merkyd amys.[2] We wate ill abowte.
II. Pastor. Ill spon weft, iwys, ay commys foull owte.[3]

[Suddenly, realizing that it is a sheep.]
   Ay, so!
He is lyke to oure shepe!
III. Pastor. How, Gyb! may I pepe?   590
I. Pastor. I trow, kynde will crepe
   Where it may not go![4]

[They lift the sheep out of the cradle.]
II. Pastor. This was a gwantt gawde, and a far cast!
It was a hee frawde![5]
III. Pastor.   Yee, syrs, wast.[6]
Lett bren[7] this bawde, and bynd hir fast.
A! fals skawde,[8] hang at the last!
   So shall thou.
Wyll ye se how thay swedyll
His foure feytt in the medyll?
Sagh I neuer in a credyll   600
   A hornyd lad or now!

Mak. Peasse byd I! What! Lett be youre fare!
I am he that hym gatt, and yond woman hym bare.

---

[1] cloth   [2] deformed   [3] an old proverb: "From an ill-spun woof
ever comes foul out"   [4] an old proverb: "Nature will walk where
it may not go"   [5] great fraud   [6] was it   [7] burn   [8] scold

I. Pastor. What dewill shall he hatt? [1]
"Mak?" Lo, God, Makys ayre!

II. Pastor. Lett be all that. Now God gyf hym care,
I sagh.

Vxor. A pratty childe is he
As syttys on a womans kne;
A dyllydowne, perde,
   To gar a man laghe. 610

III. Pastor. I know hym by the eeremarke; that is a
      good tokyn!

Mak. I tell you, syrs, hark! hys noyse [2] was brokyn;
Sythen [3] told me a clerk that he was forspokyn. [4]

I. Pastor. This is a fals wark; I wold fayn be
      wörkyn. [5]
   Gett wepyn!

Vxor. He was takyn with an elfe,
I saw it myself;
When the clok stroke twelf
   Was he forshapyn. [6]

II. Pastor. Ye two ar well feft [7] sam in a stede. 620

III. Pastor. Syn thay manteyn thare theft, let do
      thaym to dede.

Mak. If I trespas eft, gyrd of my heede!
With you will I be left.

I. Pastor.   Syrs, do my reede:
   For this trespas
We will nawther ban ne flyte, [8]
Fyght nor chyte, [9]
Bot haue done as tyte, [10]
   And cast hym in canvas.

---

[1] be named   [2] nose   [3] afterwards   [4] bewitched   [5] avenged
[6] deformed   [7] endowed   [8] curse nor quarrel   [9] chide   [10] quickly

[They toss Mak in a sheet, and then return to the fields.]

I. PASTOR. Lord, what! I am sore in poynt for to
    bryst.

In fayth, I may no more; therfor wyll I ryst.   630

II. PASTOR. As a shepe of sevyn skore he weyd in my
    fyst.

For to slepe ay-whore[1] me thynk that I lyst.

III. PASTOR. Now I pray you,

Lyg downe on this grene.

I. PASTOR. On these thefys yit I mene.

III. PASTOR. Wherto shuld ye tene?[2]
    Do as I say you!

[They lie down and fall asleep.]

An angel sings "Gloria in excelsis"; then let him say:

ANGELUS. Ryse, hyrd-men heynd![3] for now is he borne

That shall take fro the feynd that Adam had lorne:

That warloo[4] to sheynd[5] this nyght is he borne;   640

God is made youre freynd now at this morne.

    He behestys

At Bedlem go se,

Ther lygys that fre[6]

In a cryb full poorely

    Betwyx two bestys.

[The angel withdraws.]

I. PASTOR. This was a qwant stevyn[7] that euer yit I
    hard.

It is a meruell to neuyn,[8] thus to be skard.

II. PASTOR. Of Godys son of heuyn he spak vpward.

All the wod on a leuyn[9] me thoght that he gard[10]   650

    Appere.

---

[1] anywhere   [2] trouble   [3] gracious   [4] devil   [5] destroy   [6] noble
being   [7] voice   [8] relate   [9] lightning   [10] made

III. PASTOR. He spake of a barne
In Bedlem, I you warne.
I. PASTOR. That betokyns yond starne;[1]
 Let vs seke hym there.

II. PASTOR. Say, what was his song? Hard ye not how
 he crakyd it,
Thre brefes to a long?
III. PASTOR. Yee, mary, he hakt[2] it;
Was no crochett wrong, nor no-thyng that lakt it.
I. PASTOR. For to syng vs emong, right as he knakt[2] it,
 I can. 660
II. PASTOR. Let se how ye croyne.
Can ye bark at the mone?
III. PASTOR. Hold youre tonges! Haue done!
I. PASTOR. Hark after, than!

II. PASTOR. To Bedlem he bad that we shuld gang;
I am full fard[3] that we tary to lang.
III. PASTOR. Be mery and not sad; of myrth is oure
 sang;
Euer-lastyng glad to mede[4] may we fang,[5]
 Withoutt noyse.
I. PASTOR. Hy we theder for-thy,[6] 670
If we be wete and wery,
To that chyld and that lady!
 We haue it not to lose.

II. PASTOR. We fynde by the prophecy—let be youre
 dyn!—
Of Dauid and Isay and mo then I myn,[7]
Thay prophecyed by clergy that in a vyrgyn
Shuld he lyght and ly, to slokyn[8] oure syn

---

¹ star   ² sang   ³ afraid   ⁴ reward   ⁵ go   ⁶ therefore
⁷ remember   ⁸ quench

And slake it,
Oure kynde from wo.
For Isay sayd so: 680
Ecce virgo
    Concipiet a chylde that is nakyd.

III. PASTOR. Full glad may we be, and abyde that day
That lufty to see, that all myghtys may.
Lord, well were me, for ones and for ay,
Myght I knele on my kne som word for to say
    To that chylde.
Bot the angell sayd,
In a cryb wos he layde;
He was poorly arayd, 690
    Both meke and mylde.

I. PASTOR. Patryarkes that has bene, and prophetys
            beforne,
Thay desyryd to haue sene this chylde that is borne.
Thay ar gone full clene; that haue thay lorne.[1]
We shall se hym, I weyn, or it be morne,
    To tokyn.
When I se hym and fele,
Then wote I full weyll
It is true as steyll
    That prophetys haue spokyn: 700

To so poore as we ar that he wold appere,
Fyrst fynd, and declare by his messyngere.
II. PASTOR. Go we now, let vs fare; the place is vs
            nere.
III. PASTOR. I am redy and yare;[2] go we in-fere[3]
    To that bright.
Lord, if thi wyll it be—

----

[1] lost   [2] prepared   [3] together

We ar lewde [1] all thre—
Thou grauntt vs somkyns gle [2]
  To comforth thi wight.

[They enter the stable. The First Shepherd kneels before the babe.]

I. PASTOR.   Hayll, comly and clene! hayll, yong child!   710
Hayll, Maker, as I meyne! of a madyn so mylde!
Thou has waryd,[3] I weyne, the warlo so wylde;
The fals gyler of teyn,[4] now goys he begylde.
  Lo, he merys!
Lo, he laghys, my swetyng!
A welfare metyng!
I haue holden my hetyng.[5]
  Haue a bob of cherys!

[The Second Shepherd kneels.]

II. PASTOR.   Hayll, sufferan Sauyoure, ffor thou has vs soght!
Hayll, frely foyde [6] and floure, that all thyng has wroght!   720
Hayll, full of fauoure, that made all of noght!
Hayll! I kneyll and I cowre. A byrd haue I broght
  To my barne.
Hayll, lytyll tyne [7] mop! [8]
Of oure crede thou art crop.
I wold drynk on thy cop,[9]
  Lytyll day-starne!

[The Third Shepherd kneels.]

III. PASTOR.   Hayll, derlyng dere, full of godhede!
I pray the be nere when that I haue nede.

---

[1] unlettered   [2] joy of some kind   [3] cursed   [4] injury   [5] promise   [6] noble child   [7] tiny   [8] baby   [9] Sacramental cup

Hayll! swete is thy chere! My hart wold blede   730
To se the sytt here in so poore wede,[1]
> With no pennys.
Hayll! put furth thy dall![2]
I bryng the bot a ball:
Haue and play the with-all,
> And go to the tenys.

MARIA. The Fader of heuen, God omnypotent,
That sett all on seuen,[3] his Son has he sent.
My name couth he neuen and lyght[4] or he went.
I conceyuyd hym full euen, thrugh myght as he
> ment;   740
> And now he is borne.
He kepe you fro wo!
I shall pray hym so.
Tell, furth as ye go,
> And myn on this morne.

I. PASTOR. Farewell, lady, so fare to beholde,
With thy childe on thi kne!
II. PASTOR.   Bot he lygys full cold.
Lord, well is me! Now we go, thou behold.
III. PASTOR. For sothe, all redy it semys to be told
> Full oft.   750
I. PASTOR. What grace we haue fun![5]
II. PASTOR. Com furth; now ar we won![6]
III. PASTOR. To syng ar we bun:[7]
> Let take on loft!

> *[They go out singing.]*

Explicit pagina Pastorum.

---

[1] garment   [2] fist   [3] that made all things   [4] alighted (an allusion to the Incarnation)   [5] found   [6] saved   [7] bound

THE SQUYR OF LOWE DEGRE

It was a squyer of lowe degre
That loved the kings doughter of Hungre.
The squir was curteous and hend,[1]
Ech man him loved and was his frend;
He served the kyng her father dere,
Fully the tyme of seven yere;
For he was marshall of his hall,
And set the lords both great and smal.
An hardy man he was, and wight,
Both in batayle and in fyght;   **10**
But ever he was styll mornyng,
And no man wyste[2] for what thyng;
And all was for that fayre lady,
The kynges doughter of Hungry.
There wyste no wyghte in Christente
Howe well he loved that lady fre;
He loved her more then seven yere,
Yet was of love never the nere.
He was not ryche of golde and fe,[3]
A gentyll man forsoth was he.   **20**
To no man durst he make his mone,
But syghed sore hymselfe alone.
    And evermore, whan he was wo,
Into his chambre would he goo;
And through the chambre he toke the waye,
Into the gardyn, that was full gaye;
And in the garden, as I wene,
Was an arber fayre and grene,
And in the arber was a tre,
A fayrer in the world might none be;   **30**
The tre it was of cypresse,

---

[1] gracious   [2] knew   [3] property

The fyrst tre that Jesus chese; [1]
The sother-wood [2] and sykamoure,
The reed rose and the lyly-floure,
The boxe, the beche, and the larel-tre,
The date, also the damyse, [3]
The fylbyrdes hangyng to the ground,
The fygge-tre, and the maple round,
And other trees there was mane ane,
The pyany, [4] the popler, and the plane,   40
With brode braunches all aboute,
Within the arbar, and eke withoute;
On every braunche sate byrdes thre,
Syngynge with great melody,
The lavorocke [5] and the nightyngale,
The ruddocke [6] and the woodewale, [7]
The pee [8] and the popinjaye, [9]
The thrustele sange both nyght and daye,
The marlyn, [10] and the wrenne also,
The swalowe whippynge to and fro,   50
The jaye jangled them amonge,
The larke began that mery songe,
The sparowe spredde her on her spraye,
The mavys songe with notes full gaye,
The nuthake [11] with her notes newe,
The sterlynge set her notes full trewe,
The goldefynche made full mery chere,
Whan she was bente upon a brere,
And many other foules mo,
The osyll, [12] and the thrusshe also;   60
And they sange wyth notes clere,
In confortynge that squyere.

    And evermore, whan he was wo,
    Into that arber wolde he go,

---

[1] chose   [2] southernwood   [3] damson   [4] peony   [5] lark   [6] robin
[7] woodlark   [8] wryneck   [9] parrot   [10] merlin   [11] nuthatch
[12] ouzel

And under a bente he layde hym lowe,
Ryght even under her chambre wyndowe;
And lened his backe to a thorne,
And sayd, 'Alas, that I was borne!
That I were ryche of golde and fe,
That I might wedde that lady fre!   70
Of golde good, or some treasure,
That I myght wedde that lady floure!
Or elles come of so gentyll kynne,
The ladyes love that I myght wynne.
Wolde God that I were a kynges sonne,
That ladyes love that I myght wonne!
Or els so bolde in eche fyght,
As Syr Lybius that gentell knyght,
Or els so bolde in chyvalry,
As Syr Gawayne, or Syr Guy;   80
Or els so doughty of my hande
As was the gyaunte Syr Colbrande,
And it were put in jeopede [1]
What man shoulde wynne that lady fre,
Than should no man have her but I,
The Kynges doughter of Hungry.'
But ever he sayde, 'Wayle a waye!
For poverte passeth all my paye!'
And as he made thys rufull chere,
He sowned [2] downe in that arbere.   90
    That lady herde his mournyng all,
Ryght under the chambre wall;
In her oryall there she was
Closed well with royall glas;
Fulfylled it was with ymagery,
Every wyndowe by and by, [3]
On eche syde had there a gynne, [4]
Sperde with many a dyvers pynne.

[1] to the test   [2] swooned   [3] side by side   [4] fastening

Anone that lady, fayre and fre,
Undyd a pynne of yvere,   100
And wyd the windowes she open set,
The sunne shone in at her closet,
In that arber fayre and gaye,
She sawe where that squyre lay.
The lady sayd to hym anone,
'Syr, why makest thou that mone?
And whi thou mournest night and day
Now tell me, squyre, I thee pray;
And, as I am a true lady,
Thy counsayl shall I never dyscry;   110
And, yf it be no reprefe [1] to thee,
Thy bote [2] of bale yet shall I be.'
And often was he in wele and wo,
But never so well as he was tho.

The squyer set hym on hys kne,
And sayde, 'Lady, it is for thee,
I have loved this seven yere,
And bought thy love, lady, full dere.
Ye are so ryche in youre aray
That one word to you I dare not say,   120
And come ye be of so hye kynne,
No worde of love durst I begynne.
My wyll to you yf I had sayde,
And ye therwith not well apayde, [3]
Ye might have bewraied me to the kinge,
And brought me sone to my endynge.
Therfore, my lady fayre and fre,
I durst not shewe my harte to thee;
But I am here at your wyll,
Whether ye wyll me save or spyll; [4]   130
For all the care I have in be,
A worde of you might comfort me;

---

[1] reproach   [2] reward   [3] pleased   [4] destroy

And, yf ye wyll not do so,
Out of this land I must nedes go;
I wyll forsake both lande and lede,[1]
And become an hermyte in uncouth stede;
In many a lande to begge my bred,
To seke where Christ was quicke and dead;
A staffe I wyll make me of my spere,
Lynen cloth I shall none were;   140
Ever in travayle I shall wende,
Tyll I come to the worldes ende;
And, lady, but thou be my bote,
There shall no sho come on my fote;
Therfore, lady, I the praye,
For hym that dyed on Good Frydaye,
Let me not in daunger dwell,
For his love that harowed hell.'

Than sayd that lady milde of mode,
Ryght in her closet there she stode,   150
'By hym that dyed on a tre,
Thou shalt never be deceyved for me;
Though I for thee should be slayne,
Squyer, I shall the love agayne.
Go forth, and serve my father the kynge,
And let be all thy styll mournynge;
Let no man wete[2] that ye were here,
Thus all alone in my arbere;
If ever ye wyll come to your wyll,
Here and se, and holde you styll.   160
Beware of the stewarde, I you praye,
He wyll deceyve you and he maye;
For, if he wote of your woyng,
He wyl bewraye you to the kynge;
Anone for me ye shall be take,
And put in pryson for my sake;

---

[1] people   [2] know

Than must ye nedes abyde the lawe,
Peraventure both hanged and drawe.
That syght of you I would not se,
For all the golde in Christente.   170
For, and ye my love should wynne,
With chyvalry ye must begynne,
And other dedes of armes to done,
Through whiche ye may wynne your shone; [1]
And ryde through many a peryllous place,
As a venterous man to seke your grace,
Over hylles and dales, and hye mountaines,
In wethers wete, both hayle and raynes,
And yf ye may no harbroughe se,
Than must ye lodge under a tre,   180
Among the beastes wyld and tame,
And ever you wyll gette your name;
And in your armure must ye lye,
Every nyght than by and by,
And your meny [2] everychone,
Till seven yere be comen and gone;
And passe by many a peryllous see,
Squyer, for the love of me,
Where any war begynneth to wake,
And many a batayll undertake,   190
Throughout the land of Lumbardy,
In every cytie by and by.
And be avised, when thou shalt fight,
Loke that ye stand aye in the right;
And, yf ye wyll take good hede,
Yet all the better shall ye spede;
. . . .

I pray to God and Our Lady,
Sende you the whele of vyctory,

¹ shoes   ² followers

That my father so fayne [1] may be,
That he wyll wede me unto thee, 200
And make the king of this countre,
To have and holde in honeste,
Wyth welth and wynne [2] to were the crowne,
And to be lorde of toure and towne;
That we might our dayes endure
In parfyte love that is so pure;
And if we may not so come to,
Other wyse then must we do;
And therfore, squyer, wende thy way,
And hye the fast on thy journay, 210
And take thy leve of kinge and quene,
And so to all the courte bydene. [3]
Ye shall not want at your goyng
Golde, nor sylver, nor other thyng.
This seven yere I shall you abyde,
Betyde of you what so betyde;
Tyll seven yere be comen and gone
I shall be mayde all alone.'
The squyer kneled on his kne,
And thanked that lady fayre and fre; 220
And thryes he kyssed that lady tho,
And toke his leve, and forth gan go.
  The kinges steward stode full nye,
In a chambre fast them bye,
And hearde theyr wordes wonder wele,
And all the woyng every dele.
He made a vowe to heaven kynge,
For to bewraye that swete thynge,
And that squyer taken shoulde be,
And hanged hye on a tre; 230
And that false stewarde full of yre,
Them to betraye was his desyre;

[1] glad [2] joy [3] quickly

He bethought hym nedely,
Every daye by and by,
How he myght venged be
On that lady fayre and fre,
For he her loved pryvely,
And therfore dyd her great envye.[1]
Alas! it tourned to wrother-heyle [2]
That ever he wyste of theyr counsayle.   240
    But leve we of the stewarde here,
And speke we more of that squyer,
Howe he to his chambre wente,
Whan he paste from that lady gente.
There he araied him in scarlet reed,
And set his chaplet upon his head,
A belte about his sydes two,
With brode barres to and fro;
A horne about his necke he caste,
And forth he went than at the last   250
To do hys office in the hall
Among the lordes both great and small.
He toke a white yeard [3] in his hande,
Before the kynge than gane he stande,
And sone he sate hym on his knee,
And served the kynge ryght royally,
With deynty meates that were dere,
With partryche, pecoke, and plovere,
With byrdes in bread ybake,
The tele, the ducke, and the drake,   260
The cocke, the curlewe, and the crane,
With fesauntes fayre, theyr were no wane,[4]
Both storkes and snytes [5] ther were also,
And venyson freshe of bucke and do,
And other deyntes many one,
For to set afore the kynge anone:

---

[1] harm   [2] calamity   [3] staff   [4] lack   [5] snipes

And when the squyer had done so,
He served the hall bothe to and fro.
Eche man hym loved in honeste,
Hye and lowe in theyr degre,   270
So dyd the kyng full sodenly,
And he wyst not wherfore nor why.
The kynge behelde the squyer wele,
And all his rayment every dele,
He thoughte he was the semylyest man
That ever in the worlde he sawe or than.
Thus sate the kyng and eate ryght nought,
But on his squyer was all his thought.
    Anone the stewarde toke good hede,
And to the kyng full soone he yede,[1]   280
And soone he tolde unto the kynge
All theyr wordes and theyr woynge;
And how she hyght[2] hym lande and fe,
Golde and sylver great plentye,
And how he should his leve take,
And become a knight for her sake:
'And thus they talked bothe in-fere,[3]
And I drewe me nere and nere,
Had I not come in, verayly,
The squyer had layne her by,   290
But whan he was ware of me,
Full fast away can he fle;
That is sothe: here is my hand
To fight with him while I may stand.'
    The kyng sayd to the steward tho,
'I may not beleve it should be so;
Hath he be so bonayre[4] and benyngne,
And served me syth he was yinge,
And redy with me in every nede,
Bothe true of word, and eke of dede,   300

---

[1] went   [2] promised   [3] together   [4] well-bred

I may not beleve, be nyght nor daye,
My doughter dere he wyll betraye,
Nor to come her chambre nye,
That fode [1] to longe with no foly;
Though she would to hym consente,
That lovely lady fayre and gente,
I truste hym so well withouten drede,
That he would never do that dede;
But yf he myght that lady wynne,
In wedlocke to welde withouten synne,   310
And yf she wyll assent him tyll,
The squyer is worthy to have none yll.
For I have sene that many a page
Have become men by mariage;
Than it is semely that squyer
To have my doughter by this manere,
And eche man in his degre
Become a lorde of ryaltye,
By fortune and by other grace,
By herytage and by purchase: 320
Therfore, stewarde, beware hereby,
Defame hym not for no envy:
It were great reuth he should be spylte,
Or put to death withouten gylte;
And more ruthe of my doughter dere,
For chaungyng of that ladyes chere;
I woulde not for my crowne so newe,
That lady chaunge hyde or hewe;
Or for to put thyselfe in drede,
But thou myght take hym with the dede.   330
For yf it may be founde in thee
That thou them fame for enmyte,
Thou shalt be taken as a felon,
And put full depe in my pryson,

[1] child

And fetered fast unto a stone,
Tyl .xii. yere were come and gone,
And drawen wyth hors throughe the cyte,
And soone hanged upon a tre;
And thou may not thy selfe excuse,
This dede thou shalt no wise refuse;   340
And therfore, steward, take good hed,
How thou wilt answere to this ded.'
The stewarde answered with great envy,
'That I have sayd, I wyll stand therby;
To suffre death and endlesse wo,
Syr kynge, I wyl never go therfro;
For, yf that ye wyll graunt me here
Strength of men and great power,
I shall hym take this same nyght,
In chambre with your doughter bright;   350
For I shall never be gladde of chere,
Tyll I be venged of that squyer.'
    Than sayd the kynge full curteysly
Unto the stewarde, that stode hym by,
'Thou shalte have strength ynough with the,
Men of armes .xxx. and thre,
To watche that lady muche of pryce,
And her to kepe fro her enemyes.
For there is no knight in Chrystente,
That wolde betray that lady fre,   360
But he should dye under his shelde
And I myght se hym in the feldde;
And therfore, stewarde, I the pray,
Take hede what I shall to the say;
And if the squiere come to-night,
For to speke with that lady bryght,
Let hym say whatsoever he wyll,
And here and se and holde you styll;
And herken well what he wyll say,

Or thou with him make any fray   370
So he come not her chambre win,[1]
No bate[2] on hym loke thou begyn,
Though that he kysse that lady fre,
And take his leave ryght curteysly,
Let hym go, both hole and sounde,
Without wemme[3] or any wounde;
But yf he wyl her chamber breke,
No worde to hym that thou do speke.
But yf he come with company,
For to betraye that fayre lady,   380
Loke he be taken soone anone,
And all his meyne everychone,
And brought with strength to my pryson,
As traytour, thefe, and false felon;
And yf he make any defence,
Loke that he never go thence;
But loke thou hew hym al so small,
As flesshe whan it to the potte shall.
And yf he yelde hym to thee,
Brynge him both saufe and sounde to me. 390
I shall borowe,[4] for seven yere
He shall not wedde my doughter dere:
And therfore, stewarde, I thee praye,
Thou watche that lady nyght and daye.'
The stewarde sayde the kynge untyll,
'All your bidding I shall fulfyll.'
    The stewarde toke his leave to go,
The squyer came fro chambre tho:
Downe he went into the hall,
The officers sone can he call,   400
Both ussher, panter,[5] and butler,
And other that in office were;

---

[1] within   [2] strife   [3] hurt   [4] pledge   [5] pantler, servant in charge of the pantry

There he them warned sone anone
To take up the bordes everychone.
Than they dyd his commaundement,
And sythe [1] unto the kyng he went;
Full lowe he set hym on his kne,
And voyded [2] his borde full gentely;
And whan the squyre had done so,
Anone he sayde the kynge unto,   410
'As ye are lorde of chyvalry,
Geve me leve to passe the sea,
To prove my strenthe with my ryght hande,
On Godes enemyes in uncouth land;
And to be knowe in chyvalry,
In Gascoyne, Spayne, and Lumbardy;
In eche batayle for to fyght,
To be proved a venterous knyght.'
The kyng sayd to the squyer tho,
'Thou shalt have good leve to go;   420
I shall the gyve both golde and fe,
And strength of men to wende with thee;
If thou be true in worde and dede,
I shall thee helpe in all thy nede.'
The squyer thanked the kyng anone,
And toke his leve and forth can gone,
With joye, and blysse, and muche pryde,
With all his meyny by his syde.
He had not ryden but a whyle,
Not the mountenaunce of a myle,   430
Or he was ware of a vyllage,
Anone he sayde unto a page,
'Our souper soone loke it be dyght, [3]
Here wyll we lodge all to-nyght.'
They toke theyr ynnes [4] in good intente,
And to theyr supper soone they wente.

---

[1] afterwards   [2] cleared   [3] prepared   [4] lodgings

Whan he was set, and served at meate,
Than he sayd he had forgete
To take leve of that lady fre,
The kynges doughter of Hungre.   440
   Anone the squyer made him yare,[1]
And by hymselfe forth can he fare;
Without strength of his meyne,
Unto the castell than went he.
Whan he came to the posterne gate,
Anone he entred in thereat,
And his drawen swerd in his hande,
There was no more with him wolde stande:
But it stode with hym full harde,
As ye shall here nowe of the stewarde.   450
He wende [2] in the worlde none had be
That had knowen of his pryvite;
Alas! it was not as he wende,
For all his counsayle the stewarde kende.[3]
He had bewrayed him to the kyng
Of all his love and his woyng;
And yet he laye her chambre by,
Armed with a great company,
And beset it one eche syde,
For treason walketh wonde wyde.   460
The squyer thought on no mystruste,
He wende no man in the worlde had wyste;
But yf he had knowen, by Saynt John,
He had not come theder by his owne;
Or yf that lady had knowen his wyll,
That he should have come her chamber tyll,
She would have taken hym golde and fe,
Strength of men and royalte;
But there ne wyst no man nor grome

---

[1] ready   [2] thought   [3] knew

Where that squyer was become;   470
But forth he went hymselfe alone
Amonge his servauntes everychone.
Whan that he came her chambre to,
Anone he sayde, 'Your dore undo!
Undo,' he sayde, 'nowe, fayre lady!
I am beset with many a spy.
Lady, as whyte as whales bone,
There are thyrty agaynst me one.
Undo thy dore! my worthy wyfe,
I am besette with many a knyfe.   480
Undo your dore! my lady swete,
I am beset with enemyes great;
And, lady, but ye wyll aryse,
I shall be dead with myne enemyes.
Undo thy dore! my frely [1] floure,
For ye are myne, and I am your.'
   That lady with those wordes awoke,
A mantell of golde to her she toke;
She sayde, 'Go away, thou wicked wyght,
Thou shalt not come here this nyght;   490
For I wyll not my dore undo
For no man that cometh therto.
There is but one in Christente
That ever made that forwarde [2] with me;
There is but one that ever bare lyfe,
That ever I hight to be his wyfe;
He shall me wedde, by Mary bryght,
Whan he is proved a venterous knyght;
For we have loved this seven yere,
There was never love to me so dere.   500
There lyeth-on [3] me both kyng and knyght,
Dukes, erles, of muche might.
Wende forth, squyer, on your waye,

[1] lovely   [2] agreement   [3] urge

For here ye gette none other paye;
For I ne wote what ye should be,
That thus besecheth love of me.'
'I am your owne squyr,' he sayde,
'For me, lady, be not dismayde.
Come I am full pryvely
To take my leave of you, lady.'   510
'Welcome,' she sayd, 'my love so dere,
Myne owne dere heart and my squyer;
I shall you geve kysses thre,
A thousande pounde unto your fe,
And kepe I shall my maydenhode ryght,
Tyll ye be proved a venturous knyght,
For yf ye should me wede anone,
My father wolde make slee you soone.
I am the kynges doughter of Hungre,
And ye alone that have loved me,   520
And though you love me never so sore,
For me ye shall never be lore.[1]
Go forth, and aske me at my kynne,
And loke what graunt you may wynne;
Yf that ye gette graunte in faye,[2]
My selfe therto shall not say nay;
And yf ye may not do so,
Otherwyse ye shall come to.
Ye are bothe hardy, stronge, and wight,
Go forth and be a venterous knight.   530
I pray to God and our Lady,
To send you the whele of victory,
That my father so leve[3] he be,
That he wyll profer me to thee.
I wote well it is lyghtly sayd,
"Go forth, and be nothyng afrayde."
A man of worshyp may not do so,

[1] lost   [2] faith   [3] dear

He must have what neds him unto;
He must have gold, he must have fe,
Strength of men and royalte. 540
Golde and sylver spare ye nought,
Tyll to manhode ye be brought;
To what batayll soever ye go,
Ye shall have an hundreth pounde or two;
And yet to me, syr, ye may saye,
That I woulde fayne have you awaye,
That profered you golde and fe,
Out of myne eye syght for to be.
Neverthelesse it is not so,
It is for the worshyp of us two. 550
Though you be come of symple kynne,
Thus my love, syr, may ye wynne,
Yf ye have grace of victory.'

. . . .

Ryght as they talked thus in-fere,
Theyr enemyes approached nere and nere,
Foure and thyrty armed bryght
The steward had arayed hym to fyght.
The steward was ordeyned to spy,
And for to take him utterly.
He wende to death he should have gone, 560
He felled seven men agaynst hym one;
Whan he had them to grounde brought,
The stewarde at hym full sadly [1] fought,
So harde they smote together tho,
The stewardes throte he cut in two,
And sone he fell downe to the grounde,
As a traitour untrewe with many a wound.
The squyer sone in armes they hente,[2]
And of they dyd his good garmente,

---

[1] boldly   [2] seized

And on the stewarde they it dyd,   570
And sone his body therin they hydde,
And with their swordes his face they share,
That she should not know what he ware;
They cast hym at her chambre dore,
The stewarde that was styffe and store,[1]
Whan they had made that great affraye,
Full pryvely they stale awaye;
In armes they take that squyer tho,
And to the kynges chambre can they go,
Without wemme or any wounde,   580
Before the kynge bothe hole and sounde.
As soone as the kynge him spyed with eye,
He sayd, 'Welcome, sonne, sykerly!
Thou hast cast thee my sonne to be,
This seven yere I shall let[2] thee.'

Leve we here of this squyer wight,
And speake we of that lady bryght,
How she rose, that lady dere,
To take her leve of that squyer.
Also [fresh] as she was borne,   590
She stod her chambre dore beforne.
'Alas,' she sayd, 'and weale away!
For all to long now have I lay';
She sayd, 'Alas, and all for wo!
Withouten men why came ye so?
Yf that ye wolde have come to me,
Other werninges there might have be.
Now all to dere my love is bought,
But it shall never be lost for nought';
And in her armes she toke hym there,   600
Into the chamber she dyd hym bere;
His bowels soone she dyd out drawe,
And buryed them in Goddes lawe.

[1] big   [2] prevent

She sered [1] that body with specery,[2]
With wyrgin [3] waxe and commendry; [4]
And closed hym in a maser [5] tre,
And set on hym lockes thre.
She put him in a marble stone,
With quaynt gynnes many one;
And set hym at hir beddes head,   610
And every day she kyst that dead.
Soone at morne, whan she uprose,
Unto that dead body she gose,
There wold she knele downe on her kne,
And make her prayer to the Trynite,
And kysse that body twyse or thryse,
And fall in a swowne or she myght ryse.
Whan she had so done,
To chyrche than wolde she gone,
Than would she here masses fyve,   620
And offre to them whyle she myght lyve:
'There shall none knowe but heven kynge
For whome that I make myne offrynge.'
    The kyng her father anone he sayde:
'My doughter, wy are you dysmayde?
So feare a lady as ye are one,
And so semely of fleshe and bone,—
Ye were whyte as whales bone,
Nowe are ye pale as any stone;
Your ruddy read as any chery,   630
With browes bent and eyes full mery;
Ye were wont to harpe and syng,
And be the meriest in chambre comyng;
Ye ware both golde and good velvet,
Clothe of damaske with saphyres set;
Ye ware the pery [6] on your head,
With stones full oryent, whyte and read;

---

[1] wrapped   [2] spicery   [3] pure   [4] cumin, an aromatic plant?
[5] maple   [6] gems

Ye ware coronalles of golde,
With diamoundes set many a foulde;
And nowe ye were clothes of blacke,   640
Tell me, doughter, for whose sake?
If he be so poore of fame,
That ye may not be wedded for shame,
Brynge him to me anone ryght,
I shall hym make squyer and knight;
And, yf he be so great a lorde,
That your love may not accorde,
Let me, doughter, that lordynge se;
He shall have golde ynoughe with thee.'
'Gramercy, father, so mote I thryve,   650
For I mourne for no man alyve.
Ther is no man, by heven kyng,
That shal knowe more of my mournynge.'
    Her father knewe it every deale,
But he kept it in counsele:
'To-morowe ye shall on hunting fare,
And ryde, my doughter, in a chare,[1]
It shalbe covered with velvet reede,
And clothes of fyne golde al about your hed,
With damaske, white and asure blewe,   660
Wel dyapred[2] with lyllyes newe;
Your pomelles[3] shalbe ended with gold,
Your chaynes enameled many a folde;
Your mantel of ryche degre,
Purpyl palle[4] and armyne fre;
Jennettes[5] of Spayne, that ben so wyght,
Trapped to the ground with velvet bright;
Ye shall have harpe, sautry,[6] and songe,
And other myrthes you amonge;
Ye shall have rumney and malmesyne,   670
Both ypocrasse and vernage wyne,

---

[1] chariot   [2] adorned   [3] knobs   [4] fine cloth   [5] small horses
[3] psaltery

Mountrose and wyne of Greke,
Both algrade and respice eke,
Antioche and bastarde,
Pyment also and garnarde;
Wyne of Greke and muscadell,
Both clare, pyment, and rochell.
The reed your stomake to defye,
And pottes of osey set you by.
You shall have venison ybake,   680
The best wylde foule that may be take.
A lese [1] of grehound with you to strike,
And hert and hynde and other lyke.
Ye shalbe set at such a tryst
That herte and hynde shall come to your fyst,
Your dysease [2] to dryve you fro,
To here the bugles there yblow,
With theyr begles [3] in that place,
And sevenscore braches [3] at his rechase.[4]
Homward thus shall ye ryde,   690
On haukyng by the ryvers syde,
With goshauke and with gentyll fawcon,
With egle horne and merlyon.[5]
Whan you come home, your men amonge,
Ye shall have revell, daunces, and songe;
Lytle chyldren, great and smale,
Shall syng, as doth the nyghtyngale.
Than shall ye go to your evensong,
With tenours and trebles among;
Threscore of copes, of damaske bryght,   700
Full of perles they shalbe pyght; [6]
Your aulter clothes of taffata,
And your sicles [7] all of taffetra.[8]
Your sensours [9] shalbe of golde,

---

[1] leash   [2] sorrow   [3] beagles, braches (kinds of hounds)   [4] call
[5] merlin   [6] trimmed   [7] tunics   [8] taffeta   [9] censers

Endent with asure many a folde.
Your quere [1] nor organ songe shall wante
With countre note and dyscant,
The other halfe on orgayns playeng,
With yonge chyldren full fayre syngyng.
Than shall ye go to your suppere, 710
And sytte in tentes in grene arbere,
With clothes of Aras pyght to the grounde,
With saphyres set and dyamonde.
A cloth of golde aboughte your heade,
With popinjayes pyght with pery read,
And offycers all at your wyll,
All maner delightes to bryng you tyll.
The nightingale sitting on a thorne
Shall synge you notes both even and morne.
An hundreth knightes truly tolde 720
Shall play with bowles in alayes colde,
Your disease to drive awaie:
To se the fisshes in poles [2] plaie;
And then walke in arbere up and downe,
To se the floures of great renowne:
To a draw-brydge than shall ye,
The one halfe of stone, the other of tre;
A barge shall mete you full ryght
With .xxiiii. ores full bryght,
With trompettes and with claryowne, 730
The fresshe water to rowe up and downe;
Than shall ye go to the salte fome,
Your maner [3] to se, or ye come home,
With .lxxx. shyppes of large towre,
With dromedaryes [4] of great honour,
And carackes [4] with sayles two,
The sweftest that on water may goo,
With galyes good upon the haven,

---

[1] choir   [2] pools   [3] manor houses   [4] large vessels

With .lxxx. ores at the fore staven.[1]
Your maryners shall synge arowe[2]   740
"Hey how and rumbylawe."
Than shall ye, doughter, aske the wyne,
With spices that be good and fyne,
Gentyll pottes with genger grene,
With dates and deynties you betwene.
Forty torches brenynge bryght,
At your brydges to brynge you lyght.
Into your chambre they shall you brynge
With muche myrthe and more lykyng.
Your costerdes[3] covered with whyte and blewe,   750
And dyapred with lyles newe.
Your curtaines of camaca[4] all in folde,
Your felyoles[5] all of golde.
Your tester[6] pery at your heed,
Curtaines with popinjayes white and reed.
Your hyllynges[7] with furres of armyne,
Powdred with golde of hew full fyne.
Your blankettes shall be of fustyane,
Your shetes shall be of clothe of Rayne.
Your head shete shall be of pery pyght,   760
With dyamondes set and rubyes bryght.
Whan you are layde in bedde so softe,
A cage of golde shall hange alofte,
With longe peper[8] fayre burnning,
And cloves that be swete smellyng,
Frankensence and olibanum,[9]
That whan ye slepe the taste may come.
And yf ye no rest may take,
All night minstrelles for you shall wake.'
'Gramercy, father, so mote I the,[10]   770

---

[1] prow   [2] in a row   [3] hangings for a bed   [4] a fine fabric
[5] columns   [6] canopy of a bed   [7] coverings   [8] pepper   [9] fra-
grant gum   [10] prosper

For all these thinges lyketh not me.'
Unto her chambre she is gone,
And fell in sownyng sone anone,
With much sorow and sighing sore,
Yet seven yeare she kept hym thore.
 But leve we of that lady here,
And speake we more of that squyer,
That in pryson so was take
For the kinges doughters sake.
The kyng hym selfe upon a daye   780
Full pryvely he toke the waye,
Unto the pryson sone he came,
The squyer sone out he name,[1]
And anone he made hym swere
His counsayl he should never discure.[2]
The squyer there helde up his hande,
His byddyng never he should withstande.
The kyng him graunted ther to go
Upon his jorney to and fro,
And brefely to passe the sea,   790
That no man weste but he and he,
And whan he had his jurnay done,
That he wolde come full soone:
'And in my chambre for to be,
The whyles that I do ordayne for thee;
Than shalt thou wedde my doughter dere,
And have my landes both farre and nere.'
 The squyer was full mery tho,
And thanked the kynge, and forth gan go.
The kyng hym gave both lande and fe.   800
Anone the squyer passed the se.
In Tuskayne and in Lumbardy,
There he dyd great chyvalry.
In Portyngale nor yet in Spayne,

<hr>

[1] took   [2] reveal

There myght no man stand hym agayne;
And where that ever that knyght gan fare,
The worshyp with hym away he bare:
And thus he travayled seven yere
In many a land bothe farre and nere;
Tyll on a day he thought hym tho　　　810
Unto the sepulture for to go;
And there he made his offerynge soone,
Right as the kinges doughter bad him don.
Than he thought hym on a day
That the kynge to hym dyd saye.
He toke his leve in Lumbardy,
And home he came to Hungry.
Unto the kynge soone he rade,
As he before his covenaunce made,
And to the kyng he tolde full soone,　　　820
Of batayles bolde that he had done,
And so he did the chyvalry
That he had sene in Lumbardy.
To the kynge it was good tydande; [1]
Anone he toke him by the hande,
And he made him full royall chere,
And sayd, 'Welcome, my sonne so dere!
Let none wete of my meyne
That out of prison thou shuldest be,
But in my chamber holde the styll,　　　830
And I shall wete my doughters wyll.'
　　The kynge wente forth hymselfe alone,
For to here his doughters mone,
Right under the chambre window.
That he might her counseyle knowe.
Had she wyst, that lady fre,
That her father there had be,
He shulde not withouten fayle

---

[1] tidings

Have knowen so muche of her counsayle
Nor nothing she knew that he was there.   840
    Whan she began to carke [1] and care,
Unto that body she sayd tho,
'Alas that we should parte in two!'
Twyse or thryse she kyssed that body,
And fell in sownynge by and by.
'Alas!' than sayd that lady dere,
'I have the kept this seven yere,
And now ye be in powder small,
I may no lenger holde you with all.
My love, to the earth I shall the brynge,   850
And preestes for you to reade and synge.
Yf any man aske me what I have here,
I wyll say it is my treasure.
Yf any man aske why I do so,
"For no theves shall come therto":
And, squyer, for the love of the,
Fy on this worldes vanyte!
Farewell golde pure and fyne;
Farewell velvet and satyne;
Farewell castelles and maners also;   860
Farewell huntynge and hawkynge to;
Farewell revell, myrthe and play;
Farewell pleasure and garmentes gay;
Farewell perle and precyous stone;
Farewell my juielles everychone;
Farewell mantell and scarlet reed;
Farewell crowne unto my heed;
Farewell hawkes and farewell hounde;
Farewell markes and many a pounde;
Farewell huntynge at the hare;   870
Farewell harte and hynde for evermare.
Nowe wyll I take the mantell and the rynge,

[1] sorrow

And become an ancresse [1] in my lyvynge:
And yet I am a mayden for thee,
And for all the men in Chrystente.
To Chryst I shall my prayers make,
Squyer, onely for thy sake;
And I shall never no masse heare
But ye shall have parte in-feare: [2]
And every daye whyles I lyve,   880
Ye shall have your masses fyve,
And I shall offre pence thre,
In tokenynge of the Trynyte.'
And whan this lady had this sayde,
In sownyng she fel at a brayde. [3]

    The whyle she made this great mornynge,
Under the wall stode har father the kynge.
'Doughter,' he sayde, 'you must not do so,
For all those vowes thou must forgo.'
'Alas, father, and wele awaye!   890
Nowe have ye harde what I dyde saye.'
'Doughter, let be all thy mournynge,
Thou shalt be wedede to a kynge.'
'Iwys, [4] father, that shall not be
For all the golde in Christente;
Nor all the golde that ever God made
May not my harte glade.' [5]
'My doughter,' he sayde, 'dere derlynge,
I knowe the cause of your mournyng:
Ye wene this body your love should be,   900
It is not so, so mote I the.
It was my stewarde, Syr Maradose,
That ye so longe have kept in close.'
'Alas! father, why dyd ye so?'
'For he wrought you all thys wo.
He made revelation unto me,

That he knewe all your pryvyte;
And howe the squyer, on a day,
Unto your chambre toke the way,
And ther he should have leyen you bi,   910
Had he not come with company;
And howe ye hyght hym golde and fe,
Strengthe of men and royalte:
And than he watched your chambre bryght,
With men of armes hardy and wyght,
For to take that squyer,
That ye have loved this seven yere;
But as the stewarde strong and stout
Beseged your chambre rounde about,
To you your love came full ryght,   920
All alone about mydnight.
And whan he came your dore unto,
And "Lady," he sayde, "undo,"
And soone ye bade hym wende awaye,
For there he gate none other paye:
And as ye talked thus in-fere,
Your enemyes drewe them nere and nere,
They smote to him full soone anone,
There were thyrty agaynst hym one:
But with a baslarde [1] large and longe   930
The squyer presed in to the thronge;
And so he bare hym in that stounde,
His enemyes gave he many a wounde.
With egre [2] mode and herte full throwe,[3]
The stewardes throte he cut in two;
And than his meyne all in that place
With their swordes they hurte his face,
And than they toke him everichone
And layd him on a marble stone
Before your dore, that ye myght se,   940

[1] dagger   [2] angry   [3] bold

Ryght as your love that he had be.
And sone the squier there they hent,
And they dyd of his good garment,
And did it on the stewarde there,
That ye wist not what he were:
Thus ye have kept your enemy here
Pallyng [1] more than seven yere,
And as the squyer there was take,
And done in pryson for your sake;
Therfore let be your mourning,   950
Ye shalbe wedded to a kyng,
Or els unto an emperoure,
With golde and sylver and great treasure.
'Do awaye, father, that may not be,
For all the golde in Chrystente.
Alas! father,' anone she sayde,
'Why hath this traytour me betraid?
Alas!' she sayd, 'I have great wrong
That I have kept him here so long.
Alas! father, why dyd ye so?   960
Ye might have warned me of my fo;
And ye had tolde me who it had be,
My love had never be dead for me.'
Anone she tourned her fro the kyng,
And downe she fell in dead sownyng.
    The kyng anone gan go,
And hente her in his armes two.
'Lady,' he sayd, 'be of good chere,
Your love lyveth and is here;
And he hath bene in Lombardy,   970
And done he hath great chyvalry;
And come agayne he is to me,
In lyfe and health ye shall him se.
He shall you wede, my doughter bryght,

[1] languishing

I have hym made squier and knyght;
He shalbe a lorde of great renowne,
And after me to were the crowne.'
'Father,' she sayd, 'if it so be,
Let me soone that squyer se.'

    The squyer forth than dyd he brynge,   980
Full fayre on lyve and in lykynge.
As sone as she saw him with her eye,
She fell in sownyng by and by.
The squyer her hente in armes two,
And kyssed her an hundreth tymes and mo.
There was myrth and melody
With harpe, getron, and sautry,
With rote, ribible, and clokarde,
With pypes, organs, and bumbarde,
With other mynstrelles them amonge,   990
With sytolphe and with sautry songe,
With fydle, recorde, and dowcemere,
With trompette and with claryon clere,
With dulcet pipes of many cordes.
In chambre revelyng all the lordes,
Unto morne that it was daye,

    The kyng to his doughter began to saye,
'Have here thy love and thy lyking,
To lyve and ende in Gods blessinge;
And he that wyll departe[1] you two,   1000
God geve him sorow and wo!
A trewer lover than ye are one
Was never yet of flesh ne bone;
And but he be as true to thee,
God let him never thryve ne thee.'
The kyng in herte he was full blithe,
He kissed his doughter many a sithe,[2]
With melody and muche chere;

[1] separate   [2] time

Anone he called his messengere,
And commaunded him soone to go   1010
Through his cities to and fro,
For to warne his chevalry
That they should come to Hungry,
That worthy wedding for to se,
And come unto that mangere.[1]
That messenger full sone he wente,
And did the kinges commaundemente.
Anone he commaunded bothe olde and yinge
For to be at that weddyng,
Both dukes and erles of muche myght,
And ladyes that were fayre and bryght.
As soone as ever they herde the crye,
The lordes were full soone redy;
With myrth and game and muche playe
They wedded them on a solempne [2] daye.
A royall feest there was holde,
With dukes and erles and barons bolde,
And knyghtes and squyers of that countre,
And sith [3] with all the comunalte:
And certaynly, as the story sayes,   1030
The revell lasted forty dayes;
Tyll on a day the kyng him selfe
To hym he toke his lordes twelfe,
And so he dyd the squyer
That wedded his doughter dere,
And even in the myddes of the hall
He made him kyng among them al;
And all the lordes everychone
They made him homage sone anon;
And sithen they revelled all that day,   1040
And toke theyr leve, and went theyr way,
Eche lorde unto his owne countre,

[1] feast   [2] festive   [3] afterward

Where that hym thought best to be.
That yong man and the quene his wyfe,
With joy and blysse they led theyr lyfe,
For also farre as I have gone,
Suche two lovers sawe I none:
Therfore blessed may theyr soules be,
Amen, amen, for charyte!

c. 1450?

PASTON LETTERS

Agnes Paston to William Paston
(This letter, written about 1440, is given in the original.
The other letters are modernised.)

To my worshepeful housbond, W. Paston, be this
letter takyn.
Dere housbond, I recomaunde me to you, &c.
Blessyd be God I sende yow gode tydynggs of the
comyng, and the brynggyn hoom, of the gentylwomman [1]
that ye wetyn [2] of fro Redham, this same nyght, acordyng
to poyntmen [3] that ye made ther for yowr self.
And as for the furste aqweyntaunce be twhen John
Paston and the seyde gentylwomman, she made hym
gentil cher in gyntyl wise, and seyde, he was verrayly
your son.   And so I hope ther shall nede no gret trete [4]
be twyxe hym.

The parson of Stocton toold me, yif ye wolde byin [5]
her a goune, [6] here [7] moder wolde yeve [8] ther to a godely
furre.   The goune nedyth for to be had; and of colour
it wolde be a godely blew, or erlys [9] a bryghte sangueyn.

I prey yow do byen for me ij.pypys [10] of gold.   Your
stewes [11] do weel.

[1] The prospective wife of her son John   [2] know   [3] appointment
[4] treaty   [5] buy   [6] gown   [7] her   [8] give   [9] else   [10] two
rolls   [11] fishponds

The Holy Trinite have you in governaunce.

Wretyn at Paston, in hast, the Wednesday next after *Deus qui errantibus*,[1] for defaute[2] of a good secretarye.

> Yowres,
> Agn. Paston

To my right worshipful husband, John Paston, dwelling in the Inner Temple at London, in haste.

Right worshipful husband, I recommend me to you, desiring heartily to hear of your welfare, thanking God of your amending of the great disease that you have had, and I thank you for the letter that you sent me, for by my troth my mother and I were not at heart's ease from the time that we knew of your sickness, till we knew verily of your amending.

My mother vowed another image of wax of the weight of you, to our Lady of Walsingham, and she sent four nobles to the four orders of friars at Norwich to pray for you, and I have vowed to go on pilgrimage to Walsingham and to Saint Leonard's for you. By my troth I had never so heavy a season as I had from the time that I knew of your sickness till I knew of your amending, and yet my heart is in no great ease, and will not be, till I know that you be very whole. Your father and mine was this day sennight at Beccles, for a matter of the Prior of Bromholm, and he lay at Gelderstone that night, and was there till it was nine of the clock and the other day. And I sent thither for a gown, and my mother said that I should have none until I had been there, and so they could get none.

My father Garneys sent me word that he should have been here the next week and my Emme also, and play

[1] The Collect for the third Sunday after Easter   [2] in default

them here with their hawks, and they should have me
home with them. And so God help me, I shall excuse
myself of my going thither if I may, for I suppose that
I shall the more readily have tidings from you here
than I should have there. I shall send my mother a
token that she brought to me, for I suppose that the
time is come that I should send it to her, if I keep the
vow that I have made. I suppose I have told you what
it was. I pray you heartily that you will vouchsafe to
send me a letter as hastily as you may, if writing be
no pain to you, and that you will vouchsafe to send me
word how your sore does. If I might have had my
will, I should have seen you ere this time. I would
you were at home, if it were for your ease, and your
sore might be as well looked to here as it is where you
are now, rather than a new gown though it were of
scarlet. I pray you if your sore be whole, and so that
you may endure to ride when my father comes to London,
that he will ask leave and come home when the horse
should be sent home again, for I hope you shall be
kept as tenderly here as you are at London. I have no
leisure to write the quarter of what I should say to
you if I might speak with you. I shall send you another letter as hastily as I may. I thank you that you
will vouchsafe to remember my girdle, and that you
would write to me at the time, for I suppose that writing is not comfortable for you. Almighty God have you
in His keeping, and send you health. Written at
Oxnead, in right great haste, on Saint Michael's even.

Yours,

M. Paston

(1443)

To Edmund Paston, of Clifford's Inn, in London,
be this letter taken.

To mine well-beloved son, I greet you well, and advise you to think once more of the day of your father's counsel to learn the law, for he said many times that whosoever should dwell at Paston should need to know how to defend himself.

The Vicar of Paston and your father, in Lent last year was, were thorough and accorded, and boundaries set how broad the way should be, and now he has pulled up the boundaries, and says he will make a ditch from the corner of his wall right over the way to the new ditch of the great close. And there is a man called Palmer, too, that had of your father certain lands in Trunch over seven years or eight years agone, for grain, and truly has paid all the years and now he has suffered the grain to be taken for eight shillings of rent to Gimmingham, which your father never paid. Geoffrey asked Palmer why the rent was not asked in my husband's time, and Palmer said because he was a great man, and a wise man of the law, and that was the cause men would not ask him the rent.

I send you the names of the men that cast down the pits that were in Genney's Close, written in a bill enclosed in this letter.

I send you this letter not to make you weary of Paston, for I live in hope, and you will learn that they shall be made weary of their work, for in good faith I dare well say it was your father's last will to have done right well to that place, and that can I show of good proof, though men would say nay. God make you a right good man, and send God's blessing and mine. Written in haste at Norwich, the Thursday after Candlemas-day.

Learn from your brother John how many joists will serve the parlor and the chapel at Paston, and what length they must be, and what breadth and thickness they must be, for your father's will was, as I know verily, that they should be nine inches one way, and seven another way, and arrange therefore that they may be squared there, and sent hither, for here can none such be had in this country; and say to your brother John it were well done to think on Stansred Church; and I pray you to send me tidings from beyond sea, for here they are afraid to tell such as is reported.

By your mother,

Agnes Paston

(1444-5)

To my well-beloved son, John Paston, be this delivered in haste.

Son, I greet you well, and let you know, that forasmuch as your brother Clement lets me know that you desire faithfully my blessing; that blessing that I prayed your father to give you the last day that ever he spoke, and the blessings of all saints under heaven, and mine might come to you all days and times; and think verily none other but that you have it, and shall have it, on condition that I find you kind and willing to the weal of your father's soul, and to the welfare of your brethren.

By my counsel, dispose yourself as much as you may to have less to do in the world; your father said, "In little business lieth much rest." This world is but a thoroughfare, and full of woe; and when we depart therefrom, right nothing bear with us but our good deeds and ill; and there knoweth no man how soon God will call him; and therefore it is good for every creature to be ready. Whom God visiteth, him he loveth.

And as for your brethren, they will I know certainly labor all that in them lies for you. Our Lord have you in his blessed keeping, body and soul. Written at Norwich, the 29th day of October.

By your mother,

Agnes Paston.

(c. 1444)

To my right honorable master, John Paston

Right honorable and my right entirely beloved master ——. Pleaseth it, your good and gracious mastership, tenderly to consider the great losses and hurts that your poor petitioner hath, and hath had, ever since the commons of Kent came to the Blackheath, and that is fifteen years past; whereas my master, Sir John Falstolf, knight, that is your testator, commanded your beseecher to take a man, and two of the best horses that were in his stable, with him, to ride to the commons of Kent to get the articles that they come for. And so I did, and all so soon as I came to the Blackheath, the captain [1] made the commons take me; and for the salvation of my master's horses I made my fellow to ride away with the two horses; and I was brought forthwith before the Captain of Kent; and the captain demanded of me the cause of my coming thither, and why I made my fellow steal away with the horses; and I said that I came thither to cheer with my wife's brethren and others that were my allies, and gossips of mine that were present there. And then was there one there who said to the captain that I was one of Sir John Falstolf's men, and the two horses were Sir John

---

[1] Jack Cade, soldier, and leader of a popular revolt against the government. The events referred to in the letter took place in 1450; the letter was written in 1465. By that time Falstolf was dead; John Paston was his executor.

Falstolf's; and then the captain let cry Treason upon
me throughout all the field, and brought me at four
parts of the field, with a herald of the Duke of Exeter [1] before me, in the Duke's coat-of-arms, making
four oyez [2] at four parts of the field, proclaiming openly
by the said herald that I was sent thither for to espy
their puissance and their habiliments of war, from the
greatest traitor that was in England or in France, as
the said captain made proclamation at that time, from
one Sir John Falstolf, knight, the which diminished all
the garrisons of Normandy, and Manns, and Mayn, the
which was the cause of the losing of all the king's title
and right of an heritance that he had beyond the sea.
And moreover, he said that the said Sir John Falstolf
had furnished his place with the old soldiers of Normandy, and habiliments of war, to destroy the commons of Kent when they came to Southwark, and therefore he said plainly that I should lose my head; and so
forthwith I was taken and led to the captain's tent,
and one axe and one block were brought forth to have
smitten off my head. And then my master Poynyngs
your brother, with other of my friends came, and pre-
vented the captain, and said plainly that there should die
an hundred or two in case I died; and so by that means
my life was saved at that time.

And then I was sworn to the captain, and to the
commons, that I should go to Southwark and array
me in the best wise that I could, and come again to
them to help them; and so I got the articles, and brought
them to my master, and that cost me more amongst the
commons that day than 27 s.

Whereupon I came to my master Falstolf and brought

---

[1] The herald was probably forced to perform his duties.   [2] Hear!
(A signal for calling court to order.)

him the articles, and informed him of the matter, and counselled him to put away all his habiliments of war, and the old soldiers, and so he did, and went himself to the Tower, and all his household with him but Betts and one Matthew Brayn; and had I not been, the commons would have burned his place and all his tenuries; where though it cost me of my own proper goods at that time more than six marks in meat and drink, and yet notwithstanding the captain that same time let take me in at the White Hart in Southwark, and there commanded Lovelace to despoil me of mine array, and so he did. And there he took a fine gown of muster devillers[1] furred with fine beavers, and one pair of brigandines[2] covered with blue velvet and gilt nails, with leg-harness; the value of the gown and the brigandines 8L.

Item, the captain sent certain of his followers to my chamber in your house, and there they broke up my chest and took away one obligation of mine that was due unto me of 36L. by a priest of Paul's, and one other obligation of one knight of 10L., and my purse with five rings of gold and 17s. 6d. of gold and silver; and one harness complete of the touch of Milan;[3] and one gown of fine perse blue,[4] furred with martens; and two gowns, one furred with badge fur, and one other lined with frieze;[5] and there would have smitten off mine head when they had despoiled me at the White Hart. And there my master Pynyngs and my friends saved me, and so I was put up, till at night that the battle was at London Bridge; and then at night the captain put me out into the battle at the bridge, and there I was wounded, and hurt near hand to death; and there I was six hours

---

[1] probably some kind of velvet   [2] coat-of-mail   [3] i. e. made in Milan   [4] bluish gray   [5] coarse cloth

in the battle, and might never come out thereof. And
four times before that time I was carried about throughout Kent and Sussex, and there they would have smitten
off my head; and in Kent where my wife dwelled, they
took away all our goods movable that we had, and there
would have hanged my wife and five of my children, and
left her no more goods but her kirtle and her smock.
And soon after that commotion the Bishop of Rochester
impeached me to the queen, and so I was arrested by
the queen's commandment into the Marshalsea, and there
was in right great duress and fear of my life, and was
threatened to have been hanged, drawn, and quartered. And so they would have made me impeach my
master Falstolf of treason, and because I would not,
they had me up to Westminster, and there would have
sent me to the gaol-house at Windsor, but my wife's
and one cousin of mine own that were yeomen to the
crown, they went to the king, and got grace and one
charter of pardon.

Per le votre,

J. Payn
(1465)

Unto my right reverend Sir, and my good master,
John Paston.

Right worthy and worshipful sir and my right good
master, I recommend me unto you, thanking you evermore of your great gentleness and good masterhood
shown unto me at all times, and especially now to my
heart's ease, which on my part cannot be rewarded, but
my simple service is ever ready at your commandment;
furthermore, as for the matter that you know of, I have
labored so to my father that your intent as for the

jointure shall be fulfilled; and, Sir, I beseech you since I do my part to fulfill your will, that you will show me your good masterhood in her chamber as my full trust is, insomuch that it shall not hurt you or any of yours, and the profit thereof shall be unto the avail of my mistress your sister, and to me, and to no other creature.

And also my mistress your mother shall not be charged with her board after the day of the marriage, but I to discharge her of her person; and to ease me that hath her chamber may be no contradiction.

And, Sir, I am ready, and always will to perform that I have said unto you, &c.

Furthermore liketh you to know, I was on Thursday last past at Cavendish to deliver an estate to Wentworth in the land that was my brother Cavendish's, as I told you when I was last with you, and there I spake with Crane, and he besought me that I would send over to my mistress your mother for his excuse, for he might not be with her at this time; but on the Saturday in Easter week he will not fail to be with her, so he counselled me that I and my brother Denston should meet with him there, and so without your better advice I and my brother purpose us to be with you there at that time, for the sooner the better for me, for, as to my conceit the days be waxen wonderfully long in a short time, wherefore I beseech you send me your advice how you will have me ruled, &c.

Written with my chancery hand in right great haste on the Friday before Palm Sunday.

Your

John Clopton
(April 12, 1454)

SIR THOMAS MALORY (15th c.)

Le Morte Darthur

(Editor's note: A specimen with the original spelling, and with punctuation slightly modernised is given. The rest of the selection has been changed to conform more nearly to present usage.)

Book XXI, Chap. 1

As syr Mordred was rular of alle englond he dyd do make letters as though that they came from beyonde the see, and the letters specefyed that Kynge Arthur was slayn in bataylle wyth sir Launcelot. Wherefore Syr Mordred made a parlemente, and called the lordes togyder, and there he made them to choose hym kyng and soo was he crowned at caunterburye and helde a feest there XV dayes, and afterward he drewe hym unto wynchester, and there he tooke the Quene Guenever and sayd playnly that he wolde wedde hyr whyche was his unkyls wyf and his faders wyf. And soo he made redy for the feest, and a day prefyxt that they shold be wedded, wherefore quene Gwenever was passyng hevy. But she durst not discover hyr herte but spake fayre and agreyd to syr Mordredes wylle. Thenne she desyred of syr Mordred for to goo to London to bye alle manere of thynges that longed unto the weddyng, and by cause of hyr fayre speche Syr Mordred trusted hyr wel ynough and gaf her leve to goo. And soo whan she came to London she took the toure of London, and sodeynlye in alle haste pssyble she stuffed hyt wyth alle manere of vytaylle and wel garnysshed it with men and soo kepte hyt. Than whan Syr Mordred wyste and understode how he was begyled, he was passyng wrothe oute of mesure. And a shorte tale for to make he wente and layed a myghty syege aboute the toure of London and made many grete assaultes therat, and threwe many grete engynes unto theym, and shotte grete gonnes. But alle myght not prevaylle Syr Mordred, for quene Guenever wolde never for fayre speche nor for foule wold never truste to come in hys handes ageyn. Thene came the bysshop of caunterburye the wyche was a noble clerke and an holy man, and thus he sayd to Syr Mordred: Syr, what wyl ye doo wyl ye fyrst dysplese god and sythen shame your self and al knyghthode? Is not kyng Arthur your uncle no ferther but your moders broder, and on hyr hym self kyng Arthur bygate you upon his own syster? Therfor how may you wedde your faders wyf? Syr, sayd the noble clerke, leve this oppynyon or I shall curse you wyth book and belle and candell. Do thou thy werst, said syr Mordred. Wyt thou wel I shal defye thee, sir, sayd the bysshop, and wyt you wel I shal not fere me to do that me ought to do. Also where ye noyse where my lord Arthur is slayne, and that is not so, and therefore ye wyl make a foule werke in this londe. Pees, thou fals preest, sayd syr Mordred, for and thou chauffe me ony more I shal make stryke of thy heed. So the bysshop departed and dyd the cursyng in the most orgulist wyse that myght be doon. And than Syr mordred sought the bysshop of caunterburye for to have slayne hym. Than the bysshop fledde and toke parte of his goodes with hym and went nygh unto glastynburye, and there he was as preest Eremyte in a chapel, and lyved in poverte and in holy prayers, for wel he understode that myschevous warre was at honde.

Then Sir Mordred sought on Queen Guenever by letters and messages, and by fair means and foul means, to have her come out of the Tower of London; but all this availed not, for she answered him shortly, openly and privily, that she had lever slay herself than be married to him. Then came word to Sir Mordred that King Arthur had araised the siege for Sir Launcelot, and he was coming homeward with a great host, to be avenged upon Sir Mordred; wherefore Sir Mordred had letters written to all the barony of this land, and many people drew to him. For then was the common voice among them that with Arthur was none other life but war and strife, and with Sir Mordred was great joy and bliss. Thus was Sir Arthur condemned, and evil said of. And many there were that King Arthur had made up of nought, and given them lands, might not then say him a good word. Lo ye all Englishmen, see ye not what a mischief here was! for he that was the greatest king and knight of the world, and most loved the fellowship of noble knights, and by him they were all upholden, now might not these Englishmen hold them content with him. Lo thus was the old custom and usage of this land; and also men say that we of this land have not yet lost nor forgotten that custom and usage. Alas, this is a great default of us Englishmen, for there may no thing please us no term. And so fared the people at that time, they were better pleased with Sir Mordred than they were with King Arthur; and many people drew unto Sir Mordred, and said they would abide with him for better and for worse. And so Sir Mordred drew with a great host to Dover, for there he heard say that Sir Arthur would arrive, and so he thought to beat his own father from his lands; and the most part of all England held with Sir Mordred, the people were so new fangle.

CHAPTER II

HOW AFTER THAT KING ARTHUR HAD TIDINGS, HE RE-
TURNED AND CAME TO DOVER, WHERE SIR MORDRED MET
HIM TO HINDER HIS LANDING; AND OF THE DEATH OF SIR
GAWAINE.

AND so as Sir Mordred was at Dover with his host,
there came King Arthur with a great navy of ships, and
galleys, and carracks. And there was Sir Mordred ready
awaiting upon his landing, to hinder his own father from
landing upon the land that he was king over. Then there
was launching of great boats and small, and full of
noble men of arms; and there was much slaughter of
gentle knights, and many a full bold baron was laid
full low, on both sides. But King Arthur was so cour-
ageous that there might no manner of knights hinder
him from landing, and his knights fiercely followed him;
and so they landed in spite of Sir Mordred and all his
power, and put Sir Mordred aback, that he fled and all
his people. So when this battle was done, King Arthur
let bury his people that were dead. And then was
noble Sir Gawaine found in a great boat, lying more
than half dead. When Sir Arthur wist that Sir Gawaine
was laid so low, he went unto him; and there the king
made sorrow out of measure, and took Sir Gawaine in
his arms, and thrice he there swooned. And then when
he awaked, he said: "Alas, Sir Gawaine, my sister's
son, here now thou liest, the man in the world that I
loved most; and now is my joy gone, for now, my
nephew Sir Gawaine, I will discover me unto your person: in Sir Launcelot and you I most had my joy, and
mine trust, and now have I lost my joy of you both;

wherefore all mine earthly joy is gone from me." "Mine uncle King Arthur," said Sir Gawaine, "wit you well my death day is come, and all is through mine own hastiness and wilfulness; for I am smitten upon the old wound which Sir Launcelot gave me, by which I feel well I must die; and had Sir Launcelot been with you as he used to be, this unhappy war had never begun; and of all this am I causer, for Sir Launcelot and his blood, through their prowess, held all your cankered enemies in subjection and danger. And now," said Sir Gawaine, "ye shall miss Sir Launcelot. But alas, I would not accord with him, and therefore," said Sir Gawaine, "I pray you, fair uncle, that I may have paper, pen, and ink, that I may write to Sir Launcelot a note with mine own hands." And then when paper and ink was brought, then Gawaine was set up weakly by King Arthur, for he was shriven a little before; and then he wrote thus, as the French book maketh mention: "Unto Sir Launcelot, flower of all noble knights that ever I heard of or saw in my days, I, Sir Gawaine, King Lot's son of Orkney, sister's son unto the noble King Arthur, send thee greeting, and let thee have knowledge that the tenth day of May I was smitten upon the old wound that thou gavest me afore the city of Benwick, and through the same wound that thou gavest me I am come to my death day. And I will that all the world wit, that I, Sir Gawaine, knight of the Table Round, sought my death, and not through thy deserving, but it was mine own seeking; wherefore I beseech thee, Sir Launcelot, to return again unto this realm, and see my tomb, and pray some prayer more or less for my soul. And this same day that I wrote this note, I was hurt to the death in the same wound, the which I had of thy hand, Sir Launcelot; for of a more noble man might I not be slain. Also Sir Launcelot, for all the love that ever was betwixt us, make no tarrying, but come over the sea in all haste, that thou mayst with thy noble knights rescue that noble king that made thee knight, that is my lord Arthur, for he is full straitly circumstanced with a false traitor, that is my half-brother, Sir Mordred; and he hath let crown him king, and would have wedded my lady Queen Guenever, and so had he done had she not put herself in the Tower of London. And so the tenth day of May last past, my lord Arthur and we all landed upon them at Dover; and there we put that false traitor, Sir Mordred, to flight, and there it misfortuned me to be stricken upon thy stroke. And this letter was written but two hours and a half afore my death, written with mine own hand, and so subscribed with part of my heart's blood. And I require thee, most famous knight of the world, that thou wilt see my tomb." And then Sir Gawaine wept, and King Arthur wept; and then they swooned both. And when they awaked both, the king made Sir Gawaine receive his Savior. And then Sir Gawaine prayed the king to send for Sir Launcelot, and to cherish him above all other knights. And so at the hour of noon Sir Gawaine yielded up the spirit; and then the king had him interred in a chapel within Dover Castle; and there yet all men may see the skull of him, and the same wound is seen that Sir Launcelot gave him in battle. Then was it told the king that Sir Mordred was quartered in a new field upon Barham Down. And upon the morn the king rode thither to him, and there was a great battle betwixt them, and many people were slain on both sides, but at the last Sir Arthur's party stood best, and Sir Mordred and his party fled unto Canterbury.

CHAPTER III

AND then the king let search all the towns for his
knights that were slain, and interred them; and salved
them with soft salves that so sore were wounded. Then
many people drew unto King Arthur. And then they
said that Sir Mordred warred upon King Arthur with
wrong. And then King Arthur drew him with his host
down by the seaside westward toward Salisbury; and
there was a day assigned betwixt King Arthur and Sir
Mordred, that they should meet upon a down beside
Salisbury, and not far from the seaside; and this day
was assigned on a Monday after Trinity Sunday,
whereof King Arthur was passing glad, that he might
be avenged upon Sir Mordred. Then Sir Mordred
araised many people about London, for they of Kent,
Southsex, and Surrey, Estsex, and of Southfolk, and of
Northfolk, held the most part with Sir Mordred; and
many a full noble knight drew unto Sir Mordred and
to the king: but they that loved Sir Launcelot drew unto
Sir Mordred. So upon Trinity Sunday at night, King
Arthur dreamed a wonderful dream, and that was this:
that him seemed he sat upon a platform in a chair, and
the chair was fast to a wheel, and thereupon sat King
Arthur in the richest cloth of gold that might be made;
and the king thought there was under him, far from
him, an hideous deep black water, and therein were all
manner of serpents, and worms, and wild beasts, foul
and horrible; and suddenly the king thought the wheel
turned upside down, and he fell among the serpents, and

every beast took him by a limb; and then the king cried as he lay in his bed and slept: "Help." And then knights, squires, and yeomen awaked the king; and then he was so amazed that he wist not where he was; and then he fell a-slumbering again, not sleeping nor thoroughly waking. So it seemed to the king verily that there came Sir Gawaine unto him with a number of fair ladies with him. And when King Arthur saw him, then he said: "Welcome, my sister's son; I weened thou hadst been dead, and now I see thee alive, much am I beholden unto almighty Jesu. O fair nephew and my sister's son, what be these ladies that hither be come with you?" "Sir," said Sir Gawaine, "all these be ladies for whom I have fought when I was man living, and all these are those that I did battle for in righteous quarrel; and God hath given them that grace at their great prayer, because I did battle for them, that they should bring me hither unto you: thus much hath God given me leave, for to warn you of your death; for an ye fight tomorrow with Sir Mordred, as ye both have assigned, doubt ye not ye must be slain, and the most part of your people on both sides. And for the great grace and goodness that almighty Jesu hath unto you, and for pity of you, and many more other good men there shall be slain, God hath sent me to you of his special grace, to give you warning that in no wise ye do battle tomorrow, but that ye take a treaty for a month day; and proffer you largely, so as tomorrow to be put in a delay. For within a month shall come Sir Launcelot with all his noble knights, and rescue you worshipfully, and slay Sir Mordred, and all that ever will hold with him." Then Sir Gawaine and all the ladies vanished. And anon the king called upon his knights, squires, and yeomen, and charged them swiftly to fetch his noble lords and wise bishops unto him. And when they were come, the king told them his vision, what Sir Gawaine had told him, and warned him that if he fought on the morn he should be slain. Then the king commanded Sir Lucan the Butler, and his brother Sir Bedivere, with two bishops with them, and charged them in any wise, an they might, "Take a treaty for a month day with Sir Mordred, and spare not, proffer him lands and goods as much as ye think best." So then they departed, and came to Sir Mordred, where he had a grim host of an hundred thousand men. And there they entreated Sir Mordred long time; and at the last Sir Mordred was agreed for to have Cornwall and Kent, by Arthur's days: after, all England, after the days of King Arthur.

CHAPTER IV

HOW BY MISADVENTURE OF AN ADDER THE BATTLE BEGAN, WHERE MORDRED WAS SLAIN, AND ARTHUR HURT TO THE DEATH.

THEN were they condescended that King Arthur and Sir Mordred should meet betwixt both their hosts, and every each of them should bring fourteen persons; and they came with this word unto Arthur. Then said he: "I am glad that this is done"; and so he went into the field. And when Arthur should depart, he warned all his host that an they see any sword drawn: "Look ye come on fiercely, and slay that traitor, Sir Mordred, for I in no wise trust him." In likewise Sir Mordred warned his host that: "An ye see any sword drawn, look that ye come on fiercely, and so slay all that ever before you standeth; for in no wise I will not trust for this treaty, for I know well my father will be avenged on me." And so they met as their appointment was, and so they were agreed and accorded thoroughly; and wine was fetched, and they drank. Right soon came an adder out of a little heath bush, and it stung a knight on the foot. And when the knight felt him stung, he looked down and saw the adder, and then he drew his sword to slay the adder, and thought of none other harm. And when the host on both sides saw that sword drawn, then they blew clarions, trumpets, and horns, and shouted grimly. And so both hosts dressed them together. And King Arthur took his horse, and said: "Alas this unhappy day!" and so rode to his party. And Sir Mordred likewise. And never was there seen a more doleful battle in any Christian land; for there was but rushing and riding, thrusting and striking, and many a grim word was there spoken either to other, and many a deadly stroke. But ever King Arthur rode throughout the battle of Sir Mordred many times, and did full nobly as a noble king should, and at all times he fainted never; and Sir Mordred that day put him in devoir, and in great peril. And thus they fought all the long day, and never stinted till the noble knights were laid to the cold earth; and ever they fought still till it was near night, and by that time was there an hundred thousand laid dead upon the down. Then was Arthur raging mad out of measure, when he saw his people so slain from him. Then the king looked about him, and then was he ware, of all his host and of all his good knights, were left no more alive but two knights; that one was Sir Lucan the Butler, and his brother Sir Bedivere, and they were full sore wounded. "Jesu mercy," said the king, "where are all my noble knights become? Alas that ever I should see this doleful day, for now," said Arthur, "I am come to mine end. But would to God that I wist where were that traitor Sir Mordred, that hath caused all this mischief." Then was King Arthur ware where Sir Mordred leaned upon his sword among a great heap of dead men. "Now give me my spear," said Arthur unto Sir Lucan, "for yonder I have espied the traitor that all this woe hath wrought." "Sir, let him be," said Sir Lucan, "for he is unhappy; and if ye pass this unhappy day ye shall be right well revenged upon him. Good lord, remember ye of your night's dream, and what the spirit of Sir Gawaine told you this night, yet God of his great goodness hath preserved you hitherto. Therefore, for God's sake, my lord, leave off by this, for blessed be God ye have won the field, for here we be three alive, and with Sir Mordred is none alive; and if ye leave off now this wicked day of destiny is past." "Tide me death, betide me life," saith the king, "now I see him yonder alone he shall never escape mine hands, for at a better avail shall I never have him." "God speed you well," said Sir Bedivere. Then the king took his spear in both his hands, and ran toward Sir Mordred, crying: "Traitor, now is thy death-day come." And when Sir Mordred heard Sir Arthur, he ran until him with his sword drawn in his hand. And there King Arthur smote Sir Mordred under the shield, with a thrust of his spear, throughout the body, more than a fathom. And when Sir Mordred felt that he had his death-wound he thrust himself with the might that he had up to the bur of King Arthur's spear. And right so he smote his father Arthur, with his sword holden in both his hands, on the side of the head, that the sword pierced the helmet and the brain pan, and therewithal Sir Mordred fell stark dead to the earth; and the noble Arthur fell in a swoon to the earth, and there he swooned ofttimes. And Sir Lucan the Butler and Sir Bedivere ofttimes lifted him up. And so weakly they led him betwixt them both, to a little chapel not far from the seaside. And when the king was there he thought him well eased. Then heard they people cry in the field. "Now go thou, Sir Lucan," said the king, "and let me know what betokens that noise in the field." So Sir Lucan departed, for he was grievously wounded in many places. And so as he went, he saw and hearkened by the moonlight, how that pillagers and robbers were come into the field, to pillage and to rob many a full noble knight of brooches, and beads, of many a good ring, and of many a rich jewel; and who that were not dead utterly, there they slew them for their harness and their riches. When Sir Lucan understood this work, he came to the king as soon as he might, and told him all that he had heard and seen. "Therefore by my rede," said Sir Lucan, "it is best that we bring you to some town." "I would it were so," said the king.

CHAPTER V

HOW KING ARTHUR COMMANDED TO CAST HIS SWORD EX-
CALIBUR INTO THE WATER, AND HOW HE WAS DELIVERED
TO LADIES IN A BARGE.

"But I may not stand, mine head works so. Ah Sir Launcelot," said King Arthur, "this day have I sore missed thee: alas, that ever I was against thee, for now have I my death, whereof Sir Gawaine me warned in my dream." Then Sir Lucan took up the king the one part, and Sir Bedivere the other part, and in the lifting the king swooned; and Sir Lucan fell in a swoon with the lift, that the part of his guts fell out of his body, and therewith the noble knight's heart brast. And when the king awoke, he beheld Sir Lucan, how he lay foaming at the mouth, and part of his guts lay at his feet. "Alas," said the king, "this is to me a full heavy sight, to see this noble duke so die for my sake, for he would have holpen me, that had more need of help than I. Alas, he would not complain him, his heart was so set to help me: now Jesu have mercy upon his soul!" Then Sir Bedivere wept for the death of his brother. "Leave this mourning and weeping," said the king, "for all this will not avail me, for wit thou well an I might live myself, the death of Sir Lucan would grieve me evermore; but my time hieth fast," said the king. "Therefore," said Arthur unto Sir Bedivere, "take thou Excalibur, my good sword, and go with it to yonder water side, and when thou comest there I charge thee throw my sword in that water, and come again and tell me what thou there seest." "My lord," said Bedivere, "your commandment shall be done, and lightly bring you word again." So Sir Bedivere departed, and by the way he beheld that noble sword, that the pommel and the haft was all of precious stones; and then he said to himself: "If I throw this rich sword in the water, thereof shall never come good, but harm and loss." And then Sir Bedivere hid Excalibur under a tree. And so, as soon as he might, he came again unto the king, and said he had been at the water, and had thrown the sword in the water. "What saw thou there?" said the king. "Sir," he said, "I saw nothing but waves and winds." "That is untruly said of thee," said the king, "therefore go thou lightly again, and do my commandment; as thou art to me lief and dear, spare not, but throw it in." Then Sir Bedivere returned again, and took the sword in his hand; and then him thought sin and shame to throw away that noble sword, and so again he hid the sword, and returned again, and told to the king that he had been at the water, and done his commandment. "What saw thou there?" said the king. "Sir," he said, "I saw nothing but the waters ripple and waves wan." "Ah, traitor untrue," said King Arthur, "now hast thou betrayed me twice. Who would have weened that, thou that hast been to me so lief and dear? and thou art named a noble knight, and would betray me for the richness of the sword. But now go again lightly, for thy long tarrying putteth me in great jeopardy of my life, for I have taken cold. And but if thou do now as I bid thee, if ever I may see thee, I shall slay thee with mine own hands; for thou wouldst for my rich sword see me dead." Then Sir Bedivere departed, and went to the sword, and lightly took it up, and went to the water side; and there he bound the girdle about the hilts, and then he threw the sword as far into the water, as he might; and there came an arm and an hand above the water and met it, and caught it, and so shook it thrice and brandished, and then vanished away the hand with the sword in the water. So Sir Bedivere came again to the king, and told him what he saw. "Alas," said the king, "help me hence, for I dread me I have tarried over long." Then Sir Bedivere took the king upon his back, and so went with him to that water side. And when they were at the water side, even fast by the bank lay a little barge with many fair ladies in it, and among them all was a queen, and they all had black hoods, and they all wept and shrieked when they saw King Arthur. "Now put me into the barge," said the king. And so he did softly; and there received him three queens with great mourning; and so they set them down, and in one of their laps King Arthur laid his head. And then that queen said: "Ah, dear brother, why have ye tarried so long from me? alas, this wound on your head hath caught over-much cold." And so then they rowed from the land, and Sir Bedivere beheld all those ladies go from him. Then Sir Bedivere cried: "Ah my lord Arthur, what shall become of me, now ye go from me and leave me here alone among mine enemies?" "Comfort thyself," said the king, "and do as well as thou mayest, for in me is no trust for to trust in; for I will into the vale of Avilion to heal me of my grievous wound: and if thou hear never more of me, pray for my soul." But ever the queens and ladies wept and shrieked, that it was pity to hear. And as soon as Sir Bedivere had lost the sight of the barge, he wept and wailed, and so took the forest; and so he went all that night, and in the morning he was ware betwixt two wooded hills, of a chapel and an hermitage.

CHAPTER VI

HOW SIR BEDIVERE FOUND HIM ON THE MORROW DEAD IN AN HERMITAGE, AND HOW HE ABODE THERE WITH THE HERMIT.

THEN was Sir Bedivere glad, and thither he went; and when he came into the chapel, he saw where lay an hermit grovelling on all four, there fast by a tomb was new dug. When the hermit saw Sir Bedivere he knew him well, for he was but little tofore Bishop of Canterbury, that Sir Mordred put to flight. "Sir," said Bedivere, "what man is there interred that ye pray so fast for?" "Fair son," said the hermit, "I wot not verily, but by deeming. But this night, at midnight, here came a number of ladies, and brought hither a dead corpse, and prayed me to bury him; and here they offered an hundred tapers, and they gave me an hundred gold coins." "Alas," said Sir Bedivere, "that was my lord King Arthur, that here lieth buried in this chapel." Then Sir Bedivere swooned; and when he awoke he prayed the hermit he might abide with him still there, to live with fasting and prayers. "For from hence will I never go," said Sir Bedivere, "by my will, but all the days of my life here to pray for my lord Arthur." "Ye are welcome to me," said the hermit, "for I know ye better than ye ween that I do. Ye are the bold Bedivere, and the full noble duke, Sir Lucan the Butler, was your brother." Then Sir Bedivere told the hermit all as ye have heard before. So there bode Sir Bedivere with the hermit that was before Bishop of Canterbury, and there Sir Bedivere put upon him poor clothes, and served the hermit full lowly in fasting and in prayers. Thus of Arthur I find never more written in books that be authorised, nor more of the very certainty of his death heard I never read, but thus was he led away in a ship wherein were three queens; that one was King Arthur's sister, Queen Morgan le Fay; the other was the Queen of Northgalis; the third was the Queen of the Waste Lands. Also there was Nimue, the chief lady of the lake, that had wedded Pelleas the good knight; and this lady had done much for King Arthur, for she would never suffer Sir Pelleas to be in any place where he should be in danger of his life; and so he lived to the uttermost of his days with her in great rest. More of the death of King Arthur could I never find, but that ladies brought him to his burials; and such one was buried there, that the hermit bare witness that sometime was Bishop of Canterbury, but yet the hermit knew not in certain that he was verily the body of King Arthur: for this tale Sir Bedivere, knight of the Table Round, made it to be written.

CHAPTER VII

OF THE OPINION OF SOME MEN OF THE DEATH OF KING ARTHUR.

YET some men say in many parts of England that King Arthur is not dead, but had by the will of our Lord

Jesu into another place; and men say that he shall come again, and he shall win the holy cross. I will not say it shall be so, but rather I will say, here in this world he changed his life. But many men say that there is written upon his tomb this verse: *Hic jacet Arthurus, Rex quondam, Rex que futurus.*[1]

c. 1470

[1] Here lies Arthur, King aforetime, and King to be.

NOTES

Genealogical Tables to *Beowulf*

(1) *The Danish Royal Line*

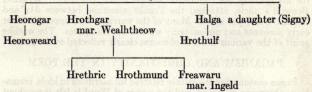

Scyld Scefing
|
Beowulf (not the hero of the poem)
|
Healfdene
|
Heorogar   Hrothgar   Halga   a daughter (Signy)
| mar. Wealhtheow
Heoroweard   Hrothulf

Hrethric   Hrothmund   Freawaru
                       mar. Ingeld

(2) *The Geat Royal Family*

Swerting
|
Hrethel
| Wægmund
| |
Herebeald Hæthcyn Hygelac a daughter mar. Ecgtheow Weohstan
                   mar. Hygd | |
                                         BEOWULF   Wiglaf

a daughter   Heardred
mar. Eofor

(3) *The Swedish Royal Family*

Ongentheow
|
Onela   Ohthere
                     |
                Eanmund   Eadgils

461

BEOWULF

THE SCENE

Heorot, the hall of the Danish king Hrothgar, was probably situated on or near the site of Leire in Zealand. In Heorot, Beowulf fights with Grendel, having come from the land of the Geats, in Southern Sweden, to do so, and later fights Grendel's mother there, too. After these contests Beowulf returns with his men to his home, where in his old age he meets his death in slaughtering another dragon. The scene is consequently not English, but Southern Scandinavian.

HISTORICAL BACKGROUND

While most of the events are mythological, certain elements in the poem are historical. Thus, Eormanric was king of the Goths, noted for his tyranny (he committed suicide about 375 A.D.). Hygelac, Beowulf's uncle, attacked the Franks sometime between 512 and 520 A.D., and was killed. Many of the warriors cited appear in other early accounts and undoubtedly were historical figures. The warlike spirit of the various tribes is of course clearly reflected in the poem.

PAGANISM AND CHRISTIANITY IN THE POEM

Pagan customs are frequently referred to: sacrifices to idols, cremation, observing of omens, and the power of Wyrd is felt throughout the poem. Side by side with these remnants of paganism, however, is a wealth of Christian material: the might of the Christian God, the terrors of hell, the power of the devil, the story of Cain and Abel, the song of Creation.

The opening lines of the poem (to line 84) record briefly the biography of Scyld the Sheaf-Child, the history of the Danish line of kings, and the building of Heorot. Scyld is the ancestor of the Danish King Hrothgar.

Page 1, l. 18. **Beowulf,** the son of Scyld, is a Dane, and must not be confused with the hero of the poem, Beowulf, a Geat (in this translation, Jute).

Page 2, l. 53. The Beowulf referred to is Beowulf the Dane (i. e., Scylding).

Page 3, l. 61. **Scylfing,** or Swede.

l. 77. **Heorot,** or Hart, so-called because hart-horns perhaps were used as ornamentation.

Page 4, l. 105. **an exile accurst,** because he is a descendant of Cain, whom God exiled for the murder of Abel.

l. 117. **æthelings,** warrior-nobles.

Page 5, l. 128. **the mighty ruler,** Hrothgar.

Page 7, l. 192. **Hygelac** (died c. 520 A.D.) was the uncle of Beowulf, the hero of the poem.

Page 8, l. 223. **Weder-folk,** or Geats (Jutes).
Page 10, l. 301. **the boar-heads** are decorations or guards on the helmets.
Page 11, l. 319. **byrnies,** coats of mail.
Page 15, l. 452. **Hrethel** was king of the Geats (Jutes).
   l. 453. **Weland,** the smith in Norse epic; **Wyrd,** Fate.
Page 16, l. 483. **Unferth,** "Spoil-Peace." His position at court, while not clearly defined in the poem, seems to be that of spokesman. In this instance he does not, of course, express the views of his lord, Hrothgar.
   l. 490. **Brecca,** leader of the Brondings. Unferth claims that Brecca defeated Beowulf in a swimming-match. Beowulf retorts that he and Brecca swam to fulfill a boast, and not as contestants, and accuses Unferth of fratricide and cowardice.
Page 34, l. 1038. **The jewelled necklace** of the goddess Freyja.
Page 37, l. 1134. **Ingwines** (the friends of Ing), Danes.
Page 48, l. 1471. **Runes** are the characters of the primitive Teutonic alphabet.
   l. 1486. **Heremod,** a king of the Danes, a mighty man, as Beowulf is, but a murderer and ungenerous. Hrothgar refers to him as a warning to Beowulf.
Page 63, l. 1929. **Wægmunding,** the family to which Beowulf and Wiglaf belonged.

DEOR'S LAMENT

This is the oldest English lyric, and is unique in the poetry of the period in that it has a refrain. Deor, a scop, has been out-rivalled by Heorrenda, and deprived of his land. In order to comfort himself Deor calls to mind instances of distress which time has cured.

The translation of this poem is by Margaret Beck McCallum. The authorship is unknown.

Page 64. **Weland.** Famous in Teutonic saga as the Smith, a worker in metal. King Nithbad hamstrung him in order that Weland would thus be obliged to stay and work for him; but Weland made a pair of wings for himself, violated Nithbad's daughter Beadohild, killed Nithbad's sons, and escaped.
  65. **Theodoric.** The Ostrogothic emperor, ruled in Italy 493–526. He was driven into exile by Attila. He is cited as an example of the suffering hero.
    Eormanric. A Gothic king (d. 375), and known as a tyrant.
    Heorrenda. A scop, and Deor's successful rival.

Two other poems from this period are added here. The one, *The Banished Wife's Complaint,* is like *Deor's Lament* elegiac. It is self-explanatory. The other, *A Love Letter*, contains a quaint conceit: the staff on which a lover has carved his message asks a high-born lady to meet the lover in the distant home which he has prepared for her. The letters at the end of the poem stand for runes, which perhaps represented the names of the lovers.

The translation of *The Banished Wife's Complaint* is by Margaret Beck McCallum; that of *A Love Letter* is by Professor F. A. Blackburn, *Journal of Germanic Philology*, vol. III, pp. 1ff.

THE BANISHED WIFE'S COMPLAINT

THIS song I sing alone most sorrowfully
Of my own fate: and truly can I say
That of the evils I have known since I grew up,
Ills new and old, no one was more than this:
Ever the shame of exile I endure!

Erstwhile my lord departing left his people,
Went o'er the strife of waves; sad in the dawn I wondered
In what far land my lord might be.
Then I went faring, followed to seek him,
A friendless wretch in my woeful need.
The kin of that man so devised a plot
With cunning thought, that they parted us,
So that we two divided should live in the world
Wretchedly, and great woe was mine.

Here my lord bade me make my home;
Few loved ones had I in this land,
Few noble friends. For this my heart is sad,
That I should find the man most meet for me
So sad a wretch, false-hearted, murderous,
Yet blithe of bearing. Full often we had sworn
That nothing less than death alone
Should part us; that is all changed now.
Now it is as it had never been,
Our friendship! I shall evermore
Endure the deep hate of my dearest love!
He bade me dwell within the wooded grove
Under an oak-tree, in an earthen cave;
Old is this earth-hall, I am full of longing;
Dark are the valleys and the hills are high,
A bitter city, overgrown with briars,
A joyless dwelling. Here often grief assails me
For my lord's faring. Friends there are on earth
Loving and living, keeping the marriage bed,

But I go alone at the dawning
Under the oak-tree, into the earth-cave!
There I must sit the whole long summer day,
There I must weep my wretched banishment,
My many troubles, since I never may
Rest from my sorrows, the desires and woe
This life has brought me.

Ever may that young man be wretched,
As bitterly sad as his bearing is blithe—
May he know breast-care, let him know suffering,
Let his joy in the world turn to woe in his heart.
May he be exiled in a strange country,
In a far folk-land, since my friend must sit
Under stone cliffs, berimed with storm—
My weary-hearted lord—water flows about
His dreary dwelling! He suffers great sorrow;
Too often he remembers a happier dwelling.
Woe is his, who longing
Shall await the beloved!

A LOVE-LETTER

My home was on the beach near the sea-shore;
Beside the ocean's brim I dwelt, fast fixed
In my first abode. Few of mankind there were
That there beheld my home in the solitude,
But every morn the brown wave encircled me
With its watery embrace. Little weened I then
That I should ever, earlier or later,
Though mouthless, speak among the mead-drinkers
And utter words. A great marvel it is,
Strange in the mind that knoweth it not,
How the point of the knife and the right hand,
The thought of a man, and his blade therewith,
Shaped me with skill, that boldly I might
So deliver a message to thee
In the presence of us two alone,
That to other men our talk
May not make it more widely known.
    Now to thee will I tell apart
That I sprang from the stock of the tree-race.
In other lands the skill of man is wont
To set on me cunning characters.
Then in a vessel I traverse the salt waves;
Oft in the prison of a ship have I visited lands,

Where my lord has sent me,
And lofty castles. Now am I come hither
In the keeled vessel, and now shalt thou know
How thou mayest think in thy heart
Of the love of my lord. I dare maintain
That there thou wilt find true loyalty.

Lo! he that carved this stave bade me
Pray thee, O jewel-decked, to remember
In thy heart the word-pledges,
Which in days of yore ye two oft spake,
While in the mead-castles ye were permitted
To have a home, to dwell in the same land,
To practice friendship. Force drove him
Out of the land. Now hath he bidden me
Earnestly to urge thee to sail the sea
When thou hast heard on the brow of the hill
The mournful cuckoo call in the wood.
Then let no living man keep thee
From the journey or hinder thy going.
Betake thee to the sea, the home of the mew;
Seat thee in the boat, that southward from here
Beyond the road of the sea thou mayest find the man
Where waits thy prince in hope of thee.
No joy of the world can be greater for him
In his thoughts, as he hath told me,
Than that the all-ruling God should grant you
That ye together should hereafter
Give out treasure to men and comrades,
Golden rings. Enough he hath
Of beaten gold, of wealth and treasure,
Since among strangers he hath a home,
A fair abode; there obey him many
Noble warriors, though here my banished lord,
Driven by necessity, pushed out his boat
And on the path of the waves was forced to run,
To journey on the water-way, eager for escape,
To stir the waves. Now hath the man
Overcome his trouble; he hath no lack of pleasures,
Of steeds or of jewels, or of mead-joys,
Or of any treasure on earth,
O prince's daughter, if he have thee
In spite of the old threat against you both.

I put together S   R
EA   W   and M(D?), to assure thee with an oath
That while he lives he will fulfill
The pledge and the love-troth
That in days of old he often spake.

THE WANDERER

His lord and patron having died, the singer of this elegy has become a wanderer and endured the hardships of exile. He reflects that life is fleeting and full of sorrow, as he regretfully submits to the power of Wyrd (Fate).

The translation of this poem and that of *The Sea-Farer* are by Professor J. D. Spaeth (Pancoast and Spaeth, *Early English Poems*, Henry Holt & Company).

The Wanderer is one of the best of the Old English elegiac poems. It belongs probably to the eighth century, and is one of the poems of the Exeter Book. (The *Exeter Book* and the *Vercelli Book* are famous collections of Old English prose and poetry. The former was given to Exeter Cathedral by Bishop Leofric, Bishop of Exeter, 1050–1071, and is still there. It contains, among other items, *Christ, Guthlac, Phœnix, Juliana, The Wanderer, The Sea-Farer,* gnomic verses, *The Address of the Soul to the Body, The Banished Wife's Complaint, Christ's Descent to Hell,* and some ninety riddles.

The *Vercelli Book,* so-called because it was found (in 1822) in the library at Vercelli in Northern Italy, dates back, as does the *Exeter Book,* to the eleventh century. Among other items, it contains homilies, *Andreas, Fates of the Apostles, Address of the Soul to the Body, Falseness of Men, The Dream of the Rood, Elene,* and a life of Guthlac, the last being in prose.

RIDDLES

The appeal of riddles is universal, and their history dates far back into antiquity. In Anglo-Saxon times some of the most famous enigmatographs (composers of riddles) were Aldhelm of Malmesbury (640–709), the author of one hundred; Tatwine, Archbishop of Canterbury (d. 734), who composed forty; Eusebius, perhaps an eighth-century divine, with sixty; and Bishop Boniface (680–755), with twenty. These authors wrote in Latin. The riddles given in the text were written in Old English, of unknown authorship. (For a full discussion, see Professor Frederick Tupper's *The Riddles of the Exeter Book,* Ginn & Company, 1910.)

CÆDMON

The *Hymn* is the only poem which modern scholars are willing to assign to Cædmon. The selection from *Genesis,* formerly attributed to Cædmon, and forming part of what is known as Cædmon's *Paraphrase,* is now considered to be of later date.

The poet has described the fall of the angels and the creation of the world. He then describes the temptation scene and the fall of man, as given in our selection.

For additional details on Cædmon, see Preface, pp. xv–xvi, and for Bede's account, pp. 106–110.

The translation is by Professor C. W. Kennedy (*The Cædmon Poems*, George Routledge & Sons, London; E. P. Dutton & Co., New York).

BEDE

The Ecclesiastical History of the English People by Bede, written in Latin, is the source of much of our information on the period, and especially for the details of the life and death of Cædmon. Bede was, for his period, an accurate historian, and shows evidence of care in selecting his material. The *History* was translated, under King Alfred's direction, into Old English.

The modern translation is by J. A. Giles.

CYNEWULF

The selection from Cynewulf (pronounced *Kin-uh-wolf*) is the third and last part of *Christ*. (Part 1, *The Advent*; Part 2, *The Ascension*; Part 3, *Doomsday*.) The original is written in the usual alliterative verse of Old English poetry. For an account of Cynewulf, see Preface, pp. xvi–xvii.

The translation is by Professor C. W. Kennedy (*The Poems of Cynewulf*, George Routledge & Sons, London; E. P. Dutton & Co., New York).

THE DREAM OF THE ROOD

The Dream of the Rood is generally considered the most beautiful of the Old English poems. It may have been written by Cynewulf. The poem consists of three parts: the description of the cross; the account of the crucifixion and of the resurrection, told by the cross, itself; and the reflections of the poet.

The translation is by Margaret Beck McCallum.

THE ANGLO–SAXON CHRONICLE

The *Anglo-Saxon Chronicle* is one of the chief sources for the history of this period. It begins with an account of the invasion of Britain by Julius Cæsar, interpolated at some much later period. Contemporary entries were probably not made until about the year 600. The last entry is for the year 1154. As the selections given in the text show, many of the entries are bare statements of fact, although two entries (*The Battle of Brunanburh* and *The Battle of Maldon*) are in alliterative verse. The entry for the year 449 (p. 137) is undoubtedly based on Bede's account (pp. 99–101).

THE BATTLE OF BRUNANBURH

This poem is found in the *Anglo-Saxon Chronicle* under date of 937 A.D. We owe it to the happy inspiration of some monk who preferred to record the event in verse rather than in prose. The poem celebrates the victory of Athelstan (grandson of King Alfred and King of Wessex and Mercia, 925–940) and his brother over a host of Scotch, Danes, and Irish.

The translation is by Alfred Tennyson.

ALFRED'S PREFACE TO THE PASTORAL CARE

Alfred (849–901), the fourth son of Ethelwulf (King of Wessex, 839–857), came to the throne in the year 871 on the death of his last surviving brother, Ethelred, and is the outstanding monarch of Anglo-Saxon times. As king of Wessex his most arduous task was the withstanding of the Danes, who persistently invaded his country, and whom he finally drove off in 896. In addition to his military exploits, Alfred reorganized the system of law, insisting on equal justice to all, and earning the title of "protector of the poor." As a stimulus to the intellectual and religious life he founded a court school for the education of clerics and laymen, and to aid him in this work imported scholars, among whom was Asser, later his biographer. (Alfred describes in the *Preface* to *The Pastoral Care* the conditions which he had to improve. See pp. 147ff.) As part of his educational program he translated, or ordered to be translated, *The Pastoral Care* of Gregory the Great, *The Consolation of Philosophy* of Boethius, *The Soliloquies* of Saint Augustine, *The Ecclesiastical History* of Bede, and *The Universal History* of Orosius.

Alfred is truly the *Great*. Of him John Richard Green, the historian, writes: "He is the first instance in the history of Christendom of a ruler who put aside every personal aim or ambition to devote himself wholly to the welfare of those whom he ruled."

The Pastoral Care (*Cura Pastoralis*) of Gregory the Great (540–604) is a handbook for the direction of priests, a treatise on clerical duties. Alfred's *Preface* is both plaintive and forceful.

The translation is by the editor.

THE VOYAGES OF OHTHERE AND WULFSTAN

These passages were inserted by Alfred in his translation of Orosius' *Universal History*, written in the early part of the fifth century. Orosius was a Spaniard and wrote his compendious work in Latin. The inclusion of these simple, first-hand accounts illustrates Alfred's interest in adding to the store of knowledge.

Ohthere should be pronounced *Ocht-hair-uh.*

The translation is by the editor.

ÆLFRIC

A selection from the *Homilies* of Ælfric is included in this volume because Ælfric is the outstanding example of Anglo-Saxon culture in its later period. Ælfric was born about 955 and died some time after 1020. His *Homilies* represent Anglo-Saxon prose at its best—lucid, direct, forceful. Because of his ability as a teacher (particularly of the Benedictine monks at Cernel in Dorsetshire), and because he was the author of a Latin grammar and glossary and of a Latin dialogue (the *Colloquium*, a manual of Latin conversation), he is sometimes referred to as *the Grammarian*.

The translation is by Benjamin Thorpe.

WULFSTAN

Wulfstan, Bishop of London in 1001, and later Archbishop of York, is after Ælfric the most important preacher of the period. He died in 1023. The *Address to the English* is a stirring message. It was delivered in 1014, about one year after the Danes had ravaged England and subdued a large part of it.

The translation is by Margaret Beck McCallum.

Page   166.   **Eadgar**, king, ruled 959–975, although only thirty-two years old at his death, restored England to a peace and strength hitherto almost unknown. Wulfstan rightly looks back to Eadgar's rule as beneficent.

Page   168.   **Eadweard, the Martyr,** was Eadgar's son, and ruled 975–978. He was assassinated.
Æthelred, the Unready, Eadweard's brother, was crowned in 979, when he was but ten years old. In 991 the Danes again invaded England, and routed the English at the Battle of Maldon. This defeat was one of a series which England suffered during Æthelred's rule. In 1013 he gave up the struggle and fled to Normandy.

Pp. 168–169.   i.e., conditions are so upset that relatives may not claim wergild (blood-money), as they ought; on the contrary, a thane must pay money for killing a thrall.

Page   171.   **Gildas** (c. 516–570), historian of the "English" conquest of Britain.

LAYAMON'S BRUT

This poem purports to be a history of England, from the supposed landing of Brutus, descendant of Æneas, to Cadwallon, supposedly the last of the English kings. As stated already (see *Preface*, p. xx) it is a reworking of Wace's *Li Romans de Brut*. Layamon follows his model in glorifying the Britons at the expense of the invading Saxons, a curious point of view to adopt at the beginning of the thirteenth century; but departs from Wace in giving emphasis to King Arthur. The account of Arthur given in the text forms part of the poem.

THE BESTIARY

The *Bestiary* treats symbolically of the habits of thirteen "animals." The habits of the lion, eagle, etc., are described, with a free fancy, and are used to symbolize some spiritual truth. The poetry is quite crude but interesting as revealing an early mode of teaching. The first twelve sections are based upon the *Physiologus* of an eleventh-century monk, Theobaldus; the thirteenth, upon the *De Naturis Rerum* of Alexander Neckam, an English scientist (1157–1217).

The modernization given in the text is by the editor. A specimen of the original (with "th" substituted for the early symbol) follows:

> The leun stant on hille; and he man hunten here,
> Other thurg his nese smel smake that he negge,
> Bi wilc weie so he wile to dele nither wenden,
> Alle hise fetsteppes after him he filleth,
> Drageth dust with his stert ther he dun steppeth,
> Other dust other deu, that he ne cunne is finden;
> Driveth dun to his den thar he him bergen wille.

SIR JOHN MANDEVILLE

The Voyage and Travel of Sir John Mandeville is a compilation from many sources. The author, whoever he was, was not an Englishman. He wrote probably at Liège, shortly after the middle of the fourteenth century, and his work is one of the most delightful of literary frauds. In the Prologue he insists on a proper reverence for the Holy Land, and gives some details about himself which we must discount. In the body of his work he describes the various roads to Jerusalem, and gives an account of the marvels he has seen in the East. This work has been translated into almost every European language, and, as an additional evidence of its popularity, has come down to us in some three hundred manuscripts.

SIR GAWAIN AND THE GREEN KNIGHT

This poem is the best of the alliterative romances, and one of the outstanding poems of Middle English literature. It was written about 1375 by an unknown author, to whom three other poems—*Pearl*, *Cleanness*, and *Patience*—have been ascribed. Whoever the author, he possessed a fine sense of symmetry and an ability not only to convey the spirit of King Arthur's court but to describe realistically the countryside as he saw it. The suspense is well sustained, and the conclusion, granting the general situation, is quite convincing.

The translation is by Jessie L. Weston.

Page 192. the traitor, Æneas, who, according to mediæval traditio
          betrayed Troy to the Greeks.
          Romulus, the founder of Rome (753 B.C.), according to
          tradition.
          Ticius has not been clearly identified.
          The Langobards, a German tribe, conquered what is now
          Lombardy, in Northern Italy.
          Felix Brutus, the founder of the "kingdom of Britain,"
          according to legend.
Page 193. Camelot, the legendary spot in England where Arthur held
          his court.
          tapestries of Tars, Oriental figured material.
Page 194. Agravain, à la dure main, Agravain, the hard-handed.
Page 196. hauberk, coat of mail (originally, armor for the protection
          of head and shoulders).
          gorget, armor for the protection of the throat.
          ell-yard, an obsolete term. An ell equals forty-five inches
          (England).
Page 200. redest, understandest.
Page 202. dossal, a hanging of heavy cloth.
Page 203. Michaelmas, September 29.
          All Hallows' Day, November 1.
Page 204. byrnie, coat of mail.
Page 205. bawdrick, a kind of belt.
          ventail, the adjustable front of a helmet (O. F., esventail,
          air-hole).
Page 207. Logres, England.
          Holyhead, west of the island of Anglesey (Wales).
          wilderness of Wirral, in Cheshire.
Page 208. matins, the morning service.
Page 209. hostel, lodging.
          corbels, ornamental brackets.
          barbican, an outer fortification.
Page 211. samite, a heavy silk.
          sodden, boiled.
Page 214. Saint John's Day, December 27.
          I wis, I know.
Page 219. rede, advise.
Page 221. tale, number.
Page 228. prime, roughly from 6 A.M. to 9 A.M.
          spinney, a small thicket.
Page 231. marks, a mark was worth thirteen shillings, four pence.
Page 232. assoiled, absolved.
          brand, sword.
Page 234. to deal the doom of my weird, to bear my fate.
Page 235. cognizance, an identifying device or emblem.
Page 238. let, hinder.

Page 239. **oratory,** a private chapel.
Page 242. **weed,** wearing apparel.
Page 246. **the book of Brutus,** a work in which the legendary history
of Britain is given, as for example, Layamon's *Brut*.

PEARL

The *Pearl*, a religious poem, written in stanzas with a complicated rhyme scheme, deserves a high place in Middle English literature by reason of its beauty and emotional appeal.

The grief-stricken poet falls asleep on the grave of a young girl, "nearer to him than aunt or niece," whom he symbolizes as his "Pearl." In a vision he sees her, and beholds the celestial country where she dwells. She expounds to him some of the mysteries of heaven, where she reigns as a queen with Mary.

THE VISION OF WILLIAM CONCERNING PIERS THE PLOWMAN

The author of this poem is unknown. Tradition assigns it, but doubtfully, to William Langland. Three versions have come down. Version A, written about 1362, contains about 2600 lines. Version B, written about 1377, is nearly three times as long. Version C, written between 1393 and 1398, is a revision of B. The poem is written in the alliterative measure.

The Vision is a series of dream-visions, under the guise of which the contemporary life in England is criticised. The indignation of the author, or authors, is stern; evil-doers of the time are castigated without reserve. The poem is one of the most important writings of the fourteenth century for a study of the period.

The translation is by Henry W. Wells.

THE BALLADS

Many of the ballads date back to the fourteenth century or earlier, but it should not be forgotten that many of them are of late origin. In 1765 Bishop Percy published his famous *Reliques of Ancient English Poetry.* (Thomas Percy, 1729–1811, was bishop of Dromore. The basis of his collection was a seventeenth-century manuscript which he found in the house of a friend, and parts of which, it is said, the servants had been using to light the fire. With the assistance of friends, Percy added other ballads to make his three-volume collection.) In 1882–1898 F. J. Child published the standard collection.

The ballad proper was not written, and consequently we do not speak of author or authors (although various literary figures have written imitations of the ballads); they were composed on subjects of popular interest and handed down from one generation to another orally. The composer does not let himself be seen in these compositions: the subject is treated quite objectively. The thought and language is simple, and repetition is used to add to the effect.

LYRICS

The Cuckoo Song is probably the best-known lyric of Middle English literature. The spontaneous joy of the unknown author is quite infectious. *Springtime* also expresses a pleasure in nature, not in the staccato manner of *The Cuckoo Song*, but still with an economy of words and gladsome effect. Both poems obviously could have originated only in a northern country where spring brings joy after winter. *A Hymn to the Virgin* is one of a large number of Middle English sacred lyrics. (See, for example, *Religious Lyrics of the XIVth Century*, edited by Carleton Brown, Clarendon Press, 1924.) *Alysoun* and *A Plea for Pity* are love-poems, the former of which is deservedly the better known.

GLOSS TO "A HYMN TO THE VIRGIN"

Page 334. **Velut maris stella.** Like a star of the sea.
           Parens et puella. A parent, though a mere girl.
           Tam pia. So good.
           Eva peccatrice. Because Eve sinned.
           De te genetrice. Having thee for mother.
           Salutis. Of salvation.
           Virtutis. Of virtue.
           Rosa sine spina. Rose without a thorn.
           Gratia divina. Divine grace.
Page 335. **Electa.** Chosen.
           es Effecta. Thou art become.
           Felix fecundata. Blessed one made fruitful.
           Mater honorata. Honored mother.
           In cruce. On the cross.
           In luce. In light.
           Ventre quam portasti. Whom thou borest in thy womb.
           Parvum quem lactasti. Whom thou didst nurse when he was small.
           Superni. Of heaven.
           Inferni. Of hell.

THE QUEM–QUÆRITIS TROPE

A *trope* is a text or a sentence or a verse which is appropriate for special days (Easter Sunday, for instance), and which may be adapted for choral rendering during the Mass. The *Quem-Quæritis* trope has been so adapted, and in dramatic form gives the conversation of the angels guarding the sepulchre with the Marys, who had come to anoint the body of Christ. Originally this trope was sung in addition to the music of the Introit of the Mass (the procession with which the Mass begins).

SEPULCHRUM

This primitive dramatic piece, with its rather full particularization of the ritual, may have been written by Ethelwold, who became bishop of Winchester in 963.

THE SHEPHERDS

Often referred to as the *Second Shepherds' Play* because it is the second of two "Shepherds" or Nativity plays in the Towneley or Wakefield cycle. It dates from the fifteenth century. Note the realism of the shepherds' complaints, the combination of horse-play and sacred theme, and the quaintness of the presents given to the Christ Child.

THE SQUYR OF LOWE DEGRE

While lacking the subtlety of *Sir Gawain and the Green Knight*, this poem has a simplicity and a freshness that makes it one of the most delightful narratives of the fifteenth century. The themes are commonplace: the poor boy who rises to wealth, and the separated lovers who are united; but the ballad-like directness of the narration adds a quaintness that compensates for the well-worn themes. Notice that the unknown narrator does not make clear the reason for placing the dead steward by the girl's door.

THE PASTON LETTERS

The Paston Letters form the most remarkable series of letters ever published. Totalling almost eleven hundred letters, they are of great value not only as a description of human nature in general but as highly interesting for the light they shed on the period which they cover (1422–1509). The first two volumes of these letters were published in 1787 by the antiquary, John Fenn (1739–1794); the third and fourth volumes appeared in 1789; and the fifth volume, years after Fenn's death, in 1823. The standard text is that of James Gairdner, vol. 1, 1872, vol. 2, 1874, vol. 3, 1875.

In the fifteenth century, at which time the Pastons first come to our attention, the family was small gentry in Norfolk. The line begins for us with William Paston, who served under Henry VI, and was called the Good Judge. His son John became executor to Sir John Falstolf.

John's two oldest sons bore, oddly enough, the same Christian name as their father. After them comes another Sir William Paston, whose son Clement, a naval commander under Henry VIII, was the most distinguished member of the family. It was he who built a fine family seat at Oxnead. Clement died childless, and was succeeded by his nephew William. His heir in turn was Christopher, an idiot. Finally the property descended to the Sir Robert Paston who proposed to the House of Commons in 1664 that the King should be given a grant of two million and a half pounds for carrying on the war against the Dutch. After him the family fortunes declined, the seat at Oxnead fell into ruins and was finally sold, and with the death of William Paxton, Earl of Yarmouth, in 1732, the titles became extinct.

SIR THOMAS MALORY

Sir Thomas Malory was born about 1400 in Warwickshire. He served under the Earl of Warwick, a staunch upholder of the customs of chivalry, from whom he undoubtedly acquired much of his enthusiasm for knightly exploits. In 1445 he was a member of Parliament. He died in 1471. His *Morte Darthur* is the most famous of the Arthurian romances, and aside from the wealth of material on the Round Table and the scope of the treatment, is noteworthy as the first treatment of the subject matter in which Arthur is made the central figure. The poem is the main source of Tennyson's *Idylls of the King*.

INDEX

477